The Mental Health Act Commission

Coercion and consent

monitoring the Mental Health Act 2007–2009

MHAC Thirteenth Biennial Report 2007–2009

Presented to Parliament pursuant to Paragraph 13 of Schedule 4 to the Health and Social Care Act 2008 (Commencement No.9, Consequential Amendments and Transitory, Transitional and Saving Provisions) Order 2009.

London: The Stationery Office

information & publishing solutions

Published by TSO (The Stationery Office) and available from:

Online
www.tsoshop.co.uk

Mail, Telephone, Fax & E-mail
TSO
PO Box 29, Norwich, NR3 1GN
Telephone orders/General enquiries: 0870 600 5522
Fax orders: 0870 600 5533
E-mail: customer.services@tso.co.uk
Textphone: 0870 240 3701

TSO@Blackwell and other Accredited Agents

Customers can also order publications from:
TSO Ireland
16 Arthur Street, Belfast BT1 4GD
Tel 028 9023 8451   Fax 028 9023 5401

Published with the permission of the Care Quality Commission on behalf of the Controller of Her Majesty's Stationery Office.

© Crown Copyright 2009

All rights reserved.

Copyright in the typographical arrangement and design is vested in the Crown.
Applications for reproduction should be made in writing to Copyright applications, The Copyright Unit, Office of Public Sector Information, Information Policy Team, Kew, Richmond, Surrey TW9 4DU.
E-mail: licensing@opsi.gov.uk

First published 2009

ISBN 978 0 11 322836 2

The Care Quality Commission has arranged for publication of this report pursuant to paragraph 13(1) of Schedule 4 to the *Health and Social Care Act 2008 (Commencement No.9, Consequential Amendments and Transitory, Transitional and Saving Provisions) Order 2009.*

Printed in the United Kingdom by The Stationery Office
6110497   C12   06/09

Acknowledgements

The author of this report was Mat Kinton.

Production was overseen by Ron Rushbrook and Vicki Eley of the MHAC Policy Unit.

Generous reading time, support and comments were provided by Gemma Pearce, Acting Chief Executive of the MHAC, despite the pressures of overseeing the last days of the organisation and ensuring that its legacy was carried on within the Care Quality Commission.

Many people helped with information, advice and discussion. Particular thanks to Janey Antoniou, Leanne Bacon, Professor Peter Bartlett (Nottingham University), William Bingley, Rob Brown, Jemma Ciplys, Luke Clapham, Jeff Cohen, Chris Conway, Chris Curran, Rowena Daw (RCPsych), Karen Early (Tribunal), Andy Evans, Professor Phil Fennell (Cardiff University), Claire Fife (Welsh Assembly Government), Pat Gregory, Professor Chris Heginbotham (University of Central Lancashire), Dr David Hewitt (Weightmans), John Horne (University of Northumbria), Phil Howes, Dr Peter Jefferies, Craig Jennings, Surrinder Kaur, Steve Klein, Sue McMillan, Professor Ronnie MacKay (De Montfort University), Christina Marriot, Camilla Parker, Francis Parker, Mike Partridge (Metropolitan Police), Rona Pickles, Richard Rook (Department of Health), Corrine Ryan (Institute of Mental Health Act Practitioners), Rose Sibley, Jo Simpson (Information Centre), Rebecca Stephens, Sue Turner, Denise Walker, Rhian Williams-Flew, and the MHAC Service User Reference Panel. Apologies to those we have not named.

This report is based largely upon the visiting work of Mental Health Act Commissioners between 2007 and 2009.

Contents

	Paragraph	Page
Foreword		
Simon Armson & Lord Patel of Bradford		11
The last 23 years in mental health		
Janey Antoniou		15

1 The Mental Health Act in Context

	Paragraph	Page
Introduction	1.1	19
Data collection and the Mental Health Act	1.4	20
The attractions of acute care	1.7	21
Service user involvement	1.13	22
General trends in admission under the Mental Health Act	1.17	24
The balance between hospital and community based services	1.20	26
The increasing relevance of the independent sector	1.25	27
Characteristics of the detained population	1.28	29
The gender mix of the detained population	1.28	29
The ethnicity of detained patients	1.36	33
Patients with learning disability	1.42	36
Children and adolescents	1.48	40
Secure services for adolescents	1.59	43
Acute ward environments	1.61	44
Locked doors	1.64	45
Bed occupancy	1.68	47
The physical environment of wards	1.71	48
Staffing	1.78	50
Activity on wards	1.86	53
The recovery model and coercive environments	1.91	55
Restrictions on smoking	1.95	56
Patient involvement and support	1.99	58
Providing patients with information about their care and treatment	1.106	60
Independent Mental Health Advocacy	1.111	62
Access to communications	1.114	63
Mobile telephones	1.114	63
Ward-based telephones	1.118	64
Access to computers and the internet	1.120	64
Patients' mail	1.123	65
Appeals against withholding of mail in High Security Hospitals	1.125	66
Access to pornography	1.128	68
Telephone monitoring in the High Security Hospitals	1.131	69
The policing of patients' mail in the High Security Hospitals	1.133	69
Observation and restraint	1.136	70
Restraint and safety	1.145	75
Police presence on wards	1.151	77
Seclusion	1.154	78

2 The Mental Health Act in Practice

The use and outcome of holding powers	2.1	82
Section 2 as a community order	2.4	86
Professional roles	2.9	87
The Responsible Clinician	2.9	87
Identifying the Responsible Clinician	2.12	87
Section 12 Approved Doctors	2.17	89
Avoidable illegal detention due to lapses of s.12 approval	2.19	89
Approved Mental Health Professionals	2.21	90
AMHPs and professional specialisation	2.22	90
Problems with assessments	2.24	90
The uncooperative patient	2.24	90
Problems with conveyance	2.28	92
Leave of absence and absence without leave	2.30	92
The planning and recording of leave of absence from hospital	2.30	92
Leave and risk assessment	2.35	94
Resource limitations and section 17 leave	2.37	95
Administering leave for restricted patients	2.41	98
Liaison with victims over leave	2.47	99
Ground leave	2.52	101
Absence without leave	2.56	102
Returning AWOL patients to hospital	2.60	104
Long-term s.17 leave	2.62	105
De facto detention	2.65	106
Supervised Community Treatment under the revised Mental Health Act	2.67	107
The impact of supervised community treatment	2.74	109
The impact on patients: MHAC experiences of SCT patients	2.77	111
The gender, age and ethnicity of SCT patients	2.79	112
SCT and deprivation of liberty	2.82	114
Residence requirements for SCT patients: the uncertain boundaries of hospital and commuunity	2.86	115
Some initial difficulties with the administration of SCT	2.89	117
Appealing against detention and SCT	2.91	117
Managers' hearings for detained patients	2.91	117
The Tribunal	2.96	119
The effects of administrative delays	2.99	120
The role of detaining authorities in adjournments of Tribunal hearings	2.101	121
Provision of social circumstances reports to Tribunal hearings	2.102	122
In-patient nursing reports	2.104	122
Informing patients about their rights to a Tribunal	2.106	123
Legal aid and Tribunal representation	2.108	123
Outcomes of Tribunal Hearings	2.111	124
The care and treatment of detained patients in acute hospitals	2.121	128
Responsibility for treatment in acute hospitals under the revised Mental Health Act	2.127	129

Police powers to remove mentally disordered persons to a place of safety under s.136	2.129	130
Defining a public place	2.138	134
Information about the use of s.136	2.140	135
Aftercare under s.117	2.141	135

3 Consent to treatment

Consent to treatment safeguards	3.1	138
The reality of consent	3.2	139
Recording consent and capacity	3.7	141
The reach of the statutory second opinion system: second opinions for consenting patients and the three month rule	3.17	145
Advance decisions	3.18	146
Access to psychological treatment	3.23	147
Safety and the administration of medication	3.24	147
Electronic records and medication management	3.27	148
The operation of the second opinion service	3.28	148
Second opinions to consider treatment with medication: patient characteristics	3.30	149
The effect of second opinion visits	3.35	154
High-dose medication	3.37	155
Concurrent certification of consent and absence of consent in detained patients	3.38	155
Emergency powers and medication	3.43	157
Electro-convulsive therapy	3.44	157
The Mental Health Act 2007's restriction on legal powers to authorise ECT without consent	3.50	161
Magnetic seizure therapy and transcranial magnetic stimulation – future treatments?	3.59	166
Neurosurgery for mental disorder	3.61	167
Deep brain stimulation	3.63	167
Consent to treatment and Supervised Community Treatment	3.64	168
The consent status of SCT patients	3.66	169
SCT and patients refusing consent to medication	3.68	170
The disjuncture in Part 4A between certification and consent	3.73	171
Issues for SOADs in certifying the appropriateness of treatment refused by an SCT patient	3.76	172
Statutory consultees for second opinions for SCT patients	3.84	174
Responsibility for the treatment of community or s.17 leave patients	3.85	174
Children and consent to treatment	3.88	175
Children and ECT treatment	3.90	177

4 The Mental Health Act and mentally disordered offenders

The diversion of mentally disordered offenders from the criminal justice system	4.01	179
Unfitness to plead and the insanity defence	4.3	179
Section 37/41 as an alternative to imprisonment	4.8	182
Probation as an alternative to Mental Health Act disposals	4.15	185
Mentally disordered women and diversion from the criminal justice system	4.20	187
Returning patients on remand or interim orders to court	4.22	188
Transfer from prison	4.24	189
Women prisoners and transfer under the Mental Health Act	4.28	191
Transfers from prison without restriction orders	4.30	192
Prison transfers in Wales	4.34	194
Treatability	4.35	195
Late transfers from prison and the fear of preventative detention	4.38	196
Rehabilitation and transferred prisoners	4.50	199

5 Deaths of Detained Patients

Deaths of detained patients	5.1	201
Total deaths recorded 2005-2008	5.2	201
Ethnicity and deaths of detained patients	5.3	201
Deaths by natural causes	5.4	202
Age at time of death	5.4	202
Cardiac and respiratory arrest	5.5	203
Natural causes deaths following ECT treatment	5.7	203
Deaths by unnatural causes	5.10	204
Accidental deaths	5.17	208
Fall prevention and mechanical restraint	5.20	209
Control and restraint deaths	5.21	209
Choking	5.27	211
Drug and alcohol intoxication or overdose	5.31	213
Iatrogenic and related deaths	5.33	214
Community patients and medicines management	5.36	214
Leave and absence without leave as a factor in unnatural patient deaths	5.39	215
Suicides	5.46	218
Observation levels	5.48	218
Deaths by hanging	5.51	219
Notable ligatures and load-bearing support	5.57	222
Doors and door hinges	5.60	223
Self-Suffocation	5.61	223
Breaking the news to relatives	5.63	224
Breaking the news to other patients	5.69	226

Epilogue – the end of the Mental Health Act Commission	227
Appendix A – in memoriam Brian D M Smith 1925-2008	229

Sir Louis Blom-Cooper QC; Elaine, Baroness Murphy of Aldgate;
Mike Napier CBE, QC; William Bingley

Appendix B – Mental Health Act Commissioners 1983-2009	231

This is not the end of this by no manners means[1].

---
[1] James Joyce (1939) *Finnegans Wake* p.373.

Foreword

Coercion and consent

The Mental Health Act Commission's Thirteenth Biennial Report

By the time that this report is published, the Mental Health Act Commission will no longer exist, and will have become a footnote in the history of mental health care in England and Wales. The quarter century allotted to the MHAC was a much shorter time than that given to the Lunacy Commission and Board of Control, our forebears from the age of the asylums, but we hope that we leave a legacy of work that will continue to influence those who come after us, just as the example of our predecessors has been both inspiration and lesson to us.

All those who have had contact with the MHAC over its lifespan will have their own ideas about the nature of that legacy. In our view, areas where the MHAC has shown a significant lead have been in addressing human rights principles to the daily lives and treatment of detainees; focussing attention on the overrepresentation of Black and minority ethnic detainees, and the sometimes inadequate provisions made to cater for these and other minorities (including women and children) of those who are detained in hospitals; raising (if not necessarily resolving) questions about consent to treatment; involving service users in our work and raising a platform for the voices of service users to be heard. It is gratifying to see the MHAC's Service User Reference Panel (SURP) being emulated across other organisations, from mental health trusts to the Royal College of Psychiatrists.

It is a great reassurance to us that the coming together of the MHAC with more broadly-focussed health and social care inspectorates under the Care Quality Commission in England, and joining with health inspection in Wales, entails no dilution of the focus on visiting detained patients in hospital, or of keeping under review the exercise of powers and discharge of duties under the Mental Health Act. We believe that our calls for the continuance of these functions – and our warnings over the lessons of their dissolution in the period following the Second World War until the creation of the MHAC – have been well heeded. It is reassuring that the United Kingdom, as a signatory to the Optional Protocol to the Convention Against Torture [OPCAT], has recognised its human rights obligations to maintain a visitorial body for those who are detained in its psychiatric facilities, whatever future arrangements may be made for the wider monitoring of quality, safety or human rights in general healthcare provision. There is a great opportunity in the joining together of the old MHAC with wider regulation of health care (and with the regulation of adult social care in England), and we hope that this will overcome some of the limitations of the MHAC remit in addressing human rights concerns over the treatment of psychiatric patients who are not formally detained. It has been a concern of the MHAC from its first Biennial Report that it was prevented from addressing problems such as the *de facto* detention of informal psychiatric patients. We hope that such frustrations will now cease.

A criticism of our predecessor, the Lunacy Commission, was that it became more concerned with patients' daily care in custody – whether they were warm; clothed; provided with adequate bedding; and appropriately fed – than with the legal powers of custody themselves, and as such reinforced the custodialism of the Victorian asylum system[2]. Or, as Andrew Scull writes of the Lunacy Commission, "to judge by the space and emphasis allotted to each topic, by the mid-1850s the question of curing asylum inmates ranked considerably below the urgent issue of the composition of the inmates' soup."[3]

There is something slightly unfair in Scull's apparent dismissal of the importance of the food provided to Victorian asylum patients: it was surely of great importance to the patients themselves[4]. Furthermore, the common-sense expectation that there is no place in a modern healthcare system for a visiting body that concerned itself with counting blankets or tasting the patient's soup is surprisingly confounded by the recent experience of the MHAC. Our reports mention many complaints from patients over the quality, quantity or choice of hospital food, including complaints that it is difficult to eat healthily whilst detained in some hospital sites. Even more strikingly, the following examples of concerns about patients' bedding are from visits in this reporting period:

> There is use of strong bedding and blankets on the unit, but the blanket had not been washed regularly and there was no bedding between the patient and the plastic mattress. The patient was also not given a pillow to use and had to use her slippers as a make-shift pillow.
>
> *East Midlands, June 2008*

> Patient X complained of being cold. She sleeps in strong bedding on a mattress and currently has two strong blankets at night. She uses one to cover the mattress and sleeps under the other. She still has no pillow. As this is a long term arrangement, please consider how she can be made more comfortable at night and ensure she is warm.
>
> *East Midlands, October 2008*

---

[2] See Scull A (1993) *The Most Solitary of Afflictions: Madness and Society in Britain 1700-1900*. Yale University Press.

[3] *ibid.*, p.303.

[4] Indeed, had the Lunacy Commission known it, some ingredients in the food and drink of asylum patients were a matter of life and death: outbreaks of cholera and similarly transmitted disease were no doubt facilitated by sanitary arrangements and pollution of water sources. There are, perhaps, some historical parallels here with the current concerns with hospital-acquired infections such as MRSA, discussed in the foreword to the MHAC's Twelfth report.

> Poor quality of bedding – very institutional and in some cases, very grubby (observed by MHAC and commented on by patient).
>
> *North-west England, May 2007*

> Patients complained that there are not enough quilts, quilt covers and pillows and pillow cases on the ward. Some patients only have a sheet … check that all patients have sufficient bedding.
>
> *London, April 2007*

What lessons should we draw from these few examples of detaining authorities failing basic (and historic) human needs of warmth and shelter? They might be presented in evidence of our belief that there is a need for continued vigilance over these matters, even if the examples above are not so common to warrant a return to counting blankets on all wards we visit. Perhaps, however, they point to a more subtle conclusion about the proper focus of visits. We do not doubt that the patients in the last example could have raised directly with nursing staff on the ward their concern about the lack of bedding, and that the matter would have been put right. That they did not do so, but raised it with an outside visiting body, points to a perception of powerlessness by the detained patients concerned. That staff had not independently noticed and resolved the lack of domestic comfort afforded patients in their care points, perhaps, to an associated lack of perceived ability or authority to make a change. Such perceived disempowerment may be even more heightened when, as in the first two examples above, the failure to provide basic comfort is partly the result of special 'clinical' interventions (in these cases the replacement of normal bedding with 'strong bedding' to reduce risks of self harm).

As such, what these examples may point to is the resilience and adaptability of the processes of institutionalisation. Like weeds breaking through concrete, institutionalisation can break out in the modern settings of today's mental health services, and one role of Mental Health Act Commissioners is to challenge this and – importantly – to help both patients and staff to challenge this themselves. We emphasise this aspect because it is important that our visits empower rather than disempower: that visiting Commissioners are seen by both patients and staff as a positive force to encourage best practice, and not just as the 'inspectorate' that picks away at the weakest parts of local mental health services. If the visiting role becomes the latter, it becomes part of the problem of institutionalisation rather than part of the solution.

The first Biennial Reports of the MHAC stressed that it was setting out matters for debate, rather than pronouncing infallible truths. Viscount Colville of Culross, the first MHAC Chairman, stated that the "real point in laying this report before parliament [is] … that it may be public and open to discussion".[5] In the conclusion to the first Biennial Report, it was stated that

> It is not to be expected that everything in this report will attract agreement. Something would be wrong if that were the outcome. Mental health services will remain a controversial area, open to constant debate and revision[6]

---

[5] MHAC (1987) *Second Biennial Report*, Chairman's foreword.
[6] MHAC (1985) *First Biennial Report*, p. 56.

Our reports have, in general, been received very much in this spirit, and we are grateful for the opportunity to test our findings and observations in the public arena. We hope that this will continue under the Care Quality Commission in England and the Healthcare Inspectorate Wales, but also that the new arrangements will be able to focus greater public attention on its findings than we have been able to do, and so enable further improvements in the quality of patients' experiences.

This foreword to the MHAC's final biennial report, which we have authored together as we both served as chairmen in the period covered, would be incomplete without paying tribute to both past and present Commissioners, Second Opinion Appointed Doctors and the Commission's staff.

At the forefront of our work, Commissioners have brought their experience, expertise and compassion to bear on their task (often well in excess of the hours for which they were remunerated), without this dedication the lives of detained patients would surely have been far less tolerable over the last twenty-five years. Our second opinion doctors have used their skill in ensuring that the treatment plans of those patients with whom they have engaged have been carefully and objectively scrutinised and where necessary challenged. Our dedicated and knowledgeable staff at our Nottingham office have kept the wheels of the Commission oiled and turning with the efficiency required to fulfil our remit under the Act. All of those who have fulfilled these functions deserve recognition and praise. We are delighted that the vast majority of Commissioners, second opinion doctors and staff are going forward to work with the MHAC's successor bodies.

Simon Armson
Chairman,
2008-2009

Lord Patel of Bradford OBE
Chairman,
2002-2008

The last 23 years in Mental Health

Janey Antoniou, service user and mental health trainer

It was near Christmas the first time I went into hospital in 1985....

I had been ill for a while and had had an initial interview with a psychiatrist. He had given me a follow-up appointment in two weeks. Before that could happen I took a huge overdose of anti-depressants. I survived the night but was much too unsteady to go into work the next day. A colleague who knew I wasn't well eventually collected me and took me to 'A and E' and then to the psychiatric out-patient clinic where I had a long "yes you will!"/"no I won't!" argument about going into hospital with the consultant and then the registrar Inevitably I lost the argument when they threatened me with a section and I was taken up to the psychiatric ward.

The ward was supposed to be for twenty-four people but it was my bad luck that they were decorating one of the other wards and we had four extra beds squashed into various corners. The whole area smelled of smoke, floor cleaner and urine – in that order. I was given a bed, one of five in a four-person room and introduced to my two neighbours. A nurse went through my things, listing my valuables and in the end confiscating my birth-control pills. I argued about that too because I couldn't see how oestrogen and progesterone could be seen to be dangerous.

I felt very helpless and vulnerable that first evening. My clothes had been were taken away and I had to wear my nightclothes, I think this was to stop me running away. The other patients terrified me; some seemed to have strange glassy-eyed expressions or shambling walks. There were people pacing the ward in silence, someone smashed a guitar against the wall, another person wet on the floor. One of my room-mates, an oldish sleepy-looking woman called Amy, told that she had entered 'The Brain of Britain' radio programme in the past but frankly I didn't believe her. And there was a young man in wheelchair who, I was informed, had jumped off a building. Most people were smoking heavily, causing a fog throughout the ward.

I ate someone else's dinner (they were on leave) because food was ordered two days ahead and I had yet to fill in menus. Then I retreated onto my bed to hide and try to read – desperately attempting to act normal so I could go home as soon as possible. I heard a weird conversation between two of my room mates who were to have a treatment in the morning, both were scared because they didn't know what to expect and I couldn't imagine what was going to happen to them. Fortunately my husband came to visit me and I felt happier for a while.

That night I had to queue at the drug trolley for my birth-control pill. The quantity of medication some of the patients were getting really surprised and shocked me. The only drug whose name I recognised was chlorpromazine because I had been given it when I was fifteen. Some people received a bright orange sticky liquid that had to be measured out carefully, others a larger amount of a brown liquid. I heard another strange conversation:

Man; "what is wrong with you then?"

Woman; "oh I used to have schizophrenia, but they cured me of that."

Afterwards there was hot milk to make a bedtime drink of chocolate or ovaltine, I was not quick enough and didn't get any. I spent the night getting up to switch the night light off because it was too bright for me to sleep, only to have the staff switch it on again. The bed was not very comfortable and creaked with every breath. It took a long time for morning to come.

The first thing the next day I was confronted with the realities of psychiatric ward bathrooms. They were always littered with forgotten shampoo bottles and small, soggy pieces of soap. There were sometimes towels and clothes too – and mould growing up the walls. I think there was some strange politics over who was supposed to clean them. Nevertheless, I showered.

I spent the next days feeling bored and frustrated because I was not allowed off the ward on my own and there was not a lot to do. The two women went for their treatment, one came back with a headache and one felt sick and was told to go and lay on her bed. There was intense drama for a while when a man abruptly kicked at one of the doors and tore it off it's hinges. Someone seeing it set an alarm off and suddenly there were nurses everywhere. The man (who never spoke the whole time I was there) was given some medication and order was resumed. We were allowed a cup of coffee as elevenses and got a cup of tea twice in the afternoon but the kitchen was out-of-bounds. Later, another man in black leather silently and inexplicably held my hand while we were watching the television.

Slowly, slowly however I settled down. I made friends and realised that there was nothing to be frightened of, all of the patients were just people. The treatment the two women received was ECT. The silence man continued to be silent and never received any visitors. Amy answered nearly all of the questions in the general knowledge section of Mastermind without turning a hair. I refused to take any medication (apart from my contraceptive pill) and left after a few days, only to be readmitted in late January of the following year and again in April.

All of this was a while ago now and of those twenty-eight patients, three that I know of have committed suicide. Amy is not her real name.

A new millennium….

In the summer of 2000 I had the misfortune to be incarcerated in the hospital after managing to stay in the community for six years. It was all terribly confused at first, but then when I became well enough to think, I was amazed that although some things had changed, others had stayed disgustingly the same as both six and fifteen years ago.

Of course the building hadn't changed and although there had obviously been several facelifts within the ward, it still has that lived-in look, with splodges of something-or-other on the floor and walls. The internal structure of the place had changed a little, so the nurses had a big room, as compared with a little one (six years ago) and a nursing station (fifteen years ago). I didn't walk into a sea of smoke this time, all smoking had been confined to one room. We had carpet in the corridor and there were more single rooms too. But other than that, the basic cubicle with bed, wardrobe and locker was the same. Drug times, ward rounds and that sort of thing seemed immutable, set in stone. Unfortunately even some of the patients had stayed the same – though I suppose they could say that of me.

The rules of the ward were stricter, with notices pinned up to remind us of them. 'No visitors until four o'clock', 'no mobile phones', 'no smoking except in the smoking room', 'drug and alcohol use will result in the police being called', etc., etc. And good behaviour was enforced with a 'sin bin' – the seclusion room (I was threatened with seclusion for kicking the door in a moments temper). Surprisingly, all of this made for a more relaxed, less dog-eat-dog atmosphere. During my previous admission I can remember mobiles ringing at mid-night, people smoking in the dormitory and the general mayhem of twenty-four people doing their own thing.

There was a mission statement on the wall by the new and bigger nurses' room now. It contained lots of long words like 'integrity', 'confidentiality' and 'valuing individuals' – the shortest was 'caring'. I guess this was a response to hospital trusts and 'the Patients Charter' though I'm not sure that practically it made any difference at all. Observation levels were more relaxed, the hell of having a nurse with one all the time (even in the loo) had disappeared completely.

And talking of loos, there were separate toilets and bathrooms for men and women. This was a welcome change because the women's bathroom was kept relatively tidy. I asked about this change and was told that it was the result of user representation on a hospital committee. The food was still bad, with few green vegetables, the queue for medication still took time to get through, and ECT was still done on Tuesday and Friday. Sadly, the suicide of those with a mental health problem had not changed at all. During my three weeks in the ward, one of my fellow patients found a way to kill himself.

And now…

My latest admission was in September 2008 and I had to wait three days for a bed. This is because one of the wards has been closed down to provide some money for the home treatment team. Next year the whole building is to be knocked around so the wards are on the ground floor and all the rooms are for one person. But for the time being there are the same dormitories, nurse's room and bathrooms as ever there was. The only real change to the infrastructure is an extra door which separates off a couple of single rooms and a bathroom so it can be called a 'women's area'. The rules governing which two women should go in this area are impossible to understand.

There are a lot more of us on a section than eight years ago and therefore a lot of things going on all the time. And the biggest change is that even though the wards are low security acute wards they are locked all day. Close observation and wall-to-wall smoke are back. The smoke shouldn't be back because the wards are theoretically smoke-free to follow government policy. But because people want to smoke more cigarettes than the nurses are willing to take them outside for, they light up surreptitiously in corners of the ward all the time. It makes things very difficult.

There are some improvements in the way patients are treated. Our clothes are not taken away anymore, though everyone is still searched when they are admitted. The kitchen is open for tea throughout the day and night and there are even biscuits and fruit occasionally. There are no menus for meals and everyone goes to a canteen, not that the food is any better. There is also now this thing called protected time, where nurses are supposed to be available for people to talk to and other people are not supposed to come onto the ward. I never learnt what time this was supposed to take place and it was not obvious when it was because nurses were talking to people or less outsiders were coming onto the ward. I guess it's a good idea that doesn't really happen.

Throughout my time on psychiatric wards the reliance has been on drugs. The medication has been in blister packs rather than loose in bottles for a while now, so it takes even longer to give out everyone's tablets. Very occasionally over the last couple of years some psychologists have been seen on the ward but it is rare. All doctors other than the consultant still change every six months which may be good for the doctor but is not for the patients.

And now we have community sections and no Mental Health Act Commission. I don't know where things are going to go from here....

1

The Mental Health Act in context

Introduction

1.1 This is the last report of the Mental Health Act Commission, collating information and our observations on the use of the powers in the Mental Health Act in England and Wales for the final two-year period (2007/08 and 2008/09) of our life. It will, by necessity, be published posthumously, given the dissolution of the MHAC on the 1 April 2009 and the merging of our functions and resources into the Care Quality Commission and Healthcare Inspectorate Wales on that date.

1.2 The MHAC was established alongside the Mental Health Act 1983 to monitor, on behalf of the Secretary of State, the operation of its powers and discharge of its duties in respect of patients detained in hospital. From November 2008 the MHAC's remit was extended to patients subject to the new Supervised Community Treatment (SCT) power. The statute requires the MHAC to visit and interview detained patients in hospital, and to visit and interview SCT patients. It is also empowered to investigate complaints and is required to administer the Second Opinion system that considers the authorisation of certain treatments (see chapter 3). These principal functions will continue to be statutory requirements and powers of the Care Quality Commission and Healthcare Inspectorate Wales after the MHAC is dissolved.

> MHAC visits are always very enjoyable, very helpful, and very useful. They are always friendly, polite and they really listen to us. They're very approachable and sympathetic to patients' fears, concerns. They listen to and act on all issues raised and you can tell they really care.
>
> *Glyn James, SURP member*

1.3 During the debates over the future of the MHAC functions, we have insisted upon the value of visiting and meeting with detained patients in private as the most effective safeguard, and argued that it should remain the core activity from which all others derive in the monitoring of the use of Mental Health Act powers. As illustrated by the quotation from Donna Gilbert, one of the members of our Service User

> I only knew about MHAC visits within the last year of my detention as far as I can remember, as this was the only time it had been announced. I did not find them very helpful and was sorry that they had very little power to help in certain circumstances and could not intervene in certain issues.
>
> *Donna Gilbert, SURP member*

Reference Panel, there will be many service users and others who nevertheless feel that the MHAC has had insufficient power to intervene over matters that arise on its visits. In contrast, the Care Quality Commission will have power to enforce compliance in certain circumstances, and yet we do not expect there to be a radical change in approach under the new organisation. There will still be matters over which the Tribunal, rather than the Care Quality Commission, must hold sway, such as when patients object to the very fact of their detention or their SCT status. We also expect that the presence of the 'big stick' of compliance notices will not prevent Mental Health Act Commissioners (as the visiting officers of the Care Quality Commission will continue to be called[7]) from working with service providers as a critical but supportive outsider. The MHAC has been instrumental in helping services make many hundreds of small steps to better practice over its lifetime, some of which were of great significance to the detainees concerned, but that cumulatively comprise some great strides in improving patient care.

> The MHAC visit was a definite positive for me. I was able to put my problems and concerns to someone who was independent, safe, who would not cause me further harm. I did wonder initially if this MHAC would be no different to everyone else – just the same old pretend to listen and understand and nothing changed. I felt instantly comfortable, given explanations of what may be possible, where differences could be made. Equally important: what was not possible for the MHAC, and signposted to where best to take those issues for resolution. The concerns which were addressed on my behalf to the ward manager led to a slight improvement in certain areas, and other issues my family and I looked to resolve outside the hospital.
>
> Monica Endersby, SURP member

Data collection and the Mental Health Act

1.4 In the First Biennial Report of the MHAC it was confidently predicted that "the computer will increasingly allow the retrieval of facts which will show society the way in which the 1983 Act is working"[8]. Later reports regretted the lack of a requirement that the MHAC, as a monitoring body, be notified of uses of the Act. Although statistics on the use of the Act have been made available through collections by the Department of Health (now through the Information Centre) and Home Office (now Ministry of Justice), these are incomplete in important respects, including the provision of data on ethnicity, age, and other important characteristics. Over the past four years we have had the annual *Count Me In* census to provide this sort of data, although this is due to end in 2010. The National Mental Health Minimum Dataset should eventually provide a complete dataset of uses of the Act relating to hospitals and community powers, and indeed could yet be the computer system anticipated by the MHAC in 1985.

---

[7] Visitors for the Healthcare Inspectorate Wales will, less happily, be called 'Mental Health Act Reviewers'. We are concerned that this may lead to confusion amongst patients between the role of such visitors and that of the Tribunal (which, for almost 50 years until November 2008, was called the *Mental Health Review Tribunal*).

[8] MHAC (1985) *First Biennial Report 1983-1985*, page 56.

1.5 There are areas of the use of the Act that may still remain uncharted. For example, we have stated before that there is no data collection capable of providing national statistics on the use of police powers to hold patients under s.136 of the Act[9]. In this case, we call at paragraph 2.139 for such data collection by the Association of Chief Police Officers.

1.6 The Care Quality Commission has the power to require health and local authorities to provide it with any information, documents, records (including personal and medical records) or other items which it considers necessary or expedient to have for the purposes of any of its regulatory functions[10]. We are greatly encouraged that the Care Quality Commission has indicated to us that it will exercise this power so as to continue and strengthen the MHAC's arrangements for it to be notified of the death of any detained patient, or the admission of a child to an adult ward under the Act. We discuss findings from both these notifications in this report. We hope that the Care Quality Commission will keep under review its exercise of the power to require information and take the opportunity to extend its monitoring practice where we have failed to tread.

The attractions of acute mental health care

1.7 Most detained patients are cared for on acute wards at some point of their admission. In recent Biennial Reports we have been critical of many aspects of these wards, and we continue to express general concerns in this report, although we recognise that there have been significant improvements in some individual services. Notwithstanding these critical comments, it is important to celebrate and appreciate the hard and demanding work undertaken by professionals in acute psychiatric care and the great improvements in the general quality of care over the lifetime of the MHAC. We recognise that criticism of services can engender or reinforce unhelpful stereotypes of both patients and staff, and as such we wish to underline what has been described as "the attractions of working in acute mental health care"[11] as the initial context of our last report.

1.8 There have been significant improvements in psychiatric treatment and care over the lifetime of the Act, such as new drugs and new hospital buildings. But more important than all such improvements in such mechanics of treatment, is the simple human compassion, humour and capacity for hope that we meet with on our visits, as expressed by both staff and patients alike.

1.9 In their ethnographic study of nursing on an acute ward, Deacon *et al* acknowledged the 'chaos' but also formulated positive aspects of nursing practice:

> Attempts to begin formal therapy were often thrown into chaos by the very combinations of problems that had brought people into hospital in the first place. Difficulties with such matters as concentration, rapid mood change, irritability, psychotic misinterpretation of therapeutic

---

[9] See MHAC (2006) *In Place of Fear? Eleventh Biennial Report 2003-2005*, para 4.167 and para 2.29 of this report.

[10] *Health and Social Care Bill 2008*, s.64.

[11] Deacon M, Warne, T & McAndrew S (2006) 'Closeness, chaos and crisis: the attractions of working in acute mental health care'. *Journal of Psychiatric and Mental Health Nursing*, 15, 750-757.

gestures, aggression, sexual disinhibition, despair, disorganization and hopelessness were all at odds with the requirements of formal therapy. This is not to suggest that nurses' work is not therapeutic, but ideas about the mandate of nursing in this environment require challenging.[12]

1.10 Thus the very act of caring for patients at times of extreme crisis or during episodes of serious mental illness is "demanding of nurses' therapeutic dexterity and repertoire of organisationally situated skills"[13] and should be afforded respect as a therapeutic activity in its own right. Acute ward nursing staff in the study by Deacon *et al* showed some difficulties in articulating their work and its value, but not in expressing affection and care for the people they work with.

1.11 As such, nursing in acute care is based on profoundly humane values that managers can and must support in the organisation of wards. Furthermore, we wish to underline here that acute care, when it is allowed to exercise these values, *works*. Even (to take a sceptical view) if the active function is one of holding and protecting patients in crisis, what Deacon *et al* say about acute services in the following passage is important and should be acknowledged as a fundamental aspect of the services discussed in much of this report:

> A paradoxical feature of acute care is that despite its unpopularity, it actually promotes the health of the majority of its service users. To play a critically important role in transforming a person from the social ravages of extreme mental illness to positive health brings enormous pleasure for nurses. During the study, for instance, over the course of about three months a mute, unkempt, distressed and socially isolative young man gradually changed into a warm, generous and funny person who was able to begin to make plans for his future. The researcher observed the nurses' huge satisfaction in witnessing his recovery having engaged in the mess of his ill health. A healthcare assistant said with great pride: "I was the first person he smiled at"[14].

1.12 We hope that those who read and reflect upon our reports will also note this 'paradoxical feature' of our subject.

Service User Involvement

1.13 One of the most welcome developments in psychiatric practice today is the increasing focus on service user involvement in making decisions about treatment and care, so that there is sense of partnership between professionals and the patient. We believe that such an approach must be aimed for even where the context of such treatment and care involves elements of coercion.

1.14 Up to its dissolution, the MHAC was working closely with the 26 members of its Service User Reference Panel to embed service user involvement in all of its activities that will pass to the Care Quality Commission. The Service User Reference Panel (SURP), which is made up of people who are currently detained or have recent experience of detention under the Act have been involved in all major projects and developments in this last reporting

---

[12] *ibid.*
[13] *ibid.*
[14] *ibid.*

period. Our project on the detention of women during 2008-09 had a service user as a part of the project team, and included visits to talk to women service users. The work on mapping how the MHAC will visit people subject to Supervised Community Treatment included a workshop with a selection of SURP members, whose further views were being sought on the draft guidance. Service users were also involved in producing a DVD, *Not Just visiting*, to explain the visiting process to service users. Service users played a significant role in Commissioner and SOAD training over the reporting period, with one of the two days new Commissioner induction training in April 2008 dedicated to service user involvement, and service user input into many of the sessions at the 2008 Commissioner and SOAD Conferences.

> The involvement of the MHAC gave me a small sense of empowerment and my self respect back ... I unashamedly admit to using MHAC at any time a serious event occurred to me. It was the Commissioner who supported me who gave me information about the Service User Reference Panel (SURP) and the forms to express interest in involvement. This became my life-line, I was determined to manage, to survive all the abusive treatment I was experiencing, so as to be able to make positive changes in future for all patients sectioned under the Act.
>
> *Monica Endersby, SURP member*

1.15 The *Acting Together* project of joint service user and Commissioner visits continued to be a significant development. These visits were piloted in 2006-07, and rolled out in 2008-2009 to aid Commissioner awareness of how mental health services are viewed by those who use them. Users of the services visited have also found *Acting Together* beneficial, with some reporting they find it easier to discuss matters knowing that, like them, one of the visitors has experience of detention.

1.16 In April 2008, the Commission held a public launch of *From Strength to Strength*, the report of the first two years of its service user involvement strategy. The purpose of this publication was both to report on the Commission's activity and to share learning on involving service users. During the year the Commission produced its third annual report on its service user involvement. This, and other information, including a regular SURP newsletter, *1983 And All That*, was made available on the 'Your Involvement' pages of the MHAC website.

General trends in admission under the Mental Health Act

1.17 In 2006/07 and 2007/08 there were, respectively, 44,590 and 45,544 uses of the Mental Health Act to detain patients in hospital in England. As is shown at figure 1 below, this level of overall use of the Act (which includes the detention of patients already in hospital as informal patients) has been relatively stable over the last decade, and has in fact dropped slightly from a peak between 1989 and 2002.

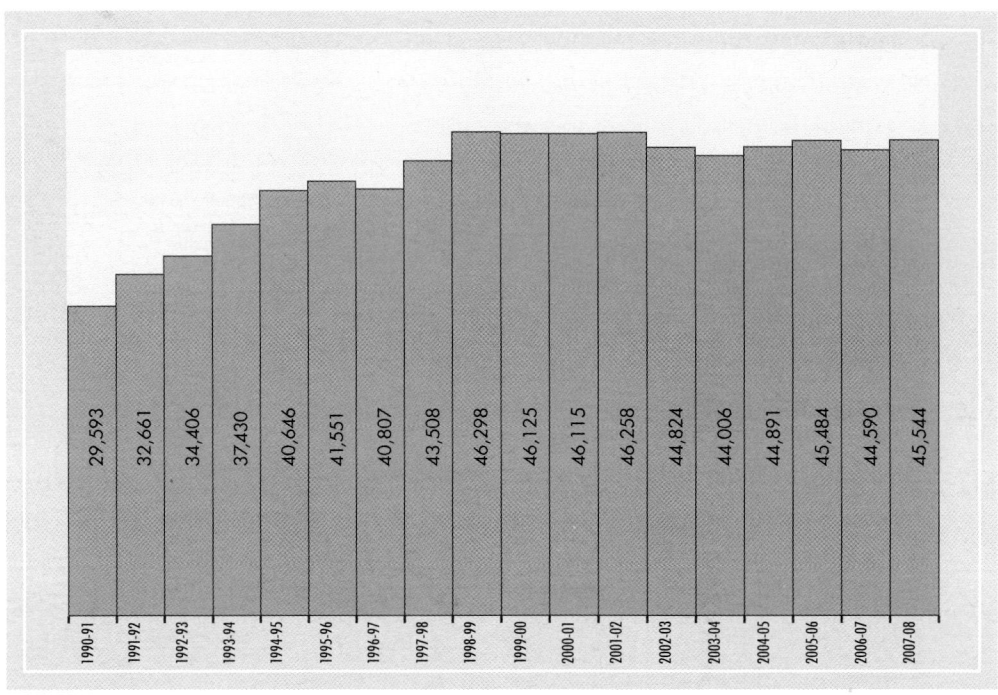

Fig 1: Detentions under the Mental Health Act 1983 (admissions and detention of informal inpatients), England, 1990/91 to 2007/08

Data source: Department of Health/Information Centre statistical bulletins "inpatients detained under the MHA and other legislation" 1986–2009

1.18 As is shown at figure 2 below, of the total admissions in 2006/07 and 2007/08, 25,806 and 26,122 uses of the Act in England were to effect admission to hospital under the 'civil' powers of Part 2 of the Act (that is, the use of s.2 or s.3, excluding such uses on informal patients who are already in hospital). This number has continued to rise, in what was suggested in our last report to be a gentle upwards trend[15]. This can be seen in the "Part 2 admissions" trend-line at figure 2 below. This rise, however, is partly offset by a fall in the numbers of times that detention under the Act is used to stop informal patients from discharging themselves from hospital, as shown by the "changes from informal admission" trend-line.

---

[15] MHAC (2008) *Risk, Rights, Recovery; Twelfth Biennial Report 2005-2007*, para 3.1.

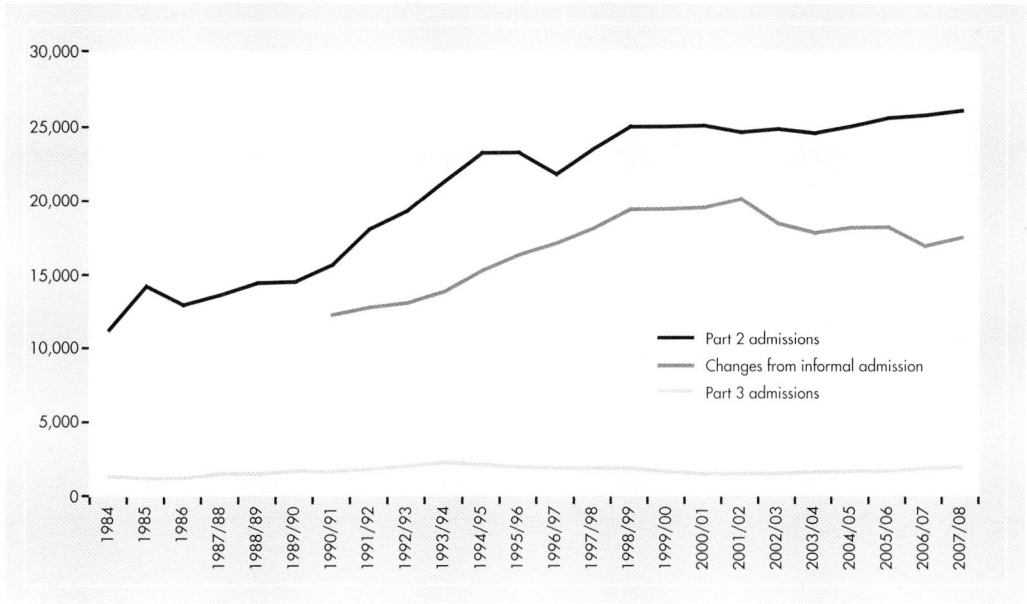

Fig 2: Mental Health Act admission trends, England, 1984 – 2007/08

Data source: as for fig 1

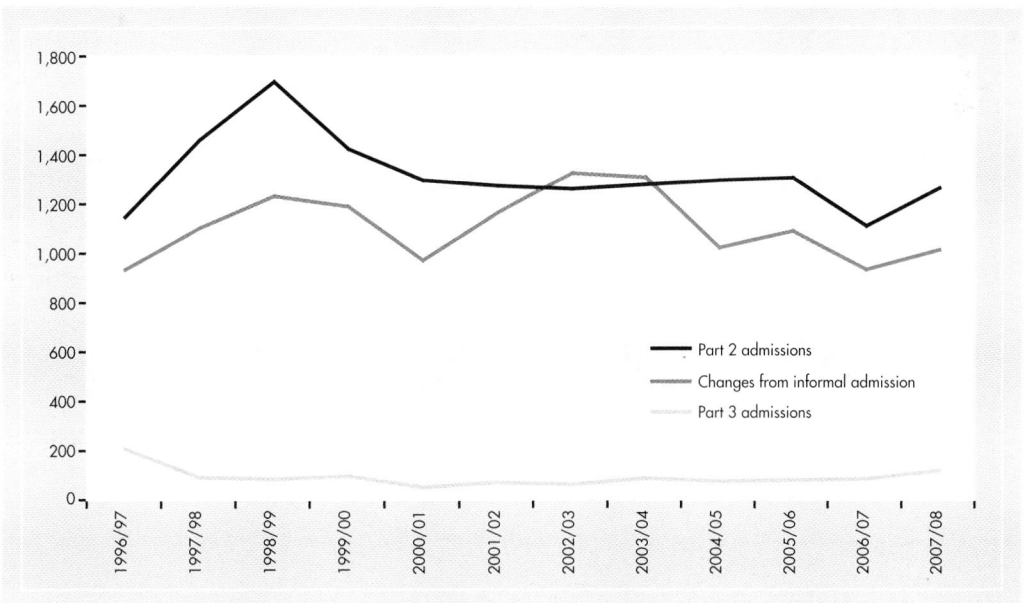

Fig 3: Mental Health Act admission trends, Wales, 1996/97 – 2007/08

Data source: Welsh Assembly Government [16]

1.19 At figure 3 we show the trends in the use of the Mental Health Act in Wales from 1996/97. Of the 2,135 uses of the Act to detain patients in 2006/07, 937 were detentions of informal patients when they attempt to discharge themselves from hospital, and 84 were detentions under Part 3 of the Act. Of the 2,403 uses of the Act in 2007/08, 1,017 were detentions of informal patients, and 118 were uses of Part 3 powers. This appears neither to represent any apparent upwards trend in the use of the Act to admit patients, nor any clear trend in the numbers or proportion of informal patients who are detained under the Act.

---

[16] *Statistics for Wales*, available at www.statswales.wales.gov.uk

The balance between hospital and community based services

1.20 We can, of course, only speculate as to any interpretation to be placed upon the apparent trend in England discussed at paragraph 1.18 above. It seems plausible, however, that this a statistical reflection of what has been termed the increased acuity of patients admitted to hospital[17]. In other words, the threshold for hospitalisation in mental health services, at least in some areas of England (and probably some areas of Wales too), may be so high that patients at the point of admission are necessarily in crisis sufficient to warrant detention. If this is the case, it may not be a bad thing, as it may simply be a reflection of development in community mental health services that are managing people who would previously have required informal admission to hospital.

1.21 Such is the interpretation provided by the World Health Organisation of the low numbers of psychiatric beds per 100,000 population of England and Wales[18]. Of the 42 countries of the WHO European Region surveyed in 2007, England and Wales (counted as representative of the United Kingdom for this purpose) was sixth from the bottom in terms of numbers of psychiatric beds per 100,000 population. Although this means that there are similar numbers of psychiatric beds proportionate to population numbers in England and Wales as there are in Greece or Albania, the WHO suggest that for England and Wales this is a reflection of "post-deinstitutionalisation", rather than low investment and inadequate infrastructure[19].

1.22 Total investment in adult mental health services in England was £5.530bn in 2007/08, an increase of £1.276bn over the five years from 2002/03[20]. The NHS spent £8.4bn on mental health services overall in 2006/07, the highest spend on any individual area of healthcare[21]. Of this, £183m was spent on crisis resolution and home treatment teams (CRHTs)[22], which are designed to avoid hospital admission if at all possible. Department of Health guidance states that:

> Only by the local crisis team assessing all people who potentially require admission, can three key objectives for crisis services be achieved:
>
> 1) Patients should be treated in the least restrictive environment which is consistent with their clinical and safety needs;

---

[17] Healthcare Commission (2008) *Review of acute inpatient mental health services*.

[18] World Health Organisation (2008) *Policies and practices for mental health in Europe – meeting the challenges*, page 48. The reported mental health beds per 100,000 population in England and Wales is 23. The only European country with fewer beds, where this is attributed in the WHO report to "post-deinstitutionalisation" rather than underdevelopment, is Italy (8 beds per 100,000). France has 95 beds and Germany 75 beds per 100,000 population.

[19] *ibid*. The only European country with fewer beds, where this is attributed in the WHO report to "post-deinstitutionalisation" rather than underdevelopment, is Italy (8 beds per 100,000). France has 95 beds and Germany 75 beds per 100,000 population.

[20] Mental Health Strategies (2008) *2007/08 National Survey of Investment in Mental Health Services*, p. 1.

[21] National Audit Office (2007) *Helping people through mental health crisis: The role of Crisis Resolution and Home Treatment services*. Report by the Comptroller and Auditor General. HC 5 Session 2007-2008. 7 December 2007, p.4.

[22] *ibid*.

2) In-patient admissions and pressure on beds should be reduced;

3) Equity of access to an alternative to admission for patients and families must be ensured.[23]

1.23 The National Audit Office found that over half of all patients admitted to psychiatric beds (including those admitted informally) had not been in contact with a CHRT, and estimated that roll-out of fully provisioned CHRTs could ultimately reduce all such admissions by one-fifth[24]. The Healthcare Commission has found that 17% of Trusts surveyed had no access to day care services, crisis accommodation or respite care services that can help CHRTs avoid inpatient admissions[25]. The development of community services is therefore an important priority in the years ahead, and it is timely that the MHAC is to be merged into the Care Quality Commission (CQC) and therefore empowered to take a broader view of care pathways than our present remit allows.

1.24 But we have warned in the past that an over-emphasis on community care initiatives can lead to relative neglect of inpatient services (a point which, to its credit, government has sought to address[26]), and we hope that the retention of specific statutory duties for CQC relating to detained patients will ensure that the patients who require in-patient treatment are given suitable attention. As the inpatient ward becomes increasingly the place of last resort, such a particular focus is all the more vital.

The increasing relevance of the independent sector

1.25 This reporting period has seen the continued increase of patients admitted under the Act to independent sector hospitals, as is shown by figures 4 and 5. The population detained in the independent sector in England has quadrupled since 1997, and peaked (so far) at 3,100 in 2007 (figure 4). In Wales, this reporting period saw a step-change in the numbers of admissions to independent sector hospitals, with over twice as many such admissions in 2006/07 and 2007/08 as the annual rate over the previous ten years (figure 5).

---

[23] Department of Health (2007) *Guidance Statement on Fidelity and Best Practice for Crisis Services*; Department of Health (2002) *Mental Health Policy Implementation Guide: Adult Acute Inpatient Care Provision*. Quoted in Paul McCrone, Martin Knapp, Jess Hudson, (2007) *Model to assess the Economic Impact of integrating CRHT and Inpatient Services*. Centre for the Economics of Mental Health, Health Service and Population Research Department, King's College London. December 2007.

[24] *ibid.*, p.22.

[25] Healthcare Commission (2008) *Review of acute inpatient mental health services*, fig.11 p.58.

[26] See MHAC (2006) *In Place of Fear? Eleventh Biennial Report 2003-2005*, para 2.28.

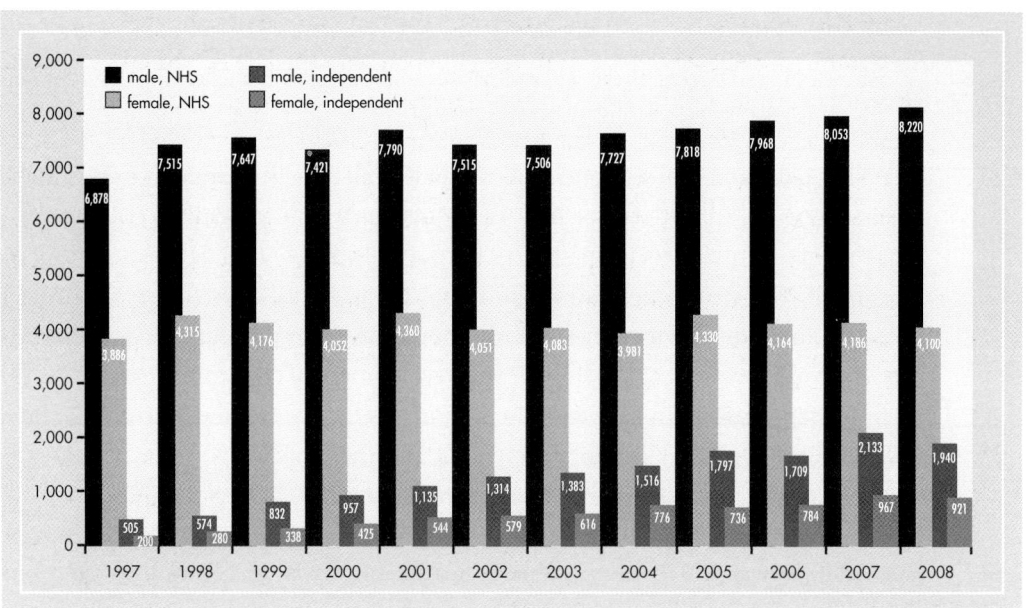

Fig 4: Resident detained population, NHS & private sector by gender, England, 1999 – 2008

Source: DH/information centre stats

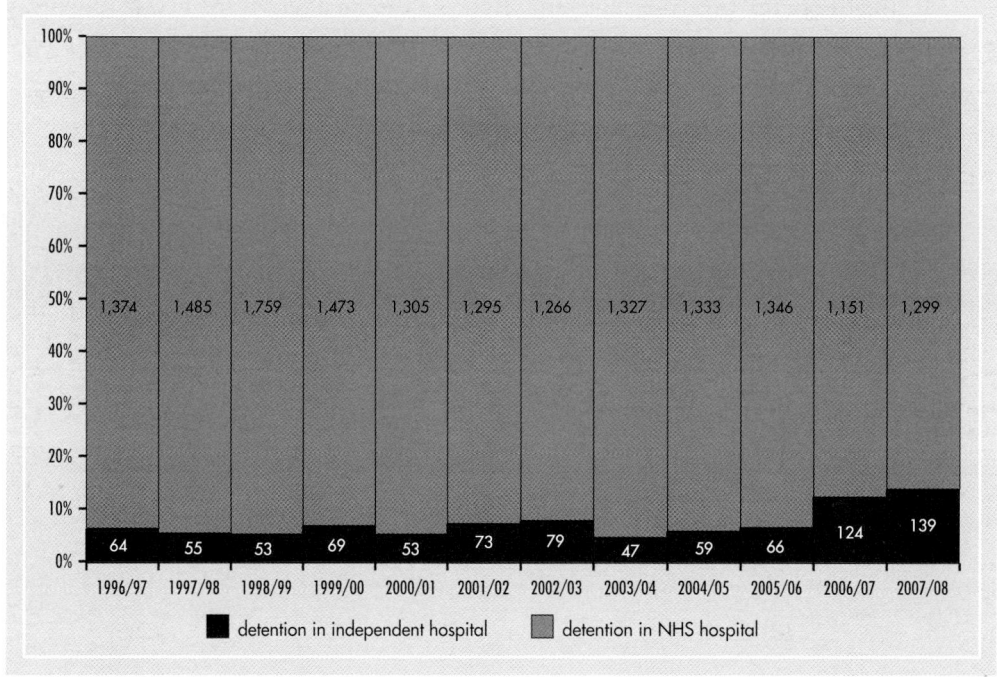

Fig 5: Admissions to NHS and independent hospitals, Wales, 1996/97 to 2007/08

Data source: Welsh Assembly Government [27]

1.26 It is likely that a significant part of the increase in use of the independent sector can be accounted for by its provision of specialist services. As such, independent hospitals are filling in gaps left in NHS provision. It is important that service commissioning bodies are competent in this environment, and alert to the dangers of commissioning expensive out of area placements for certain patients rather than developing local services[28]. We note

---

[27] *Statistics for Wales*, available at www.statswales.wales.gov.uk.

[28] See MHAC (2006) *In Place of Fear? Eleventh Biennial Report 2003-2005*, para 2.23.

some encouraging developments in collaboration between PCTs and local authorities in commissioning services from the independent sector, including, for example, a system co-ordinated by Cumbria and Lancashire Commissioning Business Service to establish a commissioner-led quality assurance framework for mental health placements in the independent sector. The framework outlines specific terms and conditions and performance standards; open and transparent pricing; and clarity about the expectations of mental health case managers to monitor the outcomes and objectives of individual placements[29]. We believe that many commissioning bodies who are spot purchasing placements from the independent sector cannot claim such a quality framework underpinning their decisions.

1.27 Some independent sector hospitals providing secure services appear to be reluctant to admit patients who have informal legal status, and we are aware of a number of cases where commissioning bodies looking for specialist beds have been told that a bed would only be available for a particular patient if that patient were detained. In one case, the patient in question was a fifteen-year old girl; in another, a patient detained in an independent hospital was initially told that a successful appeal to the Mental Health Review Tribunal against his detained status would have to leave his hospital placement. In the latter case, this was challenged as a preliminary issue at the Tribunal hearing and the detaining authority retracted from its position (the patient was, in any case, not discharged from detention). It is understandable that secure services are cautious in admitting informal patients, even if the patient contracts to abide by hospital rules and restrictions, when these aspects of the hospital regime may amount to a deprivation of liberty. Furthermore, we accept that most of the patients referred to secure services will probably meet the criteria for detention under the Act, irrespective of local admissions policies. But we are concerned that such policies have the potential to distort the assessment process for considering detention (or indeed discharge) under the Act, particularly where the patient concerned requires specialist services only available through very limited numbers of providers. We do not believe that *any* hospital can justly claim that it is bound by law to only accept detained patients. We note that Broadmoor High Security Hospital has a policy on the care of informal patients, indicating that all hospitals of any security level should be able to do likewise.

Characteristics of the detained population

The gender mix of the detained population

1.28 Although men and women are admitted under part 2 powers of the Act in roughly equal numbers(see figure 6 below), the resident population of part 2 patients (figure 7 below) is roughly two-thirds male. This indicates that male patients stay in hospital for longer periods than women patients.

---

[29] 'Bulk buy for a better deal' *Health Service Journal,* 12 March 2009, p.22-23.

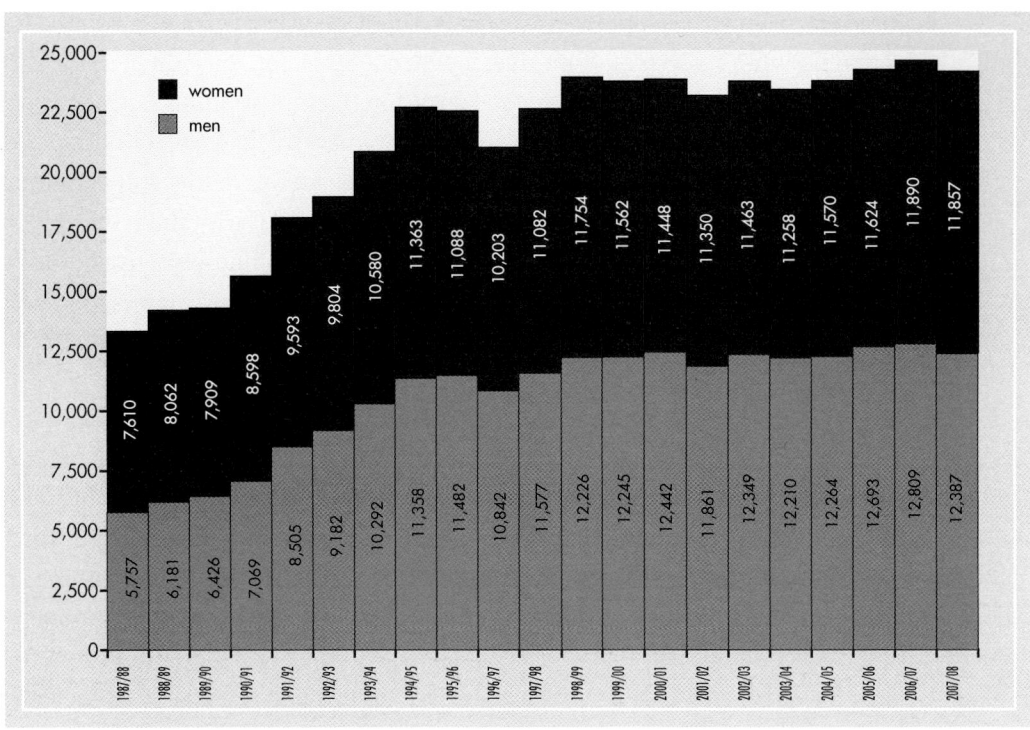

Fig 6: Male and female patients admitted to hospital under Part 2 of the Mental Health Act, England, 1997/98–2007/08

Data source: as for fig 1

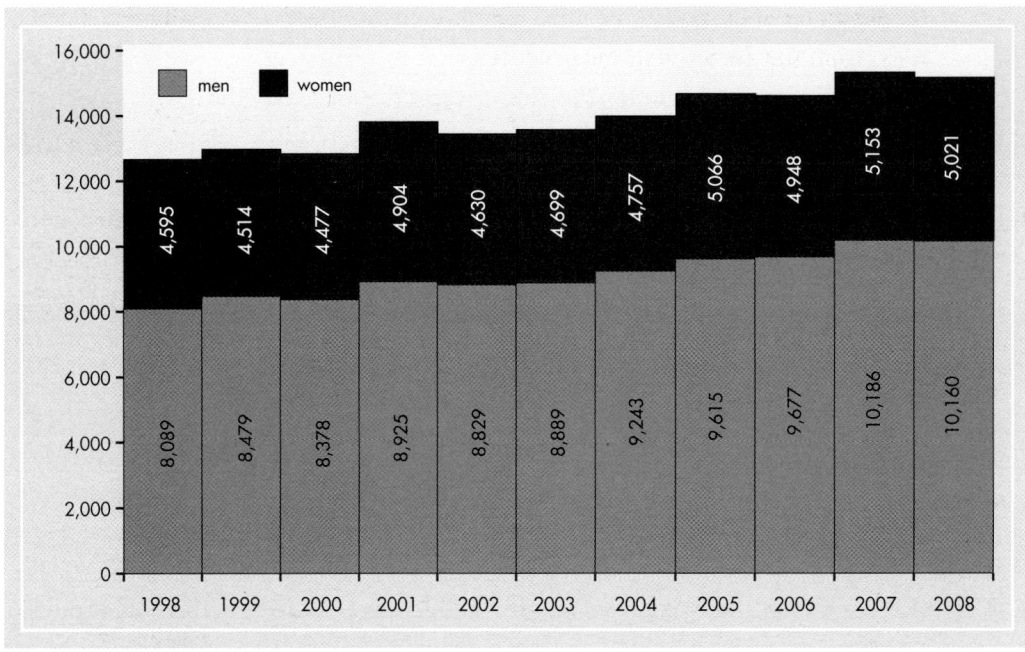

Fig 7: Male and female patients detained under Part 2 of the Mental Health Act, resident in hospital on the 31 December, England, 1998–2008

Data source: as for fig 1

1.29 Figure 8 below shows the distribution of male and female detained patients across all security levels[30].

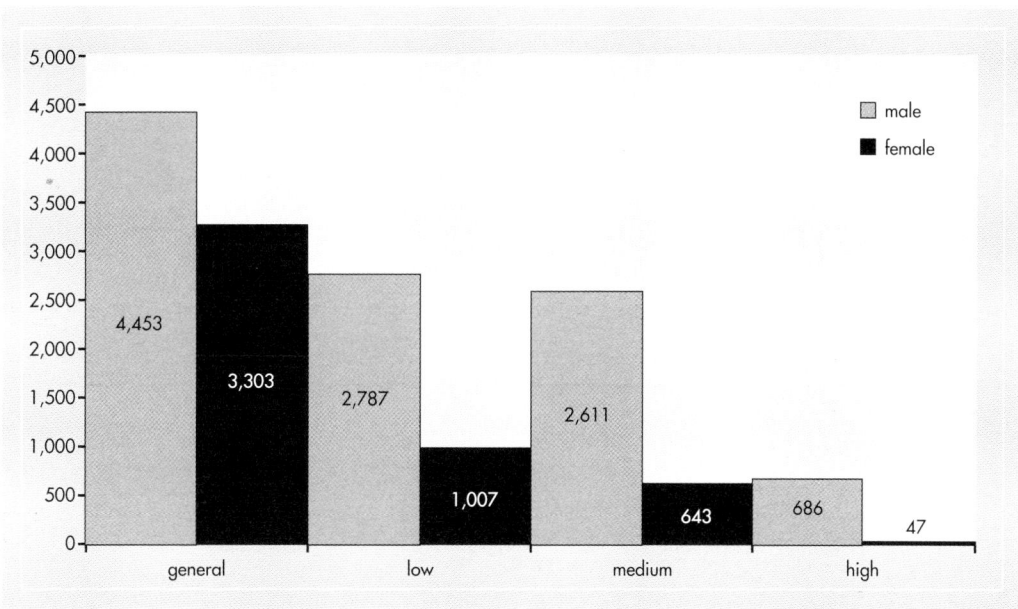

Fig 8: Male and female detained patients by security level, resident in hospital on 31 March 2008
Source: *Count Me In* census 2008

1.30 Figure 9 below shows the age ranges of male and female patients detained in hospital, according to whether they are detained in general or higher security levels. The data is taken from the 2008 *Count Me In* census.

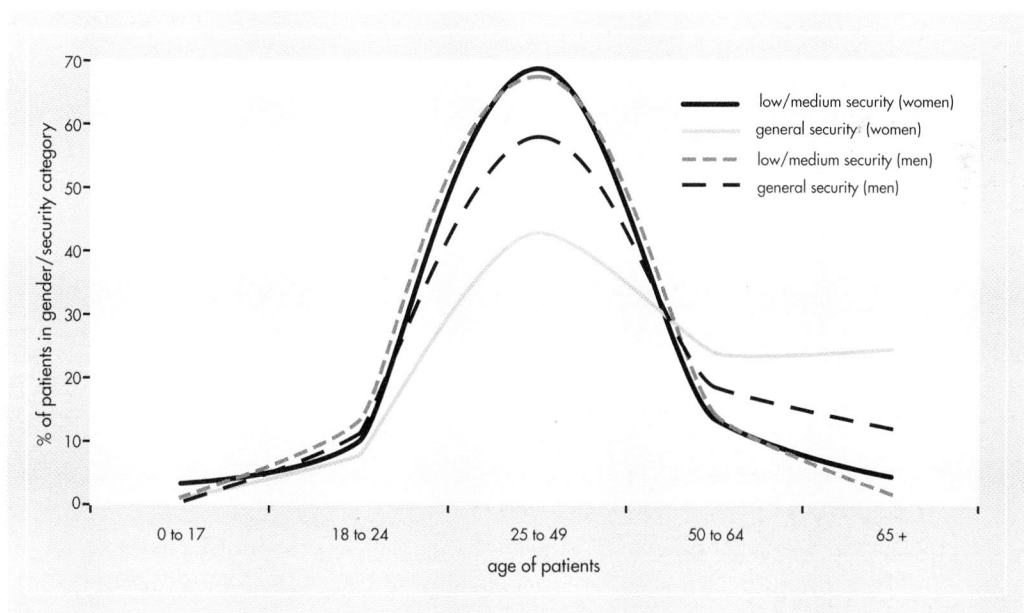

Fig 9: Age range of detained patients by gender and security level, England and Wales, 31 March 2008
Source: *Count Me In* census 2008

---

[30] The data is taken from the 2008 *Count Me In* census, rather than Information Centre statistics, and as such the overall totals do not match those shown at fig 8 above. Raw (unstandardised) data used in this report was kindly provided by the *Count Me In* census team. For published data, see Healthcare Commission (2008) *Count Me In 2008: Results of the 2008 national census of inpatients in mental health and learning disability services in England and Wales*. November 2008.

1.31 It is notable that, at general levels of security, substantial proportions of both male and female detained patients are aged over 65 years. This is especially the case for female patients in hospitals with no specified security designation (i.e. 'general' security). But in all security levels, the predominant single age group is that for patients aged between 25 to 49 years. That other age groups may be in a considerable minority, perhaps especially in the low and medium secure sector, can cause difficulties in ensuring that treatment and care is suitably tailored to their needs.

> Male staff would have to look through the observation window in the bedroom door to check that everything was alright regardless of being told that the patient was having a shower or getting dressed. At night time also the male staff would have to go into the rooms unaccompanied by a female member of staff to check if the patient was still breathing. The intrusion of privacy caused problems between patients and staff which led to many restraints or higher doses of medication being administered.
>
> Donna Gilbert, SURP member

1.32 The experiences of women patients detained in hospital are explored in more detail in the MHAC report '*Women detained in hospital*', published earlier in 2009[31], which made the following three recommendations:

1. All NHS and independent sector hospitals which admit and treat women under the powers of the Mental Health Act should read '*Women detained in hospital*' and consider their own practice in relation to its findings.

2. Commissioners of services to take the findings of the report into account when planning and commissioning services for women.

3. Our successor bodies, the Care Quality Commission and Healthcare Inspectorate Wales, in their assessment of the performance of mental health providers, should consider how duties under equalities and human rights legislation are being met, and in particular give sufficient priority through the new registration system in England (to be introduced in 2010) to assuring the safety, privacy and dignity of women detained in hospital under the powers of the Mental Health Act.

1.33 There is a culture on too many wards where women are subject to low-level harassment and exposed to men who may take advantage of them:

> I was made to feel very unsafe by a particular male patient when on section 3, he would constantly be in my room, trying to control me, and he made very improper advances. I didn't feel that I would be believed if I raised it and the staff never seemed to have time. An auxiliary nurse witnessed this and raised it with staff: the man in question was moved to another ward.
>
> All wards should be single sex, and less clinical – more like your own home with not as many rules.
>
> Deborah Hickman, SURP member

---

[31] MHAC (2009) *Women detained in hospital*, published March 2009. www.mhac.org.uk

1.34 There are also some excellent examples of specialist units where treatment and care is tailored to women's needs: as in the following report from a mother and baby unit in Homerton Hospital, London:

> The ward was pleasant, clean, well maintained. Patients had access to fresh air all day by going into the ward's own garden area. Staff were sitting with the patients and babies, with an excellent staff/patient rapport in evidence. There was access to a preparation and feeding area where mothers could be assisted by the nursery nurse always on shift, or if they were happy to breast feed and prepare their own food, they were supported to maintain independent activity and encourage bonding. The Commissioner commends the Trust and ward staff for the high level of awareness and skill in exercising the John Bowlby approach to effective attachment – the 'growth of love' as an effective measure for both mother and baby – in this setting.

1.35 Whilst the above example deals with a service that is necessarily specialist, there have been some calls from patient groups and professionals for provision of specialist women's services across all aspects of inpatient psychiatric care. One study reported in this period suggests that the clinical reality of caring for women with psychosis is different from that of men, having compared men and women inpatients treated for psychosis by one independent provider[32]. Women with psychosis are more likely to suffer concomitant affective disorders such as depression; more likely to self-harm; more likely to have difficulties with relationships and social function; and more likely to have a history of having been abused. Some of these factors may be associated with epidemiological differences in psychotic illnesses between women and men (i.e. women are statistically likely to be older at onset), although this perhaps begs the question of what causes such differences in age profile between the sexes. However, if such differences are typical (and not just limited to the patients involved in this study), then there may be an argument for specifically focussed care interventions for women with psychosis by nursing staff and psychologists; different approaches to setting aims and goals of interventions; and perhaps a more widespread use of gender-specific inpatient units for the care of psychotic illness[33]. We note this with interest and would welcome wider debate.

The ethnicity of detained patients.

1.36 The ethnic origin of patients detained as of the 31 March 2008 is given at figure 10 below. The ethnic origin of patients subject to supervised community treatment (SCT) is discussed at chapter 2.80.

---

[32] Spurrell M (2008) 'Should women be a special case when it comes to services for psychosis?' *Mental Health Today*, October 2008, p.23-26. Dr Spurrell is the clinical director of Affinity Healthcare, an independent provider of mental health services that opened a women-only unit for the treatment of psychosis near Darlington in 2008.

[33] *ibid.*

Ethnic group	Men Number	Men %	Women Number	Women %	Total Number	Total %
White British	7,515	68.7	3,904	75.0	11,419	70.7
White Irish	148	1.4	108	2.1	256	1.6
Other White	552	5.0	253	4.9	805	5.0
White and Black Caribbean	188	1.7	69	1.3	257	1.6
White and Black African	51	0.5	21	0.4	72	0.4
White and Asian	60	0.5	19	0.4	79	0.4
Other Mixed	93	0.8	30	0.6	123	0.8
Indian	160	1.5	66	1.3	226	1.4
Pakistani	218	2.0	68	1.3	286	1.8
Bangladeshi	73	0.7	26	0.5	99	0.6
Other Asian	173	1.6	44	0.8	217	1.3
Black Caribbean	762	7.0	280	5.4	1,042	6.5
Black African	385	3.5	140	2.7	525	3.3
Other Black	239	2.2	59	1.1	298	1.8
Chinese	36	0.3	25	0.5	61	0.4
Other	171	1.6	43	0.8	214	1.3
Not stated / recorded	120	1.1	53	1.0	173	1.1
Total	10,944	100	5,208	100	16,152	100

Figure 10: Patients detained in hospital under the Mental Health Act 1983 by ethnic group and gender, 31 March 2008, England and Wales

Source: *Count Me In* census

1.37 It is now well-known that, even when standardised for age, such data on admission levels show disproportionately high levels of detention amongst Black patients (in particular Black-Caribbean and Black-African patients). We discussed issues of over-representation and institutional racism in our last report[34]. Writing in the *Health Service Journal*, Heginbotham and Shah have argued that a truer measure of health inequities between different ethnic groups of patients (whatever the reason behind these) can be best measured through comparing minority groups against the majority group, rather than comparisons with the average overall as used in the *Count Me In* reports[35]. The authors criticise the Healthcare Commission for approaching the data with 'a spurious insistence on statistical significance' which mask the fact that all Black groups (including the 'Black Other' group largely comprised of second or third generation Black British young men and women) show the highest bed occupancy ratios in comparison with the White British population, and most other BME groups (with the important exceptions of Indian and Chinese patients) also have substantially higher rates of bed occupancy than the White British population.

---

[34] MHAC (2008) *Risk, Rights, Recovery; Twelfth Biennial Report 2005-2007*, para 3.79.

[35] Heginbotham C and Shah A 'Patchwork picture says volumes' *Health Service Journal*, 5 March 2009. Professor Chris Heginbotham was MHAC Chief Executive for the first part of this reporting period.

1.38   In our first Biennial Report[36], before any systematic measurement of the use of Mental Health Act powers amongst Black and Ethnic Minorities had been undertaken on the scale of the *Count Me In* census[37], we highlighted 'concerns of disadvantage' to Black and Minority Ethnic communities in the use of such powers, and suggested 'practical measures' to allay these. We urged the Department of Health and Social Security (as it then was) to undertake a translation of statutory information leaflets into various languages other than English as one such measure. By the autumn of 1986 the Department accepted responsibility for undertaking this task, but in our third Biennial Report we expressed 'profound dismay' at not having seen examples or having been given a date for their distribution[38]. In the absence of centrally available translations, some hospitals had procured their own, accepting that the duty to provide written information under s.132 cannot otherwise be met for patients who do not read English. Translated leaflets finally did become available, but not before considerable duplication of effort and unnecessary expense amongst local health authorities.

1.39   It is therefore with great regret that we have learned that the Department of Health is not to produce translations of the new information leaflets introduced following the changes to the Act in 2008, but is to leave it to individual detaining authorities to make their own provision. It seems to us a matter of great concern, especially in the light of previous criticisms of the Department of Health's fulfilment of its duties under the Race Relations (Amendment) Act[39], that the Department has divested itself of this task. The Department has explained its action to us on the grounds that it is not the detaining authority for patients; its leaflets are therefore designed only as models for detaining authorities to use, not to relieve them of their responsibilities; and that the information in the leaflets, being concerned solely with matters pertaining to the Mental Health Act, is not sufficient communication for the purposes of local detaining authorities, who will therefore need to commission other translated written communication in any case. Of course, all of these justifications could have been applied to the situation before the changes to the Act in 2008, when the Department did provide centrally translated information leaflets. We regret that the Department has taken this line. However, we commend the initiative shown by Northamptonshire Healthcare NHS Trust in organising the pooling of resources across a number of participating Trusts to provide translated leaflets, and DVDs of readings of the leaflets. We understand that these are to be provided without copyright. In the event of any future change being required to the English text leaflets provided by the Department of Health, we hope that serious consideration will be given by the Department to providing specific funding to keep these initiatives up to date.

1.40   We continue to encounter patients who require but do not appear to get translators to communicate with clinical staff:

---

[36]   MHAC (1985) *First Biennial Report 1983-1985*, p.54.

[37]   See MHAC (1987) *Second Biennial Report 1985-1987*, p.52, for the MHAC's first call for systematic monitoring of ethnicity and use of the Act.

[38]   MHAC (1989) *Third Biennial Report 1987-1989*, p.51.

[39]   MHAC (2008) *Risk, Rights, Recovery. Twelfth Biennial Report 2005 – 2007*, para 3.81. The charge against the Department of Health of 'institutional complacency' and 'probably the worst race equality record of any Whitehall department' was made in September 2007 by the Commission for Race Equality.

The Commissioner spoke with one patient who appeared to have very poor English and required an interpreter. It was noted from the patient's electronic patient records that an interpreter was required, and an interpreter had been present at a managers' hearing in July at another hospital. A recent case conference recorded 'staff report problems with communication with staff when X is trying to express her needs ... X became upset about not having leave immediately, due to language barriers.' There appeared to be some uncertainty among staff regarding interpreter input for this patient.

London, September 2007.

1.41 We also encounter failures to ensure that appropriate action is taken to protect patients from racist abuse. In the main, this will be in the form of verbal taunts from other patients, although the following example shows an unusual problem badly handled:

"The task of caring for Y was hampered by her distress due to another patient's visible Nazi tattoos and her criticism that the nursing staff did not intervene sufficiently to ensure that the other patient cover up these tattoos"

Incident report following patient suicide, West Midlands, December 2007

Patients with learning difficulties

1.42 The following statement was provided to the MHAC by one of its SURP members.

> I was detained from the age of sixteen – can you imagine being detained at sixteen until now – forty-three years. They tell you that you're institutionalised, one place to another, these sections go on too long. You're going to be institutionalised with being in these places so long. The trouble is you're told if you keep your nose clean you'll get out, and then when you go for a Tribunal you are told that you have become institutionalised and that prolongs staying in these places. I've got a City and Guilds in gardening so I can't be mentally impaired like they say I am – so how can you prove to them that you're not mentally impaired if they don't give you the chance?
>
> You don't know when you're getting out. I've been in too long. They should give me my freedom. It's not the people in the hospitals, it's the community, you don't have the back up in the community, somewhere where you can drop in everyday so they can keep an eye out for you and somewhere to go if you need to talk or are worried. Or a community nurse or social worker could come to yours to see how you're doing. Not like probation hostels where people nick your stuff to buy drugs. It pissed me off being done over in those places.
>
> When you get older you don't think about the things you did when you were young, but how do you convince Tribunals that you are no longer a risk if they don't give you the chance or the support you need outside of the hospital to prove it?
>
> I don't get any treatment – I don't get meds – we started to do 'activity folders' and nothing seems to be getting done. I made choices that nothing is being done about.
>
> *Larry Summers, SURP member*

1.43 The Healthcare Commission published its national audit of inpatient healthcare services for people with learning difficulties[40] in December 2007, as noted in our last report[41]. The audit found significant institutional failings that deprive patients of their human rights and dignity, despite the efforts of committed staff members; unacceptable variations in the quality of services; poor physical environments; and paucity of choice for patients in how they live their lives. In March 2009 the Healthcare Commission, Commission for Social Care Inspection and the MHAC published our joint review, *Commissioning Services and Support for People with Learning Disability and Complex Needs*[42], calling for improvements in the way learning disability services are planned and organised.

1.44 It is government policy that all long-stay and campus NHS provision for people with learning difficulties should be closed by 2010[43]. The emphasis of government policy is on people with learning difficulties accessing mainstream NHS services wherever possible. This can mean that some patients with learning difficulty who exhibit challenging behaviour or have concomitant mental illness[44] are admitted under the Mental Health Act to ordinary acute wards, although not always to receive very appropriate care. In other cases, specialist evaluation and assessment units are available to provide a more tailored service. As we noted in our last report, however, there has also been some growth in the independent sector provision of secure or relatively long-stay facilities to meet the gap in the market created by the closure of NHS facilities[45]. There continues to be a gap in some provision, particularly with regard to children with learning difficulties, and 'no clear planning function that links government priorities with local service provision'[46].

1.45 The number of detentions in NHS facilities under the Mental Health Act of people classified with mental impairment or severe mental impairment has decreased over the last decade, although not dramatically (figure 11). It has been relatively steady over the last six years, averaging 130 admissions per year. Such legal classifications ceased to exist on 1 November 2008, and so future admission data is unlikely to be comparable[47].

---

[40] Healthcare Commission (2007) *A life like no other. A national audit of inpatient healthcare services for people with learning difficulties in England*. December 2007.

[41] MHAC (2008) *Risk, Rights, Recovery; Twelfth Biennial Report 2005-2007*, para 3.33.

[42] Healthcare Commission, Commission for Social Care Inspection and Mental Health Act Commission (2009) *Commissioning Services and Support for People with Learning Disability and Complex Needs*. March 2009.

[43] Department of Health (2006) *Our health, our care, our say. A new direction for community services*.

[44] These are the main reasons for the admission of people with learning difficulties to assessment and treatment units. Evidence suggests that the rate of mental illness is higher in people with learning difficulties than in the general population. See Slevin E, Mcconkey R, Truesdale-Kennedy M, & Taggart L (2008) 'People with learning disabilities admitted to an assessment and treatment unit: impact on challenging behaviours and mental health problems' *Journal of Psychiatric and Mental Health Nursing* 15 537-546.

[45] MHAC (2008) *Risk, Rights, Recovery; Twelfth Biennial Report 2005-2007*, para 3.30 et seq.

[46] Wright B, Williams C, Richardson G (2008) 'Services for children with learning disabilities'. *Psychiatric Bulletin* 32 81-84.

[47] At our request, the Information Centre has agreed to collect data on admissions of persons with learning disability, as defined in s.1 of the amended Act, where that person is considered to be suffering from mental disorder by reason of that disability alone. However, such categorisation of admissions may not be sufficiently equivalent to that shown in figure 11 for the purpose of trend analysis.

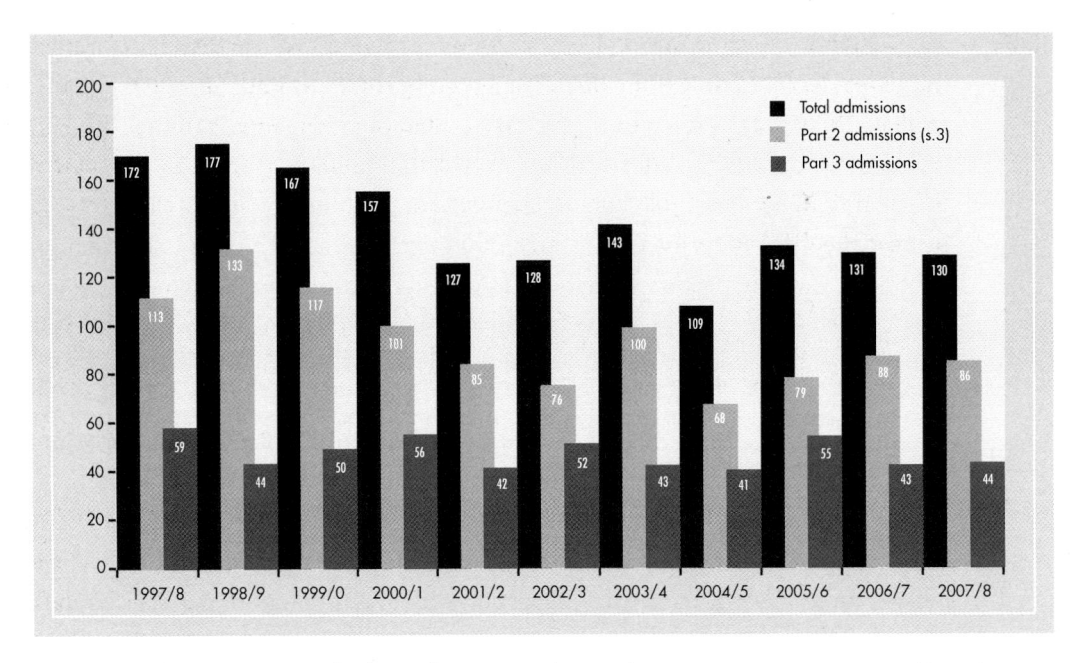

Fig 11: Admissions to NHS facilities of patients with mental impairment or severe mental impairment, 1997/98 to 2007/08, England

Data source: as for fig 1

1.46   By contrast, the number of admissions to independent hospitals of this patient group has increased over the last six years, as is shown at figure 12. We do not have admission data for independent hospitals by legal category of mental disorder for any earlier period, although it seems likely (from the resident population in independent hospitals over the last decade, as shown at figure 13 below) that the most recent data does represent an increase over the decade. It is therefore quite possible that the increase in admission to the independent sector more than compensates for the fall in NHS admissions over the decade, and that there were more detentions under the Act of patients with learning difficulties in 2007/08 than in 1997/98.

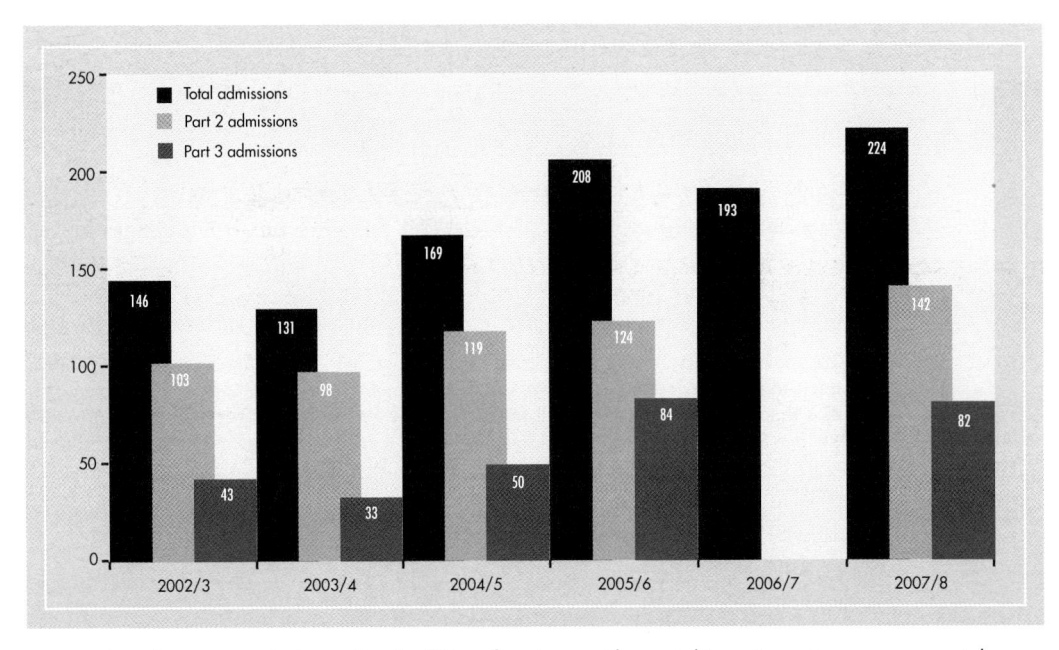

Fig 12: Admissions to independent facilities of patients with mental impairment or severe mental impairment, 1997/98 to 2007/08, England

Data source: Information Centre (KP90) on request of MHAC.
For 2006/7 data, total admissions only were available

1.47   An increase in the number of detentions of patients with learning difficulties could, perhaps, signal a success in deinstitutionalising these patients. In other words, patients who might in the past have been placed in hospital and left there are now largely managing in community settings, with multiple short admissions to hospital at time of crisis. This is, after all, the pattern for 'mainstream' detention under the Act. Two factors cast some doubt on this explanation:

- First, as can be seen in figure 12 above, a significant part of the increase is in detentions under Part 3 of the Act (in fact under s.37 court orders following conviction for an offence). Such detentions are not, of course, of short duration. Even if these are patients who have escaped institutionalisation earlier in their lives, from the point of conviction they can expect to spend considerable time within institutional settings.

- Second, figure 13 below shows an increase in the resident population of detained patients with learning difficulties over the decade, with the increase largely accounted for by placements in the independent sector. This supports the thesis (outlined in more detail in our previous report[48]) that, whatever progress may have been made towards the aim of shutting down institutional long-stay care in NHS facilities, institutions have simply shifted to the independent sector control. It may be that service-commissioning bodies are failing to identify community-based replacements for the institutional care that they used to rely upon, and perpetuating this by other means.

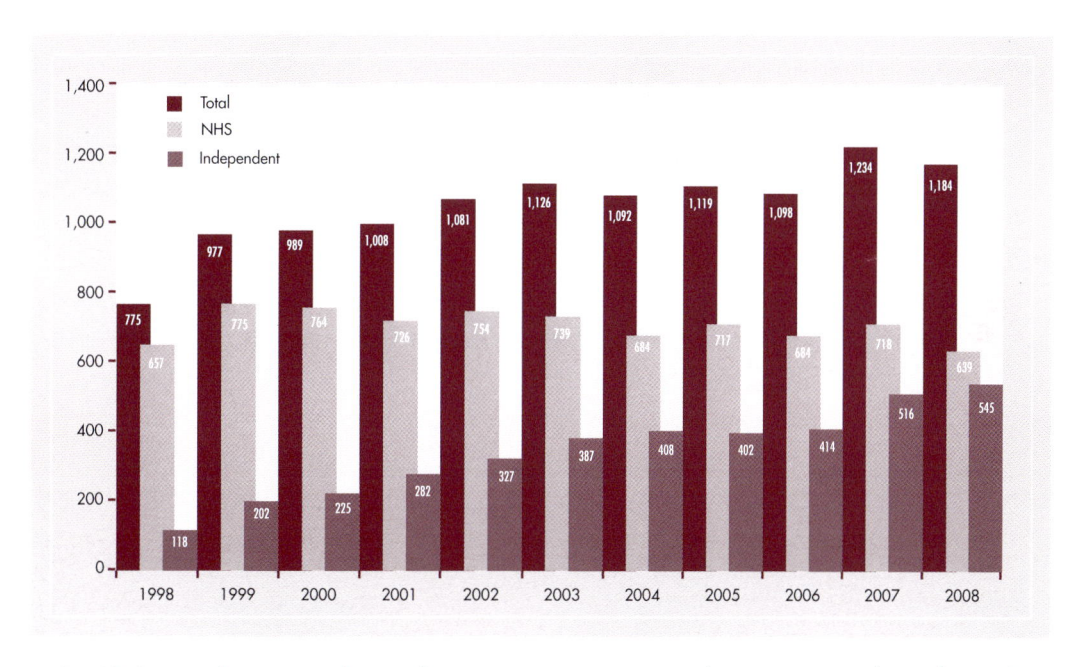

Fig 13: Detained patients with mental impairment or severe mental impairment resident in hospital, (31 March), England, 1998 to 2008

Data source: as for fig 1

---

[48]   MHAC (2008) *Risk, Rights, Recovery; Twelfth Biennial Report 2005-2007*, para 3.30 *et seq*.

Children and adolescents

1.48 New provisions in the Mental Health Act (at s.131A) will, when brought into force, provide a duty upon hospital managers when any patient under the age of 18 is admitted informally or under the Act's powers:

- to consult with a person who appears to have knowledge or experience of cases involving minors; and

- to ensure that the environment is suitable having regard to the patient's age, subject to his or her needs.

The Government has made a commitment to commence this provision in England by April 2010[49]. To meet this duty, managers will have to provide appropriate physical facilities; staff with appropriate training; and a hospital routine that will allow their personal, social and educational development to continue as normally as possible[50]. Although there is no legal requirement that the person consulted should have any particular expertise, we suggested in our last report that a doctor with specific child and adolescent mental health training should always be involved, even if only in this consultative role, in the care of any detained child or adolescent patient[51]. The Royal College of Psychiatrists has published guidelines, *Safe and Appropriate Care for Young People on Adult Mental Health Wards*[52], which we commend to all services.

1.49 In our last report[53], we welcomed the Government's commitment in England to end admissions to adult wards of all under 16 year olds from November 2008, and to end the inappropriate admission of any 16 or 17 year old to an adult psychiatric ward by the commencement of s.131A in April 2010. We noted that this was an ambitious undertaking, and it would be unhelpful to be overly critical if it was not always met.

1.50 Between 2003 and 2006 we asked to be notified of the admission of any detained child patient to an adult psychiatric ward. We set out the data from such notifications in our last report[54]. From October 2008 we have once again collected data on child and adolescent admissions to adult facilities, with the aim of monitoring closely whether the aims of government are being met.

1.51 In the four months between 3 October 2008 and 28 February 2009, we received 80 notifications of the admissions of under-18 year olds to adult facilities. The age range of these patients is shown at figure 14 below.

---

[49] 'Government invests £31m in children and young peoples' psychiatric wards', Department of Health Press Release, 14 November 2007.

[50] Rosie Winterton MP, Minister of State, Hansard HC, 18 Jun 2007: col 1144.

[51] MHAC (2008) *Risk, Rights, Recovery; Twelfth Biennial Report 2005-2007*, para 3.61, rec.21.

[52] Royal College of Psychiatrists (2009) *Safe and Appropriate Care for Young People on Adult Mental Health Wards*.

[53] MHAC (2008) *Risk, Rights, Recovery; Twelfth Biennial Report 2005-2007*, para 3.60 *et seq*.

[54] *ibid.*, para 3.63 *et seq*.

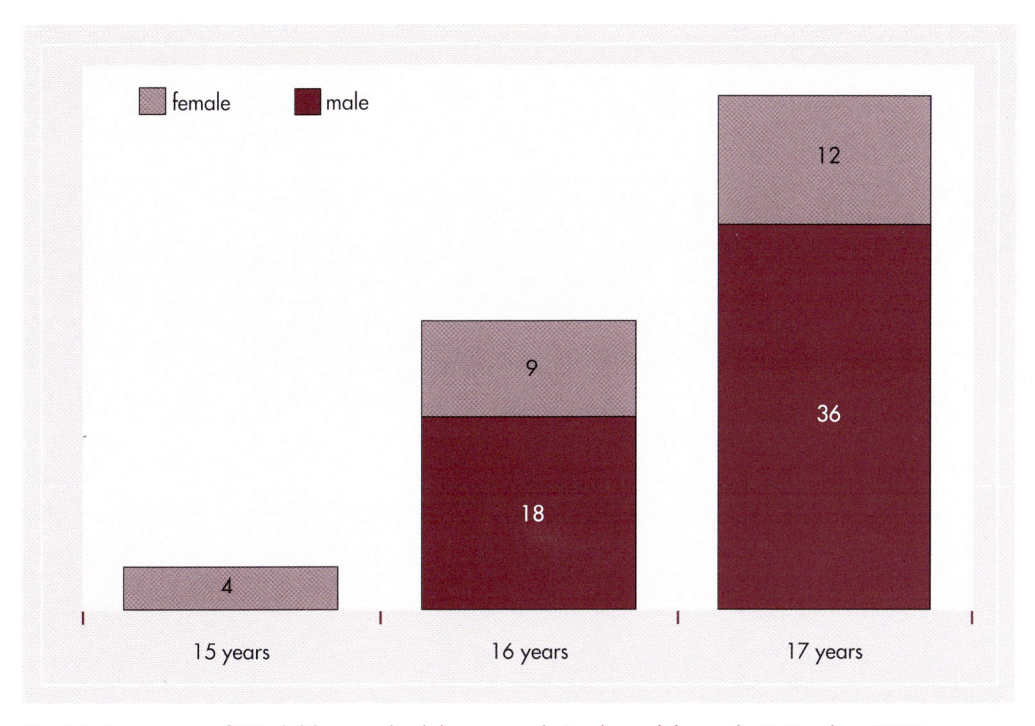

Fig 14: Age range of 80 children and adolescents admitted to adult wards, 3 October 2008 to 28 February 2009

Data source: MHAC data

1.52 The four admissions of 15 year old patients shown at figure 14 took place in 2009, and thus breached the Government commitment to end admissions to adult wards of under 16 year olds from November 2008. All four cases were female.

1.53 The majority of admissions were under s.2 of the Act, and there were twice as many male admissions as female (see Fig 15 below).

Section	2	3	37	47/49
Male	49	3	–	1
Female	24	2	1	–

Fig 15: Gender and MHA Section used to admit 68 children and adolescents to adult wards, 3 October 2008 to 28 February 2009

Data source: MHAC data

1.54 Almost one quarter of the admissions (thirteen male and four female) were to Psychiatric Intensive Care Units or other high dependency units. In theory at least, such units are likely to have higher security arrangements than the adult acute wards taking the remaining three-quarters of admissions. It is likely, however, that the arrangements for nursing care of many of these vulnerable patients quite correctly negates any practical differences that would otherwise occur between these ward regimes. Much more notable, in terms both of patient experience and, in many cases, of patient safety, is the question of whether the ward used was mixed or single sex, and whether the patient had his or her own room. As can be seen at Figure 16, nearly three-quarters of all admissions were to mixed-sex wards.

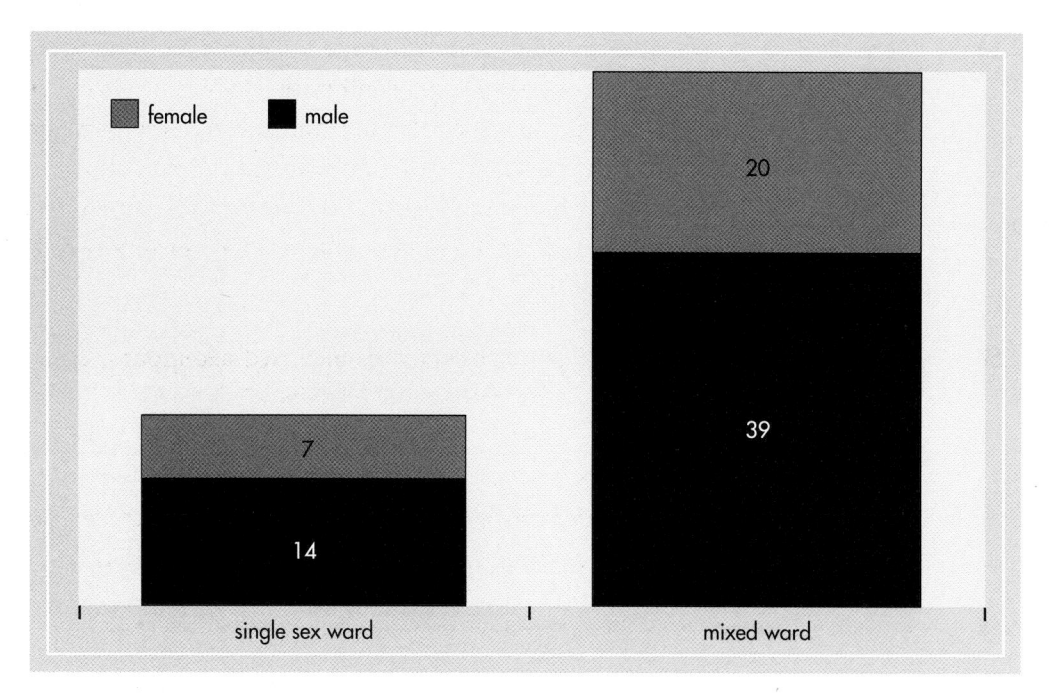

Fig 16: Mixed or single sex wards used to admit 68 children and adolescents, 3 October 2008 to 28 February 2009

Data source: MHAC data

1.55 Of the 59 patients admitted to mixed-sex wards, nine were not assigned their own room (figure 17). With the exception of one male patient, all those admitted to single-sex wards had their own room.

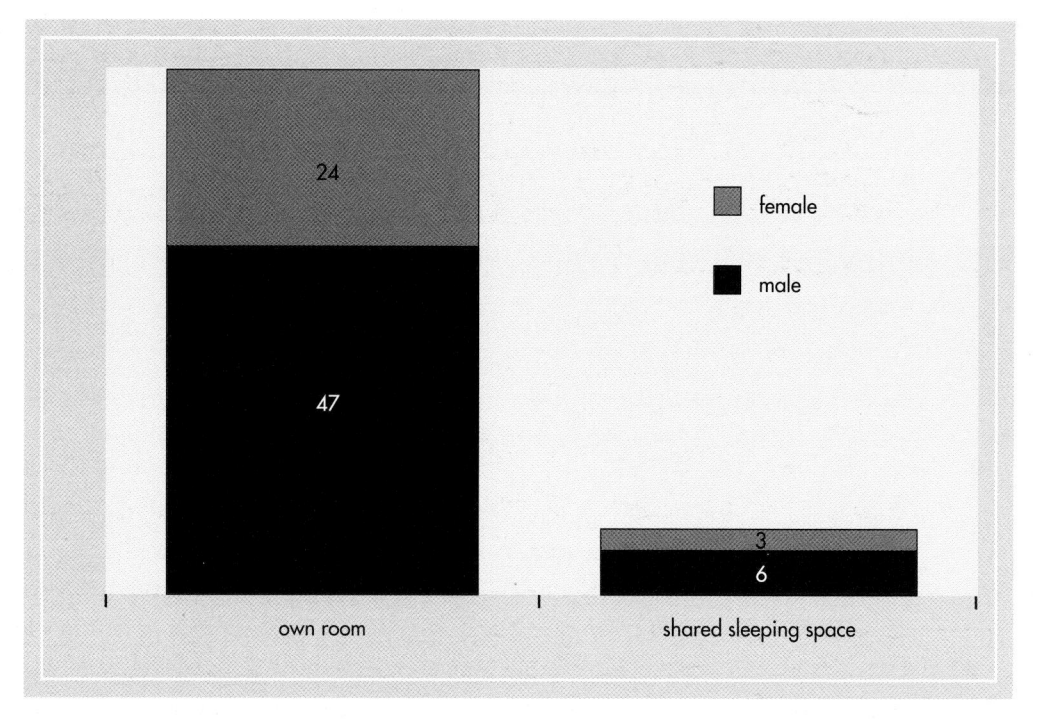

Fig 17: Sleeping arrangements for children and adolescents admitted to mixed sex wards, 3 October 2008 to 28 February 2009

Data source: MHAC data

1.56   Only 14 of the wards used (19%) to admit adolescent patients had been designated as appropriate for that purpose by the detaining authority. The Responsible Clinician for sixty-seven patients (84%) was not a specialist in Child and Adolescent Mental Health Services (CAMHS). Sixty four patients (82%) were reported to have access to advocacy, but in only seven cases (9%) was that advocacy specifically child-centred. As such, the majority of these admissions placed patients in situations where the service provided was in some sense inappropriate to their age.

1.57   We have noted some unfortunate consequences of mixed-age groups, even in wards designated as suitable for the admission of adolescents when needs arise. In October 2008 we visited a ward in the North-west of England that provided inpatient services for patients aged over 65 with functional mental illness but had also been designated as the ward for 16 to 19 year olds. Problems and conflicts had arisen, including an incident where a younger patient attempted to throw a cup of coffee over an elderly patient.

1.58   The ethnicity of patients about whom we were notified is shown at figure 18.

Ethnic group	male	female
White British	40	25
White Welsh	1	–
Other White	4	1
White and Asian	2	–
Other Mixed	1	–
Other Asian	1	–
Black Caribbean	2	–
Chinese	–	1
Not stated / recorded	2	–
Total	**53**	**27**

Fig 18: Children and adolescents admitted to adult wards, 3 October 2008 to 28 February 2009, by ethnicity and gender

Data source: MHAC data

Secure services for adolescents

1.59   On a visit to a Psychiatric Intensive Care Unit (PICU) for adolescents at Cheadle Royal Hospital in September 2008, we were impressed by efforts to ensure that patients are appropriately placed and treated in the least restrictive environment. The ward staff reported that the majority of patients were transferred when appropriate, although (as with other PICUs) a small proportion of patients are difficult to place and this had led to some delays. We saw that the patients had exercised their rights to Mental Health Review Tribunals and hospital managers' hearings, and had access to advocacy, and were satisfied that there were appropriate systems in place for patients to challenge the appropriateness of their detention. The majority of home authorities also appeared to be ensuring that patients were reviewed on a regular basis.

1.60 However, having patients placed out of area – which is perhaps inevitable with such specialised services – can lead to difficulties in ensuring full and appropriate involvement of the relevant home authorities in care and aftercare planning. In December 2007 we visited the Wells Unit in West London, a ten-bedded forensic unit for young men. Many referrals were from Feltham Young Offenders Institute, but patients came from other locations too. On the day of our visit, one patient had been referred from Nottingham. Some of these long-distance referrals limited contact with family for patients; in this case his mother could only visit once each month. Commissioning authorities should be mindful of this when referring patients, and consider ways in which they might ameliorate disadvantages of out-of-area placements (for instance, by helping relatives with travel costs for visiting). The most common problem with out-of-area specialist placements remains discharge planning, which can become complicated by arguments over who should fund after-care and the location of a suitable placement. Some of the patients have social workers from children's teams who do not have knowledge in this area, and in any case withdraw as the boys get older, even though adult services will not pick them up until they are 18 years old. Without appropriate aftercare and the involvement of the local authority, there is a significant risk of relapse and re-offending, putting the patient and others at risk and undoing the work undertaken by the forensic unit itself, which was described as a 'wonderful service' by the visiting MHA Commissioner.

Acute ward environments

1.61 In our last report[55] we stated that busy acute wards appeared to be 'tougher and scarier places' than we saw a decade ago. That phrase has been quoted by commentators and in newspaper editorials, having been highlighted by the Royal College of Psychiatrists' *Fair Deal* campaign[56]. The College's president, Professor Dinesh Bhugra, has stated to the press that he would not use these wards, nor let any of his relatives do so[57]. This has echoes of the findings of a College report from 1996, *Wish you were here?*, which looked at the ethical considerations of admitting patients to sub-standard psychiatric units, and made many of the criticisms of services that are still being made today[58]. The *Fair Deal* campaign, which was based upon a year-long consultation with psychiatrists, service users and carers, has confirmed our criticisms in stating that many inpatient units are unsafe, overcrowded and uninhabitable. For many inpatient services, these are the most pressing problems, against which all attempts at good practice in other respects will founder.

1.62 We are aware of, and have previously acknowledged, fears that voicing such criticisms of services helps to entrench the problems they face, by adding stigma to admissions, demoralising staff and forcing services into defensive practices. We recognise the possibility that we have contributed to the woes of inpatient staff by our reporting, but in our experience very many such staff members are themselves keen that the failings of infrastructure around them should be articulated. Similarly, whilst potential patients of

---

[55] MHAC (2008) *Risk, Rights, Recovery; Twelfth Biennial Report 2005-2007*, para iv, p.23.

[56] See Royal College of Psychiatrists (2008) *Fair Deal for Mental Health* manifesto, p.20.

[57] Amelia Hill 'Top Psychiatrist attacks NHS over mental health' *Observer*, 29 June 2008.

[58] Royal College of Psychiatrists (1996) *Wish you were here? Ethical considerations in the admission of patients to sub-standard psychiatric units.* Council Report CR50.

services are clearly not helped by newspaper reports of grim conditions in the hospitals that serve them, this has to be measured against the very real damage done to other patients by their experiences of acute admission. We have taken the view that the MHAC's unique access to places of psychiatric detention makes it our duty to shine light upon these very serious failings and to urge action to overcome them.

1.63 Nevertheless, it is important to recognise that there are also excellent inpatient services in the acute and other inpatient sectors, and that there has been a real increase in funding and some progress in recent years.

Locked doors

1.64 An increasing number of wards visited by the MHAC are locked. Figure 19 below shows the number and percentage of locked and unlocked acute wards visited by the MHAC from the start of 2004/05 to the end of January 2009.

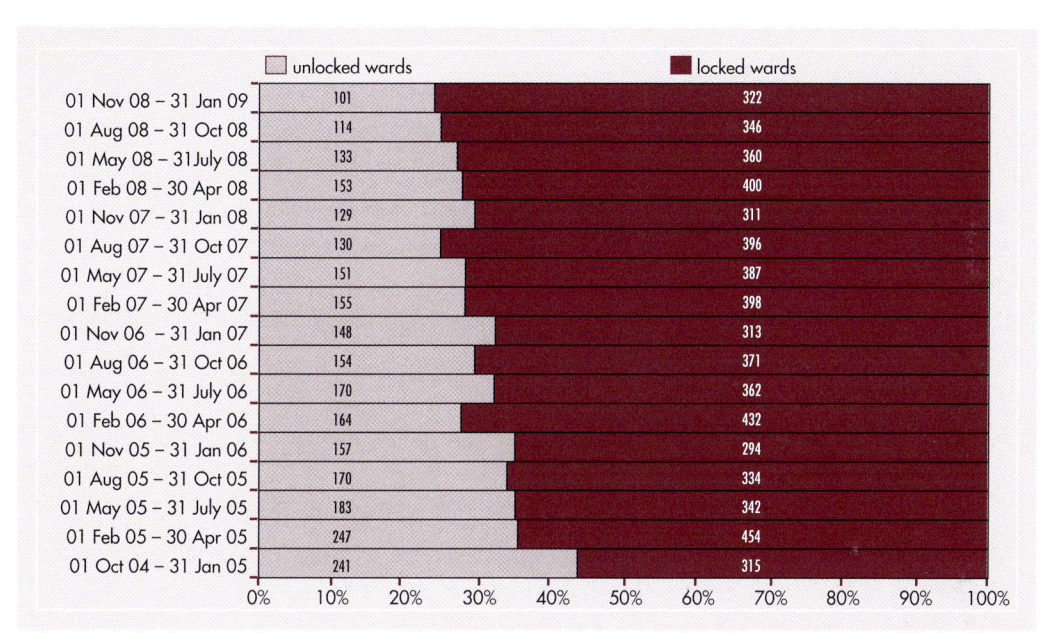

Period	unlocked wards	locked wards
01 Nov 08 – 31 Jan 09	101	322
01 Aug 08 – 31 Oct 08	114	346
01 May 08 – 31 July 08	133	360
01 Feb 08 – 30 Apr 08	153	400
01 Nov 07 – 31 Jan 08	129	311
01 Aug 07 – 31 Oct 07	130	396
01 May 07 – 31 July 07	151	387
01 Feb 07 – 30 Apr 07	155	398
01 Nov 06 – 31 Jan 07	148	313
01 Aug 06 – 31 Oct 06	154	371
01 May 06 – 31 July 06	170	362
01 Feb 06 – 30 Apr 06	164	432
01 Nov 05 – 31 Jan 06	157	294
01 Aug 05 – 31 Oct 05	170	334
01 May 05 – 31 July 05	183	342
01 Feb 05 – 30 Apr 05	247	454
01 Oct 04 – 31 Jan 05	241	315

Fig 19: Locked and unlocked acute psychiatric wards visited by the MHAC, England and Wales, 01 April 04 to 31 January 09

Source: MHAC visiting data

1.65 As we have stated in previous reports, we are concerned at the increasing trend towards locked wards in acute care[59]. Amongst the possible causes for this trend we would suggest increased levels of acuity on such wards (see paragraph 1.20), but also increasingly defensive practice may play a part. As we discussed in our last report, there are some academic studies that appear to show that having doors locked as a general, defensive measure may be counter-productive[60]. One such study, the City 128 Study of Acute Psychiatric Wards by Bowers *et al*, calls for further research into patient responses to, an evaluation of, locked wards (see figure 20 below). We support this call for more detailed research with a service-user focus.

---

[59] MHAC (2008) *Risk, Rights, Recovery, Twelfth Biennial Report 2005-2007* para 2.103 et seq.
[60] *ibid.*, para 2.103.

> **Locked wards: findings of the *City 128 Study of Acute Psychiatric Wards***
> - The positive association between self-harm rates and the locking of ward doors is of some concern, as the use of 'closed' wards is increasing.
> - Further research should be undertaken into patient responses to, and evaluations of, the locking of the ward door, and to examine further the direction of cause and effect between self-harm and door locking.

Fig 20: locked doors – findings of the *City 128 Study of Acute Psychiatric Wards*[61]

1.66 The Mental Health Act Code of Practice prior to the revisions made in November 2008 contained a section on "locking ward doors on open wards", which started from the presumption that relational rather than physical security should be the initial focus of ward managers, sand that adequate staff were available to "prevent the need for the practice of locking patients in wards, individual rooms, or any other area"[62]. Whilst some of this emphasis remains in the new Code of Practice for Wales[63], it is notable that the revision to the Code of Practice for England has removed all mention of 'open wards', and instead states that patients admitted to acute wards have complex and specific needs and that ward staff must balance competing priorities in deciding what safety measures are necessary[64]. Although the Code for England acknowledges that such arrangements should "aim not to impose any unnecessary or disproportionate restrictions on patients or make them feel that they are subject to such restrictions"[65] (and of course the Code must be read in the light of its guiding principles, including that of least restriction), this is a significant, and in our view not very welcome, change of emphasis. We hope that services in England will not overlook their Code's reminders that:

> the nature of engagement with patients and of therapeutic interventions, and the structure and quality of life on the ward, are important factors in encouraging patients to remain on the ward and in minimising a culture of containment.[66]

and

> If managing entry and exit by means of locked external doors (or other physical barriers) is considered to be an appropriate way to maintain safety, the practice adopted must be reviewed regularly to ensure that there are clear benefits for patients and that it is not being used for the convenience of staff. It should never be necessary to lock patients and others in wards simply because of inadequate staffing levels. In conjunction with clinical staff, managers should regularly review and evaluate the mix of patients (there may, for example, be some patients who ought to be in a more secure environment), staffing levels and the skills mix and training needs of staff.[67]

---

[61] Bowers L, Whittington R, Nolan P, Parkin D, Curtis S, Bhui K, Hackney D, Allan T, Simpson A, Flood C (2007) *The City 128 Study of Observation and Outcomes on Acute Psychiatric Wards. Report to the NHS SDO Programme.* City University, London.

[62] Department of Health and Welsh Office (1999) *Code of Practice, Mental Health Act 1983*, para 19.24.

[63] *Mental Health Act Code of Practice for Wales*, para 19.48 – 19.49.

[64] *Mental Health Act Code of Practice for England*, para 16.35.

[65] *ibid.*, para 16.36.

[66] *ibid.*, para 16.37.

[67] *ibid.*, para 16.40.

1.67 We also urge services to ensure that they comply with the Code of Practices' requirements that all wards have a written policy on the ward arrangements regarding locked doors that is available to patients and is explained to them upon admission[68]. Given our longstanding concern over the *de facto* detention of informal patients[69], we particularly commend the Code of Practice for England's explicit requirement that, in explaining the policy to patients and their visitors, it must be made clear to patients if they are legally free to leave the ward.[70]

Bed occupancy

1.68 In our last report, we expressed concern at the large number of wards that we visited running at over 100% occupancy, with beds managed by sending patients out on overnight leave or, in some example, setting up temporary beds on fold-out beds or even mattresses placed on the floor of some units. We continue to encounter unacceptable situations:

> On the ward there was a notice saying patients could be moved at any time due to pressure on beds, and this was very unsettling. Also in retrospect I feel that I was discharged too early.
>
> 'Elsa Monroe' (pseudonym), Portsmouth.
> Quoted in Raza Griffiths 'The patient's experience',
> Mental Health Today Oct '08, 13-15

> The ward was running at about 110% occupancy which was described by staff as a typical picture. The practice of admitting to beds of patients on s.17 leave was described as common. Staff voiced concerns that they are pressurised into admitting to 'leave beds' when they feel it is inappropriate or even unsafe. It was noted that one patient had spent a night on a beanbag in the quiet room as there were no beds available, not even the designated s.136 bed. It seems that staff feel that the reason for this situation is that there are simply not enough beds. A lack of suitable move-on accommodation, particularly for very complex or challenging service users, as well as a lack of rehabilitation facilities were also felt to be factors. There is a longer term plan for services to be re-provided, probably in 2010, but the above situation would seem to demand more immediate action.
>
> *East England, October 2007*

> Nineteen patients are admitted to the ward and only 18 beds exist. The Commissioner understands this is not unusual. A 'sleepover' sofa is provided in such cases and if s.136 patients sleepover. The sofa is not suitable for an adult. Can the Trust please advise the MHAC of their proposed action to resolve this.
>
> *Kent, July 2007*

1.69 Over 2005/06 and 2006/07, 37% of all the acute wards that we visited were running at over 100% occupancy, and a further 27% of acute wards were fully occupied. In the following two financial years that make up this reporting period, 30% of acute wards were over-occupied, and 27% were running at full occupancy. The data for this reporting period is shown in full at figure 21 below.

---

[68] *Mental Health Act Code of Practice for England*, para 16.39, *Code of Practice for Wales* para 19.50.

[69] See, in particular, MHAC (2006) *In Place of Fear? Eleventh Biennial Report 2003-2005*, para 3.18; MHAC (2008) *Risk, Rights, Recovery, Twelfth Biennial Report 2005-2007* para 2.104.

[70] *Mental Health Act Code of Practice for England*, para 16.39.

| | 2007/08 || | 2008/09[71] || |
Occupancy Band	Number of Wards	Percentage band		Number of Wards	Percentage band	
<= 90%	178	(< 100%)	42.3%	166	(< 100%)	43.8%
90%+ to <100	66			56		
Exactly 100%	151	(= 100%)	26.2%	137	(= 100%)	27.0%
100%+ to 105%	26	(> 100%)	31.5%	11	(> 100%)	29.2%
105%+ to 110%	39			31		
110%+ to 115%	26			25		
115%+ to 120%	23			20		
120%+ to 125%	13			19		
> 125%	55			42		
Total	**577**		**100%**	**507**		**100%**

Figure 21: Bed-occupancy levels on visits to 1,084 acute wards by the MHAC, 2007/08 and 2008/09

Source: MHAC visiting data

1.70 The following example from an MHAC visit report shows the additional strain that high bed occupancy can place on staff and patients:

> The Commissioner was again concerned to note exceedingly high levels of occupancy at 100% in addition to the ward having a number of leave patients. Whilst appreciating the points made previously by the Trust in relation to these issues, the Commission understood that the audit work being undertaken was designed to address and alleviate this issue. The Commissioner witnessed hard-pressed staff responding calmly to the needs of a diverse group of patients. Patient acuity was high, one patient was returned from being AWOL and staff were responding to an incident of aggression from another patient. As the Commissioner left in the early evening, one patient was being moved to another ward, with all the associated lack of continuity and upheaval, due to the need to admit a patient from the PICU so as to free up a place there. An agency member of staff had been employed to assist but was not MAPPA trained. The patient mix was also described as a matter of concern with a number of patients awaiting transfer to a more suitable environment for considerable periods of time.
>
> *West Midlands, February 2008*

The physical environment of wards

1.71 We encounter some very good ward environments on our visits, and see some important improvements being made to some other environments. The cessation of smoking inside hospital buildings (see paragraph 1.95 *et seq*) has, where it is being successfully implemented, improved the atmosphere and, in many cases, freed up a room previously designated as a smoking room for a better use. Some wards have converted such rooms into a meeting space for visitors; or a quiet space where patients can use the telephone; or, in one case, a room to house an electronic games console for patient use.

---

[71] Data incomplete for 2008/09; taken from MHAC system 19 March 2009.

1.72 We commend the King's Fund *Enhancing the Healing Environment* programme, in which multi-disciplinary teams are supported to explore practical ways in which the healthcare environment can be improved by through the use of light, colour, art and design. The teams are run by a nurse, and include service users as well as architects and estates staff. The results achieved through such groups have been published by the Department of Health[72].

1.73 On a number of visits we have promoted the *Star Wards* scheme[73] to managers and staff, both as a model against which to evaluate their services and as a source of ideas and inspiration.

1.74 In some cases, the pressures on ward beds appeared to be such that there was no time to repair facilities that were damaged by previous occupants before admitting the next patient. In two separate London hospitals in this period we have found patients housed in bedrooms whose door is missing, it having been removed for repair to damage caused by the previous occupant of the bedroom. One detained patient, who had been in such a room for four days at the time of our visit, approached us to say how unsafe he felt sleeping in his room, given that any passer-by could have immediate access to the room and there were many very disturbed patients on the ward. In another example, we found a missing bedroom door and two missing doors to toilet cubicles. It is not acceptable that patients should be compulsorily admitted to such environments that lack basic privacy and security. In these cases we asked that the Trusts to review their systems for maintenance, and ensure that repairs to the ward could be facilitated without further delay.

1.75 In other wards we encounter inadequate provision for patients that is not directly linked to over-occupancy. In one hospital in the south-east of England in 2008 we noted a ward whose general comfort level was very low, and which seemed ill-provided for the number of patients that it housed. The television room had seven poor quality plastic covered chairs, and the dining room nine chairs, although the ward had 19 patients.

1.76 There is always a danger that units which are due for reprovision or closure are allowed to decline to an unacceptable standard for the patients who are still detained there. In the autumn of 2008, for example, we visited a ward for elderly patients in a hospital in South Wales, which was due to transfer to a new purpose built unit in 2011 but at the time of the visit was wholly inappropriate for the provision of care for its elderly patients. The ward was extremely shabby; had dormitory beds with only dividing curtains between them; and was part carpeted, despite some patients suffering from incontinence.

1.77 Patients also have raised problems of security regarding their possessions. In the West Midlands over summer 2008, patients seen by a Commissioner complained about items going missing from their wardrobes and/or of other patients looking into their wardrobes. There was no personal lockable space provided for patients on the wards. Indeed, the Commissioner noted at least one patient who kept her belongings with her at all times

---

[72] Department of Health (2008) *Improving the patient experience. Sharing success in mental health and learning disabilities. The King's Fund's Enhancing the Healing Environment programme*. TSO.

[73] *Star Wards*, Bright, 356 Holloway Road, London N7 6PA, www.brightplace.org.uk

in bags, which she had brought with her into the day area. The lack of personal lockable space on the wards was therefore causing problems for, and was clearly having a negative impact on, the patients' sense of security, privacy and well being. In this case we were informed that locks had been ordered for the wardrobes: all hospitals who do not offer safe, lockable storage for patients' possessions should similarly address this. The potential negative effects of poor provision for patients' property is shown at figure 22.

> **Patient's property: findings of the *City 128 Study of Acute Psychiatric Wards***
> - Inter-patient petty theft on the ward caused considerable anxiety and irritation.
> - Lockable secure storage space for each patient should be provided in all wards.
> - All patients should be regularly informed that the stealing of others' property is not acceptable, and that when it occurs it should be reported to staff. This message should be incorporated in patient information packs and be placed on ward notice boards.
> - Staff should welcome and take seriously any reports of theft, however apparently trivial in their eyes, and should investigate and attempt to identify the perpetrator and return the items.
> - If a patient is admitted who is known to be prone to thieving, that patient should be more closely observed, and their property, locker and person searched at regular intervals.
> - Trusts may wish to consider developing a formal policy related to patients' property and theft.

Fig 22: Patient's property – findings of the *City 128 Study of Acute Psychiatric Wards*[74]

Staffing

1.78 We have previously reported having observed in some hospitals staffing levels that we have judged – often with the agreement of staff on the shift concerned – to have been unsafe[75]. We continue to see this in some services.

1.79 In our last report we cited the survey of nurses undertaken in 2007 by the Royal College of Nursing, which found that 66% of respondents considered staffing numbers to be insufficient, and 42% reporting that this regularly compromised patient care.[76] The number and percentage of trained nursing staff on wards visited by the MHAC is shown at figure 23 below.

---

[74] Bowers L, Whittington R, Nolan P, Parkin D, Curtis S, Bhui K, Hackney D, Allan T, Simpson A, Flood C (2007) *The City 128 Study of Observation and Outcomes on Acute Psychiatric Wards. Report to the NHS SDO Programme*. City University, London.

[75] MHAC (2008) *Risk, Rights, Recovery; Twelfth Biennial Report 2005-2007*, para 1.26.

[76] ibid. para 1.25: see Royal College of Nursing (2007) *Untapped Potential: a survey of RCN nurses in mental health 2007*.

	2005/06		2006/07		2007/08		2008/09	
	no of wards	% of wards	no of wards	% of wards	no of wards	% of wards	no of wards	% of wards
< 10%	19	0.95%	18	0.90%	21	0.98%	12	0.79%
10%+ to 20%	124	6.21%	124	6.18%	112	5.24%	98	6.42%
20%+ to 30%	200	10.02%	159	7.92%	231	10.81%	174	11.40%
30%+ to 40%	506	25.35%	466	23.21%	473	22.14%	369	24.18%
40%+ to 50%	507	25.40%	546	27.19%	620	29.03%	414	27.13%
50%+ to 60%	222	11.12%	248	12.35%	235	11.00%	165	10.81%
60%+ to 70%	172	8.62%	188	9.36%	191	8.94%	121	7.93%
70%+ to 80%	167	8.37%	171	8.52%	179	8.38%	127	8.32%
80%+ to 90%	13	0.65%	25	1.25%	17	0.80%	11	0.72%
90%+ to 100%	66	3.31%	62	3.09%	55	2.57%	35	2.29%
total in year	**1,996**	**100%**	**2,007**	**100%**	**2,134**	**100%**	**1,526**	**100%**

Fig 23: Number and percentage of trained staff on wards visited by the MHAC, 2005/6 to 2008/09

Data source: MHAC data

1.80 A positive practice workbook on staffing acute mental health wards was published by the Department of Health in September 2008[77], although this does not establish a minimum standard for patient/staff ratios. In our last report we noted that other jurisdictions have established mandatory staffing ratios[78], and indeed the introduction to the Department's guidance seems to acknowledge that something like this is what many services have been looking for, whilst explaining why it is not prepared to pursue this line:

> A question that has frequently been asked by people working and managing acute in-patient services has been: "How many staff do we need to run the ward?" If only it were that simple – it's more than just staffing numbers. Things have moved on from how to staff the ward towards how best to staff the overall service, paying particular attention to key interfaces and ensuring a balanced distribution of staff and skills across the care pathway. There is a need to craft local solutions to local situations to ensure the development of a workforce that is reflective of the diversity of the population served. Each area will have its distinct service configuration, own population needs and its own range of staffing skills and challenges.[79]

1.81 There are some merits to this argument, although we encounter wards where the brute fact seems to be that the staffing complement – or the complement of *qualified* staff – is simply inadequate. Nevertheless, *New Ways of Working* should encourage flexibility amongst staff when undertaking the tasks of the ward, and it is certainly our experience that, in some hospitals, what the Departmental guidance recommends is recognised as a lack by ward staff, as in the following example of a report from an MHAC visit:

---

[77] Department of Health (2007) *New Ways of Working for Everyone: A best practice implementation guide.* CSIP/NIMHE, October 2007.

[78] MHAC (2008) *Risk, Rights, Recovery,* para 1.26 & fn 55.

[79] Department of Health (2007) *New Ways of Working for Everyone: A best practice implementation guide.* CSIP/NIMHE, October 2007, p.5.

The staff I spoke to stated that staff morale on the ward was low because they felt they were not receiving appropriate training to deal with the challenging patients which are being placed on the ward. They stated that the ward has had a recent spate of serious incidents and was becoming more of a challenging behaviour unit. The staff stated that they do have not have access to CBT training, managing self harm training and training in therapeutic approaches to work with patients that use illicit drugs. The staff stated that all training apart from mandatory training had been frozen.

August 2008, London

1.82 The findings of the *City 128 Study of Acute Psychiatric Wards* that there appears to be a correlation between richer staff mix and patient self-harm and mortality (figure 24 below) indicates that poorly-staffed inpatient services are operating false economies. Such wards still use a considerable proportion of mental health service budgets, but will not be operating efficiently in getting patients fit for discharge.

> **Ward staffing: findings of the *City 128 Study of Acute Psychiatric Wards***
> - Increasing the numbers of qualified nursing staff on wards may lead to lower rates of self-harm.
> - The link between a richer staff mix and lower rates of self-harm is a pointer to the importance of nurse staffing levels and grade mix on acute psychiatric wards. A systematic review of general acute care has shown lower patient mortality with a richer grade mix.
> - A similar review of existing evidence on psychiatric nurse staffing levels and outcomes should be conducted.
> - Standards for acute inpatient care must include nurse staffing levels and grade mix.

Fig 24: Ward staffing – findings of the *City 128 Study of Acute Psychiatric Wards*[80]

1.83 The number and percentage of agency trained nursing staff on wards visited by the MHAC is shown at figure 25 below.

	2005/06 no of wards	2005/06 % of wards	2006/07 no of wards	2006/07 % of wards	2007/08 no of wards	2007/08 % of wards	2008/09 no of wards	2008/09 % of wards
< 10%	1,698	85.07%	1,777	88.54%	1,907	89.32%	1,361	89.19%
10%+ to 20%	124	6.21%	102	5.08%	105	4.92%	84	5.50%
20%+ to 30%	70	3.51%	52	2.59%	51	2.39%	26	1.70%
30%+ to 40%	63	3.16%	43	2.14%	35	1.64%	33	2.16%
40%+ to 50%	31	1.55%	14	0.70%	19	0.89%	16	1.05%
50%+ to 60%	5	0.25%	10	0.50%	8	0.37%	2	0.13%
60%+ to 70%	2	0.10%	6	0.30%	6	0.28%	2	0.13%
70%+ to 80%	–	–	1	0.05%	3	0.14%	2	0.13%
80%+ to 90%	–	–	–	–	–	–	–	–
90%+ to 100%	3	0.15%	2	0.10%	–	–	–	–
total in year	1,996	100%	2,007	100%	2,134	100%	1,526	100%

Fig 25: Number and percentage of agency staff on wards visited by the MHAC, 2005/6 to 2008/09

Data source: MHAC data

---

[80] Bowers L, Whittington R, Nolan P, Parkin D, Curtis S, Bhui K, Hackney D, Allan T, Simpson A, Flood C (2007) *The City 128 Study of Observation and Outcomes on Acute Psychiatric Wards. Report to the NHS SDO Programme.* City University, London.

1.84 One of the positive aspects of acute care nursing identified by Deacon *et al* (see para 1.9 above) is the spatial and organisational closeness of the nursing team on the ward – the sense of 'being in this together'[81]. But the authors identify that staffing pressures can damage this:

> For example, a staff nurse on the PICU returned from his days off to an early shift to discover that he was the only permanent member of staff on duty. The unit was particularly disturbed and he described the situation as: 'frightened nurses looking after frightened patients', perhaps illustrating the negative consequences of not being able to harness the comforting feature of close teamwork in this challenging environment[82].

1.85 In the following example from an MHAC report, thankfully untypical circumstances highlighted a number of concerns about staffing:

> Following a patient death on the ward, six members of staff have been suspended. A new ward manager has been appointed. In order to drive higher standards of care, the ward has had a 24 hour Modern Matron for the last two months. This has now been reduced to day time periods only. Bank and agency staff are being used to keep ward numbers up. The ward has persistent high levels of occupancy, a high proportion of detained patients, and a high incidence of foreign nationals, asylum seekers and rough sleepers. The remaining staff have naturally been affected by recent events and the continuing pressures on the ward. These difficulties are further exacerbated by failures in the recruitment process. It has been extremely difficult of late to recruit nurses of the right calibre. We were pleased to hear of the introduction of day-long interviews where both core skills and interpersonal skills can be more thoroughly appraised, and would welcome confirmation of the plans to secure adequate nursing staff for this ward.

Activity on wards

1.86 The range and quality of activities available to detained patients is in part determined by the staffing complements on wards, and the best examples appear to reflect the involvement in qualified occupational therapy teams.

1.87 In July 2008 we commended the occupational therapy team for Riverside Centre Crane Ward (Central and North West London NHS Trust) for its robust and varied activities programme. Patients that we met with spoke of going to the gym, internet café, cooking group and art group, and described activities as "very good and varied", "very helpful" and "excellent". The following aspects of the service could be emulated by other services:

- There are activities on and off the ward;
- There is evening and weekend provision;
- Volunteers and service users run some activities;
- The is a full-time activity co-ordinator for the ward;

---

[81] Deacon M, Warne, T & McAndrew S (2006) 'Closeness, chaos and crisis: the attractions of working in acute mental health care'. *Journal of Psychiatric and Mental Health Nursing*, 15, 750-757.

[82] *ibid.*, p.754.

- There is a high ratio of occupational therapists for the ward and a sports technician;
- The ward was able to evidence a high engagement rate and direct contact rate every week with patients;
- There is a follow-up service for patients discharged from the ward into the community.

1.88 Activities are not simply about helping patients pass their time on the ward, but are a vital component of the therapeutic process of recovery, without which wards may become little more than expensive places of containment for patients (see figure 26 below).

> **Activity on wards: findings of the *City 128 Study of Acute Psychiatric Wards***
> - Comprehensive programmes of patient activity may act to reduce more serious self-harm, and are highly valued by patients.
> - Those services without a programme of patient activities should take urgent steps to provide one.
> - Those with less than the mean number of patient activity sessions per week, that is, eight, should increase the numbers of such sessions.
> - Staff, equipment, and space may all need to be provided to make sure any planned programme can be put into effect.

Fig 26: Patient activity – findings of the *City 128 Study of Acute Psychiatric Wards*[83]

1.89 It is extremely important that patients have access to exercise – and to healthy diet choices – when detained in hospital. Research has shown that weight-control programmes involving both of these elements can counter weight-gain induced by antipsychotic drugs[84]. Thus exercise can not only help patients to feel better about themselves whilst in hospital, but could reduce one of the most distressing side-effects of pharmacological treatment with benefits for post-discharge compliance and possibly future readmission rates.

1.90 In several units we have visited during this period, gymnasium equipment or a designated gym room were provided within the hospital, but staffing shortages limited their availability for patient use. In some cases, this shortage related to having staff available to escort detained patients within the hospital for security reasons; in others, lack of staff trained to supervise the use of gym equipment made it available for use only at very limited times, or unavailable in practice. On a visit in London during August 2008, a young patient expressed particular frustration over having no access to such a gym facility, particularly because of her weight gain experienced as a side-effect of medication. In this unit patients also lacked access to the garden due to lack of staff to escort them, and could only access a 'smoking balcony' as a poor substitute for fresh air.

---

[83] Bowers L, Whittington R, Nolan P, Parkin D, Curtis S, Bhui K, Hackney D, Allan T, Simpson A, Flood C (2007) *The City 128 Study of Observation and Outcomes on Acute Psychiatric Wards. Report to the NHS SDO Programme*. City University, London.

[84] Poulin *et al* (2007) 'Management of antipsychotic-induced weight gain: prospective naturalistic study of the effectiveness of a supervised exercise programme' *Australian and New Zealand Journal of Psychiatry*, Volume 41, Issue 12, pages 980 - 989.

The recovery model and coercive environments

1.91 There is a considerable amount of policy and implementation guidance that outlines how mental health services should be provided and experienced[85]. A great emphasis is now placed on user involvement in planning care and treatment, and in services being responsive to patients' feedback and complaints. Values such as respect; choice; shared decision making; least restriction; and user-centred care are often cited in Trust policies as a reflection of, for example, the principles of the Mental Health Act Code of Practice. These are welcome aspirations, even if the experience of patients does not always appear to show that they are attained.

> I am acutely aware that my life is dictated for me within an institutional framework characterised by flux, control, whim and chance.
>
> *Stuart Wooding, SURP member*

1.92 A good example of a concise and clear statement of a recovery model of care has been produced by Devon Partnership Trust, and promoted by the Royal College of Psychiatrists as a part of its *Fair Deal* campaign[86]. This short paper sets out a guide for practitioners on 'values, principles, practices and standards' and emphasises a focus on working in partnership with patients to help them to build a meaningful and satisfying life, as defined by the person themselves, whether or not there are ongoing problems and symptoms.

1.93 Defensive and therefore coercive practice is not, in our view, an inevitable approach towards patients who are detained under the Act, and therefore we are encouraged that the prevailing service ethos emphasises these more consensual approaches to care. Indeed, we hope that this will be built upon and that future revisions of the Code of Practice will reflect work being undertaken to study and promote low confrontation nursing practice as a foundation for safety[87]. Values such as respect, choice, patient involvement and autonomy should be seen as integral to all aspects of psychiatric care, rather than being only a counterbalance to its more coercive aspects.

1.94 There are many services whose culture remains rooted in less forward-looking models of care. In part this can be a distortion of the culture of risk-assessment, where the risks to be assessed are all seen in a negative light, as threats to the stasis of the ward's smooth operation or of rather all-encompassing notions of 'security'. Such wards – which can be found in acute mental health services as well as medium and low secure hospitals – may be holding back patients' recovery. In autumn 2008 we visited a hospital in eastern England:

---

[85] For example, the Mental Health Act Code of Practices; *Refocusing CPA; Safety, Privacy & Dignity in Mental Health Services; Best Practice in Managing Risk; Minimum Standards for low secure/PICU care.*

[86] Available from www.devonpartnership.nhs.uk or www.rcpsych.ac.uk/campaigns/fairdeal.aspx

[87] See, for example, the work of City University Research Team as articulated by Professor Len Bowers' Skellern Memorial Lecture 2008, 'Time present, time past and time future: reflections on psychiatric nursing research'.

During interview most patients expressed some measure of dissatisfaction with what might be termed the 'culture' on the ward, which ranged from mild irritation but acceptance to feelings of abuse. In particular, patients felt that:

i) They are forced to go to 'sessions' and that privileges are withdrawn and/or punishments are meted out if they do not attend, e.g. not being allowed a takeaway; not being allowed out for a walk; being 'locked' in the wings.

ii) They are unnecessarily denied access to their bedrooms, which means that they have to sit in the communal areas when they would like some privacy or quiet time.

iii) That visitors are restricted if patients don't 'behave'.

iv) The cigarette regime is overly prescriptive and restrictive.

v) Food is limited because of 'diets' e.g. a third piece of bread being removed from a patient.

vi) Their views are not always respected; that there are too many 'rules'; one patient stated that 'they treat us like children'.

It is important to note that the concern is about the culture or ethos on the ward, and not about the range of activities available or that healthy eating and smoking cessation are promoted. It is appropriate and desirable that these are available to patients. It is also not about the management difficulties that some patients present with at times, which is not disputed. Some positive comments about staff members were also received.

The culture of the ward is a continuing concern to the MHAC and has been a consistent theme both on visits and from other complaints raised with the MHAC over the last two years. There is a discrepancy between the views of patients and those of managers who do not agree with this feedback from patients, for example it is felt that patients are 'encouraged' to attend sessions.

There is a daily patients' meeting to discuss the day ahead and to raise any concerns. The advocacy service runs a fortnightly patients' meeting. However, there was a lack of clarity as to how some issues are taken forward and also whether these meetings are sufficient and appropriate for patients to feedback their experiences, particularly concerns, of the ward.

In this case, the MHAC suggested that the culture of the unit needed to be reviewed with senior managers of the Trust, and that consideration is given to developing a regular, non-attributable and independent feedback mechanism for patients on their experiences of the ward.

Restrictions on smoking

1.95 From the implementation of the ban on smoking within enclosed spaces in psychiatric units from July 2008, being denied opportunities to smoke remains a prominent concern of many detained patients that we meet with. In some cases

> When to smoke is a problem. It hurts me. I am addicted to smoking.
>
> *Male patient aged 38, s.3, Northampton*

the volume of concern and complaint makes an interesting contrast with management views that the smoking regulations have been implemented without significant incident or deterioration in patient experience. We discussed the implementation of the smoking regulations at length in our last report[88]. We remain of the view that the most appropriate

---

[88] MHAC (2008) *Risk, Rights, Recovery, Twelfth Biennial Report 2005-2007* para 2.60 *et seq*.

management of smoking is to provide safe and well-maintained shelters outside for patient use, and many Trusts have done this. We remain concerned at those Trusts who, having declared themselves 'smoke-free' (so that smoking is permitted neither in enclosed nor open spaces on the Trust estate), are effectively making leave under s.17 the condition for detained patients to smoke, thus in practice depriving some such patients of any opportunity to do so because of their detained status. We find such a consequence of detention under the Act to be both inappropriate and discriminatory in its effect. Some Trusts who initially implemented a smoke-free policy have relented and now allow smoking in specific outdoor areas: in one such example the visiting Commissioner reported in September 2008 that "the response from patients was overwhelmingly positive". In others, staff time is spent accompanying patients on what one Trust called "perimeter leave" so that they may smoke. Such arrangements and their consequences can appear rather absurd, and pose disproportionate risks to patients and staff:

> There are a number of issues about smoking on the ward. The ward takes people out on escorted leave for smoking. Some patients abscond and then the police have to bring them back and police are now complaining about AWOL patients. The ward is monitoring serious or untoward incidents and has evidence that there has been an increase since the ban and believe that this is related. There is a rise in patients smoking illicitly with increased fire risk – patients take the batteries out of the smoke alarms in the toilets. It imposes additional strains on staffing when staff are engaged in taking patients out for smoking breaks and although such times may have therapeutic value it means staff are not necessarily engaged in meaningful activity with patients. Staff feel that if there were a change of policy so that patients could smoke in the secure gardens, then this would address some of these issues.
>
> *North-west England, October 2008*

> There are concerns relating to safety and smoking; staff have been assaulted following incidents around smoking. Lighters are being brought onto the ward, often from other service users. Also some patients are refusing to engage in activities if they are unable to smoke.
>
> *North-west England, October 2008*

1.96 A number of hospitals report an increase in surreptitious smoking as mentioned in the previous two examples. The potential consequences of this were graphically demonstrated by the devastating fire at Camlet 3 on the Chase Farm hospital site in 2008. We do not know the cause of this fire, and we acknowledge the successful and safe evacuation of all patients and staff from the burning building, but we do note the additional pressures that this has placed upon the Trust's resources, and the distress to patients caused by the experience and the loss of many of their possessions.

> Choice – Since moving from high to medium security, especially on my current rehab-discharge ward, being able to get up when I want if I've got no sessions. Making a drink when I want, i.e. 24 hour opening. Having a bath, shower or shave when and if I want. Being able to go out if I want on internal or external access. Being able to order takeaways. Being given a choice whether to engage in my current treatment pathway or not. Being given the choice of going out on s.17 leave and, until recently when I stopped, being given the choice to smoke outdoors.
>
> *Glyn James, service user*

1.97 The implementation of the regulations has increased the potential for cigarettes, or access to them, to be used as currency in wholly inappropriate ways. For example, a patient in the east Midlands complained to us in October 2008 that her access to smoking is used punitively. As a part of her risk management plan, she was only allowed a smoking break where she had been 'settled' for the previous four hours. As a consequence she was missing several smoking breaks in the day: we asked that the hospital reconsider its management of the patient, and, where it was unavoidable to prevent the patient from taking a smoking break, to have some form of nicotine replacement available to her.

1.98 It is important to remember that modern mental health care aims to support patients towards restitution of their autonomy, and that rules that are seen by patients as petty and unrelated to therapeutic requirements can have an opposite, infantilising effect. Many detained patients resent smoking restrictions, especially where these have the practical effect of depriving them of the opportunity to smoke at all. It is understandable that such patients should resent this as unwarranted paternalism, especially as no other group of adults in our society is so treated. As such, 'house rules' on wards should be reviewed to ensure that they are not unnecessarily restrictive and institutionalising:

> There is a policy of locking off the bedrooms during the daytime. As a result, at various times throughout the day, there were patients asleep in the communal areas. Additionally, there are set times for tea and coffee throughout the day and, this, coupled with the restrictions on smoking, was said to be unnecessarily controlling by some patients. Patients talked about the institutionalising effect of not being able to have a drink, smoke, or lie down when they wanted or needed to do so – particularly those patients who had been on the ward for a number of years.
>
> *North-east England, September 2008*

Patient involvement and support

1.99 From the autumn of 2008 a reorganisation of the Care Programme Approach introduced a single-level CPA, designed to be less bureaucratic and to extend only to those previously requiring enhanced support[89]. We assume that any patient deemed to meet the criteria for detention under the Act, and those who were so detained and are now subject to leave or Supervised Community Treatment, should qualify for the revised CPA. We discussed CPA at some length in our previous report[90].

1.100 The revised CPA guidance contains a statement of values and principles which reflect the best of patient experience of mental health services. The guidance states that care should aim to promote social inclusion and recovery; be respectful – building confidence in individuals with an understanding of their strengths, goals and aspirations as well as their needs and difficulties; and recognise the individual as a person first and patient second:

> Services should be organised and delivered in ways that promote and co-ordinate helpful and purposeful mental health practice based on fulfilling therapeutic relationships and partnerships between the people involved. These relationships involve shared listening, communicating,

---

[89] Department of Health (2008) *Refocusing the care programme approach: Policy and positive practice guidance.* March 2008.

[90] MHAC (2008) *Risk, Rights, Recovery, Twelfth Biennial Report 2005-2007* para 2.85 *et seq.*

understanding, clarification, and organisation of diverse opinion to deliver valued, appropriate, equitable and co-ordinated care. The quality of the relationship between service user and the care co-ordinator is one of the most important determinants of success.[91]

1.101 Whilst the use of the coercive powers of the Mental Health Act does create obstacles towards such an approach, we have seen and heard from patients and staff that such obstacles are not insurmountable:

> The best thing to come out of being in hospital, during my many months of detention on PICU, was being visited and assessed by a forensic consultant psychiatrist from my own Trust. This moment will always stay with me (although he actually was there for six hours assessing me). He genuinely and honestly wanted to work with me, when I returned into the community. There were no false illusions, very firmly placing all the future issues and treatment on the table. You cannot pretend this feeling – he really truly meant this, and I sensed this. I often look back and recall this moment, it was the first day of my positive treatment planning.
>
> *Monica Endersby, SURP member*

1.102 The Healthcare Commission review of NHS acute inpatient mental health services found that half of the care plans sampled did not record the patient's views[92]. We also find patients feeling excluded from some or all of their care planning:

> Since transfer to medium secure units from maximum I have been able to put together my care plan with my primary nurse and be part of contributing to my care and future. I would very much like to attend my CPA meetings from start to finish. At my previous hospital I was allowed to do this. Sadly at my present hospital I am only called in for ten to fifteen minutes at the end of what is often a one or two hour meeting. I feel that there should be an option [to attend] as in MHRTs. After all it's your life and you should be able to be part of it.
>
> *Mark Gray, SURP member*

1.103 Whilst there may be legitimate reasons for an element of exclusion in specific circumstances, there should be as much transparency as possible both in care planning and in any decisions to exclude a patient from planning meetings.

1.104 In some services in the general and low to medium security sector, we still encounter poor care-planning and/or limited patient involvement in their care:

> I was not consulted about my treatment at all. I was told at one point I should sell my home and enter residential care: had it not been for the intervention of my son this might have happened. Older women on these wards are treated with contempt, disregarded as a nuisance. It was a regime of compliance and punishment with the threat of increased medication or injection. You had no say with regard to your medication or the level of the dose. It was not discussed – it was forced upon you.
>
> *Gillian Brightmore, SURP member*

---

[91] Department of Health (2008) *Refocusing the care programme approach*, page 7.
[92] Healthcare Commission (2008) *The pathway to recovery: a review of NHS acute inpatient mental health services*. p.26.

1.105 An important but often overlooked source of patient support on wards comes from fellow patients, and by facilitating ward meetings or therapeutic work in groups this can be fostered and consolidated by ward staff. The *City 128 Study of Acute Psychiatric Wards* noted another aspect of this feature of ward life: the sudden removal of the warm, supportive community of patients on discharge may contribute to suicide risk. The study suggested that, alongside building and evaluating ways to enhance and consolidate inter-patient support, evaluative research into the potential role for patient safety of interventions that blur the boundary between in- and outpatient care around the time of discharge should be commissioned[93]. We endorse this call for further research.

Providing patients with information about their care and treatment

1.106 Under s.132 of the Act, detaining authorities have a statutory duty to provide detained patients about their legal position and rights[94]. Certain information – about the section that a patient is being held under; its effects; that it can be appealed against and will, in any case, end when detention is no longer appropriate etc – must be given as soon as is practicable after admission. Information about other matters, such as consent to treatment, must be given when they are relevant. The Codes of Practice for England and Wales give detailed guidance on these statutory duties, and emphasise that it is insufficient to simply give the information without ensuring that patients are given every opportunity to understand it[95]. This means that many attempts to give the information may be necessary, especially where a patient is initially incapable of receiving such information.

> On my first and second recalls I was left to stew in ignorance with no response to my insistent questioning of why I was being held and for what reason I was not able to see a psychiatrist or make phone calls ... even though I was not in isolation, I was isolated. It took me two weeks to be seen by a psychiatrist because that was when the ward round took place... I consented to medication after being told that this could be forcibly used by a SOAD.
>
> *Donna Gilbert, SURP member*

1.107 The information required to be explained to patients under s.132 must be provided orally and in writing. At paragraph 1.39 *et seq* above we discuss the availability of translated information leaflets.

1.108 The MHAC often has cause for concern over how well authorities are meeting their duties to give information. Authorities that fail to inform patients of their legal status and its consequences are effectively depriving patients of their rights under the Act, and as such we take such failure to be a very serious matter. Authorities that manage this aspect of the law well usually have some form of recording and reminder system in place, such as a form

---

[93] Bowers L, Whittington R, Nolan P, Parkin D, Curtis S, Bhui K, Hackney D, Allan T, Simpson A, Flood C (2007) *The City 128 Study of Observation and Outcomes on Acute Psychiatric Wards. Report to the NHS SDO Programme.* City University, London.

[94] Under s.132A of the Act there is a similar duty to provide information to SCT patients. We discuss one example of poor practice – where the s.132 information was simply posted to the patient after discharge onto SCT – at para 2.78 below.

[95] *Code of Practice for England*, para 2; *Code of Practice for Wales*, para 22.

completed by staff (and kept on patient files), showing when the patient was given the information; by whom; and whether the patient fully understood, partially understood or did not understand it. We would expect such a system to be able to record the initial attempt to give the information and any subsequent attempts, and provide reminders for updates (which might be triggered by key events such as managers' hearings, Tribunals, or renewal of detention, and otherwise given periodically).

1.109　In our last report we discussed our findings from a special exercise in which we interviewed over 500 patients in the summer of 2006 about the provision of legal rights. We were disappointed to find that nearly one quarter overall told us that they had not received information from nursing staff to which they had a statutory entitlement. We continue to look for records of legal rights having been explained to patients on our day to day visits and, through our private interviews with patients, check whether the records match patients' perceptions, and whether patients' understanding is as recorded. In the following examples it is possible that patients had not been informed that they could exercise their right to apply to the Tribunal, although it seemed likely that they would have done so if helped to do so. We discuss the Tribunal further at para 2.96 *et seq* below.

> The very first moment of arriving (far from home on PICU); the door slamming and locking very loudly behind me; so many emotions fighting for first place, feeling totally helpless, hopeless, vulnerable, not just scared but terrified, confused, left all alone, isolated.
> I had been informed that I was 'sectioned' before being taken to this 'out of county' hospital. However, it was not until the next day, in the new hospital, that I actually found out I was being detained in a 'secure PICU'. The revelation was extremely distressing, I had not been informed, even worse staff refused to explain why.
>
> *Monica Endersby, SURP member*

> Practice in relation to s.132 could be improved. It was not possible to find evidence that attempts to explain patient *X*'s rights to him had been made over the last year. A decision had been made then that he would not be able to understand his rights but that this would be regularly reviewed. Additionally, it was not possible to ascertain when *X* had last had a Tribunal although he had had regular managers' hearings.
>
> *Suffolk, summer 2007.*

> Patients *Y* and *Z* had completed s.132 records in their notes. However, during interview, both were unclear about their section and rights. There is no process for reminding patients of their rights, which is particularly important for patients who have difficulty retaining information. It was not possible to locate evidence that patient *Y* had had his rights explained. His primary nurse said that he regularly discusses the issue with him but *Y* did not want to appeal. There were entries in *Y*'s notes stating how unhappy he was at being on a section and having to come back to hospital from leave for his depot injection.
>
> *Cambridgeshire, September 2007*

1.110 Detaining authorities that provide internet access for patient use (see paragraph 1.120 below) should consider publicising *FLORID*, a website run by mental health service users, which aims to bring together information relating to mental health in a way that is user-friendly and simple[96]. The website includes some basic information on the Act and the effects of detention under its powers.

Independent Mental Health Advocacy

1.111 From April 2009, s.130A of the Act will place a duty on Primary Care Trusts in England to make such arrangements as they consider reasonable to enable Independent Mental Health Advocates (IMHAs) to be available to qualifying patients. Such a duty has been applicable to Local Health Boards in Wales from November 2008. Thus from the dissolution of the MHAC all detained patients (except those held under the short-term powers of ss.5, 135 or 136), including those who are on leave of absence from hospital, and all patients subject to Supervised Community Treatment, conditional discharge, or guardianship, will qualify for support from IMHAs and must be informed of this[97].

1.112 IMHAs will have a statutory duty to comply with any reasonable request to visit a patient when requested to do so by the patient's Nearest Relative, Responsible Clinician, or an AMHP who is acting for a local authority[98]. A key role of IMHAs will be to help patients understand their legal position and rights, and to help patients exercise their rights (for instance by representing them or helping them articulate their views)[99]. Although this system may not provide an automatic solution to problems that we have encountered in ensuring that patients have their legal position and rights explained to them, not least because access to the advocacy scheme may be dependent upon hospital staff taking the initiative wither to tell a patient that they may request an advocate, or (particularly in the case of responsible clinicians) to themselves request that an advocate visits the patient. Although it is a legal requirement that hospital managers provide patients with information about IMHA services, we note above that there is a significant rate of failure rate to comply with existing legal requirements over the provision of similar information. As such, we hope that IMHAs will be enabled and willing to be proactive in advertising their availability on wards where patients may be detained.

1.113 Although commissioning bodies will themselves monitor and review the operation of the IMHA services that they purchase, this will clearly be an area for particular focus in the future monitoring of the powers and duties of the Mental Health Act by the Care Quality Commission.

---

[96] www.florid.org.uk

[97] Also informal patients who are either (i) referred for possible treatment under s.57 (i.e. neurosurgery) or (ii) under 18 years of age and referred for possible ECT treatment (under s.58A).

[98] *Mental Health Act 1983*, s.130B(5).

[99] *Mental Health Act 1983*, s.130B(1) and (2).

Access to Communications

Mobile Telephones

1.114   The revised Mental Health Act Codes of Practice for England require hospitals to have policies on the use of mobile telephones by detained patients and their visitors[100]. This has been usefully supplemented by Department of Health Guidance on using mobile phones in hospital, which suggests that

> "the working presumption should be that patients will be allowed the widest possible use of mobile phones on wards, where the local risk assessment indicates that such use will not represent a threat to:
>
> - Patients' own safety or that of others;
> - The operation of electrically sensitive equipment in critical care situations; or
> - The levels of privacy and dignity that must be the hallmark of NHS care"[101].

1.115   It is particularly helpful that both this guidance and the Code of Practice for England make explicit reference to the human rights context of the debate over access to telephones. The guidance acknowledges that communication with the world outside hospital may engage rights to communicate with family and friends under Article 8 of the ECHR, but also that mobile phones equipped with cameras may pose a conflicting risk to other rights under Article 8, such as the right to privacy and dignity[102]. A photograph of a patient taken whilst they are in hospital should be treated and protected as personal medical data (although, in our view, this should not be interpreted to prevent patients and their friends or families from taking photographs of each other where the requirements of security allow this).

1.116   It is therefore important that any restriction on patient's communication with their families or friends outside of the hospital is proportionate and based upon requirements of security, privacy, or safety. Outside of the secure sector, care should be taken that policies restricting use of mobile telephones on wards do not disadvantage disproportionately detained patients who may have restricted egress from the ward:

> Due to the ward rules regarding the use of mobile phones and the continued lack of a payphone, the Commissioner is particularly concerned about patients who are unable to leave the ward being denied the right to communicate easily and privately with family, friends, solicitor etc.
>
> *West Midlands, November 2008*

1.117   Some facilities have addressed the problem of camera phones imaginatively, for example by keeping older-style telephones on the ward that can be fitted with the patient's SIM card and lent to patients upon admission. There is such a mobile telephone swap system in place at Shamrock Ward, Tolworth Hospital (South West London Mental Health NHS Trust).

---

[100]   MHA *Code of Practice for England*, para 16.5; *Code of Practice for Wales*, para 11.32.

[101]   Department of Health (2009) *Using mobile phones in NHS hospitals*. January 2009.

[102]   *ibid.*, para 3.

Ward-based telephones

1.118 The Code of Practice for England (paragraph 16.3) also states that hospital managers should ensure that patients who use any coin or card operated telephone on the ward can do so in privacy, without being overheard[103]. On a number of visits in this period, patients have made complaints about this aspect of their environment. As seen in the example above, we have visited wards where there is no telephone provision, leading to questions of how detained patients might communicate with the outside world at all. A more common complaint is that the telephone is sited in such a way that it provides little or no privacy. In some cases this could easily be resolved through installing a booth or hood, as suggested in the Code. In other cases we have asked for telephones to be relocated:

> The patients' phone has been sited in a tight corner of the lounge directly opposite the television, affording neither comfort nor privacy. Patients did remark on this and asked why it could not have been placed at the dining room end. It is suggested this is considered because the phone is not at all easy to use where it is sited now.
>
> *London area, March 2008*

1.119 Some hospitals have been found to be operating unjustifiable blanket policies restricting or preventing telephone access to all patients on a ward:

> The patient phone on the ward, situated in the old smoking room, is at present not available to patients. This is to prevent one patient making repeated nuisance calls. This means that patients are using the nursing office phone outside the office door in a very public area, which provides no privacy. … The Commission is concerned to see a blanket rule to deal with the circumstances of an individual patient. Please inform the Commission what steps the hospital will take to ensure that restrictions on the rights of patients are determined on an individual risk assessed patient basis rather than for the whole ward.
>
> *London area, March 2008*

> The patient phone is situated in a corridor which is used by patients and staff to access group/meeting rooms and the computer room. There is no privacy hood, so conversations may be overheard. The ward policy is to limit patients to a total of 15 minutes of phone calls per day between 18.30 and 21.30. All calls are supervised by a member of staff sitting further down the corridor within hearing distance. the rules on the office doors state clearly that they are not negotiable. Please inform the MHAC of the rationale for this blanket policy and consider in what circumstances it might be appropriate to allow patients more privacy when telephoning family and friends.
>
> *Midlands (secure unit), October 2008*

Access to computers and the internet

1.120 We encounter many anxieties about internet access for detained patients, even outside of secure hospitals. There are still some hospitals that do not provide any computer facilities for patients at all:

---

[103] The *Code of Practice for Wales* also requires that hospitals should ensure that patients are facilitated to make telephone calls in private wherever possible (para 19.11).

> The Commission noted that one deaf patient had considerable keyboard skills. However, there was no computer on the ward available for patient access. While the Commission accepts the need for appropriate rules for risk-assessing access to individual programs or access to the internet, a computer would increase range of options available to those patients remaining on the ward and would provide further opportunities for social and educational development.
>
> *London, April 2008*
>
> It is unclear what the Trust's policy is for internet access for patients, many of whom are accessing college courses and therefore need internet access. Others are used to using computers. There is a need for internet access and improved IT
>
> *South Wales, November 2008*

1.121 Some Trusts have addressed this issue very well. Central and North West London NHS Trust have very effective and secure internet tables on many wards, which are well used and an effective means of communication and activity for patients that is not constrained by the availability of staff. We have suggested that several other Trusts who have not provided internet access for patients might consider emulating this example. Policies on access to the internet (and other policies relating to communications or media technologies) should be regularly updated to keep track of changing technologies.

> *What would make a difference to you?*
> Internet access – I feel shut off from the world.
>
> *Nicola Pazdziersca, SURP member*

1.122 It is understandable, of course that hospitals will want to place restrictions on the content that may be accessed on their computer terminals. However, some hospitals' lists of banned websites include social networking sites and also webmail. Such blanket bans can lead to loss of contact with family or friends, including 'virtual' friends who may play a large role in an otherwise isolated person's life outside of hospital. Except in particular secure hospitals, we do not believe that blanket bans on access to the internet can be justified. Although it may be sensible to stop certain individuals from accessing the internet, or certain internet sites that would normally be considered acceptable, this should be done on basis of individual risk assessments.

Patients' mail

> These terrible despotisms would be a far less dangerous institution, were the boarders allowed their post-office rights.
>
> *E P W Packard, 1887* [104]

1.123 The current law regarding hospital managers' abilities to withhold mail to and from detained patients is a much reduced remnant of earlier legislation. Under the Mental Health Act 1959, managers could withhold any detained patient's outgoing mail if the

---

[104] Packard E P W (1887) *Modern Persecution, or Insane Asylums Unveiled, as demonstrated by the Investigating Committee of the Legislature of Illinois*, published by the authoress, Hartford. Vol 1, p.159.

addressee had requested not to receive mail; or if the mail was deemed unreasonably offensive to the addressee or defamatory to other persons (other than hospital employees); or was likely to prejudice the interests of the patient[105]. Responsible Medical Officers could lawfully open and examine mail to determine if the second criterion applied, if they considered the patient to be suffering from the kind of mental disorder that would lead him or her to send such mail[106]. The 1978 White Paper which led to the Mental Health Act 1983 proposed the complete abolition of all powers to withhold mail other than where the addressee had told the hospital that they did not want to receive it. Except in the case of patients detained in High Security Hospitals (HSHs), this is how the law now stands after the amendments enacted in 1983. But for HSH patients, managers may still open and examine outgoing mail and withhold it if, in their view, it is likely to cause danger to any person, or is likely to cause distress to the addressee or to a person other than a member of the hospital staff[107].

1.124 Under the Mental Health Act 1959, incoming mail addressed to any psychiatric patient could be withheld by the Responsible Medical Officer (or other doctor in charge) if it was thought likely to interfere with the patient's treatment or cause the patient unnecessary distress[108]. Under the 1983 Act, the right to withhold incoming mail was restricted to detained patients in High Security Hospitals, and exercisable on the grounds that it is necessary to do so in the interests of the health and safety of the patient concerned, or of the safety of other people[109].

Appeals against withholding of mail in High Security Hospitals

1.125 The 1983 Act (at s.121(7) and (8)) provided the MHAC with powers, upon receipt of an appeal, to review decisions to withhold mail to and from patients in the High Security Hospitals, and to direct that the mail be released to its addressee. This is the sole part of the Act where hospital managers are required to comply with a direction issued by the MHAC. These powers pass to the Care Quality Commission from the 1 April 2009.

1.126 Figure 27 below shows the number of appeals against the withholding of an item of mail determined by the MHAC over its lifetime. The table also shows those cases where the decision to withhold the item has been upheld by the MHAC. This is the simplest way to record the outcomes, as appeals may be wholly or partly successful, in that some but not all of the withheld item is released, or compromises may be reached, as in one case where it was agreed that the item should be released to the patient when his nursing in segregation came to an end. There have never been a large number of appeals, and numbers fluctuate from year to year, but over the lifetime of the Act roughly a third of appeals against the withholding of mail have resulted in the item being wholly or partly released to the patient or addressee.

---

[105] *Mental Health Act* 1959, s.36(2)(b).

[106] *ibid.*, s.36(3).

[107] *Mental Health Act* 1983, s.134(1)(b).

[108] *Mental Health Act* 1959, s.36 & s.134

[109] *Mental Health Act* 1983, s.134(2).

year	1983–1985	1985–1987	1987–1989	1989–1991	1991–1993	1993–1995	1995–1997	1997–1999	1999–2001	2001–2003	2003–2005	2005–2007	2007–2008
decision appealed	10	11	10	6	n/a	6	9	22	15	14	22	12	14
decision upheld	9	9	4	1	n/a	6	5	12	9	11	14	10	9

Fig 27: Appeals against decisions to withhold mail in High Security Hospitals, 1983 to 2009, with number of decisions upheld (financial years)

Source: MHAC data

1.127 The following are some examples of reviews of the withholding of mail in the High Security Hospitals during this reporting period:

- A patient suffering from a hypermanic episode wrote numerous letters, including a dozen to suppliers of die-cast model kits inviting them to consider selling their merchandise to patients and staff. The letters were withheld on the grounds that they falsely gave an impression that the patient had an official capacity for ordering items in the hospital, and so lead to distress 'in due course'. Upon the patient's appeal, the MHAC directed that the letters be released. The Responsible Clinician wrote to thank the MHAC for its review, accepted that the hospital had probably been overcautious in the application of its powers, and informed us that the patient had been given help and advice over the formulation of such letters in future.

- A patient who had recently been moved from one High Security Hospital to another wrote to another patient at the first hospital, discussing staff members in that hospital. The letter was withheld on the grounds that the inclusion of staff names and personal details could colour the second patient's therapeutic relationship with the named staff and potentially put them at risk. Both patients appealed the decision. The MHAC directed that the letter should be released, on the grounds that, however unpleasant it was for staff to know that they were being discussed in this way, or to have things said about them that could not be challenged, the letter did not compromise the safety of any person and can not be withheld on the grounds that staff members might be distressed by its content.

- A patient complained that a number of unsolicited letters from women, some of a very young age, had been withheld from him. The MHAC examined the letters but did not direct their release to the patient, finding that the hospital could justify their withholding under s.134(2): 'necessary … for the protection of other persons'. Dealing with 'fan-letters' or offers of on-going correspondence to persons who have committed notorious offences can pose difficult questions to managers and the MHAC alike. Legal advice received by the MHAC in 1997 suggested that the first ground under s.134(2) for withholding mail addressed to HSH patients ('necessary in the interests of the safety of the patient') should not be deemed to extend to include the patient's health or welfare. However, the second ground ('protection of others') might apply individually in these cases to the authors of the letters, or indeed to classes of persons, such as women or children, provided that the actual risk posed by the patient should he receive such material is clearly expressed. Such a risk could, in our view, be related to the patient's pathology and the treatment he is receiving for it, but a decision must be taken on the facts of any individual case.

Access to pornography

1.128　The issues raised in the last example are also relevant to another difficult area of boundary-setting in the High Security Hospitals and in other secure hospitals: patients' access to pornography. The legal advice referred to in that example was sought over a decade ago in relation to a now-superseded policy in one High Security Hospital that sought to ban (and therefore withhold from the mail) any material defined in the policy as pornographic. That definition was very loosely drawn[110], made no distinction between legal and illegal material, pictorial images or other media, and it had no exemption for work of artistic merit (unlike the Obscene Publications Act 1959). Whilst the policy noted that pornography may be clinically damaging to some patients, it did not seem to limit the scope of the ban on materials falling within its definition of pornography to such individuals, and indeed included within the justifications for the ban the fact that 'pornography can be seen as contrary to women's equality' and 'contrary to the spirit of the Sex Discrimination Act'.

1.129　Although the above policy is no longer in use, and the High Security Hospitals all have more sophisticated policies on pornography today, dealing with access to pornography in secure settings (and indeed on psychiatric wards of any level of security) remains a challenging subject for staff and managers alike. At paragraph 2.56 we note one example where a restricted patient, who appears to have obtained videos of violence and hardcore pornography whilst resident in a low secure unit, went AWOL from that unit and committed rape. In that case it would seem that far too little attention was paid to the risks posed by that individual, in particular in relation to sexualised behaviour prior to going AWOL. In contrast, patients on some MHAC visits to medium secure units have asked us to challenge blanket bans on pornographic material, as in the following example:

> It was brought to the Commissioner's attention that patients on this ward are not allowed the use of pornographic material for use in private. It is understood that patients on other wards in the hospital are allowed such material. Decisions to deny access to such material should be made on an individual basis … if it is a matter of general policy it could be seen as arbitrary…
>
> *Wales, April 2008*

1.130　The MHAC encourages hospitals to have policies that ensure that decisions over whether or not a patient should be allowed to remain in possession of pornography that they have lawfully obtained should be taken on an individual basis, with reference to the patient's clinical vulnerabilities, as well as his ability and willingness to ensure that the material

---

[110] The definition of pornography adopted was "the subordination of women (children, men) through images which dehumanise them as sexual objects, which reduces them to body parts and which shows them being degraded or physically hurt in a context that makes these conditions sexual" . It was unclear whether these requirements of the definition were cumulative or alternative, and it is difficult to give a precise meaning to phrases such as 'the subordination of women' or 'reduces them to body parts'.

is stored and accessed appropriately, and not kept in open view where it might cause offence to or constitute harassment of other patients. Policies and practice should not discriminate between heterosexually and homosexually orientated material.

Telephone monitoring in the High Security Hospitals

1.131   The Safety and Security Directions[111] introduced in 2000 allowed that the High Security Hospitals could record and monitor a patient's telephone calls if that patient was deemed to present a high risk of escaping or organising action to subvert security and safety in collaboration with others, or that there was a need to protect the safety of such a 'high risk' patient or others. These Directions were amended in 2003 to allow routine monitoring and recording of any HSH patient's telephone calls if there is a need to protect the safety of that patient or others[112]. A patient subject to such monitoring may appeal to the MHAC, and the MHAC is empowered to direct that it must cease.

1.132   We have received very few appeals against telephone monitoring, although a number of patients have expressed their dislike of it to us on our visits to the hospitals. Over the winter of 2008, after considering one formal appeal, we decided that the justification offered as to why the monitoring was necessary did not make a good case for its continuation, and directed that the monitoring should stop. The justification offered was that a friend of the patient had, a considerable time earlier, made threats against staff members, and that an acquaintance of the patient had been overheard in a telephone conversation with the patient remarking that he would bring Semtex into the hospital to blow it up. Further concerns had arisen when the patient was accidentally supplied with the minutes of a multi-disciplinary 'MAPPA' review of his case, which he forwarded to his solicitor. It was suggested to us that these minutes contained the names and job titles of a number of persons, not all of whom were employed by the hospital, who might now be at risk. Such arguments might well have justified the continuation of telephone monitoring, but for the absence of any recent re-evaluation of the need for this intervention or of the actual risks that the patient posed. As such, we suggested that our direction that monitoring should stop should not preclude the hospital from re-instigating it should new information come to light as a result of risk assessment.

The policing of patients' mail in Medium Security Hospitals

1.133   In 2006 we corresponded with a consultant in a medium secure unit over the management of a patient who was proposed for transfer there from a High Security Hospital. This patient had a well-known propensity to write offensive letters to persons outside the hospital, which was managed within the HSH system through the exercise of powers to withhold outgoing mail. The consultant was concerned that the law would not allow him to similarly withhold mail should the patient be transferred outside the HSH system. Indeed, there are some grounds for concluding that the lack of such powers had dissuaded other hospitals in the medium secure sector from offering a placement to this patient, so that the patient was effectively remaining in conditions of high security because of

---

[111] *The Safety and Security in Ashworth, Broadmoor and Rampton Hospitals Directions 2000*, d.29.

[112] *The Safety and Security In Ashworth, Broadmoor and Rampton Hospitals Amendment Directions 2003*, d.2(e).

his letter-writing rather than any substantive clinical need. Whilst we passed on to the Department of Health Mental Health Bill team the consultant's suggestion that the law regarding withholding of mail might be extended to the medium secure sector, we replied that we considered that such a reversal of the legislature's deliberate and progressive limitation of legal powers over patients' mail would be a disproportionate response to a difficult case. We also advised the consultant that we could see no reason why he should not write to addressees of the patient's letters advising them of their ability to request any future letters to be withheld. A number of members of the public had requested this of the High Security Hospital, and we suggested that such requests should be deemed to be transferable to the medium secure hospital managers, and that it would be unnecessarily intrusive to write to these members of the public asking them to renew their request.

1.134 Some managers and staff in the medium secure sector seem not to know the limitations of their powers to interfere with mail. On a visit in January 2009, we found unposted letters addressed to public figures in the file of one MSU patient, and upon questioning this were told by the ward manager that they had not been posted as 'it would not be appropriate to send them'. We reminded the manager that the power to withhold mail is available to MSUs under s.134 of the 1983 Act only if the intended recipient has requested this, and asked that staff should be advised accordingly and the letters posted.

1.135 Some medium secure hospital policies stipulate that, whilst it is unlawful to withhold incoming mail from a patient, or to open mail addressed to a patient without that patient's permission, if a staff member has concerns about the possible contents of a particular package or letter, it is acceptable for the patient to be advised that he or she may only open it in a controlled environment (i.e. the nurses' office) in the presence of staff. Once open, the contents may be treated like any other item of patient property and confiscated if necessary. The MHAC accepts the need for such arrangements as a last resort, but they should be carefully monitored and reviewed to ensure that they are and continue to be a justified interference with the patient's rights to privacy, and must never used as a blanket measure irrespective of individual risk assessment.

Observation and restraint

1.136 In its 2005 guidelines on the short-term management of disturbed/violent behaviour in psychiatric in-patient and emergency departments, the National Institute for Clinical Excellence sought to consolidate previous guidance on observation levels[113], and required services to adopt consistent terminology to avoid confusion. We reproduce the NICE terminology and definitions, also giving the 'levels' to which these are commonly referred, in figure 28 below.

---

[113] NICE (2005) *Violence: The Short-Term Management of Disturbed/Violent Behaviour in Psychiatric In-patient and Emergency Departments Guideline.* February 2005, para 1.7.2.

Level 1: *General observation* is the minimum acceptable level of observation for all in-patients. The location of all service users should be known to staff, but not all service users need to be kept within sight. At least once a shift a nurse should set aside dedicated time to assess the mental state of the service user and engage positively with the service user. The aim of this should be to develop a positive, caring and therapeutic relationship with the service user. This assessment should always include an evaluation of the service user's moods and behaviours associated with risks of disturbed/violent behaviour, and these should be recorded in the notes.

Level 2: *Intermittent observation* means that the service user's location should be checked every 15 to 30 minutes (exact times to be specified in the notes). Checks need to be carried out sensitively in order to cause as little intrusion as possible. However, this check should also be seen in terms of positive engagement with the service user. This level is appropriate when service users are potentially, but not immediately, at risk of disturbed/violent behaviour. Service users who have previously been at risk of harming themselves or others, but who are in a process of recovery, require intermittent observation.

Level 3: *Within eyesight* means the service user should be kept within eyesight and accessible at all times, by day and by night and, if deemed necessary, any tools or instruments that could be used to harm themselves or others should be removed. It is required when the service user could, at any time, make an attempt to harm themselves or others. It may be necessary to search the service user and their belongings, while having due regard for the service user's legal rights and conducting the search in a sensitive way. Positive engagement with the service user is an essential aspect of this level of observation.

Level 4: *Within arms length* is needed for service users at the highest levels of risk of harming themselves or others, who may need to be supervised in close proximity. On specified occasions more than one member of staff may be necessary. Issues of privacy, dignity and the consideration of gender in allocating staff, and the environmental dangers need to be discussed and incorporated into the care plan. Positive engagement with the service user is an essential aspect of this level of observation.

Fig 28: Observation terminology recommended by NICE for adoption across England and Wales[114]

1.137 At chapter 5.49 we suggest that, where hospital staff recognise an acute and high risk of suicide in any patients, it may be the case that only continuous observation should be considered a safe intervention. However, we recognise the danger in such an approach of inflating levels of observation to the general detriment of patients. Continuous observation can be very intrusive and disturbing to patients, stressful to staff, and may reinforce the patient's experience of care as being more custodial than caring[115]. Professor Len Bowers and his colleagues have estimated that between 3% and 20% of all admissions to psychiatric hospital receive some form of constant observation, and that such observations may account for up to a fifth of the nursing budgets in such hospitals[116].

---

[114] Standing Nursing and Advisory Committee (1999) *Practice guidance: Safe and supportive observation of patients at risk.* June 1999. www.publications.doh.gov.uk/pub/docs/doh/snmacobs.pdf

[115] See Buchanan-Barker P. & Barker P. (2005) 'Observation: the original sin of mental health nursing?' *Journal of Psychiatric and Mental Health Nursing* 12, 541–549; Bowles N., Dodds P., Hackney D., Sunderland C. & Thomas P. (2002) 'Formal observations and engagement: a discussion paper' *Journal of Psychiatric and Mental Health Nursing* 9, 255–260; Bowers, L. Simpson A. & Alexander J. (2005) 'Real world application of an intervention to reduce absconding' *Journal of Psychiatric and Mental Health Nursing* 12, 598–602.

[116] Bowers L. Gournay K, Duffy D, Jones J *Special observation* (City University internet resource).

The *City 128 Study of Observation and Outcomes on Acute Psychiatric Wards* found no relationship between the use of continuous observation and rates of self harm, although it did find that rates of self-harm were inversely correlated to the use of *intermittent* observation[117]. This does not mean that continuous observation is not a legitimate and necessary intervention in high risk situations, such as where a patient is actively suicidal. But it does suggest that, especially where *continuous* observation is used on a ward, managers and clinicians should evaluate their practice of *intermittent* observations, ensuring that this 'lighter touch' observation is an available option for staff and, where it is used at less than median levels (i.e. less than five patient-shifts per day), re-evaluating ward practice[118]. It may be that the effect of intermittent observations in reducing incidents and disturbance across the ward will lessen the need for continuous observations, and at the very least such evaluation should ensure that continuous observations are not being over-used where risks might be managed with lesser interventions.

> It was very annoying and uncomfortable having a nurse staring at me 24 hours a day; I felt like an insect under a microscope glass. The nurse asked me if I was okay, and I said to her "actually no, I feel like there is someone here in the room with me watching my every move, I see them all the time and they never go away and leave me alone. Occasionally, but very rarely they talk to me. It is very unnerving". I did not give this a further thought, until the ward doctor came to speak with me later that day, he made reference to hallucinations, my seeing invisible people and hearing voices. It was hard work trying to convince him that I had been joking.
>
> *Monica Endersby, SURP member*

1.138 Of course, where it is necessary to use constant observations, it is vital that it is carefully framed and justified to the patient concerned, and that staff aim to provide 'skilled companionship' rather than a custodial presence[119]. Observation and engagement with patients need not be incompatible, although patients too often complain that observing nursing staff do not talk or engage with them on an appropriately human level.

> The 'observation' by staff made you feel like a prisoner and that it was your fault that you were in hospital. If a person was paranoid this made it worse. They watched you. They did not communicate with you except to chastise you, for example for having a beaker of water in your room, or being told to have a shower in a filthy bathroom.
>
> *Gillian Brightmore, SURP member*

---

[117] Bowers L, Whittington R, Nolan P, Parkin D, Curtis S, Bhui K, Hackney D, Allan T, Simpson A, Flood C (2007) The *City 128 Study of Observation and Outcomes on Acute Psychiatric Wards. Report to the NHS SDO Programme.* City University, London. See also Len Bowers and Alan Simpson (2007) 'Observing and Engaging: new ways to reduce self-harm and suicide'. *Mental Health Practice*, vol 10 no 10, p.12-14.

[118] Bowers L *et al* (2007) *op cit*.

[119] Alland C, Gallagher A and Henderson J (2003) 'Staying close: creating distance? The ethics of constant observation'. *Mental Health Practice* vol 7 no 3, p.15-16.

1.139   Another common complaint is that insufficient thought is given to patients' dignity during observations. The following is from a visit to a hospital in the north-east of England in Autumn 2008:

> One of the patients seen talked about inconsistencies in the way in which staff respond to patients and interpret policies. At night when she is on 'arms length' observation, some female staff sit in her room but others and male staff sit outside the door. She objects strongly to being observed by male staff especially when she is wearing a strong nightdress and strong bedding.

1.140   In another case, a male patient in a medium secure unit made a parallel complaint:

> Observations have been a big issue of late. We are a 12 bedded male ward. Recently we had two patients being constantly observed…problems occurred when female staff had to observe showers and toilet usage of patients. Patient dignity was not upheld here and the patients found this difficult. Due to staff shortages and bad planning there were no male staff who could observe these areas of daily life.
>
> *Mark Gray, SURP member*

1.141   The female patient who complained of being observed by male nurses was one of two challenging patients whose care was highly disruptive to the general running of a low secure ward with no access to seclusion facilities. Some other patients had been moved out of the ward, in one case because one of the unsettled patients had threatened to kill her. Every patient we spoke with talked of feeling unsafe on the ward, and of living in constant fear and tension. Some aspects of the ward management exacerbated this. For example, weekends were better than weekdays, because patients could retreat to their rooms at weekends but had limited access to their rooms during the week, so that they were forced to witness the behaviour of the challenging patients, who had to be restrained on an almost daily basis, sometimes for lengthy periods. They reported having limited contact with familiar staff, as these were engaged in observation or restraint with the two disturbed patients, and also reported difficulties in relating to agency staff, whom they did not know and who often appeared 'out of their depth'. In our visit report we asked the hospital management to try to ensure that there were always sufficient qualified female staff on the ward to ensure patient safety, privacy and dignity, and to meet the needs of patients who were not acting out as well as those who were. We also requested a review of whether all the patients on the ward were appropriately placed.

1.142   In the following example, from a visit in north-east England in summer 2007, the patients who were subject to observation and restraint complained of being in view of other patients:

> Patients complained about being unable to access the lavatories in their rooms when they are on 'stages'. This necessitates them using the lavatory in the main ward area with the door open. Staff appear to try to facilitate this in a way which minimises embarrassment and protects patients from being observed by others but the location of the lavatory on the ward does not make this easy. Patients reported being restrained for lengthy periods in full view of others on the ward. The absence of a seclusion room means that they may be restrained in the main ward area until they are considered calm enough to be released. This is clearly upsetting not only for the restrained patient but also for those witnessing the restraint.

1.143   On another visit to a hospital in Yorkshire, patients that we met with raised concerns including: excessive use of restraint; personal belongings having been taken away as form of punishment if their behaviour was disruptive; lack of respect; feeling undervalued as patients; staff not engaging in conversation (so patients left to own devices); and not feeling safe on the ward. It seems to us that there is likely to not only be a close correlation between such patient perceptions and the high levels of 'coercive manoeuvres'[120] by staff, but that each may fuel the other. Where wards experience disruptive behaviour, the increasingly harried responses of staff may create or maintain the atmospheres of tension and fear that is so often described to and witnessed by us on our visits. It is important that ward managers audit observation and restraint levels, but, just as importantly, they should pay particular attention to the way in which observation is carried out; how much contact patients have with staff outside of confrontational situations; what actions preceded restraint; and what else was happening on the ward at the time.

> Patients complained that there was too much emphasis on control and restraint on the ward and nurses were only interested in keeping patients under their control. One patient was told that if she didn't stop crying, she would be put in her room. As this is supposed to be an 'Intensive Care' ward, I did not get the impression that there was much caring going on. Three female patients interviewed spoke about the degrading treatment of being locked in rooms without any toilet facilities.
>
> *London, October 2007*

1.144   As we have stated in previous reports[121], and as the Codes of Practice[122] and other guidance[123] recognise, much day-to-day problems of managing difficult behaviour have at root boredom and tension related to the environmental and situational aspects of ward life. As such, prioritising patient involvement in their care (see paragraph 1.91 *et seq*) and meaningful activities on wards (see paragraph 1.86 *et seq*) could lead to significant improvements in the safety of patients and staff in many services.

---

[120] See Ryan C J & Bowers L (2005) 'Coercive manoeuvres in a psychiatric intensive care unit' *Journal of Psychiatric and Mental Health Nursing*, 12, 695-702. This points to a continuum of coercive measures taken by nursing staff, including low-level physical and interactional manoeuvres to control patient's disturbed or resistive behaviour.

[121] See MHAC (2006) *In Place of Fear? Eleventh Biennial Report 2003-2005*, para 4.204; MHAC (2008) *Risk, Rights, Recovery; Twelfth Biennial Report 2005-2007*, para 2.125 *et seq*.

[122] *MHA Code of Practice for England*, para 15.5; *Code of Practice for Wales*, para 19.9 *et seq*.

[123] See, in particular, NICE (2005) *Violence: the short-term management of disturbed/violent behaviour in inpatient psychiatric settings and emergency departments*. Clinical Guidelines, 25 February 2005.

Restraint and safety

1.145 This report is being published in the year of the tenth anniversary of the death of David 'Rocky' Bennett under restraint in a Norfolk hospital. That death was caused in part by Mr Bennett being held in face-down restraint for a considerable period of time, leading to positional asphyxiation. Our last report, published five years after the inquiry into that death made its recommendations on future practice[124], commented that Government had neither established national mandatory training nor endorsed a time-limit for face down restraint, as the inquiry had recommended[125]. We also noted two further deaths through asphyxiation linked to excessive face-down restraint that may have been avoided had staff ceased prone restraint earlier.

1.146 In 2008 it was reported that the long-awaited accreditation scheme for organisations who offer training in restraint practices was again in preparation[126]. We hope that this will be progressed without further delay. The following examples show some of the concerns about restraint raised on our visits. In the first example, we were assured that training covered the areas of concern, but of course we have no reassurance over the content of such training, as we might have were accreditation in place:

> A common theme in both formal and informal discussion with patients was concern over the degree of force being used when a patient is being restrained and concern that this is overzealous on occasion. No patient wished to raise a formal complaint, but the Commissioner would like to confirm that having raised this issue with the ward manager, he has in turn raised this with his nursing staff. The commissioner suggested possibly some refresher training but was assured by the ward manager that this is a component of regular staff training.
>
> Patients identified the wearing of jewellery by staff when restraining had caused some injury and the commissioner would strongly recommend that staff do not wear jewellery on their hands or wrists whilst on duty.
>
> *East Midlands, November 2008*

1.147 We have elsewhere raised similar concerns over jewellery worn by staff who would be engaged in restraint:

> I had some concerns about the potential damage that could be caused to patients during control and restraint by a member of staff who was wearing several large rings. I asked the nurse in charge at the end of my visit about this risk and she responded that "he always removes his rings so they don't get damaged". My concerns were more about damage to the patient than the staff member's rings! Please furnish the Commission with your dress code for staff as it seems inappropriate on a PICU /any inpatient facility to wear such jewellery.
>
> *London, November 2008*

---

[124] Norfolk, Suffolk and Cambridgeshire Strategic Health Authority (2003) *Independent Inquiry into the death of David Bennett*. December 2003.

[125] MHAC (2008) *Risk, Rights, Recovery; Twelfth Biennial Report 2005-2007*, para 2.128 et seq. We do note, however, that the Welsh Assembly Government published a *Framework for Restrictive Intervention Policy and Practice* in March 2005..

[126] 'Violence increases yet staff still await training' *Health Service Journal*, 14 February 2008.

1.148 In some services we have found some staff who might be engaged in restraint practices not having received training at all. In other services, we have seen evidence of worrying, and poorly documented, practices:

> Three out of the four patients interviewed privately spoke of having been given IM medication while being restrained. All described being restrained face down. Two described their hands being held behind their backs. The Commissioner found in the individual patient notes entries confirming that these patients had had IM PRN medication under restraint. The Commissioner requested to see the incident records for these patients but they could not be produced, as no record is kept on the ward and the person with responsibility for them was in a meeting. The nursing entries did not give full details of how the restraint was carried out.
>
> *London, winter 2008*

1.149 We do recognise, of course, that ward staff should be competent and confident in restraint techniques and must be prepared to intervene physically for the safety of patients or others. The following account was sent to us by a patient in a medium secure unit, which shows how restraint might otherwise be carried out.

> This evening at 18.20 hours a police shield squad of more than twelve men heavily equipped with riot armour and accompanied by an attack dog, an Alsatian, entered "A" ward to deal with a situation in the day room. A young Black patient went beserk and the staff locked themselves in the office while he smashed the windows with a chair taken from the dining room.
>
> The police were equipped with CS gas; they used a Taser on the patient and took him to the police station where he was detained overnight and returned two days later to be detained on another ward which is empty.
>
> It is the first time I have seen a Taser used in practice although I have seen them used on the television. They rushed shouting "Taser, Taser, Taser"; after firing the Taser they took him down and dragged him into the centre of the room in front of me pinning him to the floor and dead-legging him with riot batons. I was watching everything from my doorway until the police dog handler saw me and returned up the corridor with the dog and ordered me to go back into my room.
>
> On this occasion I do not necessarily criticise the police handling of the matter. They did what they were trained and equipped to do. I criticise the fact that they were called in the first place. The hospital invests a large amount of time and energy in training staff in what are purported to be control and restraint techniques. The staff on duty locked themselves into the office (while the office was still standing that is to say) and would not even venture out. When the window gave way they evacuated the area into the next ward for a short time, leaving [a young female member of staff] with me. I am sixty-two and I have acute coronary heart disease. The senior staff in charge of the ward were clearly terrified.
>
> *A service-user in a medium secure unit, October 2008.*

1.150   A further recommendation of the Bennett Inquiry was that a doctor should be available within twenty minutes of any staff request, for example during restraint episodes[127]. This continues to be an impossibility for many units. In July 2008 we were told by one Trust that the clinical director had made a number of attempts to arrange for on-call cover for one satellite unit from a nearby hospital, but each time the primary difficulty raised had been the European Working Time Directive (EWTD), which limits the hours a doctor can work. Whether or not the EWTD is in fact the barrier to establishing workable on-call rotas for psychiatric attendance, it remains a fact that in a number of services it would take considerable time to obtain the attendance of such a doctor in the event of a psychiatric emergency, whether this is to do with urgent medication, restraint, or seclusion.

Police presence on wards

1.151   In general terms, police forces appear to attend disturbances on wards with some reluctance, taking the view (which we share, at least in cases such as the example from a medium secure unit given above), that ward staff or hospital security should be equipped and trained to deal with them. Nevertheless we accept that police intervention is necessary in situations that cannot be managed by hospital staff. The police may also be asked to attend wards for other purposes, for example where a patient or member of staff wishes to report a potential crime, or to help in searches for drugs as described in our last report[128].

1.152   St Andrews Hospital, Northampton, has funded a community police officer dedicated to the hospital site, but liable for other emergency police duties. Whilst there were initial concerns about whether having a uniformed police officer on site would make patients uncomfortable, in a published article on the scheme (written by executives and staff of the hospital and the police officer concerned) states that:

> The officer has become well integrated into the hospital community, and is welcomed as a visible, positive and friendly presence and an important resource… the officer now contributes to patient groups on personal safety and hate crimes; she pays an important role in staff induction, and supports staff and patients attending court. She co-ordinates information for defence solicitors and the Crown Prosecution Service, Police and Criminal Evidence Act interviews, intelligence on drugs misuse in site, and takes part in inter-agency liaison and policy development.[129]

1.153   Although noting an initial tendency to over-report minor incidents, which was addressed through staff training, the study reports a significant positive effect on aggressive incidents, particularly in the secure men's service. This is an interesting development, which perhaps may be emulated in other large hospital sites and would be a good subject for independent research.

---

[127] Norfolk, Suffolk and Cambridgeshire Strategic Health Authority (2003) *Independent Inquiry into the death of David Bennett*. December 2003, page 29.

[128] MHAC (2008) *Risk, Rights, Recovery; Twelfth Biennial Report 2005-2007*, para 2.120 *et seq*.

[129] Mann A, Sugarman, P, Rooney C, Goodman M and Lynch J (2007) 'Service innovation: policing mental health – the St Andrew's scheme'. *Psychiatric Bulletin*, 31, 97-98.

Seclusion

1.154   In some of the examples relating to restraint that are discussed above (see for example paragraph 1.142), it is clear that the lack of seclusion facilities on some wards leads to restraint episodes being conducted in full view of the ward, sometimes to the distress of both those who are restrained and those who are witnesess. We recognise, nevertheless, that some patients and professionals would consider that distress a lesser evil than the practice of seclusion itself. Indeed, especially when it is used for people with psychosis, seclusion may lessen the likelihood of staff injury but may increase patient distress[130].

1.155   The majority of services we visit do use seclusion. Peter Campbell (a member of the *Service User/Survivor History Group*) has written that

> The Mental Health Act Commission has been complaining regularly about hospitals' seclusion policies (inadequate, not updated, not following the Code of Practice etc) ever since it came into existence. How much real difference has that made? There is certainly more talk about the issue in the mental health nursing profession than there used to be, but it is not clear that the recipients' experience of solitary confinement has improved very much[131].

1.156   Peter Campbell's own suggestion is that "it is time the practice was covered by the Mental Health Act itself, and the involvement of advocacy services in each episode became a legal necessity". We also argued, unsuccessfully, for statutory regulation of seclusion in the debates over the revision of the Act over 2007/08[132]. We expect that this argument will come up again at a future date, but in the meantime we endorse Campbell's suggestion that

> It might be more helpful to people confined in this way if it was assumed that the practice was likely to do some harm. This might make more sensitive support for people emerging from solitary confinement more of a priority. [133]

1.157   The revised Code of Practice for England states that hospital guidelines (and therefore practice) should "ensure that the patient receives the care and support rendered necessary by their seclusion both during and after it has taken place"[134]. In our view, this requirement should be interpreted in the light of the assumption that Campbell urges us to make: all patients subject to seclusion are likely to have suffered some harm from the experience, which may be ameliorated or exacerbated through the actions of staff and the environment in which the seclusion took place. As such, the starting point of all care-planning whilst patients are in seclusion, or where seclusion might be used, should be in terminating seclusion as quickly as possible and supporting the patient throughout and after the process. It is important that the involvement of patients in their own care planning extends to restraint and seclusion where these are likely to be an issue.

---

[130] Steinert T, *et al* (2007) 'Seclusion and restraint in patients with schizophrenia: clinical and biological correlates'. *J Nerv Ment Dis* 195: 492-6.

[131] Campbell P (2008) 'Seclusion is about abandonment…', *Mental Health Today*, May 2008.

[132] See also MHAC (2006) *In Place of Fear? Eleventh Biennial Report 2003-2005*, para 4.237.

[133] Campbell P (2008) *op cit*.

[134] *MHA Code of Practice for England*, para 15.47; whilst there is no equivalent provision in the *Code of Practice for Wales*, such a requirement is in any case inherent in good mental healthcare practice.

1.158   In April 2008 we visited one women's unit in the East Midlands where nurses routinely stripped patients naked before secluding them, as a means of ensuring that they had no means to self-harm. Of course we raised objections to this and pointed out where it failed to meet Code of Practice expectations, both in terms of the clothing of secluded patients and in terms of seclusion and self-harm[135]. Just as importantly, our feedback also contained the following suggestions:

- "Please ask the women who have regular aggressive outbursts, how they would like to be treated to enable them to feel more in control of themselves.
- Help patients to keep a personal recovery book – how would they wish to maintain personal dignity and self-respect?
- Please review anger management therapy.
- Do staff have their own ideas about how to improve practice?"

1.159   We continue to see examples of unsafe practices regarding secluded patients, whether in nursing practices such as observation or the seclusion accommodation itself:

> There was a patient in seclusion on the day of my visit – and he had been there for the majority of the preceding two days. During the course of this seclusion, the patient had managed to attempt suicide by tying a ligature around his neck. The patient lost consciousness and emergency life saving techniques had been administered to the patient. This incident had not been recorded in the seclusion notes by the nursing staff on duty at the time. The incident raised serious questions about the quality of observations and record keeping when a patient is in seclusion. These concerns were acknowledged by the ward manager during the Commissioner's discussions with him.
>
> *London, September 2008*

> The Commissioner expressed concern on the previous visit about the safe observation of patients in seclusion, in that it is not possible to clearly observe a patient in seclusion without entering the separate adjacent (but not adjoining) toilet area and looking through a keyhole. The keyhole itself does not provide clear visibility: staff mentioned that the aperture is too small. As previously mentioned, the Commissioner was also concerned to see that a bedpan is still used in the seclusion room. The Commissioner raised the issue of dignity and respect in this situation and would be especially concerned if this practice occurred in the presence of a male member of staff.
>
> *Merseyside, September 2008*

We do, of course, continue to request that any failings such as these are addressed by hospital managers.

1.160   We welcome revisions to the Code of Practice in England that deal with some problem areas raised in our previous reports. We have already alluded to the clarification in the English Code over the practice of seclusion with those who exhibit self-harming behaviour. The Code for England also clarifies that detaining authorities may allow flexibility in

---

[135] On clothing in seclusion, see Code of Practices for England and Wales, paras 15.61 and 19.43 respectively. On the issue of self-harm, see *Code of Practice for England*, para 15.45. There is no equivalent reference in the Code for Wales, although we believe it to be self-evident that seclusion should never be used *solely* to prevent self-harm, and the risks and benefits of its use where a patient is liable to self-harm should be carefully considered.

reviewing arrangements at night when patients may be asleep, and specifically states that alternative terminology to 'seclusion' must not deprive patients of the safeguards established for secluded patients. Neither of these points is made in the Code for Wales (although we consider the second point to be self-evident, or at least not dependent upon being made explicit in a Code for a court of law to accept it to be so). We suggest that our successor body in Wales, Healthcare Inspectorate Wales, might keep these matters under review to see whether future editions of the Code for Wales might need revision on these points. It may that services, following the principles established in the *Munjaz* case[136], feel able to make their own arrangements for night-time reviews of seclusion without the explicit permission of the Code.

1.161 A further amendment to both Codes touches the issue at the centre of the *Munjaz* case itself, which is how the long-term seclusion of patients should be kept under review. The *Munjaz* judgment allowed that Ashworth Hospital was entitled to depart from the requirements of the Code of Practice then extant regarding the review of seclusion, where it had a cogent reason to do so and the departure did not in itself lead to a breach of the patient's human rights. Thus the hospital did not need to extend the monitoring requirements established in the Code (which required a medical review every four hours) to patients who were effectively nursed in isolation for the majority of the time.

1.162 In March 2008 we visited patient G, who was being nursed in isolation in a specially converted annex at an NHS hospital in Wales. Patient G had severe learning disability and bipolar disorder and exhibited extremely challenging behaviour, including extreme and distressing self-injurious behaviour; physical aggression towards others; high and extreme rates of environmental destruction; sexual disinhibition and deliberate incontinence. Alternative placements had been considered but rejected as providing no better clinical management and skills than those available within the Trust. Prior to the conversion of the annex, G had been nursed in his own room for much of the time, which was becoming increasingly barren as he destroyed its fittings or fittings had to be removed for safety, and was subject to very frequent restraint. It was thought that he found it difficult to manage the general noise and business of the ward, and the annex had been provided to create a separate, self-contained space to reduce stimulation. It was noted that that G had coped better in such an environment in the past. He was locked into the annex at all times, and at various times of day locked out of certain parts of the annex. He had no access to fresh air at the time of the visit, although a partitioned part of the garden was being created to remedy this. Some 'small steps' of progress had been reported since the move, with G becoming more tolerant of staff contact; beginning to participate in ball games and looking at magazines, the television, etc. Overall we were satisfied that the nursing plan had a clear rationale and that staff were caring for G with sensitivity and concern. Staff had benefited from debriefing sessions and support, and the multi-disciplinary team met weekly to review the intervention plan.

---

[136] See MHAC (2006) *In Place of Fear? Eleventh Biennial Report 2003-2005*, page 35.

1.163 Whilst the arrangements for the care of G clearly amount to seclusion, as defined in the Code of Practices relevant at the time of our visit and the revised Codes introduced subsequently, G also meets the description in the new Code for Wales of patients "who exhibit behaviours that challenge that are more sustained and therefore not amenable to short-term seclusion"[137]. The Code for England refers to such seclusion as 'longer-term segregation'[138], and both Codes allow that local policies might make special provision for multidisciplinary review of the care of patients in this situation. This is, in effect, recognition by the Codes of the *Munjaz* judgment. We accept that, for patients in long-term segregation, there could be no benefit in four-hourly reviews, and that the quality of reviews that do take place (in terms of multi-disciplinary input, detail and care planning for eventual discontinuation of seclusion) are more important than their frequency.

---

[137] *MHA Code of Practice for Wales*, paragraph 19.45.

[138] *MHA Code of Practice for England*, paragraph 15.63.

2

The Mental Health Act in Practice

The use and outcome of holding powers

2.1 Section 5 of the Mental Health Act provides 'holding powers' that can be used to prevent informal patients from leaving hospital whilst a decision whether to apply for detention is made. Section 5(4) enables a nurse to hold a patient in hospital for up to four hours, in order to facilitate the arrival of a doctor or approved clinician, and under s.5(2), a doctor or approved clinician can hold a patient for up to 72 hours. The numbers of informal patients held under sections 5(2) or 5(4) in hospitals in England between 1988/8 and 2007/08 is shown at figure 29 below, alongside the numbers of uses of these holding powers in Wales over the shorter period of 1996/07 to 2007/08 (figure 30).

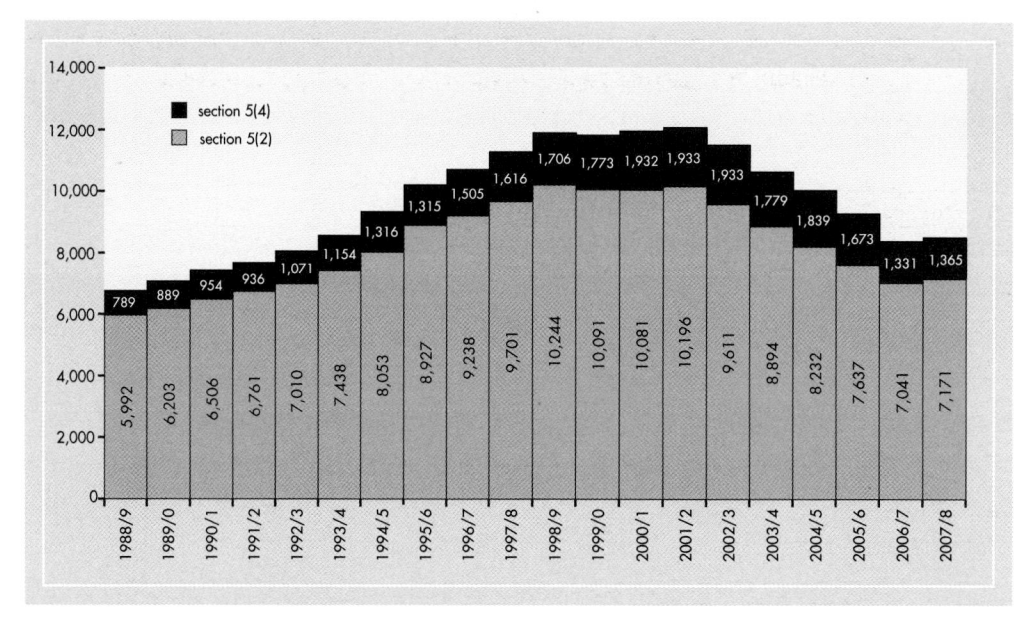

Fig 29: Changes from informal status to s.5(2) and s.5(4), England, NHS facilities, 1988/09 to 2007/08

Data source: as for fig 1

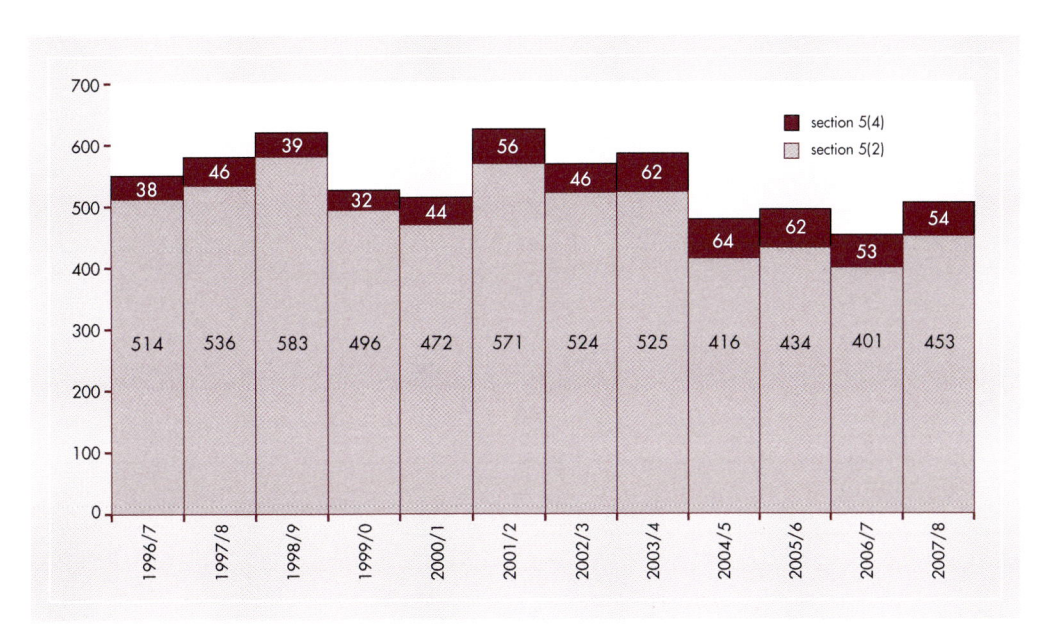

Fig 30: Changes from informal status to s.5(2) and s.5(4), Wales, NHS facilities, 1996/07 to 2007/08

Data source: Welsh Assembly Government[139]

2.2 The data shows a reduction in the annual number of uses of these holding powers in both England and Wales from the start of this new century, the difference being most pronounced in England. In terms of outcomes of the use of these holding powers, figures 31 and 32 show that roughly one third of all patients are returned to informal status, with roughly two thirds detained further under either s.2 or s.3[140]. In Wales, patients are more likely to be detained under s.2 following the use of a holding power, whereas English hospitals appear to prefer s.3. This reflects national trends in the use of s.2 and s.3 more generally, as we show at figures 33 and 34 below.

---

[139] *Statistics for Wales*, available at www.statswales.wales.gov.uk.

[140] Section 2 of the Act allows detention for up to 28 days for the purposes of assessment and/or treatment, and is non-renewable. Section 3 allows detention for treatment lasting up to six months, renewable for a further six months and then annually. Only patients detained under s.3 can be discharged onto Supervised Community Treatment (see para 2.67 below).

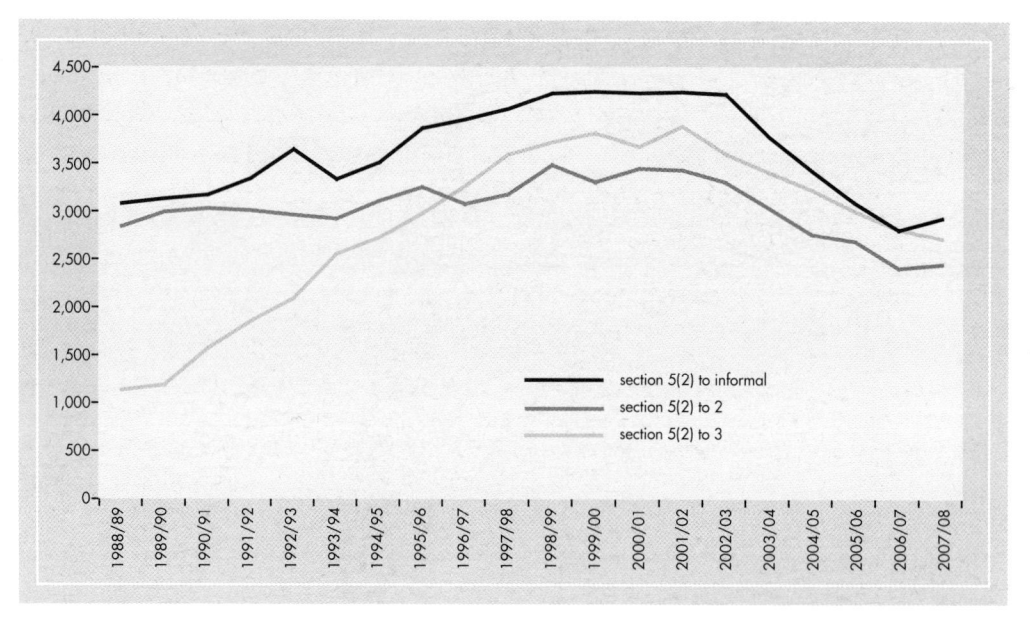

Fig 31: Outcomes of holding powers under s.5(2) and s.5(4), England, NHS facilities, 1988/09 to 2007/08

Data source: as for fig 1

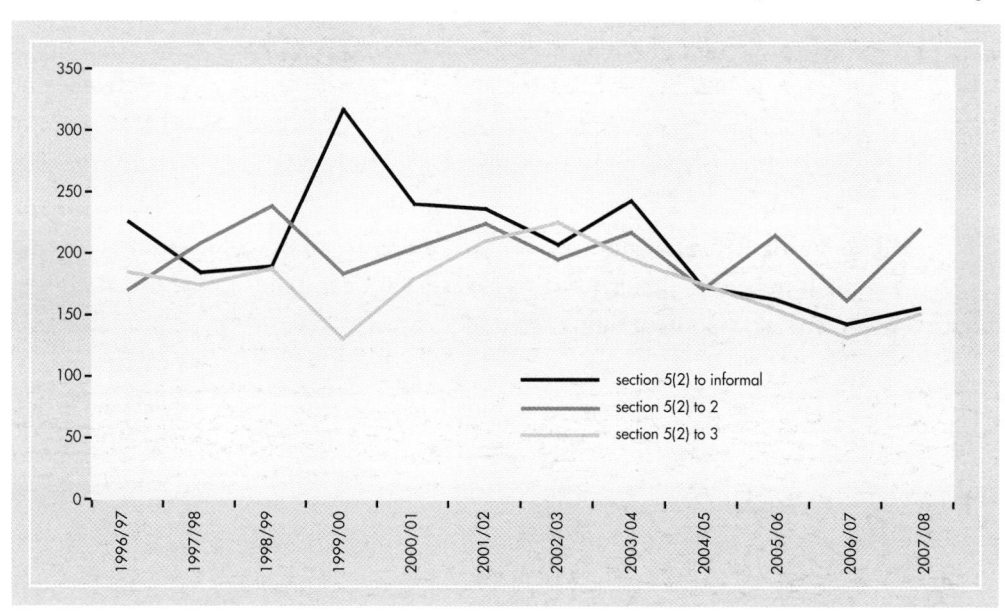

Fig 32: Changes from informal status to s.5(2) and s.5(4), Wales, NHS facilities, 1996/07 to 2007/08

Data source: as for fig 30

2.3 In respect of whether s.2 or s.3 was used as the power to admit patients to hospital from the community, or to detain patients already in hospital on an informal basis, the last two years' data (figures 33 and 34) falls into essentially similar patterns as were described and discussed in our last report[141]. Services in Wales are more likely than services in England to use s.2 as the detaining power for hospital admissions. In our previous reports we have supported the proposition that s.2 is most often the appropriate initial detention power for patients, even if they are known to services, because detention must have been

---

[141] MHAC (2008) *Risk, Rights, Recovery; Twelfth Biennial Report 2005-2007*, para 4.39, fig 51 & para 5.2, fig 57.

precipitated by some change of circumstance or clinical presentation, and this change should in most cases require a period of assessment to ensure that continued detention is warranted[142]. As might be expected, where a patient is already receiving treatment in hospital, services are more likely to use s.3 as the detaining power, presumably because the patient has been subject to a recent assessment and the clinical team are more confident of the rationale for detention.

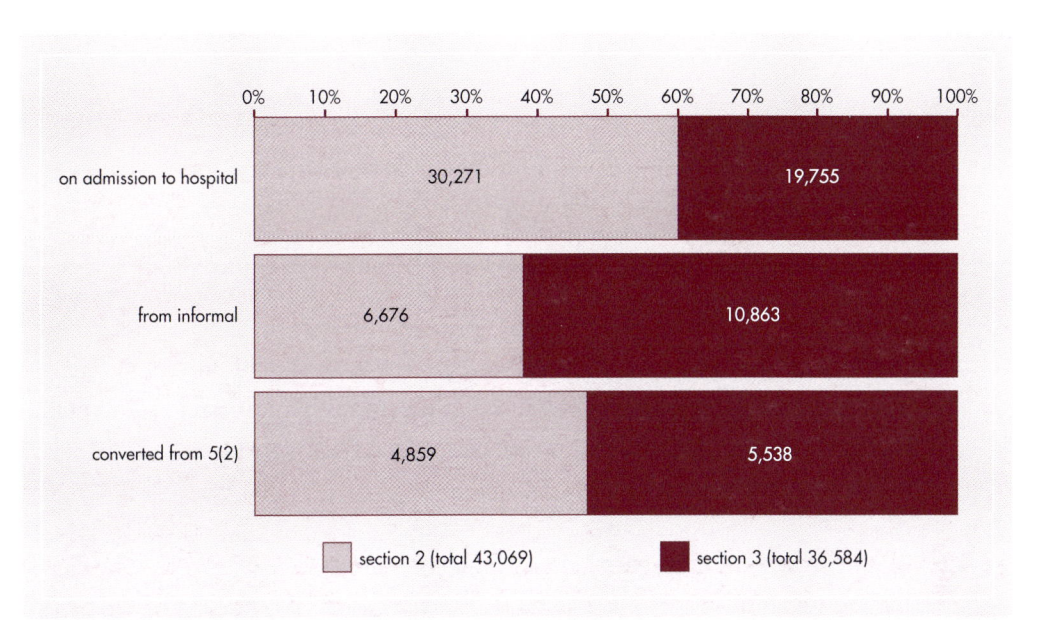

Fig 33: Uses of sections 2 and 3, NHS and independent hospitals, England, 2006/07 to 2007/08

Data source: as for fig 1

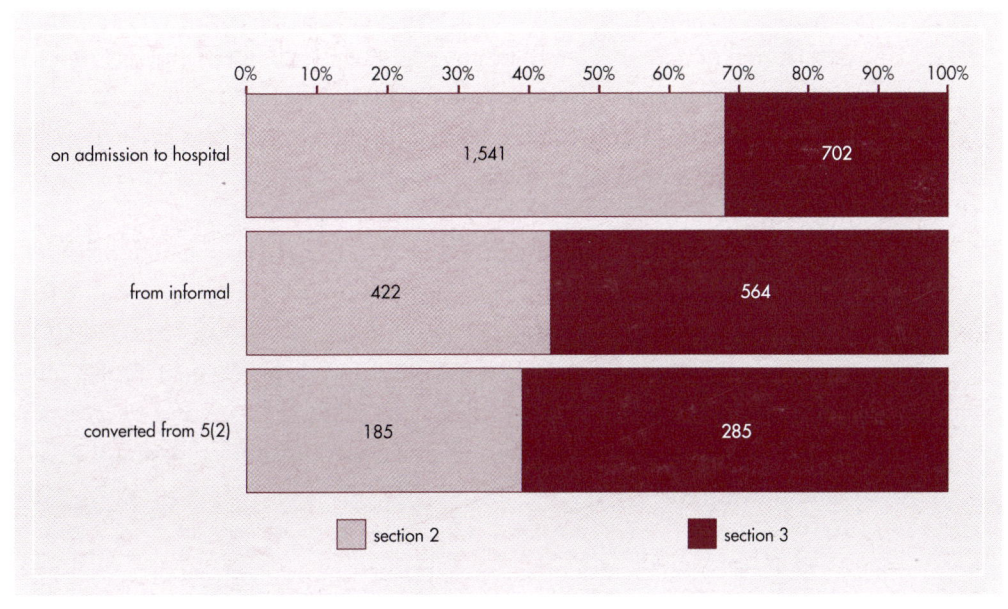

Fig 34: Uses of sections 2 and 3, NHS and independent hospitals, Wales, 2006/07 to 2007/08

Data source: as for fig 30

---

[142] See, for example, MHAC (2006) *In Place of Fear? Eleventh Biennial Report 2003-2005*, para 4.10 *et seq.*

Section 2 as a community order

2.4 In March 2008 the Tribunal considered the case of a patient who had been at home on s.17 leave for fourteen of the fifteen days that he had been subject to detention under s.2. The patient had been placed in a hospital in the south-west of England that was some 30 miles from his home, but had been sent back home on leave after less than 24 hours in that hospital. In the twenty-four hours prior to being detained he had been arrested but released with no charge on two occasions.

2.5 The patient had remained on leave for the two weeks preceding the Tribunal hearing, with his responsible clinician arguing that such assessment as he was receiving was being provided through contact with a community team. In fact the Tribunal found that the community team had visited the patient only three times in that fortnight, two of which were in the days immediately preceding the hearing. The patient, who was of Middle Eastern origin, was deemed to have pressure of speech, flight of ideas and paranoid thoughts by his original assessors and by the responsible clinician and AMHP who attended the hearing. The Tribunal found no evidence of actual mental disorder and on that ground alone was bound to discharge him. They were also not satisfied that he was being assessed in a hospital as s.2 details.

2.6 The symptoms described by the responsible clinician and AMHP to suggest that the patient was suffering from a mental disorder could as easily be explained by other factors in his life. The description that on admission he was dishevelled could be accounted for by the fact that he had been in police custody on two separate occasions, in between which he had embarked on a seven mile walk home before being arrested a second time. The description of paranoia could just as easily be explained by the fact that he had been arrested (and not charged) twice in a short period of time, as it could be by paranoid delusions. He and his family confirmed that he ordinarily spoke quickly (as did his close relative supporter) and his speech was no more rapid or pressured than usual.

2.7 In our view, even had the patient been suffering from mental disorder, his care arrangements showed that there was no justification for continued liability for detention under the Act. We do not think that detention under s.2 – the purpose of which is to facilitate assessment and/or treatment in hospital – can be justified if the patient is in fact being assessed in the community. Indeed, it is difficult to see any circumstances where detention under s.2 might be justified when a patient is subject to long-term s.17 leave in the community.

2.8 Given the very eccentric use of the Act in this case, it is of concern that a responsible clinician and an AMHP provided the Tribunal with evidence which supported continued detention.

Professional roles

The Responsible Clinician

2.9 Under the revised Mental Health Act 1983 (and for the first time in the history of the Mental Health Acts) the clinician who is in charge of a detained patient's care and treatment under the Act need not be a doctor. Provided that they are "Approved Clinicians", qualified social workers, psychologists, occupational therapists, mental health nurses or learning disability nurses may take on the role.

2.10 However, at the time of writing, the majority of Responsible Clinicians continue to be doctors, and perhaps will always continue to be so, not least because the principle medical intervention for the majority of detained patients continues to be the prescription and administration of medication for mental disorder.

2.11 We discussed in our last report the debates over whether the advice of a clinician who is not a doctor might satisfy the 'objective medical evidence' requirement for lawful psychiatric detention under to ECHR Article 5[143]. A case in October 2008 suggested that the courts may be slow to follow the Department of Health in taking the view that a broader range of professionals than doctors may determine whether a person is of unsound mind for the purposes of Article 5 of the European Convention. Lord Justice Dyson, in reviewing whether an ASBO could be imposed upon a man who lacked capacity to understand or comply with it, stated that "such incapacity being a medical matter, evidence should normally be given by a psychiatrist and not by a psychologist or a psychiatric nurse"[144] (our emphasis).

Identifying the Responsible Clinician

2.12 Many powers and duties that the Act gives to Responsible Clinicians are not delegable. For example, only the Responsible Clinician may grant leave of absence under s.17; suspend or change SCT conditions; or recall to hospital any patient who is in the community under SCT or leave arrangements. The decision of the Responsible Clinician is necessary (if not sufficient) to renew detention or instigate and renew SCT[145]. Where the Responsible Clinician is a psychiatrist, typically he or she also will be in charge of treatments falling under Part 4, and as such will be the only person (except for a Second Opinion Appointed Doctor) empowered to certify that a detained patient consents to such treatment.

---

[143] MHAC (2008) *Risk, Rights, Recovery; Twelfth Biennial Report 2005-2007*, paras 4.51 – 4.52.

[144] *R (on the application of Jamie Cook) v Director of Public Prosecutions* [2008] EWHC 2703 (Admin), para 12.

[145] As agreement that the conditions for renewal are met must be obtained from another professional (for detained patients) or an AMHP (for SCT): see ss.20 and 20A. Similarly, an AMHP must agree that the criteria for SCT are met and the conditions placed upon the patient consequent to it are appropriate (s.17A(4)).

2.13 In past years, the MHAC has been asked many times how services should manage these matters if they have to be attended to in the absence of the usual clinician in charge of treatment. The revised Code of Practice for England suggests that hospitals should have protocols to

> ensure that cover arrangements are in place when the responsible clinician is not available (e.g. *during nonworking hours*, annual leave etc). (para 14.3, our emphasis)

This is more specific than the previous edition of the Code (and more specific than the current Code for Wales), which both give as an example "...when he or she is on annual leave or otherwise unavailable"[146]. In common with other authorities[147] and many mental health services, the MHAC has in the past interpreted 'otherwise unavailable' in the 1999 Code to imply something more than simply being off-duty. Consequently, Responsible Clinicians might have been expected to be contacted by telephone when off duty to make pressing decisions about patient's care or treatment, such as authorising urgently required leave of absence. The revised Code, in England at least[148], suggests that it services must make other arrangements.

2.14 The hours that a Responsible Clinician is available by telephone when off-duty would not need to be counted as working hours for the purposes of compliance with the European Working Time Directive, although any time actually in contact with the hospital would be so counted[149]. But, clinicians may consider that a number of decisions (such as whether to administer urgent treatment for mental disorder under s.62) cannot, in any case, often be taken without seeing the patient first-hand. If the Responsible Clinician was regularly required to attend the hospital outside of working hours this might cause difficulties with the directive. Perhaps more importantly, in many cases the circumstances where such interventions might be necessary would preclude waiting for the usual Responsible Clinician to attend the hospital. As such many hospitals will already have arrangements whereby a nominated clinician is on hand to make such decisions out of hours as the 'Responsible Clinician'. Under the revised Act, it is possible to nominate another clinician to be in charge of a particular treatment in the absence of the Responsible Clinician without delegating the Responsible Clinician role in its entirety.

2.15 In any case, the relevant qualification for such 'stand-in' clinicians is that the clinician concerned is an "approved clinician". If the doctor (or any other clinician) is an approved clinician, that is sufficient irrespective of rank or grade. When standing-in for the normal Responsible Clinician, the clinician is not exercising a delegated power but rather has become the Responsible Clinician (or Approved Clinician in charge of a particular treatment) in law.

---

[146] *MHA Code of Practice*, 1999 edition, para 20.3(a), *Code of Practice for Wales*, para 12.13.

[147] See for example, Richard Jones' *Mental Health Act Manual* (tenth edition, 2006), which gave the example of being unavailable "because of sickness or annual leave" at page 212. The eleventh edition of 2008 (at para 1-410) reflects the new emphasis of the revised Code of Practice that is described above.

[148] Whilst the *Code of Practice for Wales* retains the 1999 Code of Practice construction "...on annual leave or otherwise unavailable" (para 12.13), we assume that this may be interpreted to align with the guidance in the Code for England.

[149] Case C-303/98 *Simap* [2000] ECR I-7963 Case C-151/02 *Landeshauptstadt Kiel v Jaeger*.

2.16 Services should consider protocols to set out the expectations on such 'stand-in' responsible clinicians for out of hours work which, whilst not unduly constraining them in the exercise of their legal powers, establishes that the stand-in role is primarily to react to emergency situations that cannot await resolution until the day-to-day responsible clinician is available.

Section 12 Approved Doctors

2.17 At least one of the two medical recommendations required to support an application for detention under the Act should be provided by a doctors who is approved under s.12 of the Act as having "special experience in the diagnosis or treatment of mental disorder". The 2007 amendments to the 1983 Mental Health Act made no significant changes to the provisions for the approval of doctors under s.12, although transitional arrangements (mainly until November 2009) did allow that some doctors approved under s.12 would be deemed to be approved clinicians for the purposes of the Act[150].

2.18 It seems likely that the administration of the new Approved Clinician arrangements will run alongside those for s.12 approval in many areas, although operational arrangements for training, registration and approval mechanisms are not all finalised as we go to press. In such arrangements there will need to be a technically distinct approval panel, with explicit approved clinician criteria and validation of training courses.

Avoidable illegal detention due to lapses of s.12 approval

2.19 We understand that a significant number of patients have been invalidly detained by London Trusts because approval of senior doctors had lapsed. The Trusts concerned in 2008 were Barnet Enfield & Haringey; East London; West London; and South London and Maudsley. In each case the Medical Director was informed and invited to investigate as appropriate by the London Section 12 Regional Panel. Financial compensation for invalidly detained patients – current and past – has been necessary in some cases. Some of these unlawful detentions came to light when transitional arrangements for Approved Clinicians were being considered: the most common reason was failure by the doctor to notify the s.12 Register or GMC of change of address. It is likely that similar problems occur outside London.

2.20 The London Section 12 Regional Panel has provided in its annual reports repeated reminders to Medical Directors to establish reliable systems of checking the s.12 approval status of their psychiatrists. Given that mistakes are still occurring, we endorse the Panel's recommendation that Medical Directors should include s.12 approval on their annual appraisal checklist for senior psychiatrists.

> **Recommendation:** Medical Directors should include s.12 approval on their annual appraisal checklist for senior psychiatrists.

---

[150] Such doctors must be s.12 approved and either 1) have carried out the functions of an RMO in the 12 months to November 2008; or 2) have been in overall charge of a patient's treatment in that time; or 3) have been appointed to the post of consultant psychiatrist in the twelve months prior to 3 November 2008, or in the six months following that date. See Department of Health (2008) *Implementation of the Mental Health Act 2007: Transitional Arrangements*, July 2008 for details.

Approved Mental Health Professionals

2.21 The revised Mental Health Act 1983 also opens out the role previously known as "Approved Social Worker" to other professionals. Psychologists, occupational therapists, mental health nurses and learning disability nurses may now also become "Approved Mental Health Professionals" (AMHPs), having undergone the necessary training. We have noted some take-up of training by professionals other than social workers in the initial training courses for AMHPs in certain areas of the country.

AMHPs and professional specialisation

2.22 The involvement of specialist AMHPs in Mental Health Act assessments (such as social workers from older persons' teams for elderly service users) can be commendable where this can be practically arranged, but it can lead to slow response times. On a visit to an older peoples' ward in central London in December 2007, we were told that social services' response times for unplanned Mental Health Act assessments involving older patients were still rather slow, with much longer waiting times than for other adult services. In the unit that we visited, we noted that one patient had been held in hospital for 70 of the 72 hours allowed under s.5(2) prior to an application for s.3 being made. Whilst this is lawful, it is not good practice regularly to have such holding powers run so long, as this delays exercise of rights to appeal; exercise of legal powers by Nearest Relatives; and treatment under Part 4 of the Act.

2.23 One solution to such delays would be to pool the resources of AMHPs across specialist and non-specialist teams to provide a quicker if generic service. We consider this the lesser evil than lengthy assessment delays, and indeed it can be argued that undertaking assessments out of speciality, provided the suitable mentoring support is available, is a means of keeping up general skills across services. However, we have heard of some reluctance amongst generic social workers to undertake 'specialist' assessments, and conversely reluctance amongst specialists to help out with generic work. It is unclear whether this will become more or less of an issue now other professionals as well as social workers are able to become AMHPs.

Problems with assessments

The unco-operative patient

2.24 In August 2008 the High Court considered the nature of assessment under the Act[151]. The patient concerned was detained under s.2, and had been transferred to a surgical ward in another hospital for diagnostic tests for suspected pancreatitis. Whilst on that surgical ward, she was seen by another psychiatrist and social worker for an assessment for detention under s.3, at the instigation of her Responsible Medical Officer (Responsible Clinician). The patient telephoned her solicitor, saying that she was very upset and did not feel physically well enough to participate in the assessment, and her solicitor asked that the assessment be deferred. It was not, and the subsequent s.3 detention was challenged

---

[151] *R (on the application of M) v South West London & St George's Mental Health NHS Trust* [2008] EWCA Civ 1112.

by an application for *habeus corpus*, arguing that the doctor and social worker had failed to conduct assessments or interviews with the patient as required at s.12 and s.13(2). Section 12 requires that the doctor must "have personally examined the patient"; s.13(2) requires the approved mental health professional to

> interview the patient in a suitable manner and satisfy himself that detention in hospital is in all the circumstances of the case the most appropriate way of providing the care and medical treatment of which the patient stands in need.

2.25 The application was dismissed at first instance and by the Court of Appeal. The judge at first hearing, who was extensively quoted in the Appeal Court judgment, found that "a doctor can 'examine' a patient for the purposes of reaching an opinion as to her mental health even if she refuses, for example, to answer questions or submit to a physical examination"[152]. Likewise, both courts endorsed the submission of Richard Jones that

> It is submitted that, in the context of this Act, any attempt by an [AMHP] to communicate with a patient would be sufficient to constitute an interview and that this would be the case even if the patient was either unable or unwilling to respond.[153]

2.26 Thus where a patient fails to respond, or to respond appropriately, to the approach of an AMHP attempting to communicate with him or her, it is possible for the AMHP to infer from the manner of that failure that the patient does indeed require treatment. The courts accepted that such a construction of the Act was necessary, if 'somewhat strained on a literalist approach' otherwise it would be 'inoperable in many cases where it was most obviously needed'[154].

2.27 The judgment does not mean that there can be no future challenge of applications for detention based upon cursory or otherwise restricted examinations and interviews, although (from the viewpoint of the patient in this case at least) the hurdle for such a challenge to succeed might appear to be set rather high. The patient in this case argued that the mere fact of her lack of co-operation with the assessment provided nothing to justify the conclusion that she required admission under s.3. The courts demurred, with the judge at first instance stating that he could "see nothing in the professionals' descriptions of her behaviour to suggest that they were not entitled to reach the conclusion that they did"[155]. The Court of Appeal rejected a submission that this placed the burden of proof the wrong way around, stating that the courts were entitled to take the statutory forms completed by the professionals at face value, and that, as such, there were no disputed facts in the case that would merit a hearing with cross-examination of witnesses[156].

---

[152] *ibid.*, para 15 (quoting para 12 of the first instance judgment).

[153] Jones R (2008) *Mental Health Act Manual*, eleventh edition, p.100. The court referred to the same statement in the previous edition of the Manual, at p.98.

[154] *R (on the application of M)*, para 15 (quoting para 12 of the first instance judgment).

[155] *ibid.*, quoting para 16.

[156] *ibid.*, para 30.

Problems of conveyance

2.28 The MHAC has heard that Approved Mental Health Professionals in many areas of the country experience problems in arranging conveyance for patients following assessments. Some Trusts appear to be reluctant to allow the pre-booking of transport for Mental Health Act assessments, as in the following example:

> The Trust provides a "total transport solution" which is a contract with [a private company] primarily intended to provide conveyance for detained patients. In general it works well. However, we have now been told that only senior Trust managers will authorise transport, and will be reluctant to authorise for community assessments until the person has been detained. This will lead to potential risk whereby the decision is made to detain, the person may abscond or become violent during the wait for conveyance, thereby placing the AMHP in a perilous position.
>
> *An AMHP, England, February 2009*

2.29 The most pressing problems facing AMHPs in many parts of the country appear to be such problems in accessing transport to convey patients who require detention under the Act, and, perhaps most of all, accessing available inpatient beds that such patients could be conveyed to. These problems lead to delays in admissions, and compromise the safety of patients and professionals alike. The Care Quality Commission should consider using its wide remit to focus on these areas of mental health practice.

Leave of absence and absence without leave

The planning and recording of leave of absence from hospital

2.30 In February and March 2008 the MHAC conducted 31 special visits across England and Wales to gain an insight into the arrangements made for detained patients' leave of absence from hospital. We collected data from 158 patient records in mental health units, and talked with 115 patients who had been granted leave in the fortnight prior to the visit.

2.31 The document checks showed many positive aspects of practice in recording leave. Every hospital had leave forms in use for recording the leave authorised by the responsible clinician. In 67% (105) of the leave forms, there was either an expiry date or a prompt for review of the authorisation. The parameters of that authorisation were clear for at least 90% of the 158 forms checked[157]. This meant that responsible clinicians had specified the purpose of leave, or conditions for it to take place, such as whether the patient was to be escorted or not. In the many examples where responsible clinicians had authorised the parameters of leave to be allowed on a day-to-day basis at staff discretion, MHA Commissioners felt

> "I am allowed to have a lot of two-night home leave to my mother's house. Then I report back to ward staff how things have gone. My mother also reports back to the ward".
>
> *Female s.3 patient, age 30, acute unit, Wales*

---

[157] In only eleven cases (7% of the 158) did the MHAC record that such parameters were unclear. In the remaining six cases no comment was recorded.

that those parameters were usually clear, in that they gave, for example, the maximum duration of leave, or the times of day within which leave could be allowed by nursing staff. In a few examples, however, leave had been given to places specified only as "mother's house" or "relatives in Suffolk area", where we felt that it would be sensible to specify both the address and a contact number on the leave form so that it could be easily located if needed.

2.32 According to the Code of Practice (both at the time of this review and since the issue of revised Codes for England and Wales), a copy of the leave form should be given to the patient and to other people who may need to see it, such as carers or family members. This was rarely complied with: only 19 records (12% of all 158) showed that the patient had received a copy of the leave authorisation, and there were only four records of carers or others receiving copies. However, especially in the latter case, this may simply reflect the type of leave being recorded: if it is no more than shopping time during the day, staff may feel that this is not relevant information for carers or family. It may also be the case, however, that staff members see the leave authorisation form as information for their own consumption rather than as information for the patient, especially where staff have discretion as to when or if leave can be taken that has been broadly outlined in the authorisation. In such situations staff may feel that sharing the Responsible Clinician's leave authorisation may cause tension between themselves and patients in situations where the amount of leave actually given falls short of that which has been authorised by the Responsible Clinician, whether this is because of pressures on staff or the clinical presentation of the patient (see paragraph 2.37 below). However, 32 forms (20% of the total) bore the signature of the patient, showing that the patient had seen the form even if s/he did not get a copy.

2.33 There was evidence from patients' clinical records that many hospitals were implementing, or trying to implement, the recommendations in the MHAC's own guidance on leave[158]. In particular, we found that:

- 70% of patient records showed multi-disciplinary team input into discussions about leave.

- 50% of all records showed that the patient had also been involved in planning discussions about leave arrangements. This could no doubt be improved upon: in only one case did we find a record that the patient was incapable of participating in such discussions (in that case due to advanced dementia).

- 55% of all records showed that leave was addressed in the patient's care plan: given that all these patients had taken leave in the last fortnight this was disappointing.

- 75% of records stated whether approved leave actually took place (although, of those records that showed the leave not taking place, only half stated why it had not done so).

---

[158] MHAC (2007) *Guidance Note on Issues Surrounding Sections 17, 18 And 19 of the Mental Health Act 1983* (version revised in Sept 2007). In October 2008 this was reissued as *Leave of absence and transfer under the Mental Health Act 1983*.

- In 68% of records nursing staff had made an entry to show whether the leave was completed satisfactorily, including compliance with conditions;
- In 44% of records there was evidence of a wider discussion with the patient about the outcomes of his or her leave.

2.34 At the time of our visits, the MHAC guidance on s.17 leave was more exacting than that contained in the Code of Practice extant for England and Wales[159]. As the MHAC guidance is now reflected in both the revised Codes of Practice for England and Wales[160], we are hopeful that good practice will continue to spread. We set out an example of positive practice in involving patients in good leave planning arrangements at figure 35 below.

Section 17 leave is an integral part of the patients' care in this low secure unit and is identified in all aspects of care, e.g. care plans, wards reviews, CPA etc. All relevant documentation is kept in a separate leave file as well as contained in the clinical documentation. The excellent documentation includes:
- s.17 leave policy, setting out the aims of and procedures for leave;
- a form for the Responsible Clinician's authorisation;
- a 'leave planning sheet' that is completed by the patient, demonstrating her understanding of the parameters of leave and recording a self-assessment before taking leave, and completing a further self-assessment and review of how the leave went upon return. The form asked the patient to indicate their mood on a scale of one to ten before taking leave, and again upon return, and make a note of any change and the reasons for that change. The second part of this form (i.e. the part completed on return from leave) was not always completed on the forms we saw, despite staff encouragement of patients;
- a form to record reviews by the multi-disciplinary team of leave arrangements;
- a leave of absence record sheet, which is signed by both patient and a staff member when the patient leaves and returns from that ward. This records the time due back, the time of actual return, the patient's agreed destination, any escorting arrangements and a description of the patient's clothing; and
- an audit form for checking that the procedures have been carried out properly and the above recording mechanisms used.

Fig 35: MHA Commissioner's note on good practice example, low secure female ward, Hampshire Partnership NHS Trust, March 2008

Leave and risk assessment

2.35 In many units, we find that all or most patients' leave is authorised in broad terms by the Responsible Clinician, with nurses' discretion used to determine whether or not it is appropriate for a patient to leave the ward at any particular time. This is, of course, a sensible way of managing leave, but on occasion we have questioned whether tighter procedures might be appropriate in specific circumstances. In the summer of 2008, for

---

[159] Department of Health And Welsh Office (1999) *Mental Health Act Code of Practice*, para 20.
[160] See *MHA Code of Practice* for England, chapter 21; *Code of Practice for Wales*, chapter 28.

example, we encountered a patient who, since having been authorised to take unescorted leave at nurses' discretion, had cut her wrists. Whilst the nurse in charge was clear that she would not use her discretion to allow leave since the incident, it was agreed that this was perhaps not a thorough enough system. Significant incidents in the care of detained patients should be addressed in care plans, with a proper review of leave arrangements, to ensure both that no mistakes are made in granting inappropriate leave and also to work towards a restoration of leave when it is safer to do so.

2.36 On a visit to another hospital in the autumn of 2008, we spent some time focussing on risk assessment prior to granting s.17 leave. In the previous year the hospital had lost a detained patient to suicide whilst that patient was on leave. In general it was felt that there had been considerable progress in the risk assessment process, and there was evidence of improvement. All files examined had copies of up-to-date risk assessments, and the Commissioner was also provided with sample copies of the weekly professionals' meeting, where risk issues were discussed and typed up by the consultant's medical personal assistant. There were also handwritten references in the clinical notes to the granting of s.17 leave, usually written by the junior doctor present at the ward review. Any hospital that allows detained patients leave of absence with any less of a system in place is probably running too great a risk with the lives of those patients.

Resource limitations and section 17 leave

2.37 On many occasions, patients and staff complain to visiting Commissioners about restrictions placed upon their ability to take agreed leave due to staffing pressures or other resource limitations:

'It makes me feel good when I go out'
Female s.3 patient, age 23

- On our visits in 2008 to wards in a medium secure unit for women, nurses acknowledged that staffing limitations had led, at some point, to planned escorted leave being curtailed or cancelled. In more than one example we found that such cancellations included times where arrangements or appointments had been made that heightened the injustice felt by the patient. One female patient in a medium secure unit told us that she had been unable to attend more than one dental appointment over the previous year because of lack of escorting staff, and when we met her she stated that she was waiting for a reappointment to be made and was suffering dental pain.

- In another hospital, an elderly mail patient detained under s.3 told us that he had booked two tickets to the theatre, having been informed that escorted leave had been approved and arranged, but on the day in question there was no member of staff to accompany him and he was unable to attend.

- Staff in an acute ward in the Greater Manchester area told us in February 2008 that they were concerned that many arranged escorted leave periods were cancelled due to lack of staffing, and this greatly increased patients' agitation. We were also told that bed pressures led to the use of 'leave beds' when patients were out of hospital overnight, so that the patient on leave returned to be assigned a new bed, sometimes on a different ward. We noted such problems in our previous report, including at least one occasion when patients had told MHA Commissioners that the fear of such consequences of overnight leave absences made them resistant to taking such leave. This may prolong patients' residence under detention in hospital. It was notable that all the patients interviewed who had raised this concern also complained that the ward was chaotic and sometimes frightening; that nurses had little time to much more than dispense medication; and that they felt they did not see their doctor often enough.

- In a medium secure unit in Wales, there were a large number of patients on a ward served with one vehicle to transport patients. Given the geographic placement of hospital, this was heavily used for recreational leave, but also for visits to doctors and attendance at training or academic courses. Some patients stated that they felt their rehabilitation programmes were being compromised due to unavailable transport, or due to the availability of staff, whether this was because of general staffing levels or just the availability of staff with a driving pass. The ward had a reduced medical cover (having a single responsible clinician where there had previously been four), and some patients complained that they had to wait until the fortnightly ward round to discuss or request leave.

- On one low secure ward patients are charged for petrol costs when they are taken out on some outings. The Trust makes a distinction between what it classes as 'therapeutic' and 'social' outings. For anything that they is viewed as a "social" outing (the example given was a trip to the bowling alley), the patients going on the outing would have to pay petrol costs. The ward had the use of a lease car, or hospital transport, or it sometimes used a local taxi firm for which it had a contract. It had a system where a list of the names of patients going on these social outings is kept, together with a note of the mileage, which is then sent to the finance department which sent an "invoice" at regular intervals to each of the patients concerned. The patient who raised this on our visit in March 2009 was no longer entitled to benefits, and had an income of only £16 per week provided by the hospital (see 4.53 below), and so for him it was a significant factor, even though we were told that he was often "subsidised" out of the ward budget for outings.

- On a visit in November 2008 to an NHS-run learning disability unit in the Thames Valley, we received complaints from patients about having to purchase meals for staff who escort them on trips. Patients reported being told that they could not take leave unless they paid for such meals, and also that staff had remarked that, being in receipt of benefits and having no bills to pay, patients had more money than staff. The patients said that they would like to choose their escorts if they must buy them lunch, as they did not wish to eat with, and purchase meals for, certain staff members. The nursing managers confirmed that it was unit policy to ask patients to pay for staff meals when being escorted on s.17 leave. They had explained the policy to patients by stating that the ward could not fund staff meals itself, and they could not expect staff to pay out of their own pockets for meals taken when escorting patients. The explanation had alluded to the increase in patient benefits[161] and that this was supposed to enable them to participate in increased activities. We remain deeply concerned at this, as it seems to have inherent risks of perceived or actual exploitation of patients' monies, and potentially compromising relations between patients and staff.

---

[161] See MHAC (2006) *In Place of Fear? Eleventh Biennial Report 2003-2005*, para 2.98; MHAC (2008) *Risk, Rights, Recovery; Twelfth Biennial Report 2005-2007*, paras 2.246, 7.57.

2.38 In some units, responsible clinicians' granting of leave that they consider appropriate on a clinical basis for individual patients is collectively impossible to administer for ward managers and staff. In a rehabilitation ward in Wales we heard staff remark on this problem, saying that responsible clinicians had in the past been 'generous' with leave, resulting in authorisations that had been unrealistic to facilitate for all patients. This appeared to have been resolved two weeks before our visit through the instigation of a system of leave progression, which granted leave conditional on the patient's participation with their therapeutic programme, and included a leave booking system designed to ensure that sufficient staff were available for patients to receive the leave that they had earned. The new arrangements were designed to reflect the hospital policy that the patient should be able to demonstrate to professional carers that she is likely to cope outside the hospital. The new system had, however, reduced the leave available for some women. One patient told us that she had 'lost' a month's leave through being unfairly implicated in a disturbance on the ward: another that she had had leave stopped for breaking smoking rules, and not being cooperative with her therapy and medication. The latter patient expressed concern that leave was being used as a reward for good behaviour rather than being seen as therapeutic in its own right. There are difficult ethical lines to draw, not only in rationing leave to ensure that all patients have an opportunity to benefit, but also in using leave as a therapeutic tool but not an instrument of reward and punishment. Where such issues arise we recommend that they are discussed openly when talking about individual patients' leave within multi-disciplinary teams.

> I think leave has psychological advantages. It feels like a weight off my shoulders – more relaxed, living!
>
> *Male s.3 patient, age 84, Dorset*

2.39 Some units audit leave taken and not taken to identify where additional resources are needed:

- A low secure unit in Cumbria had an excellent audit tool concerning leave taken or cancelled. This identified causes of cancellations (one of which was lack of transport) so that future arrangements could be improved where possible. Managers reported to us that staff were flexible in reducing or rearranging breaks to facilitate leave, but that problems could still occur when patients need 2:1 escort. It was a recognised priority that no home leave should be cancelled, and so extra staff would be brought in to ensure that leave was facilitated.

- One acute ward in Wiltshire kept track of times when any patient was denied leave for want of an escorting staff, and if it happens on two occasions a bank nurse is called in to take the patient out.

- On an acute unit in Wales, we were told by the ward manager that staff had shown themselves to be flexible in their shift duties, and in coming in from other wards, to help out to provide necessary escort for patients' leave.

2.40 The MHAC is aware that many units run on the goodwill of staff, who give up their own time or compromise their own working conditions for patients' benefit. Whilst we applaud this, hospital managers should not be reliant upon staff goodwill to make up for inadequate resources.

Administering leave for restricted patients.

2.41 Of the 158 patient records studied on our themed visits (see paragraph 2.30), nineteen were for patients subject to restriction orders. Two patients (one female) were transferred prisoners, and the rest (including three women) had received hospital orders with restrictions under s.37/41. In all but two cases a copy of the letter from the Ministry of Justice granting leave was available at ward level, although in five of these cases the letter was not kept alongside the responsible clinician's leave form.

2.42 We met with one patient detained under s.37/41, whose leave had been suspended three weeks earlier after he had shared with staff that he was having thoughts about his original offence. The patient told us that he accepted that it had been appropriate to suspend leave at the time, but that he was no longer experiencing these thoughts and wished the matter to be reconsidered. Being kept on the ward without leave had made him low in mood and agitated, and he felt that he had not been talking with staff as much as he should. He had also had no opportunity to use a cashpoint, meaning that he had been unable to purchase the computer magazine that he usually read and particular foodstuffs to supplement that which was provided. The visiting Commissioner passed on the patient's concerns, with his permission, requesting that his leave status be reviewed and discussed with him with his advocate present; and that something be done about his lack of access to money. She also suggested that the patient might wish to write down his feelings and what reassurances he could give regarding leave, with help from his advocate. The hospital agreed to the review and informed us that a visit to the cashpoint would be arranged.

2.43 All clinicians with responsibility for restricted patients should be familiar with the Ministry of Justice Mental Health Unit (MHU) guidance on leave of absence[162]. In the above case it was not clear whether the MHU had been informed of the suspension of leave. The MHU guidance states that it should be told immediately if leave is suspended by the Responsible Clinician, and will then decide as to whether or not to reserve to itself the ability to reinstate leave[163]. The MHU also provides a pro-forma for a report to be made to it on leave that has taken place, which it will take into account when considering further requests for leave.

2.44 It is clear that leave authorised by the Mental Health Unit can also be subject to disruption for want of resources. One young patient with a learning disability, who had been transferred from prison under s.47/49, told us that he had a fishing trip cancelled because his Responsible Clinician had forgotten to sign off the papers before going on leave, and although staff explained nicely, he had to wait for that clinician's return before he was allowed to join trips. The unit had only one consultant psychiatrist, with cover being provided by another doctor based ten miles away. The patient told us that another trip had been cancelled due to staff shortages, and that he was also 'fed up with delays in getting MHU agreement for leave'. Another patient, who was transferred from prison under s.47/49 for treatment of personality disorder in a medium secure unit, told us that

---

[162] Ministry of Justice (2008) *Guidance for RMOs: Leave of absence for patients subject to restrictions.*
[163] *ibid.*, para 19.

> I get very anxious if I am sat on the ward all the time. My RMO says I need to get off the ward as much as possible but often this does not happen due to staff shortages and lack of transport ... it's not good enough considering the amount of money being paid by commissioners.

2.45 Money issues may also limit prison transferees' access to leave and other aspects of rehabilitation, due to the withdrawal of benefits to such patients in April 2006, as we discussed in our last report[164]. For many of these patients, money that is spent on the incidental expenses of leave outside hospital (such as bus fares or meals out) will be a considerable proportion of the weekly pocket-money income now provided by the hospitals themselves, and may only be affordable by going without purchases of additional food items, toiletries or indeed clothing. At paragraph 2.37 above we note one unit where patients were expected to pay for petrol costs for social trips, and another where patients had to pay for staff meals on escorted trips.

2.46 Leave of absence can form an important part of a detained patient's treatment plan[165]: successful episodes of leave will form part of the measures of progress used to determine whether a patient may be managed at a lower level of security; and both the Ministry of Justice and the Tribunal will look to restricted patients' leave histories when considering applications against detention. It therefore seems possible that curtailment of authorised leave could hinder a patent's progress through the secure psychiatric system, and thus delay their eventual discharge from hospital. Where this happens through lack of resources (whether hospital resources or allowances paid to patients) there would seem to be parallels with the "unhappy state of affairs" described in the Court of Appeal in February 2008[166] as "a systemic failure on the part of the Secretary of State to put in place the resources necessary to implement the scheme of rehabilitation necessary to enable [imprisonment for an indeterminate period under the Criminal Justice Act 2003] to function as intended"[167]. Indeed, by requiring that patients demonstrate themselves rehabilitated to effect discharge, whilst failing to resource rehabilitative programmes necessary for such demonstration, the Courts thought that an infringement of Article 5 of the European Convention was "likely"[168].

Liaison with victims over leave

2.47 In one West Midlands forensic unit in early 2008, some restricted patients complained of lengthy delays in obtaining Ministry of Justice permission for leave, apparently due to consultation with victims of their past offending. We have discussed the relatively new legal duties towards victims of offender patients in our previous reports[169]. At the time of our visit, Victim Liaison Officers were under a duty to provide information and an

---

[164] MHAC (2008) *Risk, Rights, Recovery; Twelfth Biennial Report 2005-2007*, para 7.62.

[165] MHA *Code of Practice for England*, para 21.8; *Code of Practice for Wales*, Para 28.2.

[166] *R (on the application of the Secretary of State for Justice) v Walker, R (on the application of the Secretary of State for Justice) v James* [2008] EWCA Civ 30, Para 72.

[167] *ibid.*

[168] *ibid.*

[169] MHAC (2006) *In Place of Fear? Eleventh Biennial Report 2003-2005*, para 5.118 et seq; MHAC (2008) *Risk, Rights, Recovery; Twelfth Biennial Report 2005-2007*, para 7.81 *et seq*. See Chapter 2 of Part 3 of the Domestic Violence, Crime, and Victims Act 2004.

opportunity for representation to victims in respect of decision-making over a restricted patient's discharge, and had the power to provide such other information as was thought appropriate. It would seem reasonable to infer that the Ministry of Justice has every right, therefore, to discuss proposals for leave arrangements with victims of offenders before exercising its discretion to allow such leave to take place. This would seem to be in the spirit of the legislation, and indeed the point of the legislation would be undermined were it not the case. However, we hope that the Ministry of Justice will try to ensure that the exercise of that right does not delay decisions for unreasonable lengths of time.

2.48 From November 2008, these powers and duties in respect of victims were extended to apply in the case of unrestricted patients detained under s.37 or s.47, as a result of changes brought about by the Mental Health Act 2007[170]. They will continue to apply should any such patient be discharged onto SCT. For these unrestricted patients, the hospital managers rather than the Ministry of Justice will be the effective gate-keeper of information. The Department of Health and Ministry of Justice have issued guidance on the exercise of the powers and duties in such a role[171]. Where victims request information, hospital managers will be required by law to inform them of any plans to discharge a patient (whether absolutely or onto SCT) or to amend conditions attached to an existing SCT; or of an application to the Tribunal. The victim should be invited to submit representations over these matters. The guidance also suggests that hospital managers should also "consider using their discretion to give victims additional information (eg about patients' leave of absence, absconding, or transfer to another hospital)"[172]. It sates that this is designed to enable managers to "reassure" victims, but is not intended to permit disclosure of confidential patient information.[173] The example given in the guidance is as follows:

> ...if there is a possibility that victims may come into contact with patients who are on leave, it may be appropriate for hospital managers to exercise their discretion to disclose that a patient has been allowed leave (without giving specific details about the timing or purpose of the leave), so that the victim knows that the patient has not absconded.[174]

2.49 It seems likely that a victim who is given such information may feel justified in asking for more details: indeed precisely those that the guidance suggests might not be divulged, such as where the patient is likely to be that they might come into contact with them, and why the patient is allowed to be there. Of course, we recognise the very difficult problems that such questions pose to detaining authorities, who are under a legal duty to respect patient confidentiality, and to protect a patient in their custody from harm (given that, in some cases, the victim's request for information about where the patient is likely to be may not be motivated by a wish to avoid contact, but to facilitate it for the purposes of revenge). But we do not hard to envisage that it could be profoundly unsettling to a

---

[170] For our general concerns over the potential exercise of these powers and duties, see MHAC (2008) *Risk, Rights, Recovery; Twelfth Biennial Report 2005-2007*, para 7.87.

[171] Department of Health and Ministry of Justice (2008) *Mental Health Act 2007: Guidance on the extension of victim's rights under the Domestic Violence, Crime and Victims Act 2004*. October 2008.

[172] *ibid.*, para 2.28.

[173] *ibid.*, para 2.30.

[174] *ibid.*, para 2.31.

victim who has requested to be given information to be told only that there is a likelihood that they might come into contact with the patient, without more specific details.

2.50 It may be that clinicians or managers who have duties towards the victims of patients detained in their hospitals feel that they should emulate the practice of the Ministry of Justice, and consult with victims before granting leave. In general terms, it might only be through such consultation that the Responsible Clinician can place such conditions upon the leave as would provide reassurance to victims as is apparently required by the law. No doubt, however, any such consultation could involve considerable bureaucracy and potential delays to decisions about leave.

2.51 We suggest that the way in which hospital managers and Responsible Clinicians respond to their new discretionary power, and exercise their duties regarding discharge arrangements, should be closely monitored in the early years following this change of law.

Ground Leave

2.52 In most cases, patients do not need to be given leave under s.17 when they remain within the grounds of the detaining authority when off the ward. However, such 'ground leave' is, of course, still a matter that still needs to be negotiated between clinical staff and patients, and in many cases patients are only allowed off the ward under escort of staff. Patients may feel the consequences of withdrawal or retraction of 'ground leave' to be the most restrictive of all, as they will be literally confined to the ward.

2.53 One patient in an acute admission ward had a half-hour escorted ground leave twice daily. He told us that the short periods of time

> Really isn't enough – half an hour makes you become a time-keeper, because you are worried that if you are a few minutes late they will take notice and my privileges might be revoked. It makes me feel nervous. I have to leave exactly on the half or quarter or full hour so I can calculate when I need to be back.

2.54 The patient also explained the frustrations and disappointments that he had experienced when his short periods of ground leave were curtailed or delayed by even a few minutes through the action of his escort. He had particular complaints about one escort, and told us that, on different occasions, this escort had made him wait until the end of a televised football match before going out; had insisted on visiting a cash point; or had taken a route through the hospital to visit the shop when the patient had expected to access fresh air. The limited duration of his ground leave periods made him resent such matters to a great degree, and added to the sense of infantilisation that he reported experiencing over other aspects of his care.

2.55   In one Medium Secure Unit in Wales, we met with some patients who were allowed only short periods of escorted ground leave because of clinical and/or security considerations. One such patient, a young man who had been on the ward for six weeks and who had been asleep during most of our visit, stated that he would like more physical activity. The hospital management team agreed on the day of the visit to instigate a structured exercise programme, facilitated by gym staff, for such patients if they chose to co-operate. Where patients are confined to the ward in this way, managers should make it a high priority to ensure that there are activities such as this available for patients to exercise and feel less confined.

> I was given thirty minutes s.17 leave, and due to my disability / mobility it took me ten minutes to get out of the hospital, five minutes to cross the busy city street. The nurse then took me back again, otherwise I would be over my thirty minutes. I mentioned this to my consultant, his response: if I dared to complain again he would withdraw my leave until further notice. When he finally extended the time for me, the staff often were too busy to take me out – so still no s.17 leave.
>
> Monica Endersby, SURP member

Absence without leave

2.56   Understandable public concern was raised by the details surrounding the rape of a young girl by a detained patient who had escaped from a low-secure unit near Bristol in February 2008. The patient, then aged 20, had a diagnosis of autistic spectrum disorder, and had been placed under a hospital order with restrictions aged 12, having killed his stepbrother. The patient was given further hospital order with restrictions in September 2008, having pleaded guilty to escaping from custody, burglary and two counts of rape. In making the order, Nicholas Cooke QC, the Recorder of Cardiff, said in that the case raised several concerns, including why the patient, who had a history of absconding, was moved to a low-security unit, why staff waited nearly half an hour before informing police of his escape and why neighbouring police forces were not alerted[175]. The independent review commissioned by the National Autistic Society (the service provider in this case) found deficiencies in risk-assessment at the unit[176]. There were concerns over violent and pornographic films accessed and owned by the patient whilst in the unit, whether the risks posed by this patient were sufficiently identified and whether indications of increasingly disturbed and sexualised behaviour should have been acted upon.

2.57   The revised Code of Practice for England now makes specific mention of the need to review and analyse "incidents in which patients go AWOL or abscond ... so that lessons for the future can be learned, including lessons about ways of identifying patients most at risk of going missing"[177]. We do not doubt that such reviews of absconding should take place (and in many services they do). It is difficult to imagine that such reviews will provide much in the way of a predictive tool relating to risks of absconding amongst the detained

---

[175] At the time of writing this report, the police actions were the subject of a review by the Independent Police Complaints Commission (IPCC).

[176] *Independent external review report of the circumstances preceding the escape of DH from the Hayes Independent Hospital.* Presented to the Board of the National Autistic Society, September 2008.

[177] *MHA Code of Practice for England*, para 22.20. There is no equivalent in the Code for Wales.

population in general terms, although it may highlight particular triggers for the patient concerned and should help to identify failures in physical security management. Services undertaking such reviews may have to determine the threshold for an incident analysis, or at least ensure that such analyses are not needlessly cumbersome or time-consuming when the situation being considered does not merit this. The majority of patients who are technically AWOL simply return late, without significant incident, from an agreed period of leave. For such AWOL incidents, compliance with the Code's requirement that outcomes of leave be recorded and discussed with patients where possible (para 21.11, see also figure 35 above) should be sufficient to identify any further need for review or analysis.

2.58   The Government faces a similar problem in identifying significance in AWOL episodes in its wish to collect statistics on this aspect of the administration of the Mental Health Act. It distinguishes between "absconding", which is where a patient who is already outside the perimeter of a secure unit goes AWOL (for example by failing to return from leave),and "escaping", which is where a patient manages to get out from within the secure perimeter of such a unit[178]. The Department of Health does not routinely collect data on absconds centrally in regard to all mental health services, with the exception of High Security Hospitals[179].

2.59   During 2008 we were approached by the Department of Health asking what statistical information we held about absences without leave of detained patients. Of course, the answer was none, in that the MHAC has never been provided with the means to be systematically notified of the detention of patients, let alone incidents that happen to such patients subsequent to detention[180]. But we understand the will to have such data to hand. This is apparent from the recent inclusion in the Mental Health Minimum Data Set (MHMDS) of data requirements for patients who are AWOL. This will, we understand, take as a threshold for a notifiable AWOL episode that the patient should be AWOL 'overnight'. This is, in many respects, a rather arbitrary threshold, not least because the most likely risk to life associated with AWOL status is that to the patient's own, and patients who kill themselves whilst AWOL are not especially likely to wait overnight before doing so. Patients who are technically AWOL overnight may have failed to return to hospital from leave granted over consecutive nights, and not be considered especially high risk. It is, presumably, the aim of the Department of Health to quantify risk (although to what end is not clear), as evidenced by the Secretary of State's written answer to a question laid in the House of Commons over the numbers of absconds, that:

> an abscond can be either non-serious or a serious untoward incident (SUI). In relation to mental health patients detained under the Mental Health Act 1983, an abscond is treated as an SUI where a significant risk is posed to the patient or to others. An abscond would not

---

[178] Hansard, House of Commons, 25 July 2007 : Column 1206W.

[179] In the five years 2003 – 2007 there were three absconds from HSHs, but no escapes. One absconder was from Rampton (2003), one from Ashworth (2004) and one from Broadmoor (2005). Data source: Hansard, House of Commons, 25 July 2007: Column 1207W.

[180] Statistical data on the use of the Act cited in this report is from various sources, including Department of Health (Information Centre) data collections; Ministry of Justice data published from case files; and data from the *Count Me In* censuses of the psychiatric hospital population over the last three years.

necessarily be treated as an SUI where the abscond is unintentional, due for example to a patient missing a bus or train when returning from leave ... The reporting of SUI absconds is stringent. Individual National Health Service organisations are responsible for identifying SUIs and there must be clear local procedures at each NHS organisation to identify, report and investigate SUIs. Information is collected by, and is available on request from, each strategic health authority about all SUIs reported[181].

This appears to be a sensible approach, although any data collection of absconds relying on their SUI status, no matter how stringent are the reporting requirements for the latter, will only capture a subset determined at least in part on subjective local determinations over perceived significant risk to the patient or others, and the perceived or reported intentionality of the absconder. It is not clear that the case with which we started this discussion would have been considered a 'significant risk' prior to the offence being discovered (although there is a good argument that it should have been recognised as such). But, aside from these methodological considerations, we remain unconvinced that centralised (as opposed to local) collection of AWOL episodes is of any particular practical use above that already provided for by regional SUI collections.

Returning AWOL patients to hospital

2.60 We continue to hear of difficulties in making arrangements to return AWOL patients to hospitals, in particular when they are found some distance from the detaining hospital. In usual circumstances, we would expect the AWOL patient to be accommodated in a hospital local to where he or she was found until the detaining authority arranged transport, which in most cases should involve sending staff to escort the patient back in suitable transport. In some cases, however, we have found that such arrangements fall down. The following cases are both from 2008:

- A patient who was AWOL from detention under s.3 in south Wales was retaken in London following contact between the relevant police services. The London police ruled out transporting the patient themselves for the 250 mile journey back to Wales (both because of a reluctance to use police transport when the risk did not require such a last resort response, and because it "didn't make good operational sense"); the local mental health unit would not accept the patient into its care whilst other arrangements were made; and it had not been deemed appropriate to wait until transport and accommodation arrangements had been made before retaking the patient. The eventual police action – for lack of any alternative – was described by the police themselves as "trudge around West London looking for somewhere to accommodate him (anyone and anywhere), give up and find him a warm spot in the station office for the best part of twelve hours."

- A patient absconded from detention in a Nottingham hospital and was retaken by police in London. The Nottingham hospital requested that the patient be accommodated in a local service so that it could arrange collection from there, as we would expect. The local mental health unit initially refused to take the patient, suggesting that the patient should be accommodated at an Accident and Emergency department, which (perhaps

---

[181] *ibid.*

understandably) also refused to take the patient. In this case, however, the London-based mental health unit eventually allowed the patient to be left in its care.

2.61 The revised Codes of Practices for England and Wales make it clear that detaining authorities have responsibility for the return of their AWOL patients, and that the role of the police should be minimal[182]. Both Codes require the police to be informed when patient who is considered to be either particularly vulnerable or particularly a risk to others, or when the patient has restricted status. But the Code for England's description of the principle to be followed thereafter is well put: "the role of the police should, wherever possible, be only to assist a suitably qualified and experienced mental health professional in returning the patient to hospital."[183]

Long-term s.17 leave

2.62 In 2008 we met with some patients who were on long-term s.17 leave, usually in venues away from the main hospital site at which they remained liable to be detained. This was in a limited number of pilot visits in preparation for the extended Mental Health Act Commissioner visiting role under the Care Quality Commission[184]. Discussion of one of these visits has been published in the *Journal of Mental Health Law*[185].

2.63 The sorts of issues raised on the trial visits may give some indication of problems that CQC may encounter in the coming years, and indeed that may be common features of community patients subject to legal powers whether they are on s.17 leave or supervised community treatment:

- Due to a misunderstanding between professionals, one patient had not received his depot medication for some time (the patient thought three months, but staff informed the Commissioner that it was considerably longer).

- The authority for treating one patient under section 58, which was eighteen months old, did not fully cover the medication being given.

- A patient had been resident in supported housing for some time, although this was not stated as a condition of his leave on the leave form. The manager of the supported housing had, we were told, asked him to vacate by Easter 2008. With nowhere else to go, this was causing some anxiety, not least because of the possible need to return to hospital. It was unclear who was helping him with this.

- Another patient in supported housing unit had, as part of her leave arrangements, the condition that she was allowed out for only two hours a day. Thus for the most part she was detained in the community.

- One patient had no traceable s.17 leave form, whereby staff could determine the agreed leave parameters.

---

[182] *MHA Code of Practice for Wales*, para 29.11, *MHA Code of Practice for England*, para 22.13.

[183] *MHA Code of Practice for England*, para 22.13.

[184] The MHAC's remit was extended to SCT and Guardianship patients on the 3 November 2008 as a consequence of the implementation of the MHA 2007.

[185] Jones, B & Kinton, M (2008) 'A snap-shot of 'long-term' section 17 use in South-West England'. *Journal of Mental Health Law*, 7, May 2008.

- One patient and her advocate stated that her Responsible Clinician had advised her to withdraw her appeal to the Mental Health Review Tribunal. The doctor's comment left the patient feeling that exercising her right of appeal would be held against her in the long run.

- One patient, who was liable to be detained under s.3 but had been on long term leave in her own home for over a year, met with us at an assertive outreach team base. She told us that was pleased to be able to do what she liked, when she liked, in her own home. She described herself as 'being on section at home', and told us that she had a review every month or so and that leave was written into her care plan. She took her medication, although she didn't like doing so, but seemed not to have considered that she might be recalled to hospital if she ceased to comply, or indeed for any other reason.

2.64 In other dealings with patients on long-term leave, the MHAC has been concerned to be told that hospitals would have trouble contacting certain patients to invite them to meet with us, indicating that some patients who are allegedly receiving some aspect of inpatient treatment are, in fact, not in touch with hospitals at all. We have also noted some other, less dramatic signs of inadequate oversight of patients who are on long-term s.17 leave. In a hospital in south-west England in November 2008, we found that, while the hospital kept copies of detention papers on file, it did not appear to hold the relevant clinical notes. We were concerned over the mechanisms whereby the Responsible Clinician for this patient – who had recently changed – would make decisions about this patient's care, and indeed the patient was still being treated on a consent form signed by the old Responsible Clinician, his leave authorisation (also completed by the previous doctor) had expired two months before the visit, and there was no evidence that Supervised Community Treatment had been considered as an alternative to long-term s.17 leave.

De facto detention

2.65 On a themed visit on the subject of section 17 leave, a MHA Commissioner examined the file of a patient whom she had been told was detained, but found there a record that the patient had been made informal over five weeks earlier. She queried this, concerned that ward staff appeared to believe the patient to be detained, and at the continuing references in the file to the patient being 'given leave' in ward rounds. She was told that the patient had in fact been moved to a neighbouring ward ten days earlier. On that ward, she discovered that neither the patient nor staff had been informed of the patient's informal legal status. The hospital later told the MHAC that this had indeed been a mistake by staff in overlooking the patient's discharge, but that in any case the hospital used references to 'leave' for both detained and informal patients as a clinical rather than a legal term.

2.66 We have written in past reports of our concern over the *de facto* detention of informal patients, although such concerns are outside of our legal remit. This will not be the case when the duties of the MHAC are joined to the wide remit of the Care Quality Commission (CQC), which is to be tasked with monitoring new deprivation of liberty safeguards. It is our experience that many instances of *de facto* detention go unnoticed or unmarked under the legal structure at the time of writing (i.e. prior to the introduction of those safeguards), although in theory any patient who is deprived of his or her liberty outside of the legal powers of the Mental Health Act or other statutory regime should have been referred to the Court of Protection. It may be that services are waiting for the DOLs regime to come into force before regularising the legal position of the informal patients concerned, as is apparently the case in the example below. However, as the DOLs safeguards will, for the majority of those to whom they might apply, continue to be initiated by the detaining body itself, the CQC should be alert to instances of deprivation of liberty such as those repeatedly seen by the MHAC over the last quarter century.

> During the visit the Commissioner observed staff caring for a highly disturbed resident who is an informal patient. The regime which has been devised to meet the resident's needs involves 24 hour one to one care, with gentle restraint being applied for much of the time to guide and manage behaviour. In addition the resident is not permitted to leave the house unaccompanied, and the doors are kept locked. Although the care of informal patients is not currently part of the Commission's legal remit, the issue of Deprivation of Liberty will be included from April 2009, and the Commissioner discussed the issue with the manager, learning that some discussions have already been held with the social work team involved.
>
> *London, January 2009*

Supervised Community Treatment under the revised Mental Health Act

2.67 The new power of Supervised Community Treatment (SCT) came into effect with the implementation of the amendments to the Mental Health Act on 3 November 2008. It is applicable upon the discharge from detention in hospital of patients who are subject to section 3, or to unrestricted Part 3 detention powers, if both their Responsible Clinician and an Approved Mental Health Professional agree that the criteria are met. The criteria for SCT, and Government's advice on its purpose, are set out in the revised Codes of Practice for England (chapter 25) and Wales (chapter 30). In summary, SCT is designed for patients who still require treatment for mental disorder, on the grounds of their own health or safety or for the protection of others, but such treatment can be given outside of detention in hospital, provided that there is a power to recall them if clinicians have concerns that the community arrangements are no longer sufficient. The ability to recall to hospital must be a necessary factor in the patient being able to receive treatment in the community.

2.68 In the Mental Health Bill debates, the Secretary of State for Health (Patricia Hewitt) stated that SCT was

> designed particularly for the so-called "revolving door patients" – people who are hospitalised, whether under compulsion or voluntarily, who respond to treatment, who are released, and who then fail to maintain their treatment, producing another crisis and yet another hospitalisation.[186]

---

[186] Hansard (Commons) 16 April 2007, Col 56.

Although SCT was thus designed 'particularly' for certain patients, it may yet be applied in practice to the generality of cases which fall within its scope. The revised Codes of Practice (chapter 25.2 in England, 30.3 in Wales) states that the purpose of SCT is "to allow suitable patients to be safely treated in the community rather than under detention in hospital, and to provide a way to prevent relapse ... It is intended to help patients to maintain stable mental health outside hospital and to promote recovery". There is no mention of the concept of the 'revolving door' in any official guidance on the implementation of SCT and, although grounds must be given on the statutory forms for certifying that the use of SCT is 'necessary', there is no explicit requirement to give objective evidence (for instance of past relapse) to show such necessity. We expect that this will be an issue raised at SCT patients' Tribunal hearings, and may yet be subject to further judicial interpretation.

2.69   Practitioners and patients who are familiar with the rules regarding the 'conditional discharge' of detained patients who are subject to restriction orders will recognise that this is, in essence, a parallel system for unrestricted patients. In our Eleventh Biennial Report (2006) we reported on the rising numbers of conditionally discharged Part 3 patients[187]: patients now subject to restriction orders can reasonably expect that their eventual discharge from detention in hospital is likely, at least for an initial period, to be conditional rather than absolute. It is to be hoped that the use of SCT does not follow a similar pattern, and as such become a usual stage in the detention process of unrestricted patients. The restrictions placed upon Part 3 patients result either from them having criminal convictions and/or being identified as posing a particular danger by the courts. The unrestricted population of detainees under the Act has, in general terms, no such distinguishing features.

2.70   As such, the AMHP who has to countersign that SCT is appropriate on the statutory forms initiating the power has an important gate-keeping role. The revised Codes of Practice allow that an AMHP who is part of the multi-disciplinary team caring for the patient in hospital can undertake this role, and indeed there is nothing in law to prevent this. If such arrangements are made locally, it will be vital that the AMHPs concerned make a particular effort to ensure that they take an objective view that takes full account of the wider social context in the case, to avoid their teams developing a culture of using SCT as an automatic discharge process.

2.71   In contrast to statutory requirements regarding the time that may elapse between medical recommendations and applications for detention[188], there are no time restrictions relating to the completion of the statutory forms that discharge a patient onto SCT. That is, the law is silent, both in relation to:

- the lapse of time that make take place between the AMHP stating agreement with the responsible clinician's view that SCT and any imposed conditions are appropriate and, perhaps more importantly,

---

[187] MHAC (2006) *In Place of Fear? Eleventh Biennial Report 2003-2005*, para 5.135 *et seq.*

[188] Medical recommendations for detention must be based upon examinations that took place no more than five days apart (s.12(1)), and an application for detention based upon such recommendations must take place within 14 days of the last dated medical examination (s.6(1)(a)).

- the lapse of time between such a statement by the AMHP and the putting into effect of SCT through the Responsible Clinician's completion of the last part of the form.

As such, the law does not preclude a responsible clinician discharging onto SCT a patient who has not been seen by an AHMP for a considerable period of time, provided that an AMHP had at one time completed their part of the CTO form. Of course, such use of 'old' agreements could open a way to legal challenge of the decision to use SCT, on the grounds that the patient's circumstances had since changed. Such delays may be an issue where discharges onto SCT are delayed through last-minute problems with aftercare arrangements, although it would have to be determined on the facts of each case whether the eventual use of paperwork completed before such delays was reasonable.

2.72 On SCT-focused visits in 2009, we have been advised by clinicians of problems in making SCT arrangements 'fit' existing protocols and pathways in service delivery. In particular, the problem seems to be in maintaining a Responsible Clinician who has access to a bed should the need for recall arise, and co-ordinating the care of patients within the community based structure of assertive outreach teams, crisis and home treatment teams. In part this is simply a problem of access to services: hospital-based Responsible Clinicians cannot set conditions of engagement with community teams if there is insufficient resource in the community to provide a service. The problem also relates to the structures of community services, and in particular the functionalized service pathways introduced under National Service Framework. In effect, a patient's Responsible Clinician (defined as the clinician who is *in fact* in charge of that patient's treatment) will change as he or she moves across different care pathways. Trusts will need to establish locally agreed policies across their inpatient and community teams to coordinate such transfer of responsibility, taking particular account of the need for continuity of care.

2.73 These are areas that we consider would benefit from close monitoring as SCT practice develops in the following years.

The impact of supervised community treatment

2.74 Prior to the implementation of SCT there was some debate over its likely impact[189]. The Department of Health estimated that 2% of potentially eligible patients would be made subject to SCT in the first year of implementation, rising to 10% within 5 years[190]. Given the detained population and rates of detention[191], this implied a starting population of 200 SCT patients, rising to an annual rate of perhaps 2,250 initiations of SCT by 2013. Although we have only five month's data available to us for consideration at the time of writing, it is clear that the first estimation (of the number of patients to be made subject

---

[189] See Lawton-Smith S (2005) *A question of numbers: the potential impact of community treatment orders in Emgland and Wales*. King's Fund; Kinton M (2008) 'Towards an understanding of Supervised Community Treatment' *Journal of Mental Health Law*, 17, May 2008, 7-20.

[190] Department of Health (2006) *Mental Health Bill: Regulatory Impact Assessment*. November 2006, p.55.

[191] The last three years' *Count Me In* censuses have identified just under 10,000 patients detained in hospital on the census date under sections 3 or 37. According to Information Centre statistics, there were 22,400 uses of s.3 and 350 uses of s.37 (without restrictions) in 2007/08 (Information Centre (2008) *In-patients formally detained in hospitals under the Mental Health Act 1983 and other legislation, England: 1997-98 to 2007-08*. October 2008).

to CTO in the first year) was far too low. By the end of March 2009, over 1,700 people were known to have been subject to SCT.

2.75 The MHAC's data on the use of SCT is obtained only in the course of our administration of the second opinion system: as with the other powers of the Act, there are no requirements upon authorities to report their use to the MHAC for monitoring purposes[192]. As such, our data only includes most of those instances of SCT that involve treatment requiring certification[193] and continue, or are expected to continue, for an initial period of one month. This is because, after the initial month of treatment for mental disorder (unless the patient was still subject to the three-month period when placed under SCT), authorities must contact the MHAC with the details of the SCT patient in order to arrange for a second opinion appointed doctor (SOAD) visit. In the first five months of SCT we received over 1,722 requests for second opinions: the numbers of such requests recorded in each week is given at figure 36 below.

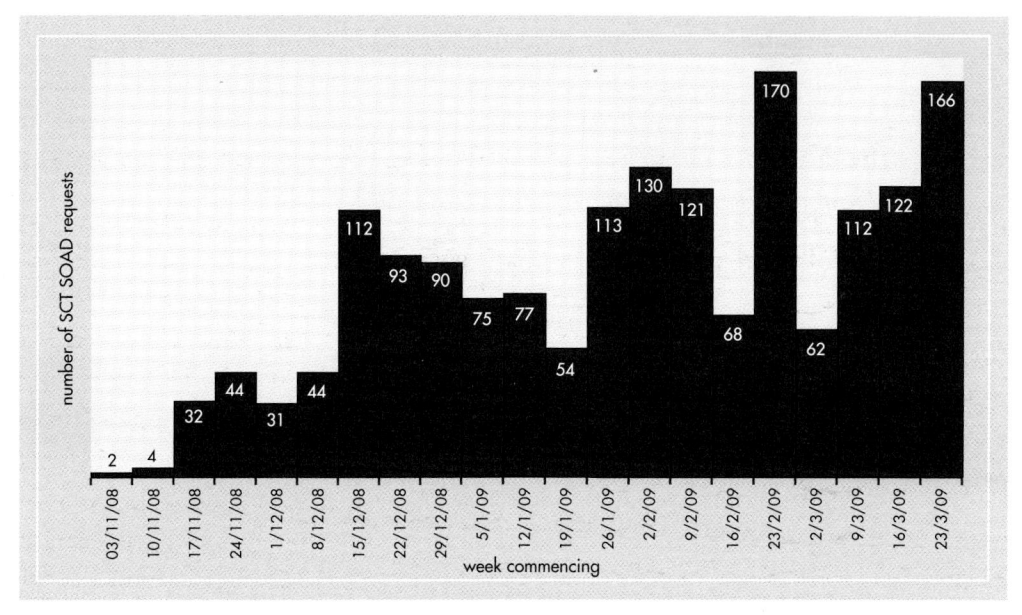

Fig 36: Number of SOAD visit requests for SCT patients, by week, November 2008 to March 2009
Source: MHAC data

2.76 The MHAC's record of SOAD visit requests should not be assumed to be a complete record of the use of SCT during this period. As is further discussed at paragraph 3.68, until mid-January 2009 the MHAC declined a number of requests for SOAD certification of treatment for SCT patients who were deemed by their responsible clinician to have capacity and be refusing consent to their treatment. These patients subsequently do not appear in our count of SCT patients based upon SOAD requests. Some requests at the end of the month may not have been recorded on the database used. The MHAC also receives many contacts from clinicians and administrators requesting advice or information on the operation of the Act, and from such contacts we gather useful if anecdotal information about other SCT use that will not show up in our data:

---

[192] Although we note that the power to request information has been given to the Care Quality Commission through the Health and Social Care Act 2008.

[193] That is, medication for mental disorder or ECT that would fall under s.58 or s.58A, were the patient detained in hospital.

- We are aware through such contact of one example where SCT has been used where the patient is not receiving any treatment that would require certification. It seems unlikely that there are very many such cases (i.e. where a patient who takes no medication for mental disorder is placed under SCT), although we have no means of knowing for certain.

- Within the first week of the implementation of the revised Act we had discussed the revocation of one patient's SCT status with their responsible clinician. It would seem likely that a number of SCTs are similarly revoked soon after initiation. This may be because the patient immediately ceases compliance with treatment that is deemed necessary (perhaps in this way testing the coercive 'teeth' of the new power). It may also be because of misunderstandings over the coercive powers of SCT, whether by the patient or by the responsible clinician and AMHP who initiated the patient's discharge onto SCT. From approaches made to the MHAC for advice, we are aware that a number of responsible clinicians assumed incorrectly that the revised Act *required* them to place all patients subject to long-term s.17 leave under SCT, and/or that SCT provided powers of coercive treatment even if such patients were capable and refused their consent.

The impact on patients: MHAC experiences of SCT patients

2.77   In the lead-up to the implementation of the revised Mental Health Act, we saw that some detaining hospitals had made good efforts to explain the changes in the law to their patients. As might be expected, there was nevertheless some confusion and anxiety amongst patients as to the possible consequences for their own care. Although we met with one detained patient in the summer of 2008 who had requested that he be discharged to a residential home under SCT when the power became available, in the main patients who were aware of the changes in the law were concerned that SCT might extend the time they were subject to legal coercion, perhaps indefinitely. It is important that hospitals include information about SCT when informing patients who are detained for treatment of their legal position and rights, so as to meet detaining hospitals' duties under s.132 of the Act.

2.78   The MHAC has initiated some SCT-focussed visits from November 2008. We aim to meet with patients who are prepared and able to attend the visit site, and examine records. In one such visit in February 2009 we talked to one SCT patient whose situation appeared to raise some general points over the operation of the power. She was quite isolated, living with her son but with no other family or friends, whose contact with services was a weekly visit from a CPN. She told us that she disliked these visits, as she felt unable to talk with the CPN assigned to her. She would have liked to engage in more activity, and had information about a gardening course but had felt unable to follow this up. She had no copy of her care plan and we were unable to find such a plan in her notes. She was unaware of her rights and understood neither the implications nor the conditions of her community treatment order (we explained these to her and advised her to seek advocacy support from a provider that she had used previously). It seemed that information from the hospital managers had been posted to her some days after she had been discharged onto SCT. We suggested that the Trust should ensure that patients have their rights explained to them before discharge, and that hospital record forms could be developed, similar to those used to record the giving of information to detained patients, to keep an auditable trail of this legal duty being performed. In this case, we also made several suggestions and requests, including that the hospital managers draw up a care plan reflecting the patient's wishes, and consider allocating a support worker to help the patient engage with activities outside her home. It is disappointing to find, so soon after the introduction of SCT, such isolation and poor provision for a 'community patient'. Whilst we have no reason to believe that this is the general situation of SCT patients, this does point to the need to be on guard against repeating past mistakes in decanting hospital patients into inadequate community situations.

The gender, age and ethnicity of SCT patients

2.79 The number of requests for Second Opinion Appointed Doctor visits to SCT patients, up to the end of January 2009, by the age and gender of the patients concerned is shown at figure 37 below. Whilst the age profile of both male and female patients combined forms a regular bell-curve, with the 35-44 year-old group most prevalent, the patterns of males and females are noticeably distinct. That women make up only one-third of the total will in part be a reflection of the gender imbalance in the detained population: twice as many males (10,200) as females (5,000) were detained in hospital at 31 March 2008, in part because males spend longer in hospital than females[194]. It is also notable that men who are subject to SCT are on average younger than women.

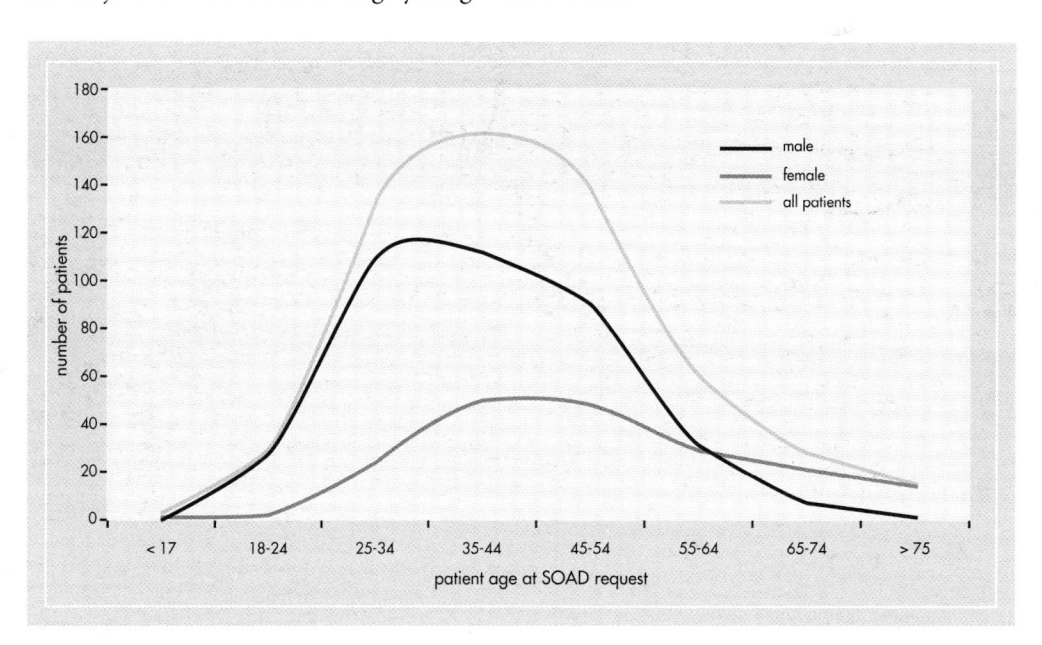

Fig 37: Age and gender of Supervised Community Treatment Order patients upon request for SOAD visits, 3 November 2008 to 16 January 2009, England and Wales

Source: MHAC data

2.80 The ethnic group of the 726 SCT patients who were referred for a second opinion between the 3 November 2008 and 30 January 2009 is shown at figure 38 below. This is 'raw' data, which has not been standardised for age, but it suggests, at the very least, that the

---

[194] Information Centre (2008) *In-patients formally detained in hospitals under the Mental Health Act 1983 and other legislation, England: 1997-98 to 2007-08.* October 2008.

overrepresentation of Black Caribbean and Black African patients amongst the detained population continues amongst patients subject to SCT. Taking the detained population at the time of the 2008 census for comparison, White British patients accounted for 72.9% of the population detained under s.3 (who make up the largest part by far of persons eligible to be placed on SCT), compared to 66.0% of those subject to SCT powers. Black Caribbean patients accounted for 5.6% of all those detained under s.3 on the 2008 census day, but 7.0% of this data set of SCT patients. Black African patients made up 3.1% of s.3 patients, but 5.6% of our SCT dataset. Interestingly, the 'other White' ethnic group is also proportionately larger in the SCT sample, accounting for 4.7% of the s.3 patients on census day, but 6.7% of SCT patients referred for a second opinion[195].

Ethnic group	Men Number	Men %	Women Number	Women %	Total Number	Total %
White British	317	65.8	162	66.4	479	66.0
White Irish	3	0.6	–	–	3	0.4
Welsh	2	0.4	–	–	2	0.3
Other White	33	6.8	16	6.6	49	6.7
White and Black Caribbean	4	0.8	5	2.1	9	1.2
White and Black African	1	0.2	1	0.4	2	0.3
White and Asian	1	0.2	1	0.4	2	0.3
Other Mixed	3	0.6	1	0.4	4	0.6
Indian	2	0.4	6	2.5	8	1.1
Pakistani	8	1.7	3	1.2	11	1.5
Bangladeshi	5	1.0	2	0.8	7	1.0
Other Asian	6	1.2	2	0.8	8	1.1
Black Caribbean	35	7.3	16	6.6	51	7.0
Black African	27	5.6	14	5.7	41	5.6
Other Black	6	1.2	2	0.8	8	1.1
Chinese	–	–	1	0.5	1	0.1
Other	3	0.6	–	–	3	0.4
Not stated / recorded	26	5.4	12	4.9	38	5.2
Total	**482**	**100**	**244**	**100**	**726**	**100**

Fig 38: Requests for SOAD visits to Supervised Community Treatment Order: ethnic group by gender, 3 November 2008 to 30 January 2009, England and Wales

Source: MHAC data

2.81   This requires continued monitoring and further investigation. The data suggests that those Black groups that are already overrepresented in the detained population may be even more disproportionately represented amongst patients subject to community powers. Although the numbers involved are small, we note that Black African or Caribbean women appear to be proportionately greater in the SCT population than in the detained

---

[195] Data from *Count Me In* census of patients detained on the 31 March 2008 under s.3. The proportions of patients in the census data set who had been *admitted* under s.3 were 72.6% (White); 6.2% (Black Caribbean); 3.1% Black African) and 4.7% (White Other).

population. Of course, there may be various explanations for such phenomena, including the age profile of Black patients, or the areas of the country where community services are more developed and therefore ready to take larger numbers of SCT patients. But an alternative possibility would simply be that, just as Black patients are more likely to enter coercive treatment, so they are less likely to leave it, in that coercion follows them out of the hospital after discharge from detention. Both local services and central government should be aware of this possibility. For local services, it underlines the great need for ethnic monitoring and race equality work to extend fully to Supervised Community Treatment.

SCT and deprivation of liberty

2.82 Writing to the Joint Committee on Human Rights in 2007, Department of Health officials stated that

> ...the Department does not consider that it would be appropriate for the Responsible Clinician and the AMHP to impose conditions on a CTO which are so restrictive in nature that they would effectively amount to a deprivation of liberty for the purposes of Article 5 of the Convention.[196]

2.83 Consistent with this view, the revised Codes of Practice do not envisage that the conditions imposed as part of SCT arrangements would themselves result in deprivation of liberty. However, the Code for England does suggest that situations which involve deprivation of liberty might arise while SCT patients are in the community, for example due to their admission to a care home for further care or treatment for their mental disorder, or to a care home or hospital for physical care[197]. In such circumstances, the Code allows that deprivation of liberty under the DOLs safeguards can "co-exist" alongside SCT, "provided that there is no conflict with the conditions of SCT...set by the patient's Responsible Clinician".[198] In our view, if there is such a conflict but Responsible Clinicians are prepared to resolve it, they should suspend the conflicting SCT conditions, rather than modify them to encompass the deprivation of liberty (that is, it might be wiser to suspend a residence requirement, rather than modify it to name the place at which deprivation of liberty is to take place). We take the view that Responsible Clinicians should avoid setting conditions at any stage of SCT which may appear to require deprivation of liberty.

2.84 The powers of supervised discharge (i.e. s.25A, the forerunner to SCT) appear to have been used in the past to discharge patients from detention in hospital to care homes, with conditions that amount to a deprivation of liberty. In the course of our pilot visits to patients on long-term leave (see paragraph 2.62 above), we learnt of two supervised discharge patients, both of whom had mental illnesses and learning disability, who had each resided in staffed community homes in Wales for between two and three years. Both were taking medication and neither was allowed to leave the home without being

---

[196] Joint Committee on Human Rights (2007) *Legislative Scrutiny: Mental Health Bill Fourth Report of Session 2006-07*, Appendix 3, para 3.38. Also referenced in Jones R (2008) *Mental Health Manual*, 11th edition, 1-196.

[197] MHA *Code of Practice for England*, paras 28.7 to 28.10.

[198] *ibid.*, para 28.8.

escorted by a member of staff. It seemed arguable that these patients were deprived of their liberty by the restrictions placed upon them. We expect that there will be many similar cases amongst SCT patients who reside in care homes, and that this may be an area that the courts will be asked to consider.

2.85 The revised Code of Practice for England makes a special case for admission to hospital for treatment of mental disorder, where such admission involves deprivation of liberty:

> where patients on SCT ... need to be detained in hospital for further treatment for mental disorder, they should be recalled under the MHA itself. The MCA deprivation of liberty safeguards cannot be used instead.[199]

The obvious conflict between depriving a patient of liberty in hospital when that patient is subject to SCT, which is a power of discharge from detention in hospital, is reflected in the exclusion of SCT patients from eligibility for authorised deprivation of liberty under the MCA where this takes place in hospital, wholly or partly for the treatment of mental disorder (see schedule 1A of the MCA as amended). This does not, of course, mean that a patient cannot enter hospital voluntarily for care and treatment of mental disorder as an informal patient. There is no reason why such informal admission cannot co-exist with SCT status, although the SCT conditions may need to be modified to encompass the change of circumstances.

Residence requirements for SCT patients: the uncertain boundaries of hospital and community

2.86 The MHAC has been asked whether, in its view, it can be lawful to require a patient to reside in a hospital as a condition of SCT (where such residence would not amount to deprivation of liberty)[200]. This question is not as surprising as it may first appear. As we have noted before[201], the distinction between supported accommodation, such as care homes or staffed hostels, and establishments that are designated as 'hospitals' may be more a question of terminology than practical difference.

2.87 Our Eleventh Biennial Report discussed court rulings relating to similar questions over the conditional discharge of restricted patients[202]. In these cases, it would appear that the court was more exercised over whether the discharge was to a situation of continued deprivation of liberty (for example in the *PH* case[203]) than it was over whether the

---

[199] *ibid.*, para 28.9.

[200] It should be noted that the MHAC has no remit to provide legal interpretation of the Act, and as such what follows is merely a view rather than authoritative guidance.

[201] MHAC (2006) *In Place of Fear? Eleventh Biennial Report 2003-2005*, para 2.56.

[202] *ibid.*, para 1.149 to 1.166.

[203] *R (on the application of the Secretary of State for the Home Department) v MHRT and PH* [2002] EWCA Civ 1868. See MHAC (2006) *In Place of Fear?* para 1.149 – 1.152: here a patient was conditionally discharged to a staffed hostel. In the case of *R (on the application of the Secretary of State for the Home Department) v MHRT* [2004] EWHC 2194, the court ruled that a similar transfer involving a different patient would not be lawful because in the new placement the patient would continue to be deprived of his liberty by the supervisory arrangements. In *MP v Nottingham Healthcare NHS Trust* [2003] EWHC 1782, the court ruled that the Tribunal, in making a conditional discharge "may not impose conditions which require the patient's continued detention (for any period) at a medium secure or other hospital"; see MHAC (2006) para 1.165 and 1.166.

patient took up residence in another hospital, or even remained in the same hospital accommodation in which he had previously been detained[204]. In a more recent case[205], Mr Justice Bean recognised the *PH* case as establishing a precedent that the 'discharge' of a patient from one state of detention to another was unlawful, although discharge to a position of restricted liberty was not. These cases appear to have overturned a previous ruling that remaining in hospital is inconsistent with the meaning of discharge in the Act[206]. But we must be cautious in assuming that this resolves the matter completely in the case of SCT patients. In our Eleventh Report, we argued against applying the principle seemingly established in the conditional discharge cases to applications for Supervised Discharge[207], on the grounds that the statutory provisions of Supervised Discharge were much more explicit in making a connection between its commencement and the patient 'leaving' hospital[208].

2.88 The revised Act does state that s.17A provides the Responsible Clinician with the power by order in writing to 'discharge a detained patient from hospital' (s.17A(1)). However, the relevant criterion for making an SCT is stated to be that "treatment can be provided without his continuing to be detained in hospital" (s.17A(5)(c)). A situation where a patient who moves from detention in hospital to residence in a hospital under SCT fulfils the literal meaning of "without ... continuing to be detained in hospital". In the cases explained to us so far, the hospital named as a place of residence is a different establishment to that in which the patient had been detained. As such, the effect of the community treatment order would certainly be to 'discharge a detained patient from hospital', albeit that they are required to take up residence in another. Whilst such a reading of the law might seem perverse, we suggest that it is no more so than a reading which allows a patient to be discharged to a staffed establishment that functions in much the same way as a hospital, provided that it is not officially designated as such. We have raised this matter with the Department of Health, and whilst officials have accepted that our reading may be correct, they did restate that SCT was designed as a mechanism for discharge from hospital, and not for transfer between one hospital and another. We share this concern that SCT should be operated within the spirit as well as the letter of the law, but the precedent of conditional discharge cases suggests that the boundaries of the law will be tested.

---

[204] *R (on the application of G) v MHRT* [2004] EWHC 2193. See MHAC (2006) *In Place of Fear?* para 1.153 – 1.157. In this case the court allowed a patient to be conditionally discharged from detention in a hospital rehabilitation flat, even though one condition of such discharge was that he continue to reside in the flat.

[205] *R (on the application of T) v Secretary of State for Justice* [2008] EWHC 1707 (Admin)

[206] *Secretary of State for the Home Department v MHRT for the Mersey Regional Health Authority* [1986] 3 All E.R. 233. See MHAC (2006) *In Place of Fear?* Para 2.56.

[207] Supervised Discharge, or Aftercare under Supervision (s.25A of the MHA 1983) was introduced by the Mental Health (Patients in the Community) Act 1995 and abolished by the Mental Health Act 2007. It was the immediate precursor to SCT, as a form of discharge from civil detention subject to conditions which "applies particularly to 'revolving door' patients..." (*Mental Health (Patients in the Community) Act 1995: Guidance on Supervised Discharge (Aftercare under Supervision and related provisions. Supplement to the Code of Practice.* Department of Health and Welsh Office, 1996, para 5).

[208] MHAC (2006) *In Place of Fear? Eleventh Biennial Report 2003-2005*, para 1.163 – 1.164.

Some initial difficulties with the administration of SCT

2.89 We have been informed of some confusion over responsibilities regarding SCT patients. In one London borough, an SCT patient was arrested by the police for offences relating to making obscene telephone calls. The police initially requested a Mental Health Act assessment, and were directed to the assertive outreach team who were responsible for his care in the community as an SCT patient. The team initially declined to attend the police station, stating that they did not have an assessment role. In the meantime, the patient was in a police cell, apparently falling into a gap between services. In our view the most appropriate response would have been for the assertive outreach team to attend the police station, on the basis that it was the team responsible for the patient's supervision in the community, to consider having the responsible clinician initiate recall to hospital (or, indeed, to support the patient without such recall if this was appropriate).

2.90 In another example of confusion of roles, we heard that Responsible Clinicians in one south-west England service sought to divest themselves of the role of prescribing SCT patients' medication for mental disorder, arguing that this could be a matter for the patients' general practitioners. The Mental Health Act Administrator (following discussion with the MHAC) argued that such divestiture of responsibility was inappropriate (although not unlawful), at least until and unless the GPs concerned were designated as the clinicians in charge of such treatment and understood their role in relation to the provisions of the Act regarding consent to treatment and second opinions (see paragraph 3.85 below).

Appealing against detention and SCT

Managers' hearings for detained patients

2.91 The revised Code of Practice for England states at chapter 31.13 that

> It is desirable that a managers' panel considers a [renewal] report made under section 20 or section 20A and decides whether to exercise its discharge power, before the current period of detention or SCT ends.

We have noted some serious delays in facilitating such managers' hearings. In June 2008, managers' hearings were taking place in one hospital in the Midlands some months after the renewal of the detention that instigated them. In a London hospital that was also experiencing delays in 2007, one patient waited for two months after the first renewal of his s.3 for a managers' hearing, and then waited over three months for a review when the time came to renew the detention again later in the year. Similar delays were experienced in a London forensic service in 2007. With such delays, hospitals cannot hope to meet the practice recommendation of the Code and may face legal challenges that they are failing human rights requirements.

2.92 It is good practice to provide patients with frequent explanations of their legal position and rights. The revised Code of Practice for England (chapter 2.25) states that triggers for consideration of whether the patient needs a fresh explanation of their rights should include a patient's request for a managers' hearing, or consideration being given to renewing a patient's detention or SCT. We suggest that an unsuccessful appeal to the managers for discharge (or to the Tribunal) should also be such a trigger: patients should also be reassured that no irrevocable decision has been made, in that their detention remains under review and they have, or will have in time, further powers of appeal.

2.93 It is also vital that patients receive an adequate explanation of the outcome of any managers' review of their detention. We have noted some variation in the standard of records made of hospital managers' hearings and in communications to patients. In some cases we see very detailed accounts of hearings, with clear reasons for the decision given. In other cases, very little was recorded: in one example it was not even clear who had attended. Reasons given by managers for their decisions must be specific to individual cases and relate to the criteria for continuing detention.

2.94 Patients should be informed of the outcome of managers' hearings in writing. It is important that letters describe the nature of the decision (and by implication the powers of the managers) accurately. In 2007, in a hospital in Yorkshire, we found standard letters in use for managers' hearings after renewals of detention that informed patients that "the managers made the decision that your section 3 should remain in place for a further twelve months and this will be reviewed again at that time". This was misleading for several reasons: not only in that it gave the false impression that the managers hearing could make such a decision (as opposed to simply determining whether or not to exercise the power of discharge under s.23), but also in that it may have led patients to assume that they had no further right of appeal over the next twelve months, or that their doctor might not discharge them from detention during that time.

2.95 Some hospitals have approached us with concerns over the availability of legal representation for managers' hearings. In contrast with representation for Tribunals, discussed below, civil legal aid for managers' hearing representation may be means-tested, in which case some patients may be ineligible[209], although usually such representation can be 'rolled up' with MHRT work and will thus not be means-tested[210]. It would appear, therefore, that problems in getting representation may be a consequence of the fee structure for such work. As discussed below, there has been some retraction in the number of legal representatives who are available for such work in some areas of the country. It appears to be the case that, for some hospitals, this is experienced as a complete withdrawal of legal representation for managers' hearings.

---

[209] Figures produced by the Ministry of Justice estimated that, in 2007, 71% of the population of England and Wales were ineligible for legal aid: in 1998 this had been 48%. See Adam Griffith (2008) 'Dramatic drop in civil legal aid eligibility' *Legal Action*, Sept 2008, p.10-11.

[210] Where a solicitor has an MHRT file open, any work related to the same period of eligibility (hospital managers' hearings, CPA meetings, etc) must be claimed as part of that MHRT file and is not means-tested. This is because non-MHRT mental health work becomes part of any MHRT case within the current period of eligibility (whether before or after the MHRT case). Guidance on matter start boundaries and "rolling-up" of files is available from the Legal Service Commission.

The Tribunal

2.96 From the 3 November 2008, with the coming into force of the Tribunals, Courts and Enforcement Act 2007, the Mental Health Review Tribunal (MHRT) in England became part of the First-tier Tribunal (Health, Education and Social Care Chamber), administered by the Ministry of Justice. The jurisdiction and powers of the "First-tier Tribunal (Mental Health)" (hereafter 'the Tribunal') remain essentially similar from the patient's point of view, and indeed patients are unlikely to have noted any change other than that the Tribunal may now recommend (but not require) that they be 'discharged' onto Supervised Community Treatment as introduced by the Mental Health Act 2007. The most significant change implemented by the Tribunals, Courts and Enforcement Act is that the overall Tribunal structure now has a second tier, which will deal with appeals on points of law, rather than such appeals going to the High Court.

> My Tribunal panel were very supportive, gave me time, explained the process to me and checked my understanding also. Although a stressful time, they did all they could to make things comfortable and safe for me, asking if I wished to comment on responses by professionals present. This was reassuring, as I felt an equal part of my Tribunal.
>
> *Monica Endersby, SURP member*

2.97 With the new title and structure, the Tribunal became subject to new Rules and (possibly the first of many) Practice Directions, replacing the Mental Health Review Tribunal Rules. A key provision of the Rules sets out an overriding objective that the Tribunal should deal with cases fairly and justly, defined to include the avoidance of unnecessary formality, seeking flexibility, avoiding delay and ensuring that the parties are able to participate fully in the Tribunal itself[211]. Such a principled grounding is very welcome, although (as our service user quotes on these pages indicate), we generally receive positive reports of patients' experience of Tribunal hearings under the previous system. As such, we expect the principles to underpin existing good practice, rather than instigate particular changes.

---

[211] *First-tier Tribunal (Health, Education and Social Care Chamber) Rules 2008*, Rule 2(1) to (3).

2.98 Parties to the Tribunal are under an express requirement to cooperate with the Tribunal to further the overriding objective[212]. This requirement, allied to the case-management powers of the Tribunal[213], may help avoid delays caused by the unavailability of witnesses or reports discussed below. The Tribunal may summon witnesses and require the production of documents, and failures to meet such summonses may be referred to the Upper Tribunal, which has the similar powers to the High Court, such as imposing a fine for a contempt of court[214]. It had been suggested that these powers will be more widely used in future, with the appointment of full-time legal members ('Judges') to support the Regional Chairmen (now called 'Regional Tribunal Judges')[215].

> My experience of Mental Health Review Tribunals is good. How they run on the day depends on the judge / chairman of the tribunal. Some are very strict and go by the book (e.g. if I want to speak to the panel I have to talk via my solicitor and nor directly). Of recent years I am invited to speak to all members openly. Some allow you to speak with them on their own at the end of the hearing, some do not.
>
> Mark Gray, SURP member

The effects of administrative delays

2.99 In past reports we have expressed great concern at the effect on patients of administrative delays in arranging Tribunal hearings[216]. At the end of March 2008, the Tribunal's administrative office in London closed and training commenced of around 80 new staff in a new Tribunals Service Mental Health Administrative Support Centre located in Leicester. Some improvements in the service were reported by the end of 2008 by the service itself[217], and we hope that these will be built upon and consolidated in the forthcoming period. However, we continue to hear of problems in Tribunal administration. Particular concerns expressed to us as we go to press are that paperwork is received late by Tribunal members; that Tribunal members continue to be booked at the last moment; and that hearings continue to be cancelled at short notice or without notice. These problems are connected. They limit the involvement of those with less flexibility in their other working arrangements[218], and presumably make the administration of Tribunals unnecessarily complex. We understand that full implementation of the Tribunal's administrative database over 2008/09 may help to resolve this problem.

---

[212] *ibid.*, Rule 2(4).

[213] *ibid.*, Rule 5. The new Rules give the Tribunal wide powers of case management, for example, to hold a case management hearing; deal with a preliminary issue; adjourn a hearing or direct a party to produce a bundle of relevant documents for the hearing.

[214] *ibid.*, Rule 22.

[215] Julie Austin (2008) 'The new MHRT – what has changed?' Hempsons Solicitors' *Mental Health News Brief*, December 2008. http://www.hempsonsonline.co.uk

[216] See, for example, MHAC (2008) *Risk, Rights, Recovery; Twelfth Biennial Report 2005-2007*, para 4.66 – 9.

[217] Sarah Gane 'Mental Health: Taking the Tribunal Forward' *Adjust Newsletter, op cit*, Dec 2007.

[218] An ongoing study by the Legal Services Commission has identified that, of adjournments that can be attributed to, or influenced by Tribunal Service actions in a random sample of 167 adjourned cases, the majority (27 of 41 cases) were due either to a failure to convene the panel, or non-attendance of one or more panel members. (From a report prepared by LSC for the AJTC MH Advisory Group Meeting, 10 March 2009: see para 2.101 below).

2.100 Mental Health Act Commissioners have been witness to some of the frustrations and management problems caused through delays to Tribunal hearings over this reporting period. The following examples are taken from feedback from MHAC visits to three different London hospitals in the summer and autumn of 2008:

> I heard of two patients who had Tribunals cancelled; one patient who may also have had some chance of discharge, for the second time. I saw the fallout for this patient who stormed out of the unit.
>
> Patient X said that he had been waiting three months for a Tribunal date. The Mental Health Act Office contacted the Tribunal whilst I was there and was told that they still do not have a date. The Mental Health Act Manager told me that the Trust is having problems with the Tribunal and have several reviews outstanding.
>
> Patient Y [a conditionally discharged patient recalled to hospital] reported an assault from another patient, witnessed by a staff member that he has reported to the police. He is also of the view that he does not need to have been recalled to a High Dependency Unit (HDU) and complained that he has had to wait 14 weeks since recall for his automatic Tribunal[219]. His central complaint was that had he either been placed elsewhere, or seen by the Tribunal earlier and moved from the HDU, this assault would not have taken place

The role of detaining authorities in adjournments of Tribunal hearings

2.101 The Legal Services Commission (LSC) has initiated a project to analyse the reasons that give rise to adjournments of Tribunal hearings. It has undertaken an initial analysis of 167 adjournments taken at random from its files, and intends to undertake similar analyses over 2009/10 to measure any improvements achieved. Figure 39 below shows our interpretation of data from the LSC's initial study, showing 91 reasons for adjournments which were classified as being beyond the control of the Tribunal Service. It is clear that the majority of these adjournments result from the Tribunal being presented with inadequate information to make a decision, either because the reports are incomplete, or because the professionals who are in attendance cannot address questions arising from such reports and other Tribunal proceedings.

Adjournment reason	Total
For further information on aftercare plan or transfer arrangements	34
RMO did not attend / inadequate clinical report	30
AMHP did not attend/ inadequate social circumstances report	17
Non-attendance of translator	5
Patient AWOL or ill	5
Total	**91**

Fig 39: Reasons for Tribunal hearing adjournments

Data source: adapted from Legal Services Commission report, Jan 2009.

---

[219] In this case the Secretary of State had met the duty under s.75(1) to refer the case to the Tribunal within a month of the recall, but the Tribunal had not met its duty under Rule 26(2) of the First-Tier Tribunal (Health Education and Social Care Chamber) Rules 2008 to list the case to start between 5 and 8 weeks from receiving the referral.

Provision of social circumstances reports to Tribunal hearings

2.102 The detaining authority of any patient for whom a Tribunal hearing is to take place is required to provide the Tribunal with a 'social circumstances' report. A considerable number of Tribunal postponements appear to be caused by the unavailability of such reports, or by reports containing insufficient information. There are, on occasions, disputes between local authorities and health authorities over who should produce the report, although such disputes invariably expose poor co-ordination over community support in the patient's care.

> Recently there have been some problems with social work reports ... but that is due to us not having a social worker for our ward, as they keep leaving. This tends to cause problems and Tribunals being cancelled.
>
> Mark Gray, SURP member

2.103 All persons involved in writing the social circumstances report must have regard to the relevant requirements set out in the 2008 Practice Direction[220]. The report must be up to date, so in the event of several weeks' delay between completion of the report and the hearing, an addendum should be added. In an article first published in *Openmind*[221], Curran and Golightley have provided a model report structure which encompasses the regulatory requirements of the Practice Direction alongside recommendations for other information to be included. We recommend this guidance to all those who complete social circumstances reports.

In-patient nursing reports

2.104 Unlike the old Tribunal rules, the new Practice Direction requires a nursing report for all inpatients, defined according to whether, at the time of the application or referral, the patient is receiving in-patient treatment for mental disorder, "even if it is being given informally or under an application, order or direction other than that to which the Tribunal application or reference relates"[222].

2.105 The report must include a copy of the present nursing plan, but also give 'full details' of the patient's understanding of and willingness to accept the current treatment; current observation levels; instances of seclusion or restraint; absences without leave; and any incidents where the patient has harmed himself or others, or has threatened other persons with violence[223]. This should be of benefit to the Tribunal (particularly in appeals against s.2[224]), but should also encourage services to ensure that proper records are kept of patient care.

---

[220] *Practice Direction on Statements for Mental Health proceedings from the Responsible Authority and the Secretary of State*, First-Tier Tribunal Health Education and Social Care Chamber, Mental Health Cases, section E. http://www.tribunals.gov.uk/Tribunals/Documents/Rules/Mentalhealthcaseshesc.pdf

[221] Curran C & Golightley M (2009) Social Circumstances Reports for a Mental Health Review Tribunal under 2008 Practice Direction. Section E *Openmind*, 156 March/April 2009, p.24-5. Also available from http://eprints.lincoln.ac.uk/1838/

[222] *Practice Direction*, para 2.

[223] *Practice Direction*, section F.

[224] Holdsworth R (2008) *The New Rules and the New Practice Direction; a Guide for all members of the MHRT*. September 2008, p.24.

Informing patients about their rights to a Tribunal

2.106 Patients detained under s.2 have a brief window (the first fourteen days of detention) to appeal to the Tribunal. On several occasions we have met with such patients who have effectively been denied the opportunity to apply themselves to the Tribunal by the detaining authorities' failure promptly to meet their obligation under s.132 to explain legal rights, or were in danger of being so denied:

- In August 2007, in north-west England, no record could be found of one patient receiving information under s.132 in a hospital that otherwise appeared to have good systems in this respect. Our private meeting with the patient appeared to confirm that she was unsure of her rights. The patient was on a s.2 and had passed the fourteen days within which she could appeal to the Tribunal.

- In May 2008, we found no record in clinical notes that legal rights had been explained to a patient who had been admitted under s.2 to one London hospital. The patient had moved wards twice from admission, and this may have been a factor in the failure to meet the legal requirements of s.132. During the meeting with a MHA Commissioner, the patient said he would like to appeal against his detention. As he had not been made aware of his legal rights in time for him to apply to the Tribunal, the Commissioner brought this issue to the attention of the Mental Health Act manager and it was agreed to arrange a managers' hearing as soon possible.

- In June 2008, we met with a Polish-speaking patient detained under s.2 in a London hospital, for whom language barriers appeared to have been a factor in delays in explaining legal rights. The patient had not at that time missed the fourteen-day window for appeals to the Tribunal, and as such we urged the hospital to avoid any further delay in arranging for an interpreter.

2.107 Where a patient has missed the chance to apply him or herself to the Tribunal for reasons such as those set out above, the potential injustice may be addressed by a request that the Secretary of State exercises the powers under s.67 to refer the case for a hearing. As anyone can request that the Secretary of State exercises this power at any time, it is open to Mental Health Act Commissioners to do this directly, and we would expect them to do so if, for any reason, they do not wish to leave this to the hospital managers.

Legal aid and Tribunal representation

2.108 In our last report, we also expressed concern over patients' ability to have their cases considered adequately by the Tribunal, because of changes in arrangements for legal aid payments[225].

2.109 The rates of remuneration to lawyers representing patients at Tribunals was announced by the Legal Services Commission (LSC) in June 2007, to immediate protest from the Mental Health Lawyers Association (MHLA), a body representing the majority of lawyers then practising in the field[226]. We recognise that the LSC strongly contest claims that the new fee system will lead to any reduction in service for patients, but it is a fact that several

---

[225] MHAC (2008) *Risk, Rights, Recovery; Twelfth Biennial Report 2005-2007*, para 4.80 – 4.83.

[226] See, for example, Richard Charlton, 'Impact of legal aid proposals on mental health representation' Administrative Justice & Tribunals Council's *Adjust Newsletter*, Dec 2008. See also response from Crispin Passmore 'Reforming legal aid' *Adjust PDR Special*. http://www.ajtc.gov.uk/

more experienced solicitors have curtailed or withdrawn from undertaking Tribunal cases, particularly for restricted or other long-term patients with complex histories. We appreciate that the LSC is keeping access to services under review; has invited feedback from practitioners; and has stated its willingness, should any problems arise, to take swift action ("including tendering for additional services, or paying supplementary remote travel payments for cases where clients are resident at specific hospitals")[227].

2.110 The Administrative Justice & Tribunals Council (AJTC) Stakeholder Advisory Group, upon which we are represented, has discussed concerns over the withdrawal of some specialist solicitors from Tribunal work, and over concerns that the changes may have led to some deterioration in the standard of representation at Tribunal hearings. In an opinion piece published in the AJTC newsletter, the mental health lawyer Sheila Carrick has written of legal representation in south-west England "hanging by a thread" as a result of a "critically low number of mental health representatives" following retraction in local firms offering representation. The use of out-of-area firms, according to Carrick's report, has been criticised by Mental Health Act Administrators who cite poor communication and changing representation where "service users require a flexible, supportive and recognisable representative to give them confidence in the difficult process of making an appeal and appearing before the Tribunal"[228]. The AJTC aims to continue to monitor the situation carefully[229]. Given the fundamental issues at stake in a Tribunal hearing, we think that these changes should be subject to systematic monitoring, and as such we repeat the call, made in our last report[230], for government to commission and fund an independent review of the effects of the revised fee system, with a particular focus on Tribunal representation.

Outcomes of Tribunal Hearings

2.111 The outcomes of Tribunal hearings which reach decision are set out at figure 40 below. On average, about 14% of all hearing decisions result in some form of discharge, although in some cases this may be deferred until some condition has been met. The data in figure 40 does not include the considerable number of cases that are adjourned to another date. The Tribunal secretariat reported to us that there were 15,089 Tribunal hearings in total during 2007, and 18,099 during 2008. The data below shows, respectively, 9,964 and 7,295 decisions in these years, which suggests that up to one third of hearings may have been adjourned in 2007, rising to a possible 60% in 2008. Although we recognise that Tribunals may be adjourned as a means of deferring the decision for a relatively short period (for example, until a particular part of treatment is completed or some aftercare provision arranged), as we discussed at paragraph 2.101 above, a great many hearings appear to be adjourned for want of sufficient information to make a decision, whether this is the fault of the Tribunal secretariat or the detaining authority. As such this requires further monitoring.

---

[227] Crispin Passmore 'Reforming legal aid' *op cit* above.

[228] Sheila Carrick 'Opinion: Legal representation at MHRTs in South West England hanging by a thread', *Adjust Newsletter, op cit*, Dec 2008. this account was challenged by the LSC.

[229] Penny Letts 'The AJTC's Stakeholder Advisory Group on the Mental Health Review Tribunal' *Adjust Newsletter, op cit*, Dec 2008.

[230] MHAC (2008) *Risk, Rights, Recovery; Twelfth Biennial Report 2005-2007*, rec 29, para 4.83.

Decision of MHRT	2000	2001	2002	2003	2004	2005	2006	2007	2008
Absolute discharge	858	854	744	923	709	784	655	643	535
Delayed discharge	342	334	427	518	317	364	287	298	215
Conditional discharge	39	89	90	141	145	222	195	265	132
Deferred conditional discharge	97	74	101	265	180	217	224	196	85
Total discharge	1,336	1,351	1,362	1,847	1,351	1,587	1,361	1,402	967
No discharge	10,199	10,229	8,637	9,906	10,546	7,935	7,417	7,158	6,328
% of discharges to hearing decisions	12%	12%	14%	16%	11%	17%	16%	16%	13%
Withdrawn applications	---------- n/a ----------					1,843	1,960	2,744	2,448
Discharged by clinician prior to hearing	---------- n/a ----------					4,790	4,629	6,344	5,862

Fig 40: Outcomes of applications to the Tribunal, 2000 – 2008

Data source: Tribunal secretariat

2.112 Figure 40 above also shows, for the years 2005 to 2008, the numbers of withdrawn applications and the number of discharges prior to hearings by the responsible clinician (or responsible medical officer prior to November 2008). This is discussed further at paragraph 2.119. Data for years prior to 2005 was not available.

2.113 In a study of Tribunal hearings and outcomes in Goodmayes Hospital in the period 1997 to 2007, Singh and Moncrieff noted that both the number of detentions and the numbers of appeals to the Tribunal had risen, although appeals were no more likely to be successful at the end of the period than at the start[231]. The number of annual detentions at the hospital rose from 203 in 1996 to 279 in 2006, and the percentage of such detentions that went to appeal rose from 34% to 81% over the period. But the rate of successful appeals (in terms of discharge from detention) remained at 12%. In their discussion of this finding, the authors suggest two possible factors, neither of which need be exclusive of the other. One of these seems to us uncontroversial: patients are more aware of their legal rights now than ten years ago, and advocacy services and nursing practice probably help to encourage patients to exercise those legal rights in making an appeal.

2.114 Singh and Moncrieff's further posited explanation for the unchanging rate of discharge despite increased applications starts with an assumption that there is an "increasingly liberal use of psychiatric detention" today than was evident ten years ago. It is true, of course, that there are more psychiatric detentions. But by "increasingly liberal", the authors appear also to assume that "the threshold for detentions has fallen" and that "the Act is being applied to people who are less severely ill". This could, of course, account for the increase of appeals, but it would also mean that the Act was being applied in "more disputable situations, possibly more often with people who maintain the capacity to understand and challenge its use", which would lead us to expect that the proportion of successful appeals would also increase. To explain why this is not the case, the authors

---

[231] Singh D K & Moncrieff J (2009) 'Trends in Mental Health Review Tribunal and hospital managers' hearings in north-east London 1997-2007'. *Psychiatric Bulletin*, 33(1), January 2009, pp.15-17.

suggest that maybe "the threshold for discharge by appeal hearings has risen, in the same way and possibly for the same reasons that the threshold for detentions has fallen".

2.115   This is an alarming suggestion, and deserves attention. Is it the case that it is increasingly easy to be detained as a psychiatric patient, and increasingly hard to be released from such detention? If so, we should be very concerned, not least because it is at least arguable that the amendments made to the Act in November 2008 have broadened the scope for such detention even further[232], and (although this is perhaps a slightly different matter) the introduction of Supervised Community Treatment has provided a new intermediate stage of coercion akin to 'conditional discharge' for a potentially large number of detainees. Have these extensions of the reach of the Act have been introduced during a period of its increasingly coercive application in the sense suggested by Singh and Moncrieff? In our view, it is likely that the position is more complex than such a reading would suggest.

2.116   As we have remarked in previous reports, and discuss briefly in chapter 1.20 *et seq* above, the rise in the number of detained patients admitted and resident in acute psychiatric facilities must be seen in the context of much broader changes to service provision, including the retraction of inpatient bed numbers. Put crudely, a number of patients who once would have been admitted to hospital informally are now managed through community teams, and hospital admission is reserved for patients at times of acute crises. As such, hospital admission would be more likely to take place under detention, and lead to a relatively short stay, perhaps with multiple admissions over the course of a year. This is not indicative of the threshold for detention being lowered, but rather a rise in the threshold for hospitalisation under any legal status. Indeed, whereas Singh and Moncrieff suggest that wards might be taking in a greater proportion of less severely ill patients under the powers of the Act, our impression is rather that a greater proportion of hospital inpatients on admission wards are very acutely disturbed than was the case a decade or more ago.

2.117   The increased acuity of inpatient admissions under the Act, coupled with an increasing awareness of patients' rights to appeal detention (whether this awareness comes from the patients themselves, or from nursing staff or advocacy workers) could, in our view, be sufficient explanation for Singh and Moncrieff's statistical finding that the rate of discharge has not increased with the number of appeals against detention. It may be that the increase in applications is in part made up of patients who are in more acute stages of their illness, and in past years would either not received help to appeal, or would have been actively discouraged from appealing by staff, and whose appeals are unlikely to succeed.

2.118   Even if this is sufficient explanation, Singh and Moncrieff's concluding comment still highlights a very pertinent issue:

---

[232] See Fennell P (2008) *Mental Health: The New Law.* Jordans, p.69 ('conclusion'), and Bowen, P (2008) *Blackstone's Guide to the Mental Health Act 2007*, Oxford, p. 54 for debates over whether the revised Act extends the criteria for detention.

> The low rate of success of Mental Health Act appeal is not widely publicised. Patients should be informed about this before they embark upon an appeal. We also need to think about whether the system is an adequate check on ... use of psychiatric detention.

This would be a fruitful area for wider debate. Whilst we rather doubt that it would be helpful for any individual considering making an application to the courts to be guided by aggregate rates of success of others, and we recognise that the appeal mechanisms under the Act are necessary components of lawful detention under human rights principles, it seems to us that there *may* be a danger that professionals could urge patients towards the Tribunal when they have no hope of success, and thus deny them opportunities to make such an appeal at a more apposite time. For this reason, it is vital that specialist lawyers are available to advise patients when to apply in the duration of the detention, and when it may be wiser to withdraw an application that has already been made.

2.119 In any case, counting Tribunal decisions to discharge against hearings is a rather crude measure of the success of the utility of the Tribunal system. At the very least, some account must also be taken of withdrawn applications and discharges whilst an application is outstanding. As was shown at figure 40:

- for every three patients who proceeded to a Tribunal hearing and were subject to a Tribunal decision during 2007 and 2008, another patient had withdrawn an application before the hearing; and, similarly,

- for every four patients who proceeded to a Tribunal hearing and were subject to a Tribunal decision in 2007 and 2008, another three patients had already been discharged by their responsible clinician in the period between making an application and the Tribunal hearing date.

Of course, we cannot tell why over 5,000 patients withdrew their applications to the Tribunal over 2007 and 2008, nor do we know why responsible clinicians chose to discharge over 12,000 patients who had applied to the Tribunal over that period. However, the patients who withdrew their applications would have thereby reserved their right to apply again during the same period[233]; the patients who were discharged whilst their application was still pending would probably have had a good chance of a 'successful' appeal. This may suggest that patients are not so poorly advised after all.

2.120 Given that the resettlement of the Tribunal secretariat for England is now complete, and a new computer system is being established in the Leicester office, we believe that it is now appropriate for the Tribunal to address our past recommendations of the collection and publication of data on hearings. This is a matter in which we believe the Care Quality Commission and Healthcare Inspectorate Wales usefully could take an interest.

Recommendation: The Tribunal secretariats should collate and publish data on applications against detention or SCT under the MHA, including appellants' gender, ethnicity and the section of the Act to which they are subject.

---

[233] MHA 1983 ss.66 and 69.

The care and treatment of detained patients in acute hospitals

2.121 The Mental Health Act Commission focuses its funding on visits to detained patients in mental health and learning disability units. It does not undertake routine visits to try to meet with those who are detained by Acute Trusts. Indeed, it is not even clear how many such detentions take place. Only a small number of Acute Trusts complete the Information Centre's 'KP90' statistical return on the use of the Act. In 2000/01 the MHAC obtained statistics from fifteen Acute Trusts on their use of the Act over the year, finding that collectively they had used the Act on 66 occasions (32 times for Section 5(2), 24 for Section 2, and 10 for Section 3).

2.122 In August 2001 we first published our guidance note, *the use of the Mental Health Act 1983 in general hospitals without a psychiatric unit*, last updated in October 2008[234]. We welcome the publication in 2008 of the Academy of Medical Royal Colleges' guidance document *Managing Urgent Mental Health Needs in the Acute Trust*, described as 'a guide by practitioners, for managers and commissioners in England and Wales'[235]. We concur with the Academy in stating that there is an urgent need for national standards to inform the commissioning of mental health services in A&E departments, medical and surgical wards. The guidance concludes that liaison psychiatry teams are best placed to provide multi-disciplinary psychiatry services for such wards.

2.123 Such multi-disciplinary teams should include administrators familiar with the law. Because they will only infrequently operate powers of the 1983 Act, staff in general hospitals should have access to advice and support from a competent Mental Health Act Administrator. Acute Trusts are unlikely to have either appropriately skilled staff to scrutinise statutory documentation relating to detention under the Act, nor the sorts of administrative systems used in psychiatric hospitals to ensure that the duties of a detaining authority are met and the rights of the detained patient are upheld. They have frequently not known how many patients they have detained in the previous year. One Trust which had detained some 25 patients over the year took four months to put together a list and provide the files for MHAC scrutiny.

2.124 From time to time, the MHAC continues to be informed of hospitals where elderly care wards, psychiatric liaison wards, or Clinical Decisions Units are using the Mental Health Act to detain patients. In 2007/08 we made a number of specialist visits, concentrating on scrutinising the paper records of such detentions. These visits reinforced our concern about the use of the Act in the non-psychiatric sector, as we discussed in our previous report[236].

2.125 Acute Trusts have a number of obligations when they detain patients under Mental Health Act powers, which imply the following requirements upon their organisation:

---

[234] Available from www.mhac.org.uk

[235] Academy of Medical Royal Colleges (2008) *Managing Urgent Mental Health Needs in the Acute Trust; a guide by practitioners, for managers and commissioners in England and Wales.*

[236] MHAC (2008) *Risk, Rights, Recovery; Twelfth Biennial Report 2005-2007*, para 4.8 *et seq.*

- They need a system for receiving the documentation and scrutinising it for errors
- They need to have staff trained and capable of understanding and explaining to detained patients their rights in line with the requirements of s.132 of the Mental Health Act
- They need to understand that the requirements of s.58 of the Mental Health Act place extra burdens on staff when dealing with negotiating consent to treatment alongside the extra powers that detention confers.
- They need to have managers to undertake those functions required under the Mental Health Act.

2.126   For Trusts where the numbers are relatively small the most effective way of ensuring that they manage their statutory obligations under the Mental Health Act, and the simplest way to ensure compliance and high quality practice is to make a Service Level Agreement with the local Mental Health Trust to provide the service on their behalf. Such an arrangement is in place, for example, between Surrey & Borders Partnership NHS Foundation Trust and Frimley Park NHS Foundation Trust (contact: Miranda Allen, Mental Health Act Manager).

Responsibility for treatment in acute hospitals under the revised Mental Health Act

2.127   Prior to its amendment in 2008, the 'Responsible Medical Officer' in charge of a detained patient's treatment needed no qualification beyond registration as a medical practitioner. It was therefore possible, if not always very good practice, for that role to be taken by a non-psychiatric specialist in an acute hospital or other establishment. Such a doctor could therefore exercise the powers of granting leave of absence, directing initial or emergency psychiatric treatment, and so on. Under the revised Act, the new role of 'Responsible Clinician' that replaces 'Responsible Medical Officer' can only be taken by a doctor or certain other professionals[237] who are 'approved clinicians', having completed a training course for that purpose. As such, Acute Trusts will need to ensure that those clinicians who might be deemed responsible for the care and treatment of detained patients are provided with Approved Clinician training. In some services it may be impractical to train in-house clinicians in this way, in which case service agreements could arrange to outsource responsibility for the psychiatric care and treatment of any patient detained by the non-psychiatry facility to local mental health services.

2.128   The revision of the 1983 Act has not, however, altered the position whereby any registered medical practitioner may exercise the 'doctor's holding power' under s.5(2), or provide one of the medical recommendations required to support an application for detention under ss.2 or 3.

---

[237] Either social workers, first-level nurses registered to practice mental health or learning disabilities nursing, occupational therapists or psychologists. See *Mental Health 1983 Approved Clinician Directions 2008*, Schedule 1.

> **Recommendation:**
> 1. Acute Trusts which detain patients should complete the KP90 return.
> 2. Acute Trusts which detain patients should formalise Service Level Agreements with their local Mental Health Trust to ensure that they comply with the Mental Health Act.
> 3. An annual report should be made to the Board on the Trust's use of detention under the Mental Health Act.
> 4. Both hospital Boards and commissioning authorities should follow the guidance in Managing Urgent Mental Health Needs in the Acute Trust.
> 5. Acute Trusts which detain patients should arrange 'Approved clinician' training for those staff who might be required to act as Responsible Clinicians, or arrange for such roles to be provided by mental health trusts as part of the SLA.
> 6. Mental Health Trusts should make contact with their local Acute Trusts to ensure that they understand the legal requirements on them.

Police powers to remove mentally disordered persons to a place of safety under section 136

2.129 Section 136 of the Act allows a police officer to remove from a place to which the public has access any person appearing to be mentally disordered and in need of care or control. Such a person may be held at a place of safety for up to 72 hours to enable examination by a doctor and an AMHP and the making of necessary arrangements for further treatment and care.

2.130 Statistics gathered by the Independent Police Complaints Commission for 2005/06 show that the majority of such detentions – 60% – took place at places of safety located in police cells, rather than in health care settings[238]. This is, of course, contrary to the guidance of the Codes of Practice, both in England and Wales. We recognise that additional funding has been provided to some Trusts in England to establish hospital-based places of safety, and welcome this. As we noted in our last report, establishing hospital-based places of safety is yet to be identified as a priority in Wales[239], although in parts of the country there is very poor provision.

2.131 In 2008 the MHAC collaborated, alongside many other organisations, in a multi-agency working group led by the Royal College of Psychiatrists, to revise the College's report 'Standards on the use of s.136 of the Mental Health Act 1983'[240]. We hope that all services involved in the exercise of the powers under this section will obtain a copy and ensure that their policies are informed by its recommendations.

---

[238] Independent Police Complaints Commission (2008) *Police Custody as a "Place of Safety": Examining the use of section 136 of the Mental Health Act 1983.* IPCC research and statistic series: Paper 11. Maria Docking, Kerry Grace and Tom Burke. September 2008.

[239] MHAC (2008) *Risk, Rights, Recovery. Twelfth Biennial Report 2005-2007*, para 5.22 et seq.

[240] Royal College of Psychiatrists *(2008) Standards on the use of Section 136 of the Mental Health Act 1983 (2007)* (version for England): Report of the multi-agency group led by the Royal College of Psychiatrists. College Report CR149. September 2008.

2.132 We also very much welcome the revision to the Act enabling, from the end of April 2008, transfer between places of safety during the 72-hours allowed for assessment. We expect that this will be used, primarily, to avoid unnecessarily long detention in a police cell where alternative accommodation can be obtained. On page 132 we reproduce in full a service-user account, '24 hours in a police cell' which was read out at the launch of the Royal College of Psychiatrists' report in September 2008. This articulates very well why it is necessary to avoid keeping mentally disordered people in police cells wherever possible.

2.133 The following example from an MHAC visit in November 2007 shows how practical requirements of patient care (and, as in this case, responses to untoward events) forced detaining authorities to breach the law before the power to transfer s.136 detainees was introduced:

> On the night prior to the Commissioner's visit a patient had been admitted on a s.136. The patient had been taken to the general hospital at 19.30 hours as there were concerns about his physical well-being. Presumably this was on his way to the designated place of safety, but there was no evidence found that, at this point, the ward was informed of a possible s.136 admission. The patient arrived on the ward at 23.40 he absconded, apparently through a window, and was returned to the ward by the police at 02.40 and at this point it seemed it was agreed that his behaviour could not be managed on the ward. He was taken to the police station as another place of safety. At the time of the MHAC visit he was awaiting assessment at the police station.
>
> *Surrey, November 2007*

2.134 The new power of transfer has not prevented some inappropriately lengthy detentions in police stations rather than hospital-based places of safety, as is shown in the following example. On this visit, we urged the Trust to provide a dedicated place of safety suitable for the needs of people detained with mental illness for all areas that the Trust serves, taking account of both the new Code of Practice and the RCPsych guidance.

> It was very disturbing to hear an account by a patient – a 70 year old lady – of being arrested by the police and taken to the police station. The patient described in detail how she was locked in a cell with a concrete floor and was not given food or drink for some considerable time so that by the time she was given this she had not eaten for over 24 hours. The patient also says that she was not advised of her rights. She was not happy with how the police interacted with her and was made to feel like a criminal. She also described the police van that she was transported to the police station and to the hospital in – very narrow benches and with no lights. This account ties in with an account by another patient that was heard recently on a MHAC visit to an acute ward at a neighbouring hospital. It is possible that the experiences described could amount to a breach of human rights.
>
> *Cambridgeshire, October 2008*

24 hours in a police cell – a service-user's account

Upon arrival you are aware that you are entering into a very secure environment. The last "outside" things you see are high metal gates sliding closed behind you. All doors from here on in are metal, loud and interlocked with the next. At the custody desk, you are stripped of all personal belongings, shoe laces, belts, watches etc. You receive a full external body search.

I received some basic information about the booking-in process, none of which I was in any way in a proper state to absorb. I was given a two-page A4 leaflet explaining my rights and the availability of the [Police and Criminal Evidence Act] "Code of Practice" book. It transpired that none of this information related to someone being sectioned.

The cell was lit, moderately clean and warm. Within the cell was a dirty metal toilet, a dirty metal washing aperture and a bench with a PVC mat. For probably very good reasons, there was no soap, towel or toilet tissue.

Drinking water could be requested via a cell "call" button. Response times varied depending on how busy the staff were and, as I was to discover, on their attitude towards the detainee. Meals were offered but had to be taken in the cell, adjacent to an open toilet. I declined all meals.

There was no bedding, no pillow. You sleep on the PVC mat, sat and stood on by countless others. I used my A4 leaflet as a pillow of sorts to keep my face off the mat.

I had no awareness of time. I had to use the call button to ask what time it was.

The custody officers were not able to advise me of what was going on. It was pretty much a case of "social services are dealing with your case. When we know, you will know". I did not know how long I would be detained for. When 24 hours was up I asked if I could leave and was told that did not apply to me.

The majority of conversations with staff took place through a glass pane of a locked metal door. My call button was switched off after I had kicked the door in frustration.

After 20 hours and several requests I was allowed out into a small square compound for fresh air. I was told that visitors were not permitted in the custody suite, although at the time of my release and transfer my wife was allowed in the cell.

A police station cell, by its very nature has to be a bare, controlled environment, for obvious reasons. As a place of safety for a vulnerable person it offers no comfort, poor communication, little interaction and a sense of extreme solitude.

All in all an extremely unpleasant experience. It provides only a place of safety. The staff are trained to detain people only. I do not have cause or reason to blame them or complain about how I was "processed". They operated the facility in a manner appropriate for its purpose. At the end of the day the agencies concerned provided me with a place of safety, not ideal in many ways, but I am, and will forever be, thankful that it was there.

Although the physical environment was harsh a little discomfort never harmed anyone. The lack of suitably qualified supervising staff was, in my opinion, a very major shortcoming. The sense of extreme solitude would have been lessened if what conversations there were had not taken place through a locked door.

I requested a solicitor at one point but was told that I did not need one and they could not help as I was under the authority of social services.

2.135   We are not complacent over the suitability of all hospital-based places of safety. The hospital in the this example has now de-commissioned the place of safety described here, and provided a new facility:

> I saw a patient 'marooned' in the s.136 room. It is welcome that this room will not be used any more. The patient, who had already been in overnight awaiting assessment, was lying on a bed, in a soulless room, with the door open. This patient spoke Farsi, and had little English. She complained to me about the lack of privacy. For someone in a vulnerable state, this is not a welcome experience of admission into hospital.
>
> *London, April 2007*

2.136 The revised Codes of Practice for England and Wales contain generally useful guidance on the operation of s.136 in a police station, about which we make the following comments:

- Police services in England as well as Wales should take note of the Welsh Code's reassurance (at chapter 7.23) that, consequent to detention under s.136 being counted as an arrest for the purposes of the Police and Criminal Evidence Act (PACE), police are empowered to search the detainee at any place other than a police station, and the custody officer at a police station is entitled to identify what the detainee has in his or her possession. We have heard of a number of instances where nursing staff in hospital-based places of safety have found that the person delivered to them by police has not been searched and has concealed about their person a knife or other potential weapon.

- The advice on powers and duties under PACE contained in the Code of Practice for England may be misinterpreted to lead to the premature release of detainees upon inadequate medical assessment. The Code advises at chapter 10.32 that 'in no case may a patient continue to be detained in a police station under section 136 once a custody officer deems that detention is no longer appropriate.' This is, of course, correct in law, as the custody officer has a statutory duty under PACE to determine who shall or shall not be detained in police custody. However, we doubt that there will be many circumstances in which the custody officer is able to make such a determination, unless he or she has the advice of a suitably qualified medical professional who can determine whether or not the person is suffering from mental disorder. We therefore support the Royal College of Psychiatrists' recommendation that, before reaching a decision that detention is no longer appropriate, the custody officer should first discuss the case with a doctor or an approved mental health professional[241]. Custody officers must keep in mind that the purpose of detention under s.136 of the Mental Health Act is distinct from that behind most other detentions in police custody, in that it to facilitate a professional assessment with a view to making any necessary arrangements for treatment and care. Such arrangements are not limited to further detention under the Mental Health Act.

2.137 In other circumstances we have noted incomplete assessments of s.136 detainees. In the following examples, the informal admission of the patient to hospital may or may not have been appropriate, but it should not, in our view, have taken place without the patient being seen by an Approved Social Worker (Approved Mental Health Professional):

---

[241] *ibid.*, p.33.

Patient X was brought to the hospital by the police on s.136 and assessed by one doctor only who admitted him informally. X was not seen by an ASW at that time. Two days after admission, X was placed on s.5(2) and three days later on s.3, when he was first interviewed by an ASW. This is contrary to the Act and the Code of Practice. Anyone detained under s.136 must be assessed by both a doctor and an ASW (unless the doctor concludes that the person is not mentally disordered), even if the patient is agreeing to informal admission.

London, May 2007

Police brought patient Y to the ward under s.136. The nursing notes record that he was assessed and "admitted" under s.136 at 23.40 on 3/9/07 and that his doctor was informed of the same the next day. An ASW was not contacted until sometime on 4/9/07 and an assessment for s.3 completed on 5/9/07 at 12.00. The Duty Doctor has recorded on the s.136 Receipt Form that Y was assessed at 01.00 on 4/9/07 and agreed to be admitted informally.

London, September 2007

Defining a public place

2.138 In our last report we noted having seen an audit from one London-based social services authority in which 30% of s.136 arrests took place at or just outside the detainee's home[242]. This audit was referred to in another visit during this period:

> I read the most recently produced s.136 audit and was dismayed to note that 30% of arrests under s.136 by police are made at the person's home (or outside) – this is not the spirit of the Mental Health Act and the local police need to urgently review this situation and remind themselves of the law and guidance in relation to the use of this section. Indeed on this visit I found evidence on the file of patient Z. The police had been called to a disturbance inside a dwelling and rather than use other powers available to them had waited until Z stepped outside and arrested her using s.136.

London, May 2007

2.139 We have previously assumed from dicta in the case of *Seal v Chief Constable of South Wales Police* [2007][243] that, in asking or otherwise contriving to have a person 'step outside' so as to arrest that person in a public place, the police would be likely to render the arrest unlawful. A case in this reporting period, *McMillan v Crown Prosecution Service* [2008][244] suggests that, in certain circumstances, the courts might find otherwise. In this case, the court accepted that an officer acted lawfully when he arrested a person for being drunk and disorderly in a public place when he had physically escorted that person out of her own garden. This judgment has been highlighted by the mental health lawyer David Hewitt as a possible precedent in any similar challenge to s.136 detention, although we note the qualified circumstances in which the court accepted the lawfulness of the action:

> the High Court noted that at first instance, the magistrates found that the officer had been attempting to reach a negotiated conclusion that would have been in the woman's best interests, and that they rejected the suggestion that he did what he did so as to justify an arrest for an offence that could only be committed in a public place. The High Court said that

---

[242] MHAC (2008) *Risk, Rights, Recovery. Twelfth Biennial Report 2005-2007*, para 4.63.

[243] *Seal v Chief Constable of South Wales Police* [2007] UKHL 31.

[244] *McMillan v Crown Prosecution Service* [2008] EWHC (Admin) 1457.

he could properly be said to have acted in conformity with generally acceptable standards of conduct.[245]

Information about the use of s.136

2.140 Detention under s.136 remains the sole example of a civil power to detain a patient that requires no completion of a statutory form. We note that both the Royal College of Psychiatrists and the Independent Police Complaints Authority have backed our earlier call for the collation of reliable statistics on the use of s.136. The IPCC report suggests that there is very high overrepresentation of people from Black and Minority Ethnic groups in those subjected to s.136. We therefore repeat our recommendation on data collection, and its rationale, as first published in 2006 in our Eleventh Biennial report[246]:

> **Data on the use of police powers under the Mental Health Act**
>
> The lack of data on the use of police powers in dealing with mentally disordered persons prevents adequate assessment of service needs and trends in the use of the Act. The lack of centrally collated and audited data with regard to ethnic monitoring cannot but set an obstacle to fulfilment of police authority duties under the Race Relations (Amendment) Act 2000. We accept that some elements of recording the use of Mental Health Act holding powers could fall to social services and NHS authorities, and urge social service and police authorities to co-ordinate efforts to address the lack of monitoring in this area. However, not all uses of sections 135 or 136 can be captured by data collections through other agencies, as on occasion the use of a power may be terminated before their involvement.
>
> **Recommendation:** We recommend that ACPO should consider issuing guidance on data collection and audit of the use of police powers under the Mental Health Act.

Aftercare under s.117

2.141 Under s.117, health and local authorities have a combined duty to assess the requirement for, and then provide, after-care services for patients upon their discharge from detention under sections 3, 37, 45A, 47 or 48. This includes patients on leave of absence under s.17 and patients discharged into Supervised Community Treatment.

2.142 In 2002 the House of Lords clarified in the *Stennett* case[247] that there was no provision within s.117 that allows authorities to charge for services provided. We outlined this case in detail in our Tenth Biennial Report[248]. It was noted by their Lordships that the judgment created different funding rules for detained patient and informal patients upon discharge from hospital. For patients being discharged from detention in hospital (where they had

---

[245] Hewitt, D (2008) 'Court accepts acting in best interests' *Jane's Police Review*, 14 November 2008.

[246] MHAC (2006) *In Place of Fear? Eleventh Biennial Report 2003-2005*, fig 79, page 285.

[247] *R v Manchester City Council, ex p. Stennett and two other actions* [2002] UKHL 34.

[248] MHAC (2003) *Placed Amongst Strangers: Tenth Biennial Report 2001-2003*, para 9.62 *et seq.*

been detained under one of the sections mentioned above) authorities have no legal right to charge for aftercare services deemed to be required, including domiciliary care, whereas (subject to means-testing) authorities can and must charge patients in receipt of domiciliary care upon discharge from informal admission to hospital. In his judgment Lord Steyn rejected as 'simplistic' the suggestion that this created an anomaly between patients, although, as we discussed in our Eleventh Biennial Report, other commentators disagree[249].

2.143   In its proposals for the Mental Health Bill 2004, Government indicated that it intended to limit the period for which charging could not be applied to patients subject to s.117 to a period of six weeks. We wrote of our concern at this proposal in our Eleventh Report[250], and are pleased to record that it was one of the measures to fall when the draft Bill was replaced by the Mental Health (Amendment) Bill. As such, the changes to the Act effective from November 2008 do not alter the effect of the *Stennett* judgment and aftercare under s.117 must remain free at the point of delivery.

2.144   In this reporting period, some local authorities have continued to question their inability to charge for aftercare services provided under s.117 of the Act. We were able to intervene in one case, having been alerted to it by the local MIND group, where a local authority had indicated to care managers and some patients that, in order to avoid discrimination between those patients subject to s.117 who are living in their own homes and those who are subject to s.117 service living in residential care, patients in the latter situation would be expected to pay (subject to means-testing) for rent, food, lighting and heating costs. At our intervention the local authority took further legal advice and withdrew the proposal.

2.145   The Local Government Ombudsman gave a ruling on a case in December 2007 that is helpful in establishing criteria for the discharge of patients from s.117 aftercare[251]. A local council and health authority had established a policy whereby the question to be addressed in reviews of patients' continued need for such aftercare services was "whether the services were necessary to prevent further admission to hospital i.e. if the s.117 were discharged, would the person be eligible for services under other legislation". The "pointers to determine whether to discharge s.117" in this policy included, in the case of persons with dementia, whether that person was settled in a nursing home and so unlikely to be readmitted to a hospital, and the policy suggested that the longer the time elapsed between the hospital stay and the review, the more likely it was that s.117 could be discharged. This policy was applied in the case of Mrs Fletcher, who had been detained under s.3 in July 2003 before being moved to a nursing home in September of that year. In a review in February 2006, the multi-disciplinary team, guided by the local policy, agreed that Mrs Fletcher no longer met the criteria for s.117 aftercare as her mental state was stable, she was accepting of her residential place and the care she needed, and she

---

[249] MHAC (2006) *In Place of Fear? Eleventh Biennial Report 2003-2005*, para 4.132.

[250] *ibid.*, para 4.134 *et seq.*

[251] *Local Government Ombudsman Report on an investigation into complaint no 06/B/16774 against Bath and North East Somerset Council.* 12 December 2007.

was not at risk of readmission to hospital. The Ombudsman found this reasoning to be maladministration:

> Whether or not a person is 'settled in a nursing or residential home' is an irrelevant consideration. The key question must be, would removal of this person (settled or not) from this nursing or residential home mean that she is at risk of readmission. If the answer is yes then the person cannot be discharged from aftercare.
>
> These defective criteria fatally flawed the decision that Mrs Fletcher was no longer at risk of readmission to hospital because it ignored the vital contribution of the residential home to her s.117 aftercare.
>
> The practical effect of the council's criteria is to remove long-term nursing or residential home accommodation from the definition of aftercare services. If that were to remain the position, the council's criteria would allow it to avoid its public responsibilities under s.117 of the Mental Health Act 1983.[252]

2.146 The most significant practical effect of a decision that a person's continued residence in a nursing home can no longer be considered to be part of their s.117 aftercare would be that the person would become liable, subject to means-testing, to contribute towards its cost. In the case under review, Mrs Fletcher had not suffered any financial loss as a result of the flawed decision that her residential care was no longer being provided under s.117 of the Act, as the council had agreed to continue to meet her fees whilst the appeal against the decision was considered by the Ombudsman. The Ombudsman ordered the council to review other cases determined using its flawed criteria to ensure that no other person had been wrongfully caused a financial loss.

2.147 It may therefore be very difficult to establish any point at which s.117 ceases to apply in the case of patients who are discharged from detention under s.3 or relevant Part 3 powers into long-term residential, especially where such patients suffer from the illness is either progressive, or where the nature of the illness is unchanging over time.

---

[252] *ibid.*, paras 18-20.

3

Consent to treatment

Consent to treatment safeguards

3.1 A major innovation of the Mental Health Act 1983 – and indeed one important impetus behind its introduction – was to regulate not only detention in hospital, but also the medical treatment of the detained patient's mental disorder[253]. The system of second opinions was introduced under the 1983 Act, and given to the MHAC to administer. The initial arrangement from September 1983 relied upon 20 consultant psychiatrist members of the MHAC to undertake visits, although this soon proved inadequate and in January 1984 a 'panel' of 70 consultants was created from whom second opinion appointments were made. As we go to press in March 2009, that panel consisted of 110 consultants, although recruitment continues. The number of visits undertaken has increased at a much greater rate. For the first four years of the Commission there was an average of 183 requests for second opinions in any month[254]. In February 2009 there were 1,383 second opinion referrals in total, the highest number ever received since the Act was implemented 26 years ago. Second opinion requests over the lifetime of the MHAC are shown at figure 41 below.

---

[253] Under the Act today (i.e. as revised by the Mental Health Act 2007), detained patients who do not or cannot consent to medication for mental disorder must, after an initial three months of such treatment, receive a visit from a SOAD who must consider whether it is appropriate to continue that treatment and certify accordingly. Detained patients who are incapable of giving consent to treatment with ECT cannot be given such treatment without a similar certification that the treatment is appropriate. Neither of these procedural safeguards is necessary if the treatment with medication or ECT is an emergency. The consent to treatment procedures for patients subject to Supervised Community Treatment is described at paragraph 2.75 & 3.64 below.

[254] Data from MHAC first and second Biennial Reports (see figure 41 above). The first report counted 4,032 second opinion requests in the 22 months from September 1983 to the end of June 1985. The second report counted 4,369 requests. The first step-change increase in numbers of second opinion requests was recorded in the third report, and the rise has continued ever since.

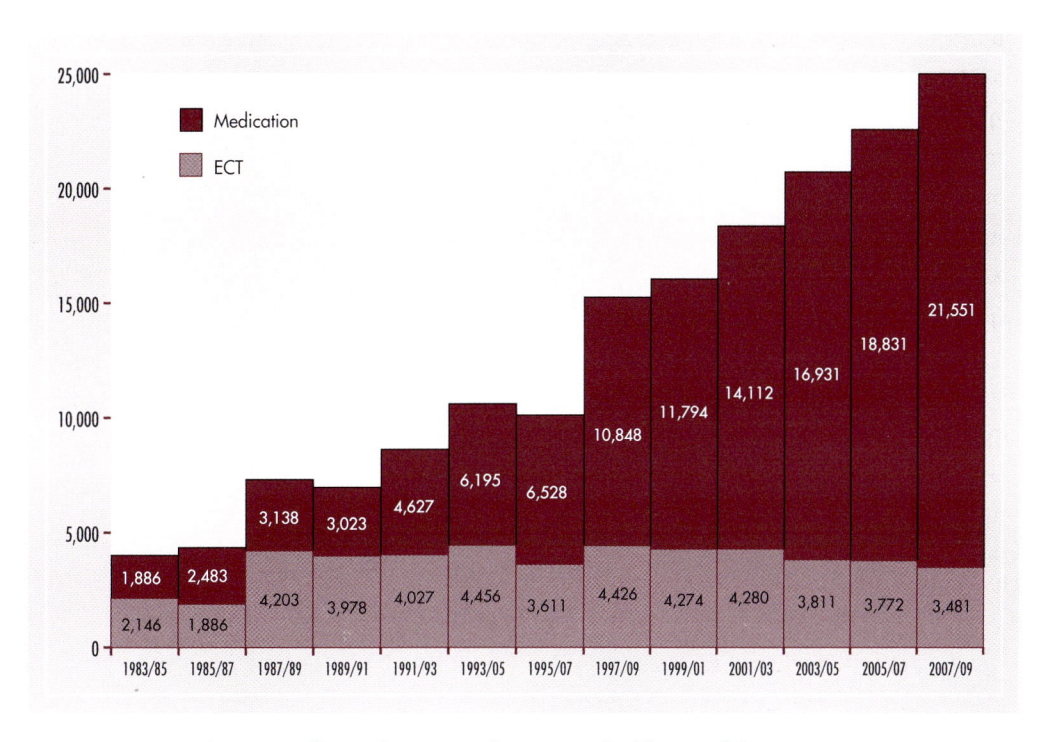

Figure 41: Second opinions for medication and ECT over the lifetime of the MHAC

Data source: MHAC [255]

The reality of consent

3.2   The majority of detained patients never receive a second opinion. This is because the safeguard of a SOAD visit after the first three months of treatment is conditional upon responsible clinicians' recognition that the patient does not, or cannot, give consent to the treatments being prescribed. We have no doubt that there are many patients who, throughout their detention, are erroneously described as giving consent to their treatment, mainly because they have been asked to agree to treatment without it being explained sufficiently to allow for informed consent, but also because of unrecognised mental incapacity or refusal of consent.

3.3   As we observed in our last report[256], the position is rather different for patients subject to Supervised Community Treatment, who all receive a SOAD visit after a certain period, whether they consent or not to treatment. We discuss this further at paragraph 3.66.

3.4   The safeguard provided for many detained patients who do receive a SOAD visit can itself be relatively fragile or transitory:

- As discussed at paragraph 3.38 below, a patient who is refusing certain treatments that have been certified by a SOAD may subsequently consent to other treatments and have these certified concurrently by the clinician in charge of the treatment. As a result, SOADs may find it difficult to establish an upper limit of preparations or dosages although part of the treatment is being administered without consent.

---

[255] Some data will be missing for 2007/09 as not all requests received in March 2009 had entered onto the MHAC database as this report went to print. Data from Nov 2008 includes 1,290 patients on SCT.

[256] MHAC (2008) *Risk, Rights, Recovery; Twelfth Biennial Report 2005-2007*, para 6.23 *et seq.*

- Any SOAD certificate stating a patient to be incapable of consent to a particular treatment is only valid – or should only be valid – insofar as the patient continues to be incapable of consent[257]. A patient who regains capacity during the course of the treatment with medication authorised whilst they were incapable of consent should, in law, be asked if they will now consent to the treatment and, should they decline to do so, be provided with a fresh SOAD visit to consider its certification in the face of a refusal of consent. If the treatment in such a situation is ECT, the patient who regains capacity but refuses consent to further treatment could only be treated under emergency powers under the revised Act (see paragraph 3.50 *et seq* below). But, of course, the patient's regained capacity must be recognised by the clinician in charge of the treatment for it to have such an effect on the perceived authority for ongoing treatment.

3.5 The safeguards available to detained patients are therefore conditional upon detaining authorities' good practice in the area of consent to treatment. The General Medical Council's guidance on consent was reissued in May 2008[258], and includes core principles that emphasise the concept of partnership between patient and doctor in making treatment decisions. Detained patients should not be excluded from the application of such principles. For detained patients, the Codes of Practice also require that patients' consent should be sought before any treatment is given (even if that treatment may be given without consent), with the patient's consent or refusal recorded in their notes alongside the treating clinicians' assessment of the patients capacity to consent[259]. The Codes also note that the compulsory administration of treatment is

- *invariably* an infringement of Article 8 of the European Convention on Human Rights (respect for family and private life, in this case encompassing integrity of the person), and as such that infringement must be proportionate and in accordance with the law; and

- *potentially* a breach of Article 3 (as inhuman treatment) if its effect on the patient reaches a certain level of severity, but not if the treatment can be convincingly shown to be a therapeutic necessity from the point of view of established principles of medicine [260].

Good consent to treatment practice is integral to ensuring proportionality; acting in accordance with the law; and in determining therapeutic necessity. As such it is a safeguard necessary for practitioners as well as patients.

3.6 It is important that such good practice is evident across the whole care pathway of patients, and we hope that this is something that the Care Quality Commission and Healthcare Improvement Wales will be able to focus upon, using their wide legal remit concerning psychiatric care and its registration powers.

---

[257] MHA 1983, ss.60(1C), 60(1D).

[258] General Medical Council (2008) *Consent: patients and doctors making decisions together.*

[259] MHA *Code of Practice for England, para* 23.37; *Code of Practice for Wales*, paras 16.38 – 16.40.

[260] *ibid.*, above, paras 23.40 & 16.42 respectively.

> I often hear patients arguing about wrong doses and being given the wrong tablet etc. Obviously some patients do not consent to their medication but it is not until a SOAD or a followed-up complaint happens that this is discovered. You are usually told that a medication has been chosen for you rather than having a chat with clinical staff on options and side effects of a drug. I see very few SOADs called in to the ward. I do see patients upset at medication time though. …on the question of being deemed consenting, refusing or incapable, on my ward because of bad communication it really makes no difference, sadly.
>
> *Mark Gray, SURP member*

Recording consent and capacity

3.7 Responsible Clinicians are not always recording the consent and capacity of patients during the first three months of treatment, when certification for medication is not required, nor is there always a clear recording of a discussion with the patient in relation to treatment plans during that time. Where insufficient attention is paid to this aspect of patients' treatment during the initial three-month period, it is common to find that questionable assumptions about patients' capacity or consent continue once certification of treatment is required, leading to dubious certification of consent on Forms T2 (CO2 in Wales) and questionably lawful treatment.

3.8 Good recording of capacity and consent to treatment reviews can also provide a useful tool for risk assessment, especially in terms of future treatment compliance, as this allows consideration to be based upon records of patients' past attitudes and concerns rather than simple legal facts about the authority to treat. Predictors are less arbitrary when based upon a chronology of past behaviour and understanding. For example, it is relevant to risk assessment that a patient consents to treatment because of an acceptance that it will prevent relapse, rather than on a reluctant realisation that the treatment will be given anyway. For this reason, clinicians should document consent discussions that lie behind their completion of Forms T2/CO2 denoting patients' consent, as well as documenting discussions where a patient does not or cannot consent.

3.9 Hospital managers and medical directors should particularly ensure that, in the case of any patient for whom the presumption of mental capacity to take treatment decisions is in doubt, a full mental capacity assessment is carried out and kept under review. The following example of poor practice, from a visit to a London hospital in the summer of 2008, shows the importance of capacity and consent assessments, not only for patients' benefit and protection, but as a part of the clinical governance of hospital procedures:

> There was little evidence in the notes of assessments of capacity in terms of consent to treatment. Medication was listed in the notes but nothing about the person's capacity or not to give consent. Although the MHA generally overrides the Capacity Act in terms of treatment for mental disorder, the Code of Practice states that consent should always be sought and in the absence of consent an assessment/record of the patients' capacity made. Please can the Trust confirm what guidance is being given to medical staff in this area to ensure compliance with the Code of Practice. Some examples from the notes seen:

Patient 1: Medication was prescribed and given twice whilst the patient was under s.136. This section is not covered by Part 4 of the Act, so treatment can only be given if the patient consents or if they lack capacity through the powers of the Mental Capacity Act 2005. No assessment of capacity was recorded in the notes but the patient was described as 'unwell, elated, formal though disorder, partial insight'.

Patient 2: The patient was described in notes as having paranoid delusions, visual hallucinations and no insight – but on the same day was written up for medication with no assessment of her capacity to consent.

Patient 3: On three occasions the patient was described as 'compliant' to medication but in the same assessment was described as having 'no insight to her illness'. The term 'compliant' provides no indication of whether a person has capacity or not and is not evidence of an assessment of capacity.

3.10 Mental Health Act Commission visits often reveal a mismatch between what the patient tells us and that patient's purported consent status. Where this is the case, we request that the patient's documented consent is reviewed by the clinician in charge of treatment. A number of 'consenting' patients that we encounter state that they do not want to receive their antipsychotic medication by depot injection, sometimes because of pain resulting from the injection itself, or else because of the perceived humiliation of being injected, whether this is because of the physical act or the implication that the patient cannot be 'trusted' to comply with oral medication.

3.11 It may be that some patients are reluctant to voice such concerns to members of the clinical team, for fear of being considered non-compliant and of hindering their eventual discharge from coercion, whereas MHA Commissioners provide a safer space for such discussions. As such, it may be that patients may be providing new information about their view on the day of our visit to them. In some cases, however, we have reason to doubt that the patient has previously been given either sufficient explanation of the treatment, or a sufficient hearing regarding the patient's own concerns and wishes.

3.12 In one example, two patients on a ward in eastern England were both deemed to be consenting to their medication, but upon meeting with them we found that neither was aware that they were being administered antipsychotic drugs in doses over the BNF limit. In both cases the high-dose was a result of two antipsychotic drugs given in combination: one patient was not even aware that he was taking two different preparations.

3.13 A report from one London visit in summer 2007 stated that one patient

… had a Form 38 [equivalent to Forms T2 or CO2] on his file and medicine chart stating that he was consenting to Clozapine, but when I interviewed him, he made it quite clear that he strongly objected to it due to the bad side effects he was experiencing. He said that he had made this clear to the doctors but they would not listen to him and said that if he doesn't take his medication then he cannot go out on leave.

3.14 In Suffolk during the summer of 2007 we reported that

During interview some patients who were being treated under a Form 38 appeared to have minimal knowledge and understanding of the medication they were taking. A particularly concerning example was patient *D* who could only name one of the drugs he was taking and initially said he did not know why he was taking them and then said "to get off illicit drugs". He was unaware that he was consenting to "up to 3 anti-psychotics drugs" as specified on his Form 38 and which additionally could in total, using the percentage method, exceed BNF maximum doses. *D* was described in his notes as "very thought disordered" and during interview was difficult to engage due to poor concentration.

3.15 In another example, a patient was (rather unusually) regretful of having been taken off a depot injection upon transfer from a high to a medium security hospital. The cause of his regret was the prescription of four different oral antipsychotic drugs in place of the depot injection, and the fact that he felt 'drugged up' under the new treatment plan. However, the patient stressed to us that he was eager not to be seen as defying the wishes of his responsible clinician and could certainly have been described as 'compliant'. It was far less certain that he could be described as having given consent within the meaning of the Act and its Codes of Practice, although the statutory documentation recorded him to be consenting. We have noted before the relative high levels of 'consent' in patients admitted from the criminal justice system in contrast to patients detained under the 'civil' powers of Part 2 of the Act [261]. As shown at figure 42 below, there continues to be significantly higher rates of Part 3 'consenting patients' than other detainees, and (as shown at figure 43) restricted patients have the highest rates of consent overall. In many cases such consent may be genuine and given for very good reason, but the example above shows a need for caution on the part of clinicians not to confuse compliance with consent. It would probably be helpful to the therapeutic relationship of all involved if such patients were reassured that raising concerns about particular treatments will not be assumed to indicate lack of insight, or withdrawal of cooperation with the clinical team, but should be a part of the care planning process. Effective risk assessment and care planning will be hampered where patients are afraid to reveal their true feelings about their treatment.

	(n=15,902)	s.2 number	s.2 % of legal category	s.3 number	s.3 % of legal category	Part III number	Part III % of legal category	Total number	Total % of legal category
consent status	consenting	654	56.8	5,492	56.7	3,558	70.1	9,704	61.0
	capable but refusingng	161	14.0	1,324	13.7	550	10.8	2,035	12.8
	incapable of consent	298	25.9	2,648	27.4	794	15.7	3,740	23.5
	not known	38	33.0	215	2.2	170	3.4	423	2.7
all consent status in legal category		1,151	100	9,679	100	5,072	100	15,902	100

Figure 42: Consent status of all patients on the 31 March 2008, all hospitals, England and Wales

Source: *Count Me In* 2008

---

[261] See MHAC (2008) *Risk, Rights, Recovery; Twelfth Biennial Report 2005-2007*, figs 28, 38 & 75, and accompanying commentary.

(n=4,983[10])		s.37		s.37/41		s.47		s.47/49		s.48		s.48/49		CPIA[263]	
		number	% of legal category	number	% of legal category	number	% of legal category	number	% of legal category	number	% of legal category	number	% of legal category	number	% of legal category
consent status	consenting	783	67.9	1,997	71.4	65	63.7	467	74.8	11	50.0	122	65.6	56	55.4
	capable but refusing	125	10.8	317	11.3	10	9.8	58	9.4	4	18.2	17	9.1	10	9.9
	incapable of consent	223	19.3	402	14.4	21	20.6	66	10.6	6	27.3	31	16.7	32	31.7
	not known	22	1.9	79	2.8	6	5.9	33	5.3	1	4.5	16	8.6	3	3.0
all consent status in legal category		1,153	100	2,795	100	102	100	624	100	22	100	186	100	101	100

Figure 43: Consent status of patients detained under the main Part 3 powers on the 31 March 2008, all hospitals, England and Wales

Source: *Count Me In 2008*

3.16 To be able to give genuine consent to a treatment, patients should have had the opportunity to understand its nature, purpose and likely effects, including the likelihood of its success and any alternative treatment options. We frequently meet with patients who appear to have little understanding of their medication, where the cause would seem to be paucity of information rather than mental incapacity. In some instances, clinical teams appear to assume that 'too much' information about drugs will undermine treatment compliance, although there is no evidence that this is the case[264] and this belief, in the context of iatrogenic sexual dysfunction, has been described as a having 'mythical status' without evidential basis[265]. Where patients are not provided with adequate information about their treatment, genuine consent, and any opportunity to develop treatment models of partnership between patients and doctors as required under GMC guidance, will remain an unachievable ideal. As indicated at paragraph 3.24 below, pharmacists can play a useful role in enabling patients to understand and discuss medication and side-effects, but it is important that members of the day-to-day clinical team and those responsible for giving the treatment in question engage with patients on these issues as well. For some practitioners, this may require enhanced technical knowledge about medication[266], and a willingness to discuss areas of patient experience, (such as weight gain [267], sexual

---

[262] Excludes 89 patients detained under Part 3 powers other than those listed in the table.

[263] Excludes patients detained subsequent to a finding under the Criminal Procedure (Insanity) Acts after March 2005, who would be detained under s.37. (For the changes to the CPIA in 2005, see MHAC (2006) *In Place of Fear? Eleventh Biennial Report 2003-5*, para 5.25 et seq).

[264] Gray R et al (2002) 'From compliance to concordance: a review of the literature on interventions to enhance compliance with antipsychotic medication' *Journal of Psychiatric and Mental Health Nursing* 9, 277-284.

[265] Higgins A et al (2006) 'Iatrogenic sexual dysfunction and the protective withholding of information: in whose best interest?' *Journal of Psychiatric and Mental Health Nursing* 13, 437- 446;

[266] Jones M & Jones A (2007) 'Delivering the choice agenda as a framework to manage adverse events: a mental health nurse perspective on prescribing psychiatric medication.' *Journal of Psychiatric and Mental Health Nursing* 14, 418-423.

[267] Up to 80% of individuals treated with antipsychotics suffer from medication-induced weight gain. See Alvarez-Jiminez M et al (2008) 'Non-pharmacological management of antipsychotic-induced weight gain: systematic review and meta-analysis of randomised controlled trials' *British Journal of Psychiatry* 193, 101-107. See also para 1.89 above.

functioning[268] or hyperprolactinaemia[269]) that are often pushed aside when the powers of the Mental Health Act have been used to address acute mental disorder.

The reach of the statutory second opinion system: second opinions for consenting patients and the three month rule

3.17   The MHAC owed its very existence to a political compromise over the nature of the second opinion system during the Mental Health (Amendment) Act 1982[270]. The subsequent expansion of the second opinion system (most notably in its extension as a safeguard for consenting SCT patients) was the result of further political compromises aimed at meeting concerns of lobbying groups over later amendments to the 1983 Act[271]. We doubt that the current system would have been created from a blank slate. We accept, of course, that providing every consenting *detained* patient with a second opinion would involve a huge amount of resources (not least in doctors' time), which might be better used elsewhere[272]. Indeed, as there are indications that the numbers of patients subject to SCT may greatly exceed government forecasts (see paragraph 2.74), similar concern for the effective use of resources may suggest a reconsideration of providing second opinions to consenting SCT patients. It could be, for example, that resources would be more effectively channelled into reducing the 'three month period' before second opinions are required upon the first administration of medication to detained patients, as we discussed in our previous report[273]. It is seems quite possible that the absence of an external safeguard in relation to the imposition of medication without consent for such a period will, at some future point, be found incompatible with human rights obligations[274], given modern medical practice and pharmacopoeia.

---

[268] Many antipsychotic and antidepressant drugs have effects on sexual function, most commonly arousal problems. See Higgins A *et al* (2006) and Jones M & Jones A (2007) *op cit* above.

[269] i.e. the heightened production of prolactin which can lead to breast enlargement and milk production in males and females. This is a potential side-effect of some atypical antipsychotic drugs. See Jones M & Jones A (2007) *op cit* above for an account of treatment negotiation (or 'concordance therapy') with a patient who was experiencing this and other side effects.

[270] See Cavadino M (1995) 'Quasi-government: the case of the Mental Health Act Commission' *International Journal of Public Sector Management*, Vol 8 No 7, pp. 56-62. The compromise was over the nature of the 'second opinion' required under the Act: MIND lobbied for a fully multi-disciplinary process, but the Royal College of Psychiatrists argued that the final decision must rest with a psychiatrist. The compromise was that the SOAD (a doctor) would be appointed by the multi-disciplinary MHAC, and the creation of 'statutory consultees', one of whom just be neither doctor nor nurse.

[271] As such, the fact that second opinions are not provided for conditionally discharged patients is in part the result of the powers of conditional discharge predate the 1983 Act (and therefore the SOAD system), and in part because no political lobby has yet called for this. It may be that the precedent of SCT second opinions instigates such a call. For both SCT and conditionally discharged patients, legal authority for medical treatment is fundamentally a question of common law (if the patient consents) or the Mental Capacity Act (if the patient cannot consent due to incapacity). Only for SCT patients is there an additional legal requirement of certification by a SOAD.

[272] For example, it was suggested in our First Biennial Report (p.12) that the second opinion system might be extended to incapacitated patients receiving treatment for mental disorder in hospital on an informal basis. This too, of course, would have significant resource implications.

[273] MHAC (2008) *Risk, Rights, Recovery; Twelfth Biennial Report 2005-2007*, para 6.27 – 6.31, recommendation 33.

[274] Especially ECHR Article 8: see para 3.5 above.

Advance decisions

3.18 The Mental Health Act recognises the authority of advance decisions directly, in that;

- treatment with ECT cannot be given in conflict with an advance refusal of consent (except under emergency powers, of which see paragraph 3.56 *et seq* below)[275]; and

- treatment with medication cannot be given to a patient subject to supervised community treatment where it would be in conflict with an advance refusal of consent, unless that patient is recalled to hospital[276].

3.19 Those operating the powers of the Act should also follow the guidance of the MHA Codes of Practice, which require practitioners to try to comply with the patient's wishes as expressed in an advance decision wherever possible, even if they may lawfully override it using the powers of the Act[277].

3.20 Hospital managers must therefore ensure that systems are in place to recognise and flag up to staff any advanced decision made by a patient. Such systems must have a broad reach, to extend across hospital and community-based services. Such systems are not in evidence across all services, and patients may be treated unlawfully as a result. For example, during a visit to a London hospital in the summer of 2008, we noted a solicitor's letter regarding an advance decision in one detained patient's records, but no details of that advance decision in the notes. Neither staff nor the MHA administration were aware of the advance decision's existence.

3.21 It seems likely that many patients' statements of preference or dislike regarding their treatment are not recognised as constituting advance decisions by medical professionals. There may, indeed, be situations when it is not clear whether or not a refusal to consent to treatment constitutes an advance decision to continue such refusal after any future loss of mental capacity: this may be a particular problem with patients who have fluctuating capacity, especially where the treatment in question is ECT. But we feel that most such difficulties could be resolved at an individual level through attentive listening to and open discussion with the patient concerned.

3.22 Adherence to the advice of the Code of Practice should help instil a better cultural understanding of advance decisions across services. Staff should be expected to inform patients with capacity to make decisions that they could make advance decisions, and of course the statutory advocacy services should be used to help patients express their wishes. Bisson *et al* have published easy to follow care pathways to empower individuals who may lose capacity to make advance decisions and/or confer powers of attorney.[278] The Codes of Practice rightly underline that setting out statements of advance wishes can be a helpful therapeutic tool, promoting collaboration and trust between patients and

---

[275] MHA s.58A(95).

[276] MHA s.64D(6).

[277] MHA *Code of Practice for England*, para 17.8; *Code of Practice for Wales* para 15.5.

[278] Bisson J I, Hampton V, Rosser A & Holm S (2009) 'Developing a care pathway for advance decisions and powers of attorney: qualitative study' *British Journal of Psychiatry* 194, 55-61.

professionals[279]: indeed research discussed in our last report suggests that, where such statements take the form of crisis plans, they may reduce the incidence of Mental Health Act detentions [280].

Access to psychological treatment

3.23   Many patients tell us that they wish to access psychological treatments, and consider that access to 'talking therapy' could lessen their need for psychiatric medication. In many cases this perception is undoubtedly correct. Professionals have described to us that they may well follow Department of Health[281] and NICE[282] guidance and refer people with depressive disorders for psychological therapies, but the waiting lists are such that they are unlikely to be able to benefit whilst they are inpatients. Indeed, it may be that many patients so referred do not take up 'talking therapy' opportunities at all, as these only become available after discharge when the immediate crisis is past and the patient feels relatively well. We recognise that the government wishes to increase access to psychological therapies, although there may be a danger that such increased access focuses too exclusively on community-based services and primary care, so that detention in hospital actually becomes a bar to access.

> The manager did agree that there was a need for psychotherapy in the hospital, but that the budget would not deliver this.
>
> *Gillian Brightmore, SURP member*

Safety and the administration of medication

3.24   We welcome the work of the Care Services Improvement Partnership during this period in evaluating medicines management schemes[283]. We hope that medicines management will be given a priority across the acute sector and all mental health services. In particular we hope that services will ensure that:

- Resources are available to fund clinical pharmacy services as part of routine patient care, including using all inpatient admissions as an opportunity for a pharmacist-led medicines review;

- Admissions are used as an opportunity to provide access to face-to-face and written information about medication, and for patients to discuss concerns about medication and side-effects as an integral part of the application of Care Programme Approach principles to their treatment planning and overall care;

---

[279] *MHA Code of Practice for England*, Chapter 17.4; *Code of Practice for Wales* 15.7.

[280] MHAC (2008) *Risk, Rights, Recovery; Twelfth Biennial Report 2005-2007*, para 4.25 *et seq*. See King's College London (2007) *Towards Mental Health; Health Service and Population Research at the Institute of Psychiatry* Number 2, 2007, p.11: *Can crisis plans reduce coercion?*

[281] Department of Health (2001) *Treatment Choice in Psychological Therapies and Counselling: evidence based clinical practice guideline.*

[282] National Institute for Clinical Excellence (2004) *Depression: management of depression in primary and secondary care – NICE guidance.*

[283] South Staffordshire and Shropshire Healthcare NHS Foundation Trust & CSIP (2008) *Evaluation of Medicines Management Schemes in Acute Adult and Acute Older Age Mental Health Wards, Final Report*, Dr Eleanor Bradley, Cathy Riley & Diane Thompson.

- Detained patients have rapid and assured access to medication when given periods of leave from the ward, and

- A tiered approach towards patients' self-administration of medication is adopted, with the aim of allowing all detained patients an opportunity to self-administer medication prior to discharge. We recognise that for some patients self-administration of medication may not be practicable, but these should be considered as exceptions to a general assumption in favour of self-administration as a therapeutic goal.

3.25 We are pleased to see some examples of good practice in medicines management. In one independent hospital in the north-west of England, a pharmacist reviews all detained patients' treatment authorised on Forms T2 or T3 at six week intervals. No errors of unauthorised administration of medication were found on our most recent visit to this hospital.

3.26 It is important that hospitals' arrangements with their pharmacy services are sufficiently flexible to serve the needs of patients and staff. On a visit to one Lancashire hospital in spring 2007, staff complained that it was difficult to get emergency and *ad-hoc* medication, due to the opening hours of the pharmacy. The pharmacy also required 24 hours notice to provide medication to patients going on leave. This had led, in some cases, to patients being unable to access leave as it had been granted, due to delays in receiving their medication. We suggested that the managers review pharmacy arrangements to ensure that the pharmacy is not causing unnecessary delays (or preventing) patients from accessing s.17 leave.

Electronic records and medication management

3.27 We are pleased to note that the *RiO* web-based electronic care record system[284] will include facility for the electronic prescription of medication. As a part of the prescription process, *RiO* will check the detention status of the patient, whether the three-month rule applies, and whether the medication is being prescribed lawfully. If it is not, a warning will appear on the screen. In order to allow for emergencies, it is still possible to prescribe, and a standard report can be run regularly within the Trust to audit such treatments.

The operation of the second opinion service

3.28 As discussed at paragraph 3.1 above, the MHAC arranged an average of less than 200 second opinions each month in the first four years of its existence. Demand for second opinions has increased five-fold since that time, and the MHAC received an average of over 1,000 requests every month in this reporting period. The average monthly requests over the last five years are shown at figure 44 below.

---

[284] For a description of the system see www.e-health-insider.com/comment_and_analysis/369/its_name_is_rio.

	Med	ECT	Med & ECT	Total
2004/05	679	148	7	833
2005/06	759	160	9	928
2006/07	810	154	6	970
2007/08	845	144	10	996
2008/09	865	142	9	1,017

Fig 44: Average monthly number of second opinion requests by type of treatment, 2004/05 to 2007/08

Source: MHAC data

3.29   Over the winter of 2008/09 MHAC administrators struggled to meet this demand, especially in relation to requests for second opinions for SCT patients, and some services encountered significant delays in obtaining the services of a Second Opinion Appointed Doctor. We very much regret this. As this report is being prepared, are undertaking a number of measures designed to address this problem, including putting in additional staff resources. The difficulties are not only caused by the rise of numbers of second opinion requests: requests for visits to SCT patients are taking more time to both allocate and complete, and the number of "no shows" is higher than would happen in hospital, using up additional SOAD time in repeat visits. We are still actively recruiting SOADs to respond to the increase in demand for second opinions, and wrote to all Chief Executives and Medical Directors in summer 2008 and March 2009 seeking their support in encouraging experienced Consultant Psychiatrists to apply to join the panel. We have been pleased with the positive response received from many Trusts, which has generated a number of new applications, but at the time that this report was in preparation we still needed more appointments to the panel to meet the growing numbers of referrals.

Second opinions to consider treatment with medication: patient characteristics

3.30   Figure 45 below shows that male detained patients account for about 63% of second opinion requests involving medication in this reporting period. This proportion is unchanged from that noted in our last two reports.

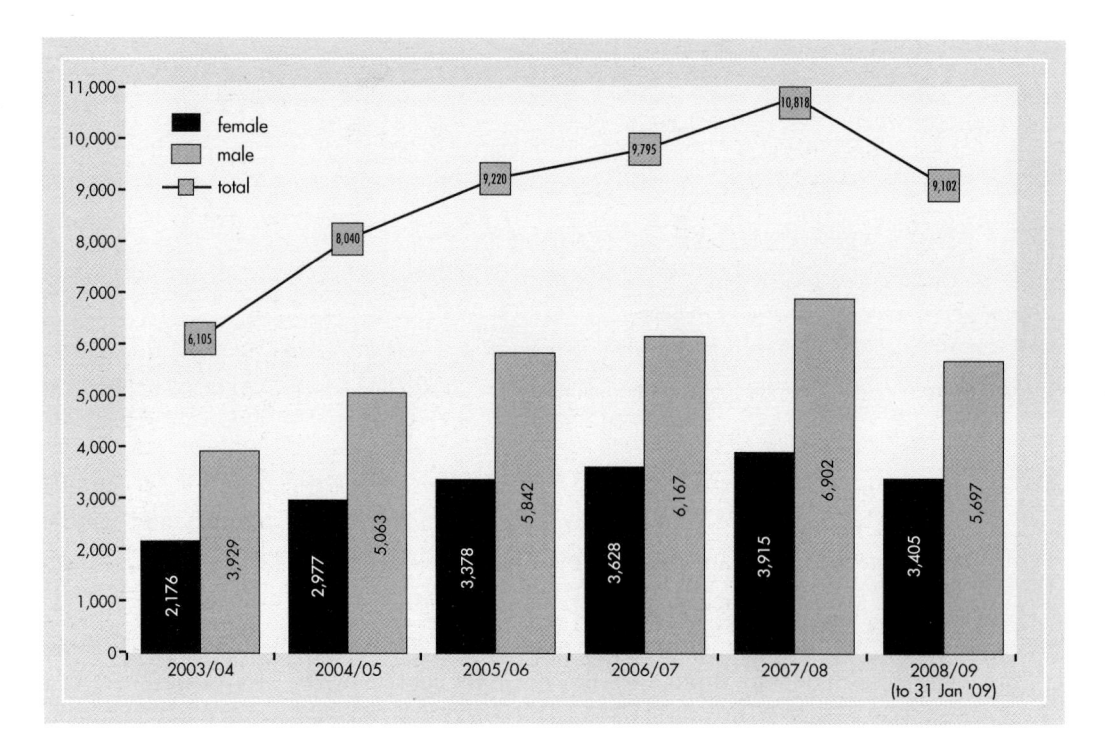

Fig 45: Second opinion requests for medication by patient gender, detained patients, 2003/04 – 2007/08

Source: MHAC data

3.31 By contrast, there has been a marked rise in the number and proportion of patients from this group who are deemed to lack capacity to consent to treatment over the six years shown at figure 46 below. For the first four years of this data, the average percentage of incapable patients was 53%, although it was slowly rising from year to year. In this reporting period the average percentage of incapable detained patients amongst all requests for second opinions for medication is 63%. We do not know why this should be the case, but possible factors could include rising acuity amongst detained patients, or improved clinical practice in assessing and recognising incapacity. If the latter, this may be due to Mental Capacity Act training undertaken consequent to that Act's implementation in 2007.

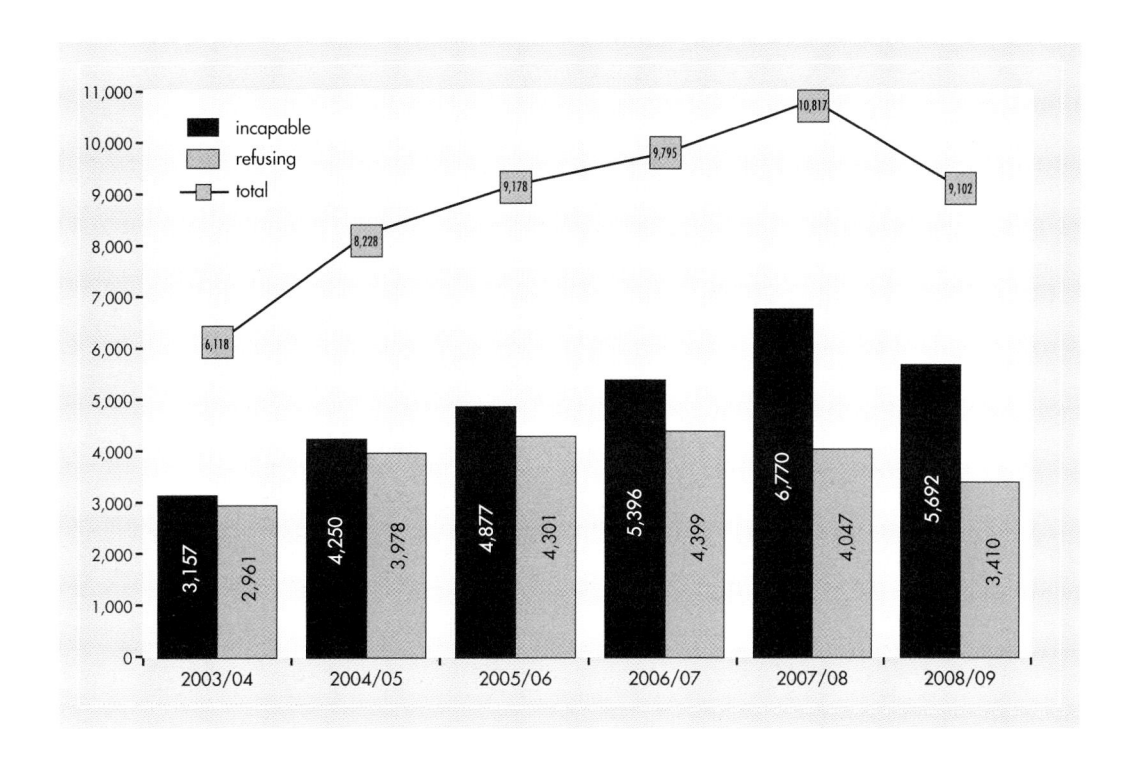

Fig 46: Second opinion requests for medication by capacity status, detained patients, 2003/04 – 2007/08

Source: MHAC data

3.32   Figure 47 below shows the age range of patients referred for a second opinion regarding medication in this reporting period, whilst figure 48 shows this data with the White British ethnic group excluded. The differences in age profile between the two sets of data is not great, although (as might be expected), the Black and Minority Ethnic group taken as a whole is marginally younger[285]. More dramatic differences would be apparent for certain individual BME groups.

---

[285]   i.e. 12% of referrals are for patients under 25 years in both sets of data; patients aged 25-34 account for 27% of the BME group and 22% of the total group; ages 35-44 for 26% BME and 23% total; 45-54 for 18% of both BME and total; 55-64 for 8% of BME group and 11% total; over 65s for 9% BME and 14% total.

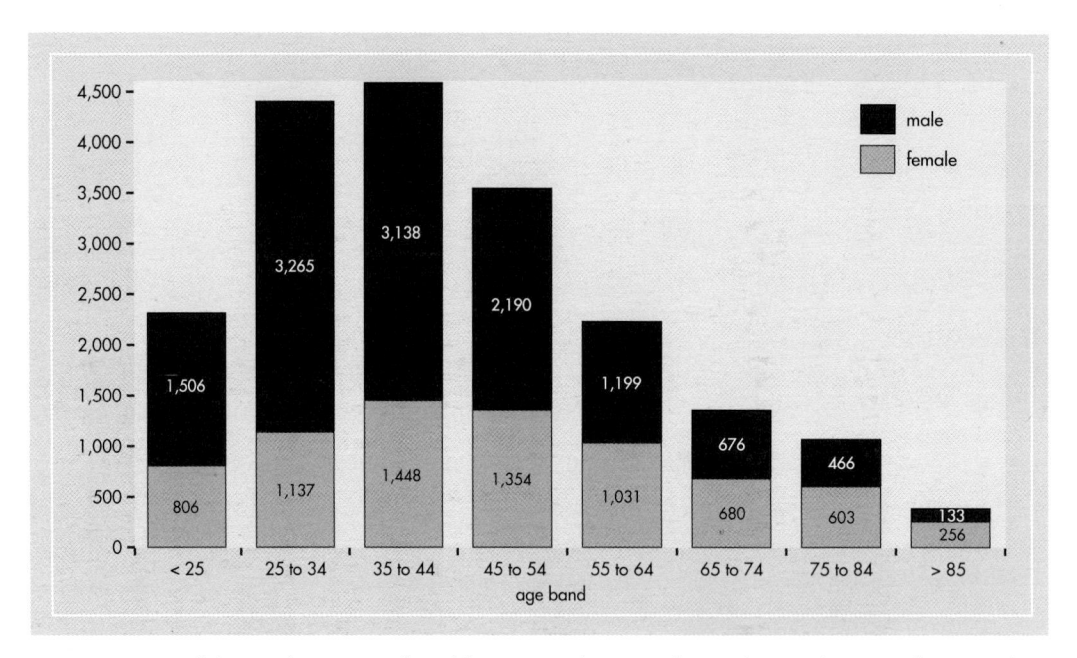

Fig 47: Age of detained patients referred for a second opinion for medication between the 1 April 07 and 31 January 09

Source: MHAC data

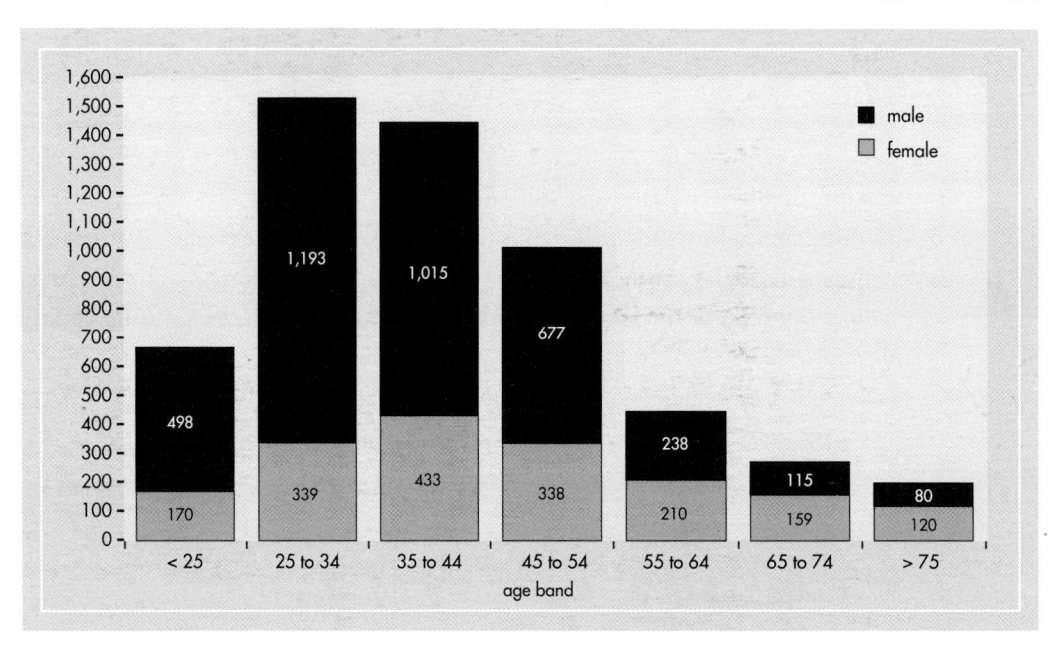

Fig 48: Age of patients referred for a second opinion for medication (excluding White British group and missing data)[286] between 1 April 2003 and 31 January 2009

Source: MHAC data

3.33 Figure 49 below shows the ethnic groups represented in figure 48, giving numbers and the percentage of the data set at figure 48 that such numbers represent. This shows, for example, that just over one-quarter of all patients in the data set at figure 48 are from the Black Caribbean group.

---

[286] White British group = 13,515 (5,252 female); Ethnicity not stated = 813 (298 female).

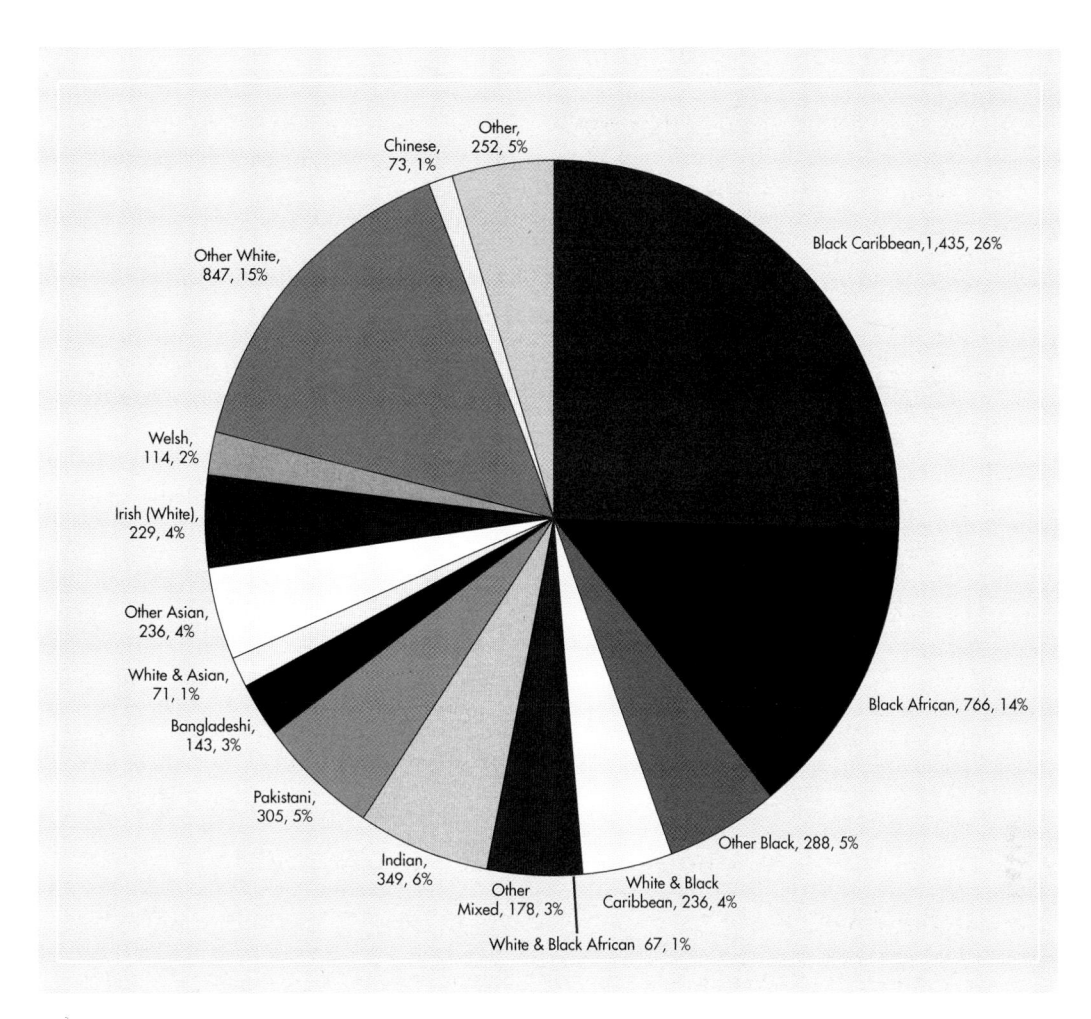

Fig 49: Composition of data shown at Fig 48 by category of Black and Minority Ethnic Group

Source: MHAC data

3.34 If, however, we compare the numbers of certain BME groups against the total data set in figure 47, we can see that Black groups, taken as a whole[287], comprise roughly 14% of all second opinion requests. This is proportionate to the percentage of patients from such groups represented in the detained population as a whole (see figure 10). Taken individually, two groups in particular have higher representation in the second opinion data than in the detention data[288]: Black Caribbean patients represent 6.5% of all detained patients, but 7.2% of all second opinions; and Black African patients 3.3% of all detained patients, but 3.9% of all second opinions. Similar differences were noted in our last report.[289] We do not assume significance in these relatively small differences, although factors accounting for them, if they are significant, could be the age profile of these patient groups or their average length of stay in hospital, or even factors relating to assessment of risk, capacity or likely compliance with medication.

---

[287] i.e. Black Caribbean, Black African, Black other, White & Black Caribbean, White & Black African.

[288] The other BME groups with slightly higher percentages of second opinions to detained population are 'other mixed' and Bangladeshi (only 0.1% higher) and Indian (0.4% higher).

[289] MHAC (2008) *Risk, Rights, Recovery; Twelfth Biennial Report 2005-2007*, para 3.77.

The effect of second opinion visits

3.35 In his study of 1,009 second opinions between December 1991 and August 1992, Fennell reported less than 1% (7) resulting in significant changes to the treatment plan, and 6% (60) resulting in slight changes[290]. Fennell's examination of the sixty 'slight changes' revealed that only eleven (eight drug-related and three for ECT) had limited the original proposal by the patient's doctor: in 13 cases the second opinion visit resulted in a more permissive authority to treat than had been sought, and in 35 cases the 'slight change' made no substantive difference to the parameters of the treatment authorised[291]. Fennell's finding the 'slight change' does not necessarily equate with a restriction of the parameters of treatment from that sought is important, and no doubt continues to be relevant today.

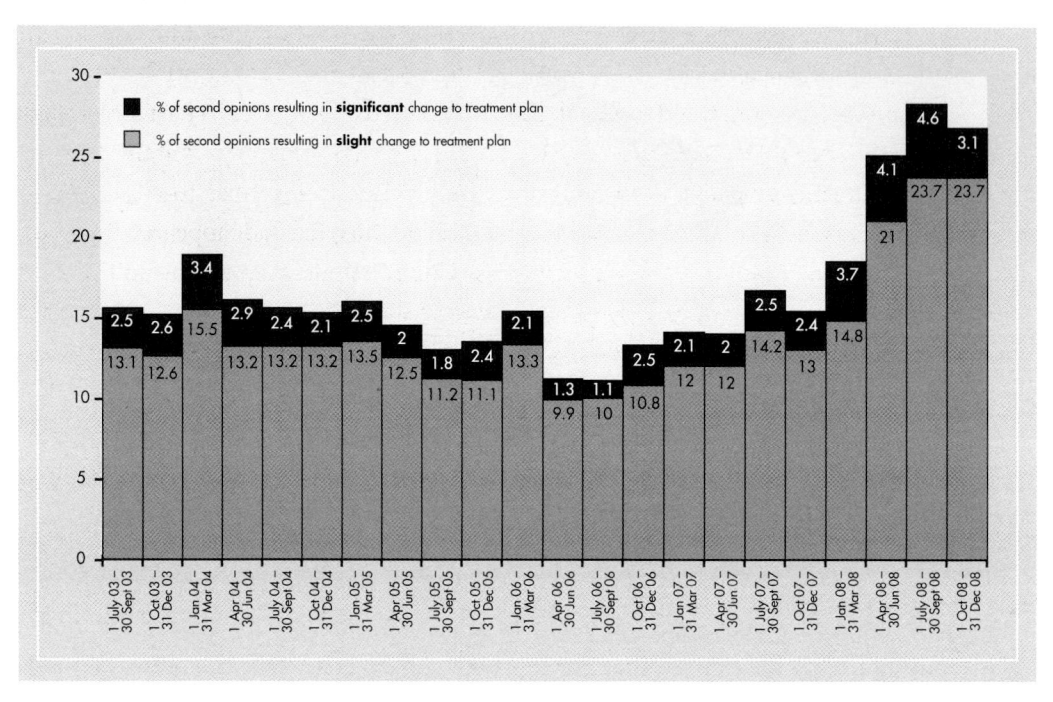

Fig 50: Percentages of second opinions resulting in slight or significant change to the patient's treatment plan, July 2003 – December 2008

Source: MHAC data

3.36 By 1997, the MHAC was able to report that 15% of all second opinion visits over the previous two years had led to some change to the proposed treatment plan[292]. Until recently, this proportion of changes resulting from second opinions remained roughly the same[293]. As can be seen from figure 50 above, 2008 saw a significant rise in the number of changes made as a result of SOAD visits. In the nine months from April to the end of December

---

[290] Fennell, P (1996) *Treatment without consent; law, psychiatry and the treatment of mentally disordered people since 1845.* Routledge, p. 208. As with the recent data given above the occasions where the SOAD refused to certify any treatment at all (4% of all second opinions in Fennell's study) are not counted in the categories of significant or slight change to the treatment plan.

[291] *Ibid.*, p.211.

[292] MHAC (1997) *Seventh Biennial Report 1995-1997*, para 5.2.4, p.106.

[293] As shown at fig 50. For data prior to 2003, see MHAC (1999) *Eighth Biennial Report 1997-1999*, para 6.33, p.178; MHAC (2003) *Placed Among Strangers: Tenth Biennial Report 2001-2003*, Fig 27, p.154, where between 13 and 15 per cent changes were reported.

2008, the percentage of changes increased to an average of 27%. We cannot tell from this data what was the nature of such changes, and so this would be a useful area for further monitoring and analysis by the Care Quality Commission and Healthcare Inspectorate Wales when they take over the administration of the second opinion service.

High-dose medication

3.37 During our visits in this reporting period we have been promulgating the Royal College of Psychiatrists' *Consensus statement on high-dosage antipsychotic medication and polypharmacy*[294], having issued guidance to MHA Commissioners on the consensus statement and its application to MHAC monitoring in 2006[295]. Some hospitals have implemented the Consensus statement's recommendations very effectively, introducing standard checklists and forms to ensure that high-dose medication is recognised and appropriate health-checks and monitoring provided as a result. In September 2008, for example, we commended Camlet Lodge (Barnet, Enfield and Haringey Mental Health NHS Trust) for developing systems of reviewing statutory consent forms, and for monitoring all patients on high-dose medication, in response to comments from our previous visit. In other cases, even in late 2008, hospital staff appeared to be unaware of the document and its content and MHA Commissioners left a copy on the ward visited. Other hospitals showed signs of management-level action (such as having standard forms available for use) that was not being translated into daily practice. In some wards we found that pharmacists had attached forms for recording health-checks to the records of patients receiving high-dose antipsychotic medication, but such forms had remained entirely uncompleted by other clinical staff. In such cases we requested assurances that basic health checks as recommended in the guidance had been carried out.

Concurrent certification of consent and absence of consent in detained patients

3.38 For a number of years the MHAC has discouraged the certification of a patient's consent for some aspects of his or her treatment with medication alongside concurrent certification of that patient's refusal of other aspects of that treatment. We have argued that it would be better for the treatment with medication to be considered as a plan of treatment which the patient may accept or reject in total. Such an approach has been criticised in Richard Jones' *Mental Health Act Manual*[296], and we acknowledge that these criticisms are based upon a defensible legal opinion. It is not, therefore, possible for the MHAC to take a position that concurrent forms must never be used, and as such we have been faced with the difficulty of preserving the protective function of the SOAD in setting limits to treatments that, at least in part, will be given in the face of patients' capacitous refusal of consent.

---

[294] Royal College of Psychiatrists (2006) *Revised consensus statement on high-dosage antipsychotic medication.* RCPsych Council Report 138.

[295] MHAC *Guidance for Commissioners: The RCPsych consensus statement on high-dose antipsychotic medication.* Issued October 2006, revised October 2008.

[296] Jones R (2008) *Mental Health Act Manual*, eleventh edition, para 1-667.

3.39 In the first three months of treatment of any detained patient, when no SOAD certificate is required, it is, of course, the sole responsibility of the approved clinician in charge of the treatment by medication to determine the patient's capacity, and to determine whether or not the patient consents if capable to do so, even though treatment may be given without formality in the absence of consent during that time. As a consequence, the approved clinician in charge of prescribing medication will know what the patient's capacity and consent is – indeed that clinician must know this to decide whether SOAD certification is needed at the end of the three month period, or whether the clinician him or herself can certify on Form T2[297] that the patient gives capacitous consent to all their medication.

3.40 It follows from this that, should the approved clinician in charge of prescribing medication decide that the patient gives capacitous consent to some medications but not to others, there can be no reason why he or she should not authorise those treatments for which consent is given on Form T2.

3.41 However, the MHAC expects that a SOAD would be bound to take a view as to whether certified consent offered for certain medications is still valid at the time of the SOAD visit. If the patient continues to consent to a part of the treatment in the SOAD's view, then we suggest that the SOAD should issue a new certificate T2 whilst certifying treatment without consent on Form T3 (indicating on each form that it to run concurrently with the other). If the SOAD chooses to leave extant a Form T2 issued by the clinician in charge of the patient's treatment, then he or she should ensure that it is clearly stated on the Form T3 that they do issue that it is to run concurrently with the earlier form.

3.42 In the majority of cases, if not all, we believe that the second opinion visit should establish the limits of treatment. We therefore suggest that SOADs may indicate that both Forms T2 and T3 must be deemed to have been withdrawn if a fresh T2 is issued later to cover an altered treatment plan. In this way a SOAD can ensure that the issue of a new T2 by the approved clinician in charge of the treatment triggers a further SOAD visit. That visit should reconsider the authority for treatment without consent in the light of the revised treatment to which the patient consents. However, it will be for the SOAD in question to decide whether this safeguard is necessary. It may be that a SOAD will be prepared to issue a Form T3 that is not interdependent with a concurrent Form T2, so that the approved clinician in charge of treatment has a free hand to certify in addition any treatments to which the patient gives capacitated consent.

---

[297] i.e. form CO2 in Wales. To avoid over-complexity in the following discussion, we refer to forms by their English titles (i.e. with a prefix 'T'). In Wales, the title should be read as though the prefix was 'CO'.

Emergency powers and medication

3.43 Figure 51 shows an apparent rise in the number of uses of emergency powers to give medication for mental disorder to detained patients without the safeguard of a second opinion. Whilst some of the rise towards the end of 2008 is undoubtedly as a result of delays in arranging second opinions caused by administrative problems within the MHAC itself (see paragraph 3.29 above), this cannot account for the rise in 2007. We hope soon to return to a position where the administration of second opinions is rarely the cause of the use of emergency powers, so that effective monitoring of possible other causes is possible.

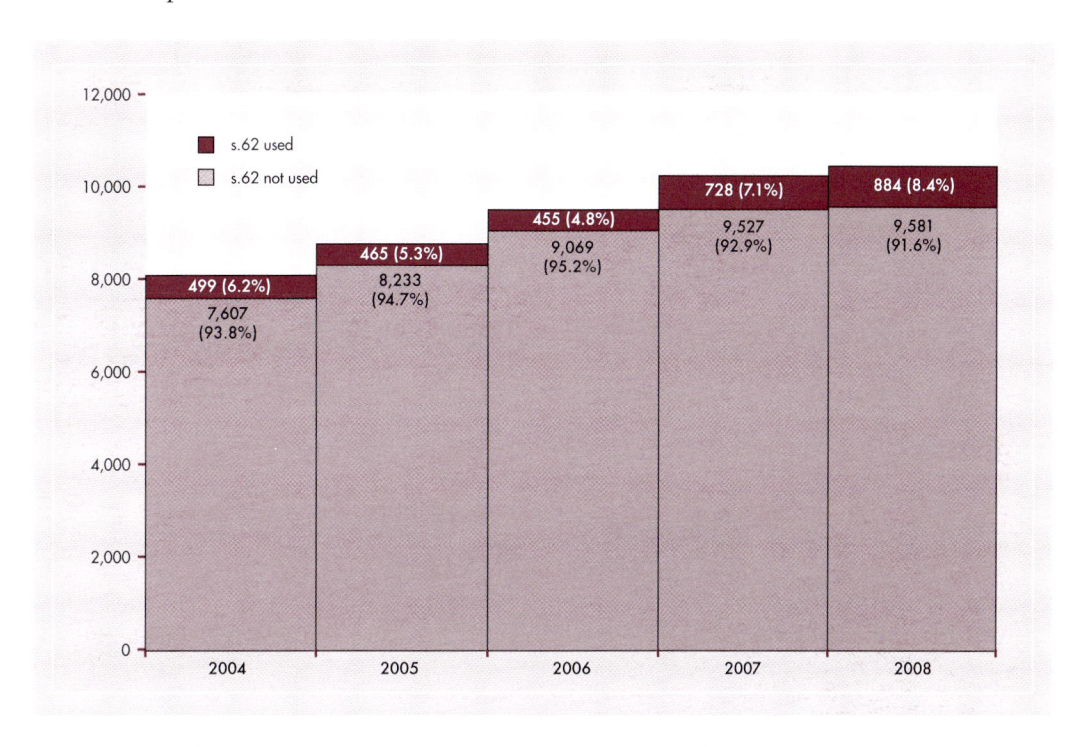

Fig 51: Use of emergency treatment powers (s.62) prior to second opinion visits for medication, by calendar year, 2004 to 2008

Source: MHAC data

Electro-convulsive therapy

3.44 The number of requests for electro-convulsive therapy (ECT) over the last six financial years is shown at figure 52. It is immediately notable that approximately twice as any women than men were referred for second opinions (see paragraph 3.48 below for discussion). The number of requests in each month in 2008/09 is shown at figure 53.

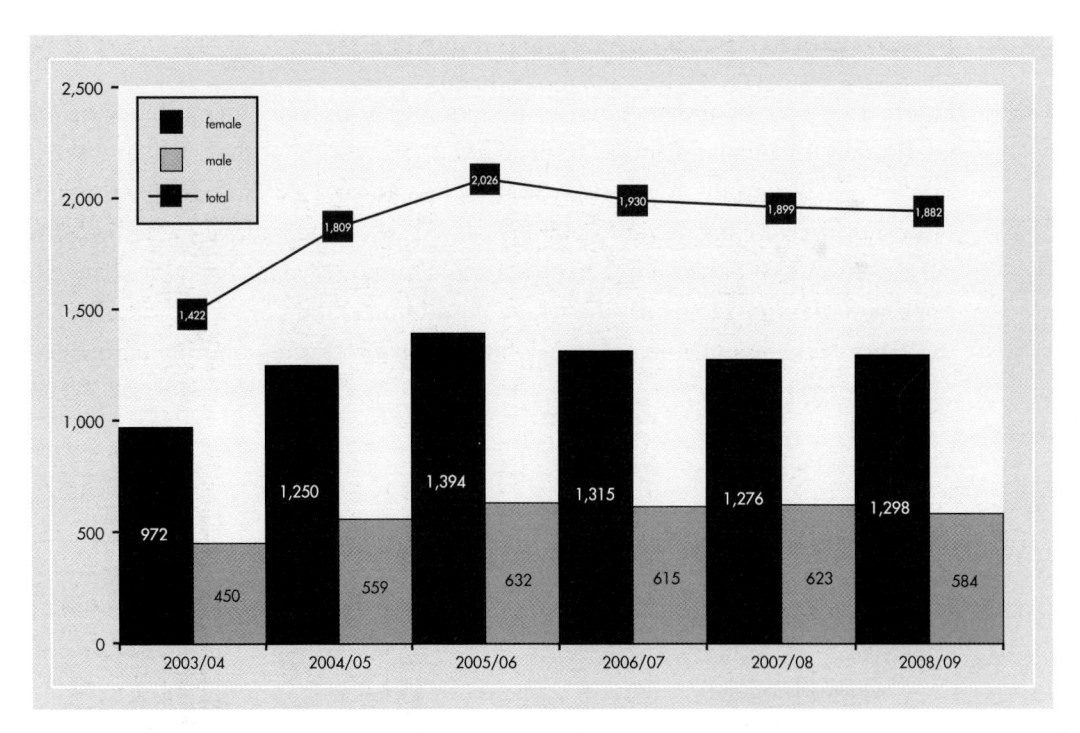

Fig 52: Second opinion requests for ECT by patient gender, 2003/04 to 2008/09

Source: MHAC data

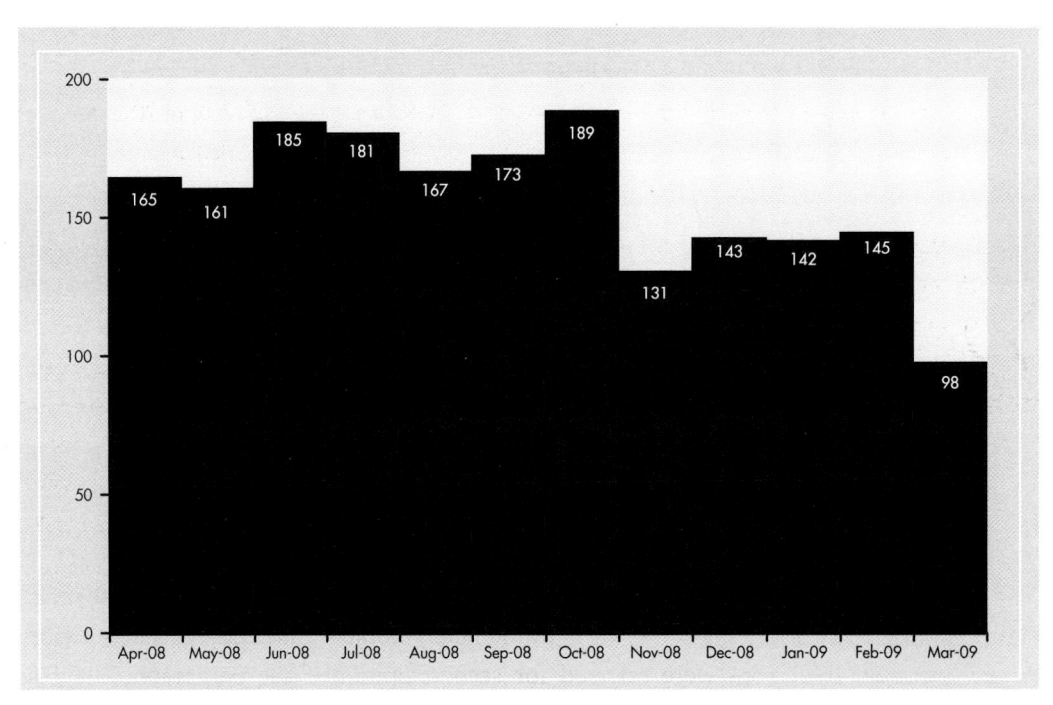

Fig 53: Second opinion requests for ECT, April 2008 to March 2009

Source: MHAC data

3.45 The data at figure 53 shows a marked fall in numbers of ECT requests from November 2008 (although it is likely that the total for March 2009 is slightly incomplete). This fall coincided with the change in the Act regarding ECT and capacitated refusal discussed at paragraph 3.50 below. There was a monthly average of 132 second opinion requests for ECT in the first five months of the operation of the revised Act, compared to a monthly average of 175 requests in the preceding months of that financial year.

3.46 The outcome of second opinion visits to consider ECT treatment in this reporting period, up to November 2008, is shown at figure 54 below.

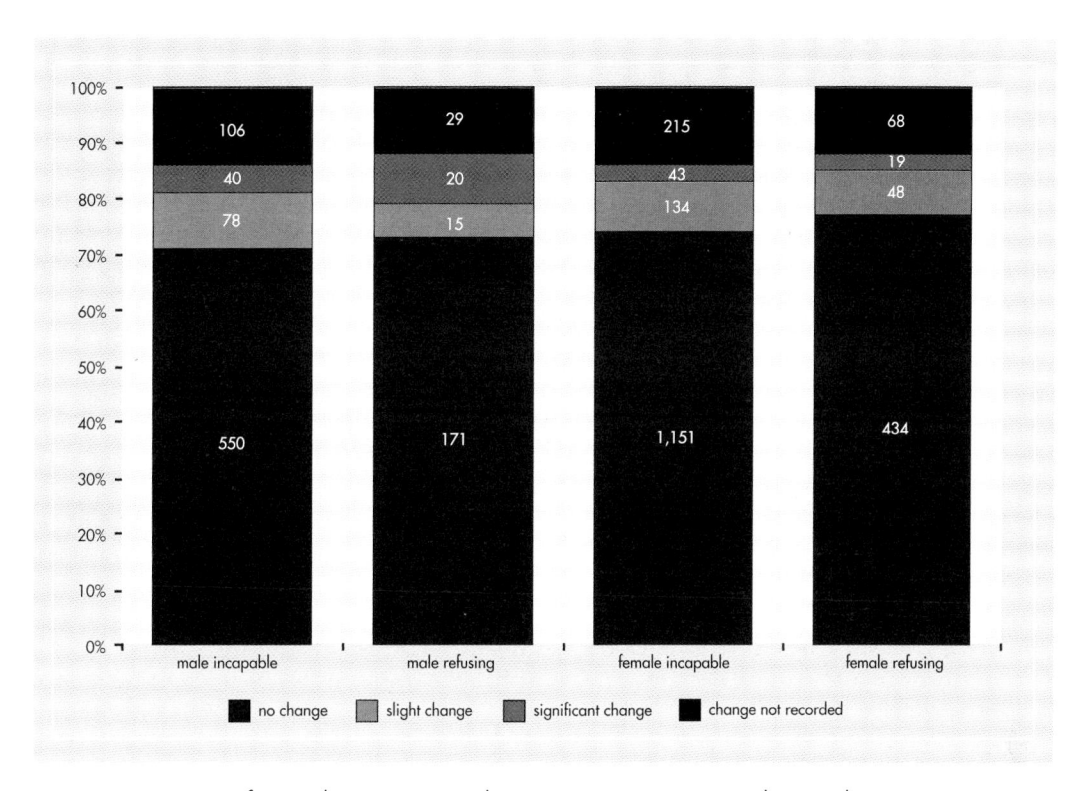

Fig 54: Outcome of second opinion visits where ECT treatment proposed, 1 April 2007 to 2 November 2008, by gender and reported capacity/consent status reported upon request

Source: MHAC data

3.47 The data at Figure 54 is incomplete, the outcome being absent in roughly thirteen per cent of returns. However, such data as we have suggests that male patients were, generally speaking, twice as likely to have treatment plans involving ECT significantly changed as female patients, with the difference most marked in capacitated patients who refuse consent[298]. A 'significant' change relating to an ECT treatment plan is likely to denote, in some cases at least, a refusal to authorise the treatment at all (although we cannot assume that some lesser alteration was not deemed 'significant' by the SOAD completing his or her report). There is not, however, a marked difference between male and female patients in relation to the proportion incapacitated by their illness (see figure 55 below).

---

[298] Whilst 3.3% of females refusing consent to ECT had a significant change to their treatment plan, 8.5% of refusing males had a significant change made. Significant changes were made to 2.8% of the treatment plans for incapable females referred, and 5.2% of incapable males.

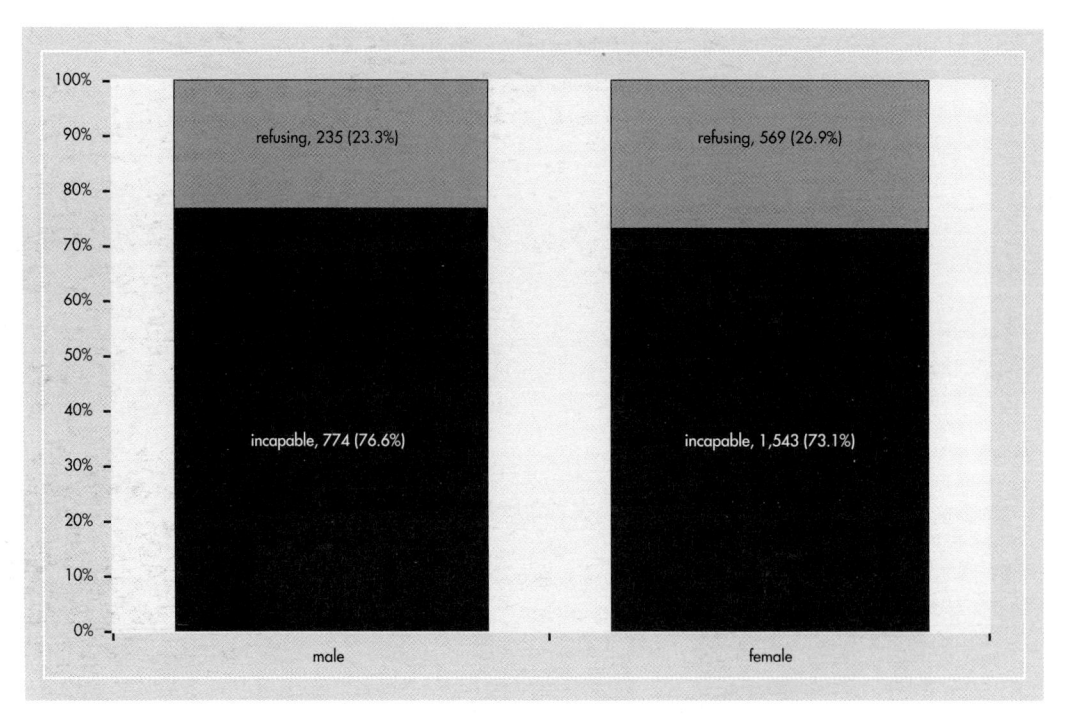

Fig 55: Second opinion visits where ECT treatment proposed, 1 April 2007 to 2 November 2008, by gender and reported capacity/consent status reported upon request

Source: MHAC data

3.48 The age profiles of the male and female groups (figure 56) are clearly relevant to any explanation of the unequal numbers of ECT referrals for men and women. As can be seen in figure 56, just over half of ECT SOAD requests relate to patients aged over 65 years. Male patients make up just over a quarter of this group. This is likely to reflect differences in longevity between men and women, although referrals of men are also substantially lower in all but the younger age groups. The differing proportions of men and women referred for ECT may also reflect objective differences between the sexes in clinical presentation, relating to the nature or degree of the illness being treated. But we do not rule out possible influence of gender stereotypes, and suggest that these differences would be a suitable subject for further research.

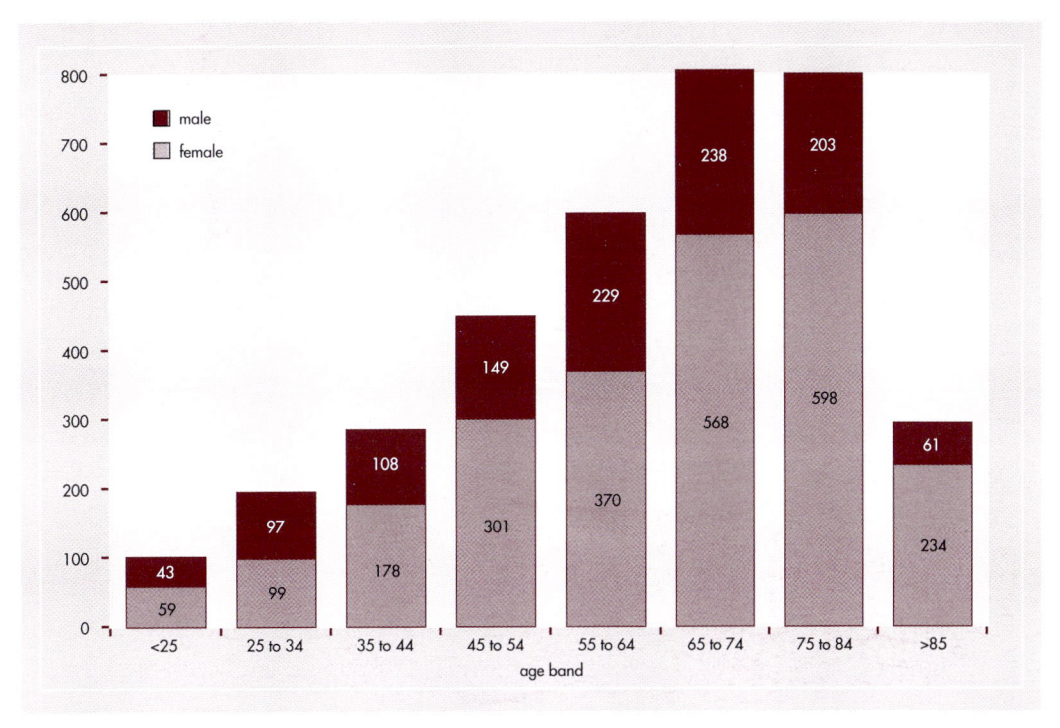

Fig 56: Second opinion requests for ECT by patient age and gender, 1 April 2007 to 31 Jan 2009
Source: MHAC data

3.49   The change in the law regarding ECT in November 2008 discussed below does not seem to have had any specific effect on any particular age group, nor on either gender, as we have seen no disproportionate falls in any one or more of these categories. However, we have only three months' data available to us, and more research in this area would be useful. With mental incapacity now forming the effective threshold for giving ECT without consent under the Act, it could be revealing to compare this data with the age and gender patterns of detained patients deemed to be consenting to ECT, and indeed with the age and gender profile of informal patients who receive ECT, whether this is with consent or using the Mental Capacity Act as the legal authority[299].

The Mental Health Act 2007's restriction on legal powers to authorise ECT without consent

3.50   The 2007 amendments to the Mental Health Act changed the legal rules for authorising ECT in the absence of consent. From the 3 November 2008, a detained patient who had capacity but refused consent to ECT can no longer have that refusal overridden on the basis of a SOAD authorisation, but can only be given the treatment in an emergency. In this way, although a SOAD authorises treatment of ECT on the basis that it is 'appropriate', just as with authorisations of medication, there is in effect a prior capacity-based threshold for considering such authorisation for ECT that does not apply in the case of medication.

---

[299] See the discussion of Rose D S et al 'Information, consent and perceived coercion: patients' perspectives on electroconvulsive therapy' *British Journal of Psychiatry*, 2005 186: 54-59 in MHAC (2006) *In Place of Fear? Eleventh Biennial Report 2003-2005*, para 4.74.

3.51 In previous reports (and in submissions to the debates over the revision of the Mental Health Act) we have highlighted the fact that, in recent years, roughly one third of all patients referred to the SOAD service for consideration of ECT authorisation have been described as refusing consent by their doctor[300]. We recommended that the practical result of the change in the law be studied carefully to determine (insofar as it possible to do so) what happened to such patients when the law effectively removed the option of treatment with ECT[301]. Although we discuss below some initial observations on the first three months of the new law's implementation, we continue to recommend this area to the close scrutiny of our successor body.

3.52 3.52 At figure 57 we show, for the five years prior to the change in the law, the monthly total of ECT second opinions requested for capacitated patients refusing consent. Two patterns emerge. The first (for which we cannot suggest any explanation) appears as a cyclic, seasonal pattern that peaks in early summer. We will pass over this. The second, which is more easily accounted for, is a declining rate of requests for SOADs to consider ECT treatment for refusing patients, as the date approaches whereby SOADs are no longer empowered by the Act to do this. Nevertheless, it should be noted that in the month before the change there was still an average of two such requests for every working day. Indeed, we received one such request on the afternoon of Friday 31 October, but declined to accept it on the grounds that we would be unable to arrange a SOAD visit before the law changed, even if we were minded to do so. That request is not counted in the data below.

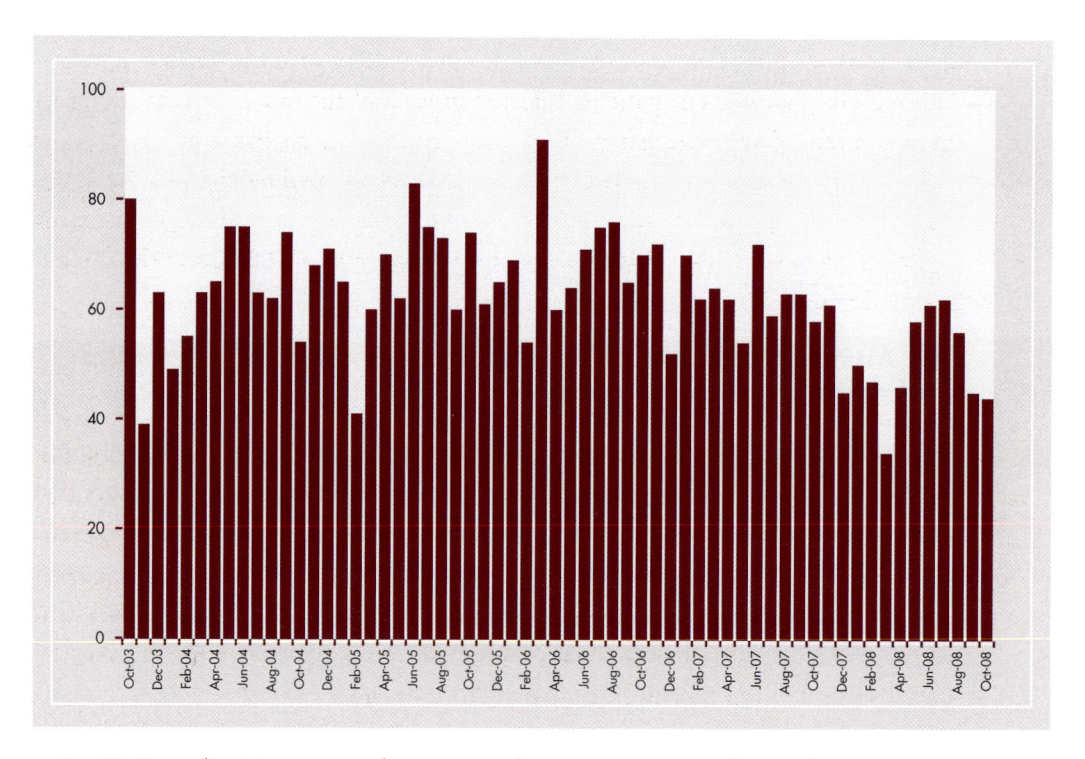

Fig 57: Second opinion requests for patients refusing consent to ECT, by month, Oct 2003 to Oct 2008

Source: MHAC data

---

[300] MHAC (2008) *Risk, Rights, Recovery; Twelfth Biennial Report 2005-2007*, para 6.76 – 6.7.

[301] *ibid.*, recommendation 38, p.221.

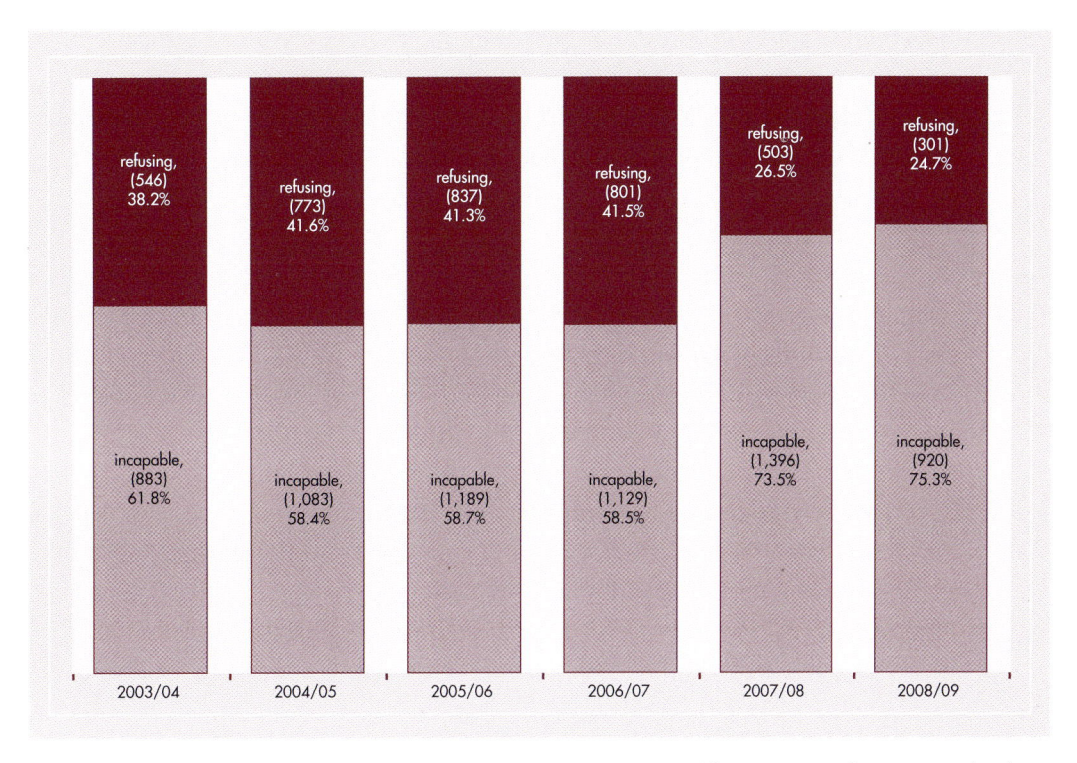

Fig 58: Reported capacity status of patients when request received for ECT second opinion, calendar years from 1 April 2003 to 3 November 2008

Source: MHAC data. Note that data for 2008/09 is only for the seven months to 3 November 2008

3.53   Figure 58 shows the proportion of patients who were either refusing or incapable of giving consent in each financial year from 2003/04 until the change in the law in November 2008. Although the numbers of patients referred in each of the first four years differ slightly, there is a remarkably consistent 60/40 proportion of incapable to refusing patients in each year. There appears to have been a step-change in the financial year 2007/08, when the proportion appears to shift towards 75/25 of incapable to refusing patients, and this proportion was again shown in data for the seven months of 2007/08, at the end of which the law changed to make obsolete the category of 'refusing' ECT patients.

3.54   We cannot, of course, provide any certain explanation for this change, and indeed it may be argued that such high-level statistical views of individual patients' presentations are little more than the accumulation of essentially random data. But we are mindful that the categories of 'incapable' and 'refusing' are inherently value-judgments (however much they may claim to be standardised by assessment procedures), and as such these findings are, potentially at least, a cause of some concern. For it appears to show an increase in the percentage *and number* of patients deemed incapacitated (it certainly shows this for the full financial year 2007/08), in a period immediately leading up to the introduction of a capacity threshold to the imposition of ECT treatment.

3.55   In our previous reports we have discussed our concern over the adoption of thresholds for intervention based upon detained patients' perceived mental capacity or incapacity to give or withhold consent[302]. In effect, there is a danger that the threshold becomes

---

[302] MHAC (2006) *In Place of Fear? Eleventh Biennial Report 2003-2005*, para 4.71 - 4.75; MHAC (2008) *Risk, Rights, Recovery; Twelfth Biennial Report 2005-2007*, para 6.76 - 6.79.

whether or not professionals are prepared to recognise as valid a patient's resistance to treatment. As such, the implantation of the revised Mental Health Act's rules regarding the imposition of ECT may be seen as a testing-ground for future moves towards capacity-based thresholds of coercion. This is an area where the operation of the law requires very careful scrutiny.

3.56   In past reports[303] we have also expressed concern that the new rules regarding ECT could lead to an increase in the use of emergency powers[304]. The debates in Parliament showed that it was envisaged that such emergency powers would be used rarely if at all for patients who retained capacity to refuse ECT. Baroness Murphy, who has a background as a psychiatrist and past vice-chairman of the MHAC, stated that

> ECT has been used much less often in the past 20 years. It is good to see how little it is used now in most services. But the evidence is that for people with profound depressive, biological types of illness – particularly those in later life, over the age of 60 – those illnesses are life-threatening. People die of depression. The mortality rate among those in a depressive stupor is quite high. If you have seen someone near death because they stopped eating and drinking get a little toehold on life again, to enable you to give them the intravenous medications which might enable them to respond over a longer period to medicine, it is very difficult to say, "I will never give that treatment again".
>
> Unfortunately, it is also true that many of those who do respond relapse within three or four months. But although that sometimes happens, ECT is sometimes the only option that one can think of. Nevertheless, as other noble Lords said, we recognise the deep fear, anxiety and revulsion that this treatment creates in many patients' minds. It seems essential that people should be able to refuse it when they have full capacity.
>
> As for emergency ECT under section 62, only very rarely does it seem necessary to give such treatment. I am rather sceptical about it. Someone would have to be profoundly dehydrated to warrant it, and ECT would be a long shot. One would not be able to wait until Monday or a second-opinion doctor was available. I cannot envisage a scenario where a fully capacitated patient who was able to consent would fall into the need for urgent treatment.[305]

3.57   Over the last five calendar years, emergency powers were invoked to give ECT treatment immediately prior to 23% of *all* SOAD visits to consider ECT treatment. Of those years, 2008 showed the lowest use of emergency powers when measured both by number of times the power was used prior to a SOAD visit (319) and by that number as a percentage of all ECT cases referred to a SOAD (19%). This data is shown below at figure 59.

---

[303] *ibid.*, see especially MHAC (2006) *In Place of Fear?* para 4.73.

[304] MHA 1983, s.62(1A): As from the 3 November 2008, any detained patient who is recognised as refusing consent to ECT could only be given that treatment if the clinician justified it on the grounds that it was either (1) necessary to save the patient's life; or (2) necessary to prevent a serious deterioration of the patient's condition.

[305] *Hansard* HL, 15 Jan 2007: Col 474 -475.

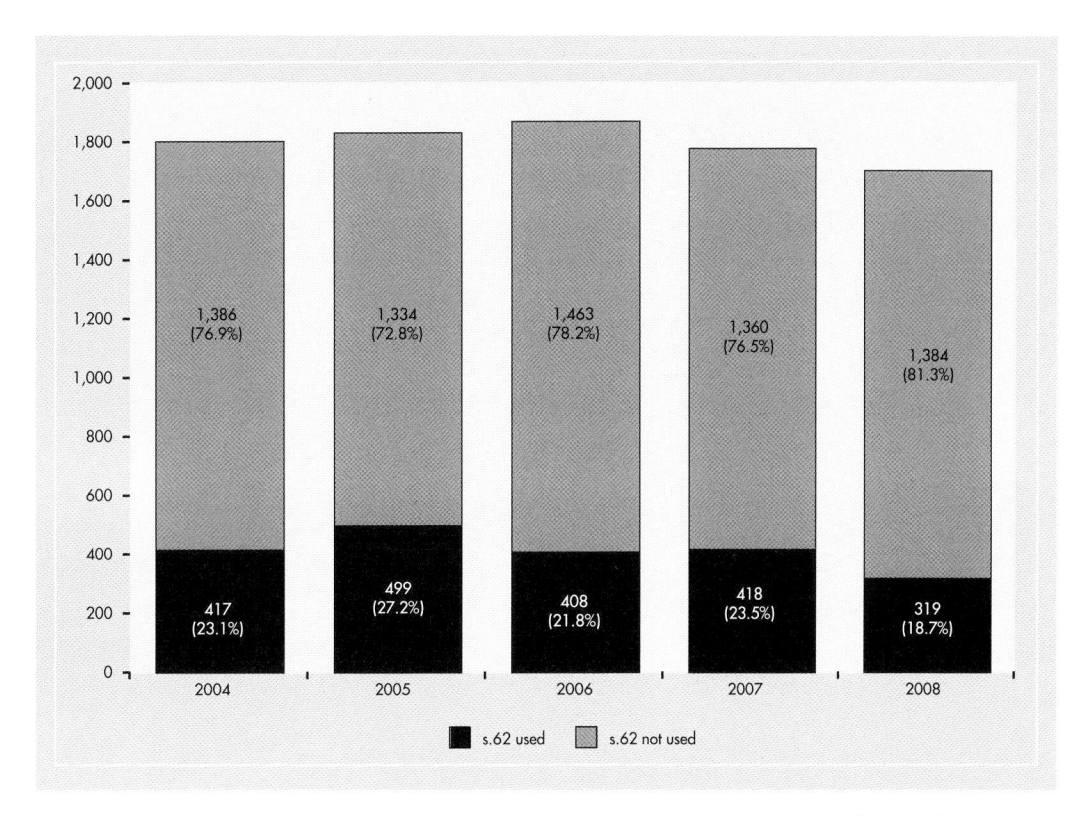

Fig 59: Use of emergency treatment powers (s.62) prior to Second Opinion visits for ECT, by calendar year, 2004 to 2008

Source: MHAC data

3.58 Figure 60 shows the data on the use of emergency powers to give ECT before a SOAD visit from May 2007 to the end of March 2009. The data is shown in columns representing periods of three-months (except the last column, which shows two months). The final two columns therefore represent data from the period after the implementation of the revised Act until the end of our reporting period (i.e. from the 3 November 2008 to the end of March 2009). This shows an initial fall in the use of emergency ECT prior to a second opinion, followed by a return to pre-revision levels. There is therefore, no sign of an increase in the use of s.62 in this reporting period. We must qualify this statement, however, in that we cannot be sure that all uses of s.62 lead to SOAD requests, and are therefore brought to our attention.

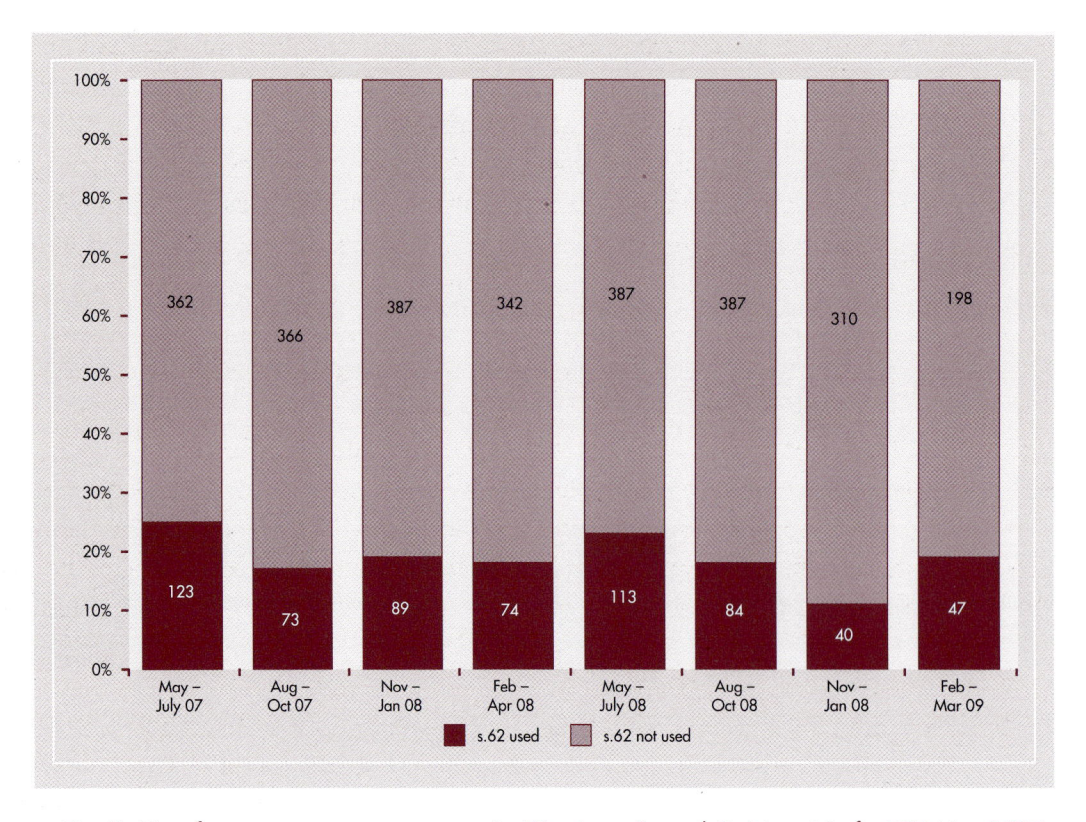

Fig 60: Use of emergency treatment powers (s.62) prior to Second Opinion visits for ECT, May 2007 to Jan 2009

Source: MHAC data

Magnetic seizure therapy and transcranial magnetic stimulation – future treatments?

3.59   Promising studies relating to the use of magnetic stimulation in the treatment of major depression were published in this reporting period:

- Kirov *et al* have tested a prototype device for inducing therapeutic seizure with a high-frequency magnetic field[306]. Eleven patients underwent treatment, all but one of whom were receiving or about to receive ECT. The patients all appeared to have a shorter recovery time than with ECT-induced seizures, and suffered less neurocognitive effects. Many patients reporting that they felt as it they had received no treatment, in that they remembered details of what happened immediately before the therapy and experienced little or no post-therapy confusion.

- O'Reardon *et al* reported a large randomised trial in which 301 patients with treatment-resistant depression were given either active or sham transcranial magnetic stimulation (TMS) – a procedure that does not induce seizure – with encouraging results: the study implies that this may be a well-tolerated and effective treatment for the future[307].

---

[306] Kirov G *et al* (2008) 'Quick recovery of orientation after magnetic seizure therapy for major depressive disorder' *British Journal of Psychiatry*, 193, 152-155.

[307] O'Reardon, J P *et al* (2007) 'Efficacy and Safety of Transcranial Magnetic Stimulation in the Acute Treatment of Major Depression: A Multisite Randomized Controlled Trial.' *Biological Psychiatry* Volume 62, Issue 11, Pages 1208-1216 (1 December 2007).

3.60   If the use of such treatments becomes more widespread, there will be a need to consider where, or if, they should be placed within the hierarchy of treatments falling within parts 4 or 4A of the Act. This should perhaps be the subject of further debate whilst the treatments are still in development. We note that neither trial showed significant side-effects, although the UK study did involve inducing seizure, which might suggest regulating it on par with ECT. However, as TMS would seem to be entirely non-invasive, there may be a case for having no particular safeguards for this procedure.

Neurosurgery for Mental Disorder

3.61   Under s.57 of the Act, any surgical operation with the aim of destroying brain tissue or the function of brain tissue for the treatment of mental disorder cannot be given unless the patient consents to it, and a team comprising a doctor and two other persons have authorised that the patient's consent is based upon an understanding of the nature, purpose and likely effects of the treatment, and that it is appropriate for the treatment to be given.

3.62   In this reporting period, MHAC-appointed multidisciplinary teams have authorised two such operations, and have not been asked to consider any cases that they have refused to authorise. The patients operated upon were a hospitalised (although informal) male with a diagnosis of obsessional-compulsive disorder, and a woman presenting with treatment-resistant depression and intrusive thoughts. In both cases, the panel had no difficulty in reaching the decision to authorise treatment, but in the latter funding problems delayed the process and the patient eventually had the operation privately following certification. Both patients show positive results from the surgery (bilateral stereotactic anterior capsulotomy), conducted under general anaesthesia at the University Hospital of Wales[308]. In the former case, the patient was preparing to leave hospital for supported accommodation as we were writing this report (this had seemed a very remote prospect before the operation), and both patients, although by no means free of all their original symptoms, stated their feelings about their improvement in terms of 'got my life back' and 'I feel I have got a life'.

Deep brain stimulation

3.63   In our previous report we suggested that deep-brain stimulation (DBS) – a procedure related to leucotomy but effected through the placing of electrodes on the brain rather than cutting brain tissue – should be afforded the protections of s.57[309]. The governments in England and Wales have yet to pass any regulation concerning NMD, although the Scottish Parliament has done so. This means that the treatment can only be given in Scotland following certification that the patient gives informed consent and it would be appropriate to give it, whereas in England and Wales the procedure remains unregulated

---

[308] The University Hospital of Wales is the only operating site in England and Wales at present, although there is another operating site (Dundee) in Scotland. We are not aware of any patient from England or Wales undergoing treatment at Dundee: if they did so they would be subject to the safeguards of the Mental Health (Care and Treatment)(Scotland) Act 2003 rather than the Mental Health Act 1983.

[309] MHAC (2008) *Risk, Rights, Recovery; Twelfth Biennial Report 2005-2007*, para 6.89 *et seq*.

and could, in theory, be given against a detained patient's will under the direction of a Responsible Clinician, or under the Mental Incapacity Act to any patient lacking capacity to refuse it. Whilst DBS remains at an experimental stage, and is certainly not likely to be in widespread use in the immediate future, there seems to us to be a good argument for regulating such procedures as soon as cases appear or are likely to appear, no matter how rarely.

Consent to medication and Supervised Community Treatment

3.64 The treatment of patients subject to Supervised Community Treatment (SCT) falls under Part 4A of the revised Act. This is a convoluted and extremely complex addition to the new Act and we regret that it is not easily understood from the text of the Act itself. In essence, Part 4A provides no new powers of treatment to an SCT patient *whilst that patient is in the community*, and authority to treat such patients must therefore be had from the common-law (where the patient consents) or the Mental Capacity Act (where the patient is unable to consent). Part 4A does, however, provide powers equivalent to those available for the treatment of detained patients where an SCT patient is recalled to hospital. But even this aspect cannot be said to have extended the coercive reach of the Act, given that SCT is effectively a replacement for the practice of allowing patients long-term s.17 leave of absence from detention in hospital. Patients who stay in the community under long-term s.17 leave continue to be subject to Part 4 of the Act as this applies to detained patients, and as such can not only be forcibly medicated upon recall to hospital, but theoretically can be compelled to accept treatment to which they refuse consent whilst in the community. As the barrister Paul Bowen points out, this makes the new Part 4A of the Act not so much a coercive mechanism as a *protective* one: it requires that the treatment of SCT patients is regulated and applies the safeguard of the SOAD procedure to it[310].

3.65 This is not to say that we see no need to keep this mechanism under close review. As noted below, we are concerned at the asymmetry of protections provided under the 1983 Act. It would also be naive to assume that coercion of SCT patients into taking medication to which they refuse consent will not occur because the law makes no formal provision for this. In chapter 2.82 above we show initial testing of the limits of coercive power of SCT regarding accommodation and deprivation of liberty, and it may be that there will be similar straining at the limits of coercive power with regard to treatment. Perhaps more importantly, we note below that some practitioners seem to be unaware that they could not compel their SCT patients to take medication, and the boundary between coercion and consent is in any case not always clear. Noting a 1998 study that found unlawful stipulation of a requirement to take medication in one-third of all patients subject to Aftercare under Supervision[311], Bartlett and Sandland have suggested that it is

---

[310] Bowen P (2008) *Blackstone's Guide to the Mental Health Act 2007*. Oxford, para 6.61.

[311] Knight A, Mumford D & Nichol B (1998) 'Supervised Discharge Order: the first years in the South and West Region' *Psychiatric Bulletin*, 22:418. Supervised Discharge Order in this case refers to the order initiating Aftercare under Supervision, s.25A of the Mental Health Act 1983 that was repealed by the Mental Health Act 2007. The MHAC's legal remit never extended to patients subject to s.25A.

not necessary to deny any benevolent intent in the interpretation of this tendency to push the legal boundaries of coercion: indeed "benevolence is a key conduit for the spread of control".[312]

The consent status of SCT patients

3.66 The consent status of SCT patients, according to the judgment of the Responsible Clinician at the time of the request for a SOAD visit, is shown at figure 61 below. Just over half of all these requests were for patients who were deemed to be capable and consenting to their treatment. It is a curious anomaly in the revised Act that patients who have capacity to consent and do so are afforded the safeguard of a second opinion when released from detention in hospital onto SCT status, but no such safeguard applies to patients deemed to be capable and consenting whilst detained in hospital. If the purpose of such a safeguard is to protect against hidden coercion (which we see as a real possibility where the decision as to whether a patient is capable and consenting is left entirely to the treating clinician), or to ensure than inappropriate treatment is not offered to and accepted by the patient who is subject to legal coercion, then such dangers are almost certainly more acute for a patient who is physically detained in hospital than for a community patient. The asymmetry of protections afforded by the Act is compounded by the fact that second opinions are not available to restricted patients who are conditionally discharged from hospital, although such patients are, in effect, subject to a regime essentially equivalent to that of patients on SCT, including being required to comply with treatment upon pain of recall to hospital.

3.67 This is perhaps an issue for consideration by future legislators. However, given that any extension of the SOAD safeguard to all consenting patients who are subject to the consent to treatment provisions of the Act would entail a substantial increase in resources (possibly beyond what could or should be made available), we suggest that there should be close monitoring of the changes made to treatment plans as a result of SOAD visits to consenting SCT patients, so as to help evaluate whether this safeguard is of value. This could also be a useful subject for wider research, taking account of the experience of patients and professionals.

---

[312] Bartlett P & Sandland R (2007) *Mental Health Law: Policy and Practice*, third edition, Oxford, p.494.

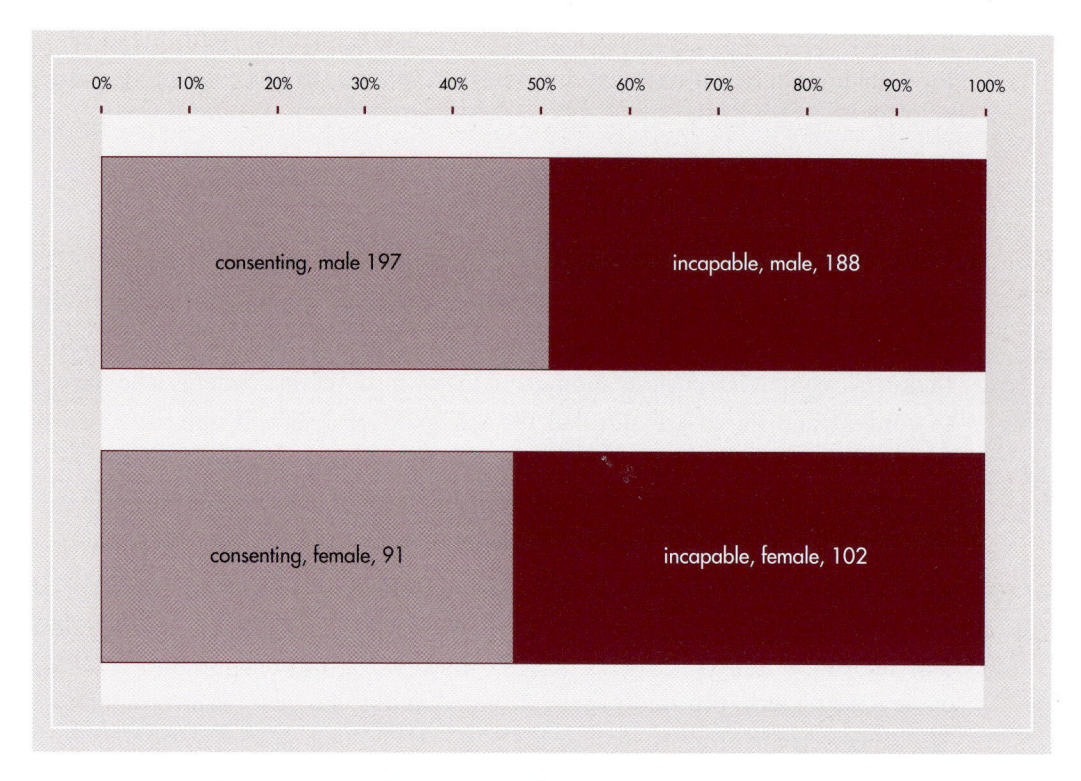

Fig 61: Reported consent status of SCT patients when SOAD visit request accepted, November 2008 to January 2009, England and Wales

Source: MHAC data

SCT and patients refusing consent to medication

3.68 The Code of Practice for England (chapter 25.14) states that:

> Patients do not have to consent formally to SCT. But in practice, patients will need to be involved in decisions about the treatment to be provided in the community and how and where it is to be given, and be prepared to co-operate with the proposed treatment.

3.69 It goes on to suggest (at chapter 28.6) that a factor suggesting the use of SCT (rather than long-term s.17 leave) is that "the patient appears prepared to consent or comply with the treatment that they need".

3.70 Where a patient subject to SCT has mental capacity and refuses consent to take medication for mental disorder, that refusal cannot be overridden using the consent to treatment provisions of Part 4A of the Mental Health Act, unless the patient is recalled to hospital.

3.71 As indicated at paragraph 2.76, there has been some uncertainty amongst practitioners as to the scope of SCT powers in the face of a patient's capable refusal to comply with medication. The MHAC received a small number of requests to arrange SOAD visits to refusing SCT patients who have not been recalled to hospital, but remain in the community. A number of practitioners seemed to be genuinely unaware that, in contrast with powers over those liable to be detained, the refusal of an SCT patient cannot be overridden using the consent to treatment provisions of the Act. Other practitioners in charge of such patients' treatment accepted that the treatment could not be administered to a refusing SCT patient, they nevertheless wanted the SOAD to certify what treatment would be appropriate should the patient's consent status change. The MHAC initially declined to arrange such visits, arguing that the patient's refusal of consent would preclude such certification that "it is appropriate for treatment to be given"[313] or would be so under any specified conditions.

3.72 Our view was challenged and, after discussions with the Department of Health, we accepted the validity of that challenge. We have issued guidance on this matter[314] and do now arrange SOAD visits to consider issuing a certificate where an SCT patient is refusing consent and has capacity to do so. The outcome of such visits is entirely a matter for the SOADs concerned (who act independently of the MHAC and of any other body), although our guidance note explores some of the issues that arise from such visits, which we outline below.

The disjuncture in Part 4A between certification and consent

3.73 Department of Health officials have advised us that the revised Act creates a deliberate disjuncture between the SOAD's test of whether treatment is appropriate and whether there is legal authority for such treatment:

> "Appropriateness" does not include [legal] authority. The Act itself provides that treatment cannot lawfully be given unless there is authority to do so, and sets out when such authority will exist. So it is not necessary … for SOADs to concern themselves with the question of whether there would be authority to give the treatment. So, in effect, the SOAD is required to consider whether it would be appropriate for the treatment to be given, assuming there were legal authority to give it[315].

3.74 We have been informed that it is for this reason that a SOAD, in certifying treatment as appropriate under Part 4A, does not have to certify the patient's consent or capacity status with regard to that treatment.

3.75 The MHAC does therefore arrange SOAD visits to consider certification of treatment where an SCT patient is reported to us as refusing consent to that treatment. The SOAD has to consider whether treatment would be appropriate should there be legal authority to give it, and give consideration to authorising treatment should the patient need to be recalled[316].

---

[313] The Act defines 'appropriate for treatment to be given' to a patient 'if the treatment is appropriate in his case, taking into account the nature and degree of the mental disorder from which he is suffering *and all other circumstances of the case*' (s.64(3), applied to Part 4A by virtue of s.64K(8), our emphasis).

[314] MHAC (2009) *Second Opinions for Supervised Community Treatment patients who are refusing medication for mental disorder. Interim Guidance for Second Opinion Appointed Doctors and Hospital Administrators.* January 2009.

[315] Advice to MHAC from Department of Health, 22 January 2009.

[316] MHAC (October 2008) *Guidance for SOADs: Consent to treatment & the SOAD role under the revised Mental Health Act (p.8):* The law allows SOADs to certify on form CTO11 (CTO7 in Wales) not only what treatment is appropriate whilst the patient is in the community on SCT, but also to authorise treatment to be given in the event of the patient's recall to hospital. A patient may be 'recalled' to hospital from an SCT for assessment, and held there for a period of up to 72 hours, by the end of which he or she should have either been released back into the community on the SCT, or readmitted formally to hospital upon the revocation of the SCT … The Code of Practice further states that SOADs should only authorise treatment to be given upon recall "where they believe they have sufficient information upon which properly to make a judgment". The MHAC urges SOADs to take particular care when considering the exercise of this power, and to be mindful that an SCT patient's recall to hospital may take place long after the certificate is issued under quite different circumstances than the SOAD encounters during the second opinion visit.

Issues for SOADs in certifying the appropriateness of treatment refused by an SCT patient

3.76 We are aware that SOADS (and other professionals) may have a number of questions about a test of the 'appropriateness' of treatment that has been decoupled from consideration of the patient's own wishes and consent. Although we have been advised that it is 'not necessary' for SOADs to concern themselves with whether there is currently authority to give the treatment when certifying in the case of an SCT patient that treatment is appropriate, or would be appropriate under certain conditions, the patient's willingness and capacity to consent to the treatment nonetheless remains one of the factors to be considered. The MHA Code of Practice for England gives examples of where consent or capacity status is named as a condition that must be met for treatment to be appropriate:

> When giving Part 4A certificates, SOADs do not have to certify whether a patient has, or lacks, capacity to consent to the treatments in question, nor whether a patient with capacity is consenting or refusing. But they may make it a condition of their approval that particular treatments are given only in certain circumstances. For example, they might specify that a particular treatment is to be given only with the patient's consent. Similarly, they might specify that a medication may be given up to a certain dosage if the patient lacks capacity to consent, but that a higher dosage may be given with the patient's consent.[317]

3.77 As the above example shows, in some cases it will be very difficult or impossible to put aside the patient's willingness and capacity to consent when making a judgment as to whether it would be appropriate at some future point to give a certain treatment. Some interventions may be appropriate only provided that a patient actively consents to them, but not where a patient has only lost capacity to refuse consent.

3.78 The Code of Practice for England also states that:

> when deciding whether it is appropriate for treatment to be given to a patient, SOADs are required to consider both the clinical appropriateness of the treatment to the patient's mental disorder and its appropriateness in the light of all the other circumstances of the patient's case.
>
> SOADs should, in particular:
>
> - consider the appropriateness of alternative forms of treatment, not just that proposed;
> - balance the potential therapeutic efficacy of the proposed treatment against the side effects and any other potential disadvantages to the patient;
> - *seek to understand the patient's views on the proposed treatment, and the reasons for them;*
> - *give due weight to the patient's views, including any objection to the proposed treatment and any preference for an alternative;*
> - take into account any previous experience of comparable treatment for a similar episode of disorder; and
> - give due weight to the opinions, knowledge, experience and skills of those consulted.[318]

---

[317] MHA *Code of Practice for England*, para 24.27.
[318] *ibid.*, para 24.57, 24.58, our emphasis.

3.79 The MHAC takes the view that, in the light of this guidance in the Code of Practice, and in the general spirit of good medical practice, making a clinical judgment about the appropriateness of treatment cannot be undertaken without at least talking to the patient about their consent and taking that information into account.

3.80 Indeed, where an SCT patient with capacity to do so refuses consent to a certain treatment, it should have been ascertained whether that patient is also making an advance decision to refuse that treatment should s/he lose capacity in future. This is important information for the clinical team (although in our experience it may not have been considered), and may well have relevance to the question of whether or not the treatment may be clinically appropriate for the time that the patient remains in the community under SCT.

3.81 Given that we view a patient's consent or capacity status with regard to a particular treatment to be potentially relevant to whether such treatment is clinically appropriate, we continue to encourage SOADs to refer to the patient's views on treatment in these terms when giving reasons for certifying treatment as appropriate on Form CTO11 (CO7 in Wales). [319]

3.82 If a SOAD certifies that treatment with medication for mental disorder "is appropriate" at the point when an SCT patient refuses consent to it, that SOAD is in effect stating that the treatment will be appropriate at some future date when the patient's consent or capacity circumstances have changed. As such, the MHAC encourages SOADs to make explicit on the certificate that the treatment would only be appropriate on condition that the patient consents to it, or on condition that the patient no longer refuses consent, etc. We also suggest that SOADs may also wish to consider time-limiting the certificate, or suggesting to the MHAC a date at which it might use its powers to request a report on the patient's treatment.

3.83 We do not rule out the possibility that SOADs, having visited an SCT patient who is refusing treatment whilst in the community, will feel unable to certify that the proposed treatment is appropriate and will therefore refuse to issue a Form CTO11 (CO7 in Wales). Similarly, patients for whom a CTO11 certificate has been completed may continue to refuse consent so that the certified treatment cannot be given. It is legally possible for a patient who is refusing consent to treatment to be placed upon SCT, and there is no direct legal consequence for the patient's SCT status if he or she refuses consent having been placed upon the power. However, whilst the patient who has capacity and is refusing consent to medication for mental disorder remains in the community on SCT, there can be no legal authority to enforce that treatment. The options (if the patient continues to refuse consent) would appear to be either that the patient remains on SCT without taking medication until circumstances change, or, if the Responsible Clinician considers this to

---

[319] MHAC (October 2008) *Guidance for SOADs: Consent to treatment & the SOAD role under the revised Mental Health Act* (p.7/8): the [CTO11 or CO7] form does not require SOADs to certify whether the patient is consenting or incapable of doing so, nor whether a patient with capacity is consenting or refusing. However, it will almost certainly be appropriate to address these questions when giving reasons for the decision to authorise any treatment using this form. A statement of reasons is required by the statutory form irrespective of the whether the patient has capacity, and irrespective of, if so, he or she consents to the treatment in question.

be inappropriate, that the patient is recalled to hospital (where such treatment refusal may be overruled). It may be that patients who are refusing consent could be managed in the community through the use of s.17 leave rather than SCT.

Statutory consultees for second opinions for SCT patients

3.84 Section 64H(3) of the Act requires that any SOAD certifying that treatment is appropriate in the case of an SCT patient must first have consulted with two persons who have been professionally concerned with the patient's treatment, at least one of whom shall not be a doctor, and neither of whom may be the responsible clinician or approved clinician in charge of the treatment in question. As such, there is no positive requirement to consult with a specific type of professional, in contrast to the arrangements for SOAD visits to detained patients, where one of the statutory consultees must be a nurse. Regrettably, both the Codes of Practice for England and Wales misrepresent the law in this area, implying that a nurse must be one consultee for all second opinions[320]. We have raised this matter with the Department of Health, who have accepted that this is not the intention of the Code. As such, we have advised SOADs that they should disregard the apparent implication of the Code and are free to choose or not choose to consult with a nurse for SCT visits, as they wish.

Responsibility for the treatment of community or s.17 leave patients

3.85 For patients who are subject to compulsion outside the hospital environment, confusion over medication management can arise, especially where the 'Responsible Clinician' is not the prescriber of medication for mental disorder. We discuss dangers in having uncertain arrangements for medication management of community-based patients at chapter 5.37 *et seq* below. From the introduction of SCT we have been asked in various ways how, for example, "other doctors" seeing a patient on s.17 leave or SCT "who properly want to initiate treatment on the basis of capacity and consent" can do so. Of course, there is nothing in the Mental Health Act to prevent this where the treatment in question is for physical (rather than mental) disorder, and as such patients on SCT or s.17 leave should be under the care of a general practitioner just as any other person requiring primary care services. However, in the case of treatment for mental disorder of patients on s.17 leave, the Act specifies that such treatment is the responsibility of the Approved Clinician in charge of any s.58 type treatment (who will, in practice, usually be the "Responsible Clinician" under the Act, unless the latter role is performed by a non-medic). For an SCT patient, there is no such legal restriction where a patient consents to treatment for mental disorder. In either case, unless the 'other doctor' is prescribing treatment within bounds established by Part 4 or 4A of the Act, the other doctor has no legal authority to do so.

---

[320] *MHA Code of Practice for England*, para 24.49; *Code of Practice for Wales*, para 18.19. Both Codes state of statutory consultees that "one must be a nurse; the other neither a nurse nor a doctor" as if this applies to SCT as well as detained patients.

3.86 Thus, the consent of a detained patient on s.17 leave is not sufficient legal authority for any doctor to prescribe medication for mental disorder outside the terms of a Form T2 (or Form CO2 in Wales). Any such prescription should first be discussed with the Approved Clinician in charge of the treatment of the patient, so that a new Form T2 can be issued providing authority. If such a patient is still under the three-month rule and has no certificate, it is still a legal requirement that the treatment is given under the direction of the Approved Clinician with responsibility for it.

3.87 In the case of an SCT patient, within the initial period where no certification is required the law does not require any 'other doctor' to have the authority of the Approved Clinician in charge of the treatment of the patient for prescription of medication for mental disorder to have a sound legal basis, provided that the patient gives consent. Once a certificate is required, any such prescription must be within the terms established by a SOAD on CTO11 (CO7 in Wales). In practice, however, it would seem to be extremely poor practice and potentially dangerous for SCT patients if there is no close co-ordination between any prescribing physician and the Responsible Clinician who retains power to recall the patient, and who must therefore monitor treatment and progress whilst the patient remains in the community (see chapter 5.37 below).

Children and consent to treatment

3.88 Figure 62 shows the number of SOAD visits to detained children and adolescents over the last four financial years. It is important to note that the data for 2008/09 is incomplete, as it covers only visits made in 2008. Nevertheless, the available data does indicate that the detention and treatment of under sixteen year olds is very rare, and the treatment of such children with ECT is even rarer. Of the 16 and 17 year olds who receive ECT, almost invariably these are female patients whose clinical presentation includes eating disorders.

			2005/06		2006/07		2007/08		2008/09[321]	
			Med	ECT	Med	ECT	MED	ECT	Med	ECT
Age of detained patient	12 yrs	visits (patients)	1 (1)	–	–	–	1 (1)	–	–	–
	13 yrs	visits (patients)	9 (8)	–	3 (3)	–	6 (6)	–	3 (3)	–
	14 yrs	visits (patients)	10 (6)	–	10 (7)	–	14 (11)	–	10 (9)	1 (1)
	15 yrs	visits (patients)	34 (22)	2 (1)	26 (21)	–	21 (20)	–	20 (18)	–
	16 yrs	visits (patients)	67 (51)	3 (2)	85 (56)	1 (1)	73 (47)	9 (6)	48 (32)	–
	17 yrs	visits (patients)	61 (50)	3 (3)	87 (76)	1 (1)	110 (80)	4 (4)	64 (50)	2 (2)
Total (Total not authorised)			182 (5)	8 (3)	213 (8)	2 (1)	225 (11)	13 (2)	145 (n/a)	3 (2)

Fig 62: Number of second opinion visits to children and adolescents, 2005/06 to 2008/09

Source: MHAC data

3.89 The outcomes of such SOAD visits are shown at figure 63 below. The data for 2008/09 is limited both in that it runs only to the end of December 2008, and in that a significant number of outcomes for visits in 2008 had yet to be recorded when it was collected. We are unable to distinguish between visits whose results were yet to be recorded, and those that result in no certification of treatment, although we have shown those recorded visits that resulted in a slight or significant change to the treatment plan proposed to the SOAD.

	2003/04	2004/05	2005/06	2006/07	2007/08	
Total visits to consider authorisation of medication to patients aged 12 to 17 yrs	117	141	182	213	225	145
Treatment authorised as requested	77 (65.9%)	107 (75.9%)	154 (84.7%)	175 (82.2%)	202 (89.8%)	n/a
Treatment not authorised	13 (11.1%)	9 (6.4%)	5 (3%)	8 (3.8%)	11 (5%)	n/a
Treatment authorised with slight change	24 (20.5%)	20 (14.2%)	17 (9.3%)	27 (12.7%)	10 (4.4%)	20 (13.8%)
Treatment authorised with significant change	3 (2.6%)	5 (3.5%)	6 (3.3%)	3 (1.4%)	2 (0.9%)	2 (1.4%)

Fig 63: Outcome of second opinion visits to children and adolescents to consider treatment with medication, 2003/04 to 2008/09

Source: MHAC data

---

[321] Data only available up to 31 December 2008 for 2008/09. As all results of visits were not all known at this time, an accurate count of medication treatments not authorised cannot be given.

[322] Data only available up to 31 December 2008 for 2008/09. As all results of visits were not all known at this time, an accurate count of medication treatments not authorised cannot be given, and the total figures for slight or significant change are likely to be incomplete.

Children and ECT treatment

3.90 Under the revised Act, treatment with ECT of any patient aged under 18 years must be certified by a SOAD, whether that patient is detained or not. From the implementation of this new legal requirement on the 3 November 2008 to the time of writing this report (March 2009) no request for SOAD certification of ECT for an informal child patient has been received. SOAD visits to the three detained patients seen to date in 2008/09 (shown at figure 62 above) took place before the change in the law.

3.91 The SOAD role in certifying the appropriateness of ECT treatment to an informal patient who is less than 18 years old is subtly different to their role in certifying treatment for detained patients. In certifying that the treatment of a detained patient is appropriate, the SOAD provides sufficient legal authority under the Mental Health Act for that treatment to be given under the direction of the clinician in charge of that treatment. In contrast, whilst a SOAD's certification of the appropriateness of ECT treatment for an informal child patient is a *necessary* requirement for lawful treatment, it is not itself *sufficient* legal authority for the treatment to be administered. For such authority, the clinician in charge of the treatment must look to the common law (where a patient consents or is under 16 years of age) or the Mental Capacity Act, where consent is precluded by the patient's mental condition and the patient is at least 16 years old. In this way the SOAD role in considering the ECT treatment of child patients is similar to the SOAD role in considering treatments proposed for patients subject to supervised community treatment (SCT). As we discuss at para 3.73, the Department of Health has informed the MHAC that it considers such a role to be essentially concerned with the clinical aspects of the treatment, and not with the legal aspects (including whether or not the patient's consent status at the time of the second opinion would preclude the lawful administration of treatment). Our concerns about disentangling issues of capacity and consent from issues of clinical appropriateness are outlined at [x-ref above]. These concerns are perhaps even more acute when the treatment in question is ECT.

3.92 Indeed, the Code of Practice's guidance on considerations relevant to the legal authority for ECT to under-16s appears, quite correctly in our view, to conflate the legal and clinical issues as indivisible aspects of the authority to treat. Chapter 36.60 of the English Code suggests that it would be prudent to obtain court authorisation to give ECT to a child who is under 16 years of age and neither detained in hospital nor subject to SCT. The Code remarks that "the issues [that] the court is likely to address will mirror those that the SOAD is required to consider". In our view this is correct. Either body must in effect apply a broadly-focussed 'best interests' test, and the essential distinction between the court and the SOAD in carrying out such a test is that the latter applies his or her own specialist medical knowledge to determine medical necessity, whilst the former relies upon evidence from specialists (including SOADs). Rather more dubiously, the Code goes on to state that court authorisation should be obtained "before a SOAD is asked to approve the treatment" (chapter 36.60, our emphasis). We doubt that the High Court would wish to determine whether authority should be given without the matter having been previously considered by a SOAD, especially as they are addressing the same issues and would want the expert view of the SOAD as evidence before them. In the Code's scheme, the court is reduced to providing an authority that may be exercised only with the agreement of a SOAD, but we submit that the court may be likely to wish that order of priority reversed[323].

---

[323] See the three-stage process identified in *R (on the application of JB) v Dr A Haddock and others* [2006] EWCA Civ 961. Although this case relates to a detained patient (and as such the SOAD certificate, being sufficient authority in itself for treatment, had a greater legal weight than in the situation discussed above), the Court of Appeal reserved to itself the role of conducting a full-merits review of the lawfulness of the SOAD's certificate. The relevant part of the judgment is summarised in Jones R (2008) *Mental Health Act Manual,* eleventh edition, p.302.

4

The Mental Healt Act and mentally disordered offenders

The diversion of mentally disordered offenders from the criminal justice system

4.1   The production of this final report of the MHAC falls on the centenaries of two significant historic reports laid before Parliament: that of the *Royal Commission on the Care and Control of the Feeble Minded* (1904-1908) and the famous *Minority Report of the Poor Law Commission* (1909)[324]. These reports highlighted the large number of people of "unsound mind" – the *Minority Report* suggested 60,000 across the United Kingdom, "including not a few children" – who were being kept inappropriately in the general workhouses of the day "without education or ameliorative treatment, and herded together with the sane". Concurring with the Royal Commission's view that "the mental condition of these persons, and neither their poverty nor their crime," was "the real ground of their claim for help from the state", the *Minority Report* concluded that the situation was "a public scandal"[325].

4.2   One hundred years on, if we substitute the word *prison* for *workhouse*, a similar 'public scandal' continues in the care of the mentally disordered. This report goes to press upon the publication of the review by Lord Bradley of the diversion of individuals with mental health problems from the criminal justice system and prison, which we hope will prove to be a watershed for measures to address this scandalous position.

Unfitness to Plead and the Insanity Defence

4.3   In recent Biennial Reports[326] we have highlighted concerns over the legal formulation of the insanity defence (also known as the *M'Naghten* rules[327]) and the rules governing

---

[324] The Minority Report was published in public edition (complete but minus footnote apparatus) in two volumes by Longmans, 1909: see *The Break-Up of the Poor Law: Being Part One of the Minority Report of the Poor Law Commission*, ed. Sidney & Beatrice Webb, Longmans & co., 1909. We have used this edition.

[325] All quotations from the *Minority Report (The Break-Up of the Poor Law)*, p.307-8.

[326] MHAC (2006) *In Place of Fear? Eleventh Biennial Report 2003-2005*, para 5.15 to 5.24; MHAC (2008) *Risk, Rights, Recovery; Twelfth Biennial Report 2005-2007*, para 7.49 *et seq*.

[327] "To establish a defence on the ground of insanity, it must clearly be proved that, at the time of the committing of the act, the party accused was labouring under such a defect of reason, from disease of the mind, as not to know the nature and quality of the act he was doing; or if he did know it, that he did not know he was doing what was wrong" *M'Naghten's case* [1843] UKHL J16 (19 June 1843).

unfitness to plead (as established in the *Pritchard* case[328]). A consequence of either finding in the courts will usually be a court order under the Mental Health Act[329], and as such these are important mechanisms to ensure treatment in hospital under the Act for a small number of mentally disordered offenders. Beyond their practical effect as such mechanisms, it is arguable that these legal formulations give an important symbolic indication of the law's approach to mentally disordered offenders, and in both respects we find them wanting. In our last report we pointed to a case where the House of Lords, sitting as the Judicial Committee of the Privy Council to hear an appeal from St Lucia, was able to apply a more sophisticated insanity test than would be available were they hearing a case from England or Wales[330]. We stated then that this underlined the need for a review of the domestic law.

4.4   We are very pleased that the Law Commission has stated its intention to undertake a review of the insanity defence and the rules regarding fitness to plead:

> Given the vulnerability of the mentally ill and the increasing frequency with which they are coming into contact with the criminal justice system, modern criminal law should be informed by modern science, and in particular by modern psychiatric thinking.
>
> The problems with the existing law are many and serious... The application of these antiquated rules is becoming increasingly difficult and artificial ... the stringent test of capacity for the purposes of fitness to plead also needs to be reconsidered and should be contrasted with the much wider test contained in the Mental Capacity Act 2005[331].

4.5   In two separate cases from this reporting period, judgments in the Court of Appeal have expressed disquiet about the unfitness to plead and insanity rules:

- In July 2008, the Court of Appeal was asked to review the conviction for murder of Ms *M*, who had killed her young daughter five years earlier under the influence of delusions arising from paranoid schizophrenic illness[332]. At the time of trial, medical advice was that she was fit to plead, on the grounds that she met the essentially cognitive criteria of the *Pritchard* test – although the doctor noted that

  > I do not think that she is able to plead with understanding to the indictment. By this I mean that she does not appear able to weigh up appropriately the contribution of mental illness to her behaviour ... if she were able to plead with understanding to the indictment she would plead guilty to manslaughter with diminished responsibility.[333]

  It was therefore acknowledged that the legal test for fitness to plead was inadequate to this situation, in that the law could not recognise *M*'s inability to 'weigh' information

---

[328] *R v Pritchard* [1836] 7 C&P 303. The test is whether the accused can (1) understand the nature of the charge; (2) distinguish between a plea of guilty or not guilty; (3) instruct a lawyer; (4) follow the evidence in court; and (5) challenge a juror to whom he might object. See MHAC (2006) *In Place of Fear?* para 5.17 for a discussion of the limitations of this test.

[329] See MHAC (2006) *In Place of Fear? Eleventh Biennial Report 2003-2005*, para 5.25 *et seq* for a description of changes to the Criminal Procedure (Insanity) Acts in 20004.

[330] MHAC (2008) *Risk, Rights, Recovery* para 7.49 *et seq*.

[331] Law Commission, statement issued July 2008 on www.lawcom.gov.uk/insanity.htm

[332] *R v Murray* [2008] EWCA Crim 1792.

[333] *ibid.*, para 4.

relevant to the decision-making process. It seems that all parties hoped that *M* would in any event plead guilty to manslaughter with diminished responsibility (and the trial judge indicated that he would have accepted this), but when the time came she pleaded guilty. This left the judge with no option but to convict for murder and sentence to life imprisonment. That this was inappropriate disposal was indicated both by the judge's expression of regret at the time, but also by the fact that *M* was soon transferred from prison to psychiatric hospital under s.47/49.

The Court of Appeal accepted in these circumstances that there was medical evidence of both the plea and the offence being affected by mental disorder, and therefore quashed her conviction for murder, substituting a conviction for manslaughter with diminished responsibility and making a hospital order under s.37/41. Lord Justice Toulson noted the likely Law Commission review of the law regarding fitness to plead, and remarked that "this case, although unusual, may be an appropriate case for it to study, for it illustrates in acute form the potential mismatch between the legal test and psychiatric understanding in these matters".[334]

- In July 2007 the Court of Appeal dismissed an appeal against a conviction for wounding with intent to grievous bodily harm[335]. The appellant, who had been made subject to a hospital order under s.37/41 following conviction (and so in essence was unlikely to gain any material change of circumstance if successful), wanted the conviction substituted for a verdict of not guilty by reason of insanity, on the grounds that he did not know that what he did was wrong at the time of the offence. Such an outcome had been rejected in the preliminary hearing to his trial because, although his actions were motivated by delusions subsequent to paranoid schizophrenia, he was deemed to have known that what he had done was against the law. The court, following legal authorities (and in particular the 1952 *Windle* case[336]), stated that "did not know he was doing what was wrong" in the *M'Nagthen* rules is a test of whether the accused knows that the action is contrary to law and not of whether he felt it to be justified as a result of delusional belief. Lord Justice Latham acknowledged that legal experts (in particular Professor Ronald MacKay) had demonstrated that other courts had "on occasions been prepared to approach the issue on a more relaxed basis", but although "there is room for reconsideration of rules … it does not seem to us that that debate …can properly take place before us at this level in this case".[337]

4.6   In our Eleventh Biennial Report we discussed the case of John Straffen as an example of the potential for illogicality in the application of the insanity defence[338]. Straffen was accused of killing a child during his brief escape from Broadmoor hospital in 1952. He was convicted of murder, despite having been found unfit to plead to the offences that originally had him sent him to Broadmoor, and despite agreement at the time of his trial

---

[334] *ibid.*, para 6.

[335] *R v Johnson* [2007] EWCA Crim 1978, 9 July 2007.

[336] *R v Windle* [1952] 2QB 826. Windle killed his suicidal wife then telephoned the police and said, "I suppose I'll hang for this." It was held that this was sufficient to show that although the defendant was suffering from a mental illness, he was aware that his act was wrong.

[337] *R v Johnson* [2007], paras 23 – 24.

[338] MHAC (2006) *In Place of Fear? Eleventh Biennial Report 2003-2005*, footnote 82, p.366.

that he had a mental age of less than ten years due to mental impairment. Straffen died during this reporting period, having become Britain's longest serving prisoner, although we understand that at the time of his death he was due for transfer to a secure psychiatric facility outside of the prison system[339].

4.7 It seems to us that one lesson of the Straffen case is that the insanity defences – and indeed other forms of diversion of mentally disordered offenders from the criminal justice system – are too easily pushed aside when the offence being considered has some notoriety or shocking aspect. Also in this reporting period, Mr Justice Calvert-Smith rejected defence applications for Mohammed Saeed-Alim (Nicky Reilly) to be assessed in Broadmoor hospital before sentencing him to life imprisonment for his attempted suicide bombing in Exeter. Although Reilly has diagnosed learning disability and Asperger's Syndrome, the conviction for attempted murder was justified by the court on the grounds that he was aware of his actions and their consequences[340]. Unfortunately, insofar as this might be put to a legal test in the law of England and Wales, the test that would be applied is far from congruent with psychiatric understanding of mental disorder.

Section 37/41 as an alternative to imprisonment

4.8 The Court of Appeal heard a case in October 2007 that highlights one example of how sentencing judges can push aside mechanisms for the diversion of mentally disordered offenders from the criminal justice system out of misplaced concerns over the future control of risk[341]. The judgment is particularly valuable, in addition, for the fact that it identifies such concerns as misplaced, and states clearly that public protection can be as well served when a mentally disordered offender is ordered to hospital under restrictions as it would be by the passing of a sentence of life imprisonment.

4.9 The appellant had been sentenced to life imprisonment, with a minimum of six years to serve less time on remand, for the attempted murder of a woman that he had attacked whilst suffering from a delusional disorder. The sentencing judge in this case had accepted that the offender met the criteria for a hospital order under s.37, and indeed had recommendations from two doctors that such a disposal would be appropriate. He declined to make such an order

> …in the light of the wider interests of public protection, to which I am bound to have regard. Section 37 and section 41 of the Mental Health Act, as [one of the recommending doctors] recognises, do not provide the same level of public protection as a custodial sentence.[342]

4.10 It was stated in the Court of Appeal that the judge's particular concerns over a psychiatric disposal related, firstly, to the possibility of escape, and, secondly, to the possibility that the discharge provisions under the Mental Health Act might in certain circumstances be

---

[339] Bob Woffinden, "John Straffen" [obituary], *The Guardian*, 22 November 2007.

[340] Owen Boycott "Life sentence for inept bomber who targeted restaurant", *The Guardian*, 31 Jan 2009. See also "Sentencing of Nicky Reilly shows up our justice system" *The Guardian*, Letters, Monday 2 February 2009.

[341] *R v Jonathan Paul Simpson* [2007] EWCA Crim 2666.

[342] *ibid.*, para 1.1.12.

less stringent than the criteria applied by the parole board. On the first issue, the Court of Appeal determined that the identified medium secure psychiatric unit (Reaside Clinic) would be able to manage the risks posed by the patient, both because it had sufficiently stringent security measures and also because an important part of managing that risk would be psychiatric treatment. On the question of discharge criteria, the Court of Appeal, following Lord Bingham of Cornhill in *R v Offen*[343], found that it was incorrect to assume that a hospital regime guaranteeing psychiatric treatment afforded less protection to the public than a regime of custody for life:

> …the best chance of minimising the danger lies in a hospital order rather than imprisonment… the danger emanates substantially from a deep seated mental illness and it is treatment for that illness accompanied by secure conditions which give the best chance of eliminating or minimising the risk and, if ever appropriate, of rehabilitating him into society.[344]

4.11 Being satisfied that a place was still available at Reaside Clinic, the court quashed the life sentence and substituted a hospital order with restrictions, asking that its judgment "accompanies the appellant and is drawn to the attention of all those concerned in his management and treatment, and in any future consideration of his possible release".[345]

4.12 At figure 64 below we show the use by the courts of hospital orders under s.37, with or without an accompanying restriction order, over the last two decades. Whilst the recent upturn in the use of the power is a welcome sign (on the grounds that every individual case is a diversion from the criminal justice system), it must be recognised in the light of the massive increase in prison population during this period that the overall proportion of diversions may have fallen considerably over this period.

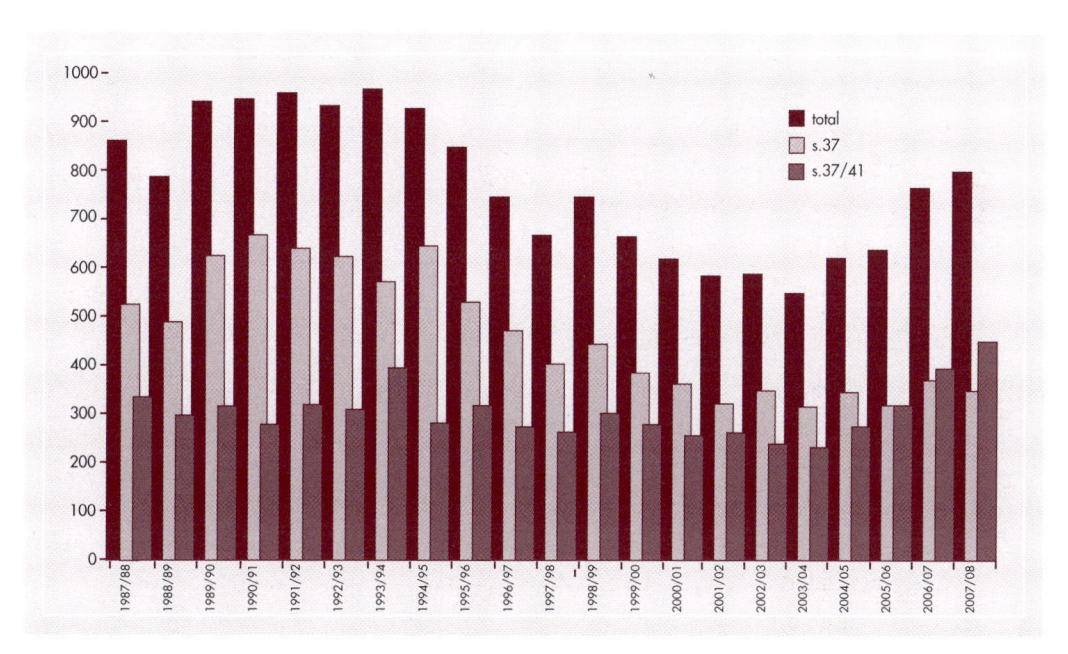

Fig 64: Hospital orders under s.37 passed by the courts, restricted (s.41) and unrestricted, England, 1987/8 to 2007/8

Source: as for fig 1

---

[343] *R v Offen* [2001] 1 WLR 253, cited by Mance LJ in R v IA [2006] 1 Cr App R(S) 521.

[344] *R v Jonathan Paul Simpson* [2007], para 1.1.30.

[345] *ibid.*, para 1.1.33.

4.13 It is also notable that the recent increase is accounted for by court orders with restrictions, and that the numbers of unrestricted court orders have fallen considerably over the period. There are several possible interpretations of this. It may be argued that these are both phenomena of increasingly risk-averse judicial disposals, or even of 'reinstitutionalisation'[346]. Alternatively, a more positive – and extremely speculative – interpretation might view the fall in unrestricted hospital orders as indicative that the courts are using more community sentences where they would previously have required hospital treatment.

4.14 Statistics on hospital orders under s.37 in Wales (figure 65 below) are difficult to interpret because of the relatively low numbers involved. Over the last decade, there have been an average of about 50 admissions per year as a result of s.37 hospital orders, of which about 30 were subject to an additional restriction order. If there is a discernable trend in the use of hospital orders in Wales, it may be in the increasing proportion of independent sector hospitals receiving such patients from the courts (figure 66).

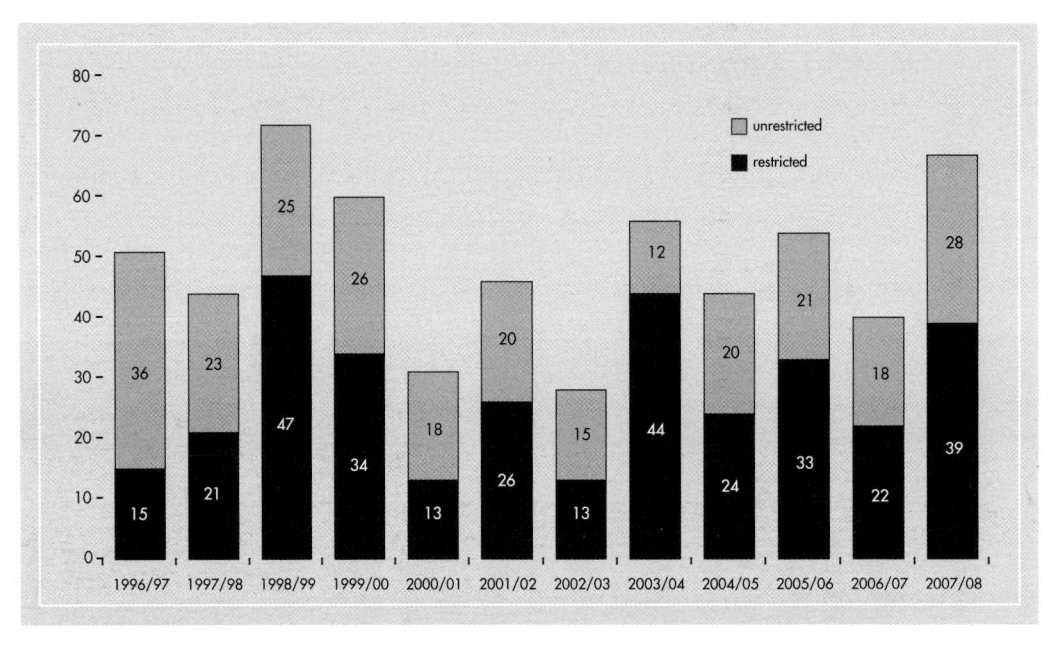

Fig 65: Hospital Orders (s.37), NHS and independent hospitals, Wales, 1996/97 to 2007/08 – restricted and unrestricted orders

Data source: Welsh Assembly Government Statistics for Wales

---

[346] MHAC (2006) *In Place of Fear? Eleventh Biennial Report 2003-2005*, para 2.53 *et seq*; MHAC (2008) *Risk, Rights, Recovery; Twelfth Biennial Report 2005-2007*, para 1.19 *et seq*.

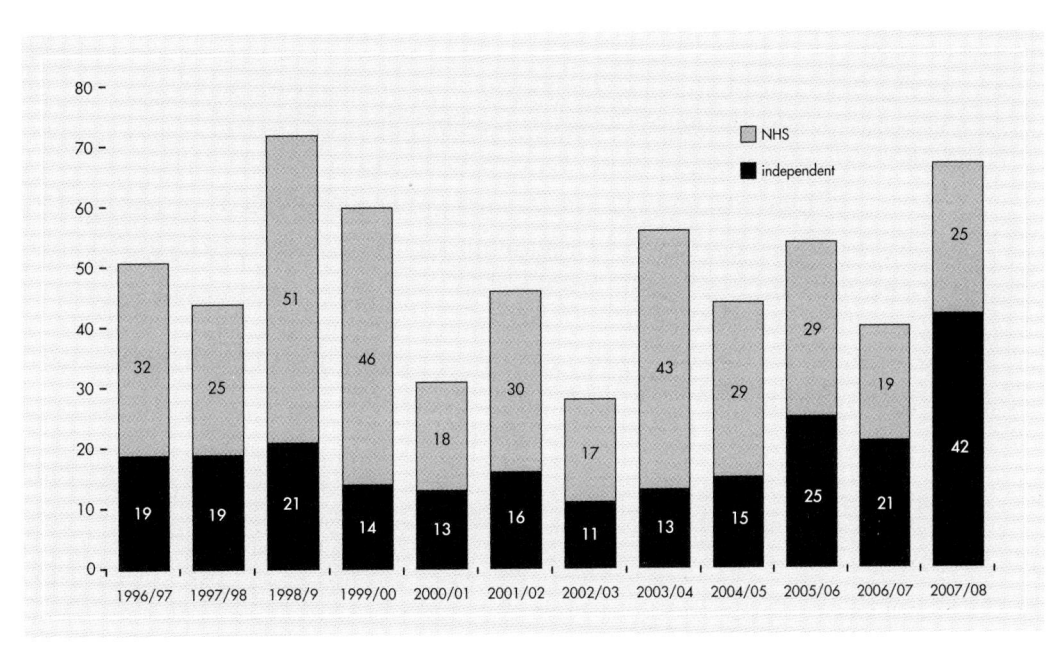

Fig 66: Hospital Orders (s.37, restricted and unrestricted), Wales, 1996/97 to 2007/08 – NHS and independent hospital provision

Data source: Welsh Assembly Government Statistics for Wales

Probation as an alternative to Mental Health Act Disposals

4.15 Ministry of Justice data does appear to show a significant increase in the number of offenders starting probation services' supervision with a requirement of mental health treatment for 2006 and 2007 (figure 67).

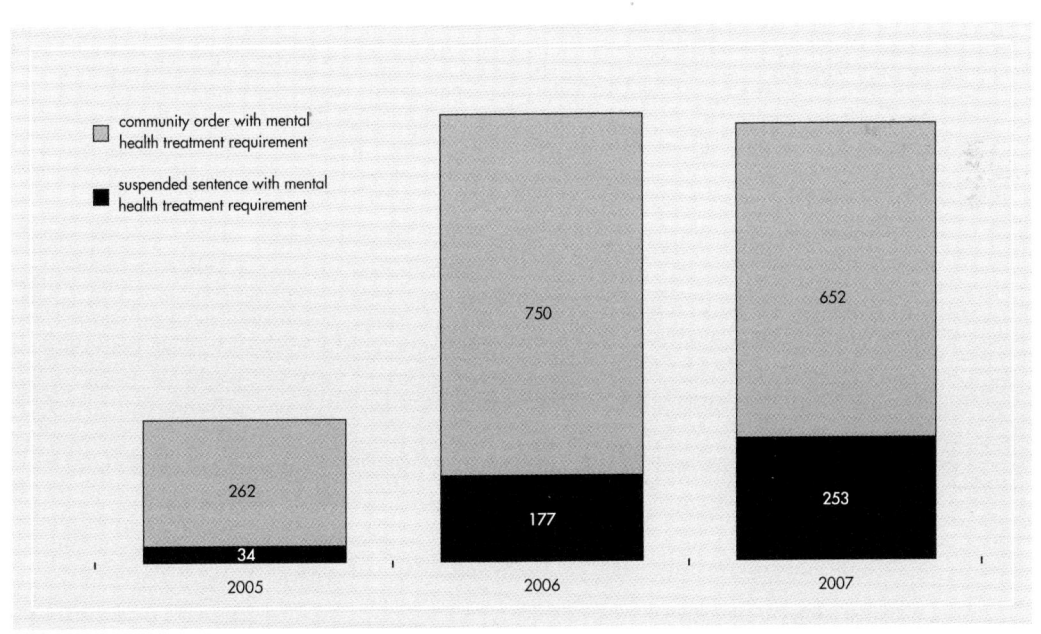

Fig 67: Mental health treatment requirements commenced under community orders and suspended sentence orders, 2005 – 2007

Data source: Ministry of Justice[347]

---

[347] Ministry of Justice (2008), *Offender Management Caseload Statistics 2007*. For earlier data see MHAC (2006) *In Place of Fear? Eleventh Biennial Report 2003-2005*, Fig 166, page 424.

4.16 The data shown at figure 67 above is not directly comparable with that published for earlier years by the Home Office, due to the introduction of new community orders in April 2005, and differences in data collection. Nevertheless, we have shown the Home Office data at figure 68 below as a rough comparison. Such a comparison suggests that the levels of mental treatment requirements ordered in 2006 and 2007 are not unprecedented, although they may represent a significant upturn in courts' use of probation services to deliver mental health treatment and divert mentally disordered offenders. As the Sainsbury Centre report *The Community Order and the Mental Health Treatment Requirement* has shown[348], there was a steady increase in 2005/06 in the use of the newly-introduced community orders (which were effectively a re-launch of the probation order with psychiatric treatment).

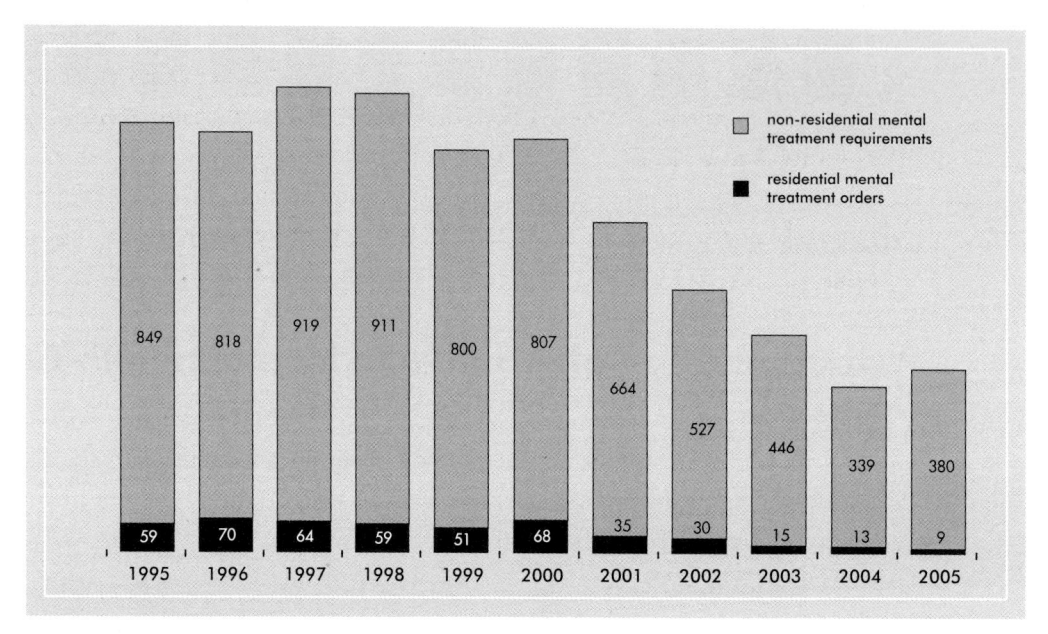

Fig 68: Mental health treatment requirements commenced under community rehabilitation orders and community punishment and rehabilitation orders, 1995 – 2005

Data source: Home Office[349]

4.17 The grounds for making a community order with a mental health treatment requirement are that;

- treatment to improve the offender's mental health problem will be provided;

- any hospital treatment is not given in a high secure psychiatric unit;

- the offender's mental health problem requires and may be susceptible to treatment, but is not serious enough to invoke the sections of the Mental Health Act 1983;

- the practitioners and services are available to carry out the treatment; and

- the offender is willing to comply with the requirement.

---

[348] Sainsbury Centre for Mental Health (2008) *The Community Order and the Mental Health Treatment Requirement*. Linda Seymour and Max Rutherford. Jan 2008, fig 5 p.14.

[349] Home Office (2005) *Offender Management Caseload Statistics, England & Wales, 2005*.

4.18 Whether or not an offender's mental health problem is serious enough to invoke sections of the Mental Health Act (i.e. detain that person in hospital) will in part depend on what level of services are available in the community. As such, given development in suitable community-based services, there is some potential for community orders to be used much like the stand-alone community treatment order envisaged in the failed Mental Health Bill of 2002. It may be that such developments are some way off, however.

4.19 The National Audit Office has suggested that offenders who leave court with a mental health treatment requirement are likely to have already been in receiving treatment when they went in: the NAO sample found no instances of mental health treatment itself being instigated by the court[350]. There are a number of reasons to doubt that the courts are effectively identifying mental health treatment needs for those people who receive community disposals[351]. Research by King's College has shown the use of mental health treatment requirements (less than 1% of all community order requirements) does not correspond with the incidence of offenders exhibiting mental health needs who are given community orders (43%)[352].

Mentally disordered women and diversion from the criminal justice system

4.20 Figure 69 below shows the total court disposals under the Mental Health Act (sections 45A, 35, 36, 37 and 37/41) from 1987/88, according to Information Centre data.

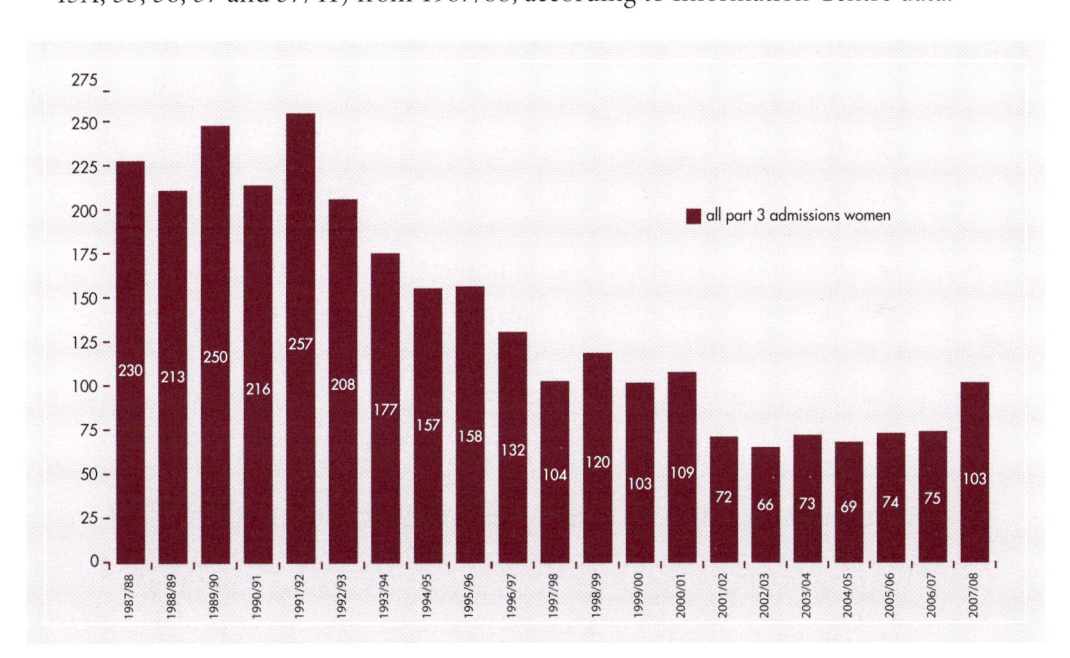

Fig 69: Court disposals under the MHA of mentally disordered women, 1987/88 to 2007/08, England

Data source: as for fig 1

---

[350] National Audit Office (2008) *National Probation Service – The Supervision Of Community Orders In England And Wales.*

[351] Enver Solomon and Arianna Silvestri (2008) *Community Sentences Digest,* second edition, Centre for Crime and Justice Studies, King's College London. November 2008, page 32.

[352] House of Commons Committee of Public Accounts (2008) *The Supervision of Community Orders in England and Wales. Forty-eighth report of session 2007-08* HC 508, p.15.

4.21 The overall decline in court disposals under the Mental Health Act over the last two decades is a matter of some concern, given the rising numbers of women in prison (and of rising recognition of psychiatric morbidity in women prisoners) during that time. We discuss this further in relation to prison transfers at paragraph 4.28 below.

Returning patients on remand or interim orders to court

4.22 In our Eleventh Biennial Report[353] we raised the problem of who should be responsible on court premises for patients who have been brought there from detention in hospital, whether this is under an interim order of the Act, following transfer from imprisonment on remand, or for other reasons. The Mental Health Act Code of Practice, prior to its revision in 2008, stated that it was the responsibility of the detaining hospital to convey the patient to court as required, although "once on the court premises, the patient will come under the supervision of the police or prison officers there".[354] This did not reflect actual practice as it developed subsequent to publication, as court security was contracted out under a condition that excluded mentally disordered offenders detained under Mental Health Act powers from the responsibility of court security services. The revised Codes of Practice now both state that "if possible, and bearing in mind the patient's needs, medical or nursing staff should stay with the patient on court premises, even though legal accountability while detained for hearings remains with the court".[355]

4.23 In reality, it appears to be the case that mental health and hospital security professionals continue to be expected to take charge of the security of patients throughout the court proceedings, irrespective of any clinical needs that the patient may have. This has raised some concerns over the actual legal accountability in the event of an incident, and in our Eleventh report we recorded concerns over practical arrangements made within some courts where hospital staff have been only reluctantly given access to secure facilities, or have been unable to obtain food for the patient whilst on court premises, or where nursing staff have been left without adequate help whilst on court premises. In our Eleventh report we urged government to look again at this matter, but have heard that no progress has been made on addressing these concerns. We therefore repeat our request.

Recommendation: Government should look address the concerns of mental health services over court-based security provision with a view to ensuring that court administration fufils its legal duties towards the custody of defendants.

---

[353] MHAC (2006) *In Place of Fear? Eleventh Biennial Report 2003-2005*, para 5.80 *et seq*.

[354] *MHA Code of Practice* (1999 version), para 29.6.

[355] *MHA Code of Practice for England*, para 33.26; *Code of Practice for Wales*, para 32.32.

Transfer from prison

> At the start of my stay in hospital I felt very alone, scared, frightened and disorientated. A prison officer came to my ward and told me to pack my things as I'd been sectioned and was on my way to hospital. I have been told by another patient who was there at the time that I literally climbed the walls and had to be sedated when they told me the night before transfer. On the day of transfer I woke up in a strip cell, after being given liquid cosh (largactil) the night before.
>
> Upon arriving I was strip searched, given a welcome pack (baccy, soap, rizlas) then met by three large men in white smocks and a lady in a suit. I thought, oh my god, what's this? There's no hope for me now, I'm never getting out. I was frogmarched by the reception committee down long bare corridors through many locked gates to Cavendish acute admissions. Given medication. No choice, drink this. Swallow these. Shown room which was bare, dark, and grimy, with locked shutters on windows, bare floor, bed and a cupboard. Told to leave my stuff and then taken to a day room where there were nineteen other patients, none of whom I knew, mostly heavily sedated. I felt I had walked into a living nightmare.
>
> *Glyn James, SURP member.*

4.24 The immense challenge of providing appropriate hospital places for prisoners suffering from serious mental disorder has been detailed very clearly in the Prison Reform Trust publication *Too Little, Too Late: an independent review of unmet mental health need in prison*.[356] Whilst recognising Department of Health initiatives to reduce waiting times for transfers to hospital of such prisoners under the Mental Health Act, it reports that just over half Independent Monitoring Boards for prisons reported serious delays in arranging transfers, and fewer than a quarter of such Boards felt that transfers were achieved in a timely and therapeutic way. The quarter of Boards who provided more positive reports described various improvements in therapeutic work with prisoners leading up to transfer, and better communication and links with NHS services. The majority still felt that administrative delays – including in arranging PCT funding for prisoners' hospital places – were still unacceptable. Boards continued to report the misuse of segregation facilities in prison to contain those awaiting transfer: arrangements that, whilst possibly unavoidable for the containment of an acutely disordered prisoner prior to transfer, may well be extremely damaging to the prognosis of the disorder and the speed or effectiveness of recovery.

4.25 Although the 'principle of equivalence' means that prisoners should have access to the same quality of healthcare as people in the community, including access to a hospital place in the event of severe mental disorder, the Prison Reform Trust concludes that

> the problems with transfers (delays, lack of available places, disputes about eligibility or which PCT is responsible) highlight the 'prisoner or patient' gulf. There is a huge gap between what happens to a severely mentally ill person person in prison and one who falls ill in the community.[357]

---

[356] Prison Reform Trust (2009) *Too Little, Too Late: an independent review of unmet mental health need in prison.* Kimmett Edgar and Dora Rickford, see especially Chapter 5, *Transfers*.

[357] *ibid.*, p. 22.

4.26 In our last report we welcomed a renewed focus in Government departments on increasing the number and speed of transfers to hospital of seriously mentally disordered prisoners using powers of the Mental Health Act[358]. As in our last report, we are able to cite Mental Health Unit statistics showing that a record number of prisoners have been transferred under restriction orders in this way (see figure 70 below). On the 31 December 2007, there were 968 patients detained following transfer from prison (either after sentence or while unsentenced or untried). This represents a 21 per cent increase on the 2006 figure, and the highest figure and largest yearly increase over the last decade[359].

> I was first detained under the Mental Health Act in 1991 after waiting for 18 months in prison. At the start of my stay I was pleased to be out of prison and in a hospital, where food and conditions were better. Prior to this I had never experienced mental health services. While I was in prison I had a visit and interview from a staff nurse who was from the hospital I was going to be sent to. He did leave me with hope and feeling more positive. On arrival to the hospital I was informed by admin staff that I was detained under the Mental Health Act.
>
> Mark Gray, SURP member

4.27 As we discussed in our last report[360], we are very pleased that the number of prison transfers appears to be rising, but it must also be acknowledged that, with the rise in the prison population, there are likely to be a great many more prisoners with serious mental disorders who require such transfer. It remains the case that the transfer rate of restricted patients per 1,000 prisoners is lower now than in the mid-1990s, when it peaked at over 17 such transfers for every 1,000 prisoners[361]. The prison population in June 2006 was 77,982[362], and so the 894 restricted patients that were transferred in that year represent an average of just over 11 such transfers per 1,000 prisoners. If we assume that 10% of the prison population suffer from psychotic illness[363], this leaves 6,900 prisoners whose psychotic illness is managed – or perhaps not managed – in prison. Alongside prisoners with psychotic illnesses, there are of course a great deal more who have personality disorders or learning disabilities that could warrant their removal to places of appropriate care and treatment (see paragraph 4.6 above).

---

[358] MHAC (2008) *Risk, Rights, Recovery; Twelfth Biennial Report 2005-2007*, para 7.6.

[359] Ministry of Justice (2009) *Statistics of Mentally Disordered Offenders* 2007, p.5.

[360] MHAC (2008) *Risk, Rights, Recovery; Twelfth Biennial Report 2005-2007*, para 7.6.

[361] ibid.: see para 7.6 and fig 74 of *Risk, Rights, Recovery*. The peak level of transfers (17.3 per 2,000) was in 1993.

[362] National Offender Management Scheme (2006) *Population in Custody, Monthly Tables*, June 2006.

[363] MHAC (2008) *Risk, Rights, Recovery ibid.*, see para 7.6 and footnote 583 of *Risk, Rights, Recovery*: 10% "is a modest assumption given current estimates", such as that of the Home Office (2005) *Memorandum submitted to the Select Committee on Home Affairs* (HC-656-I, October 2005), which suggested rates of psychosis amongst prisoners of 11% (men) and 15% (women).

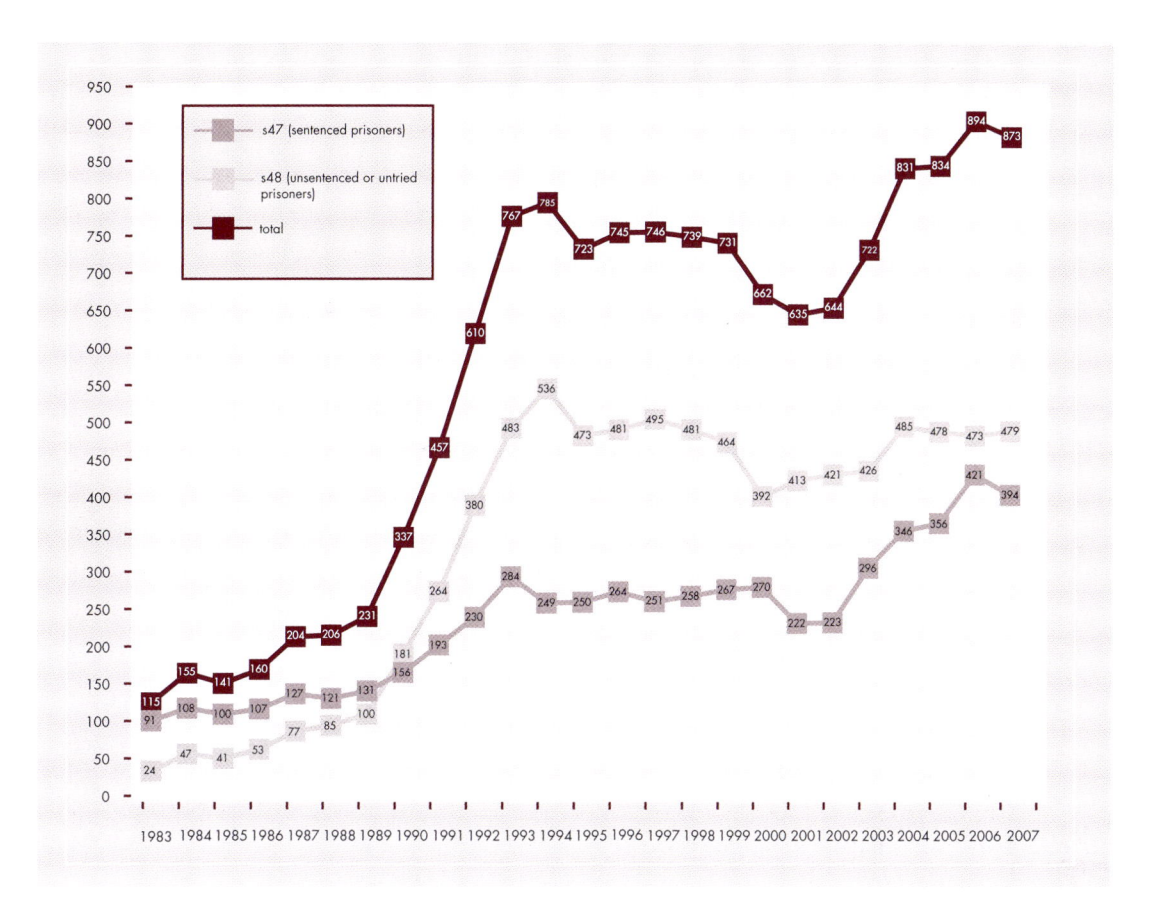

Fig 70: Prison transfers under restriction orders, 1983 – 2007

Source: Mental Health Unit Statistics of Mentally Disordered Offenders 1985 – 2008

Women prisoners and transfer under the Mental Health Act

4.28 The women's prison population more than doubled between 1995 and 2001[364], and has averaged roughly 44,000 since 2002[365]. The mental health needs of such prisoners are acknowledged to be high, with 70% of sentenced women prisoners estimated to have at least two mental disorders, and 37% reporting previous suicide attempts[366]. Thirty per cent of women have had previous psychiatric admission before they come into prison[367], and at least five to eight per cent of women in prison – and probably a greater percentage than this – are likely to suffer from serious and enduring mental disorder[368]. As such, we can estimate that, at any time since 2002, the prison estates have housed a changing population of at least 350 seriously mentally disordered women at any one time. This is seven times the average number of women prisoners who transferred to hospital under the powers of the Mental Health Act in any year during that period.

[364] Melcott D "Women in Prison" in Jewkes Y, (ed) (2007) *Handook on Prisons*. Willan Publishing.

[365] Home Office / Ministry of Justice (1998 – 2008) *Population in Custody, England & Wales: monthly tables* (we have used October for each year in this calculation).

[366] Melcott *op.cit*, citing data from Social Exclusion Unit (2002) *Reducing re-offending by ex-prisoners*, London: Social Exclusion Unit.

[367] Department of Health, Conference Report, *Sharing Good Practice in Prison Health*, 4/5 June 2007: see Prison Reform Trust (2008) *Bromley Briefings Prison Factfile*, page 29.

[368] Department of Health (2000) *The NHS Plan: a plan for investment, a plan for reform*. The figure of 5–8 % of prisoners with serious and enduring mental disorder applies to male and female prisoners. Given the higher incidence of previous psychiatric admission, etc, in women patients, it is likely to be an underestimate.

4.29 Data collected by the Information Centre, and presented at figure 71 below, suggests that women prisoners have benefited less, if at all, from the increasing rate of transfers from prison than their male counterparts. Given the above facts about imprisoned women, this is unlikely to be for want of any need, and therefore implies that a greater focus on women's prisons could be required.

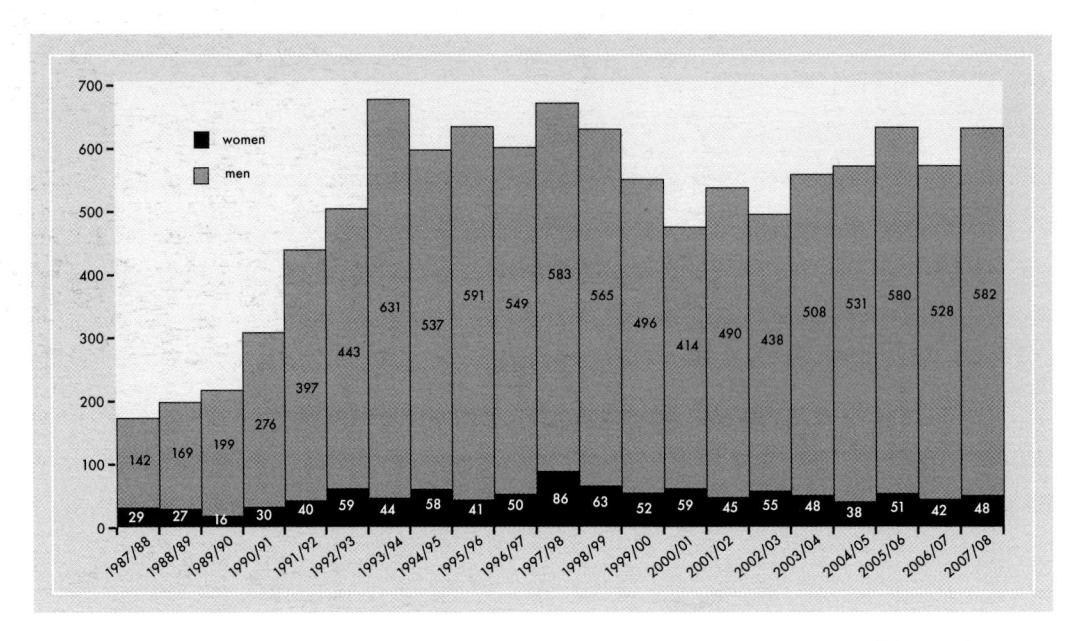

Fig 71: Transfers from prison under the Mental Health Act, 1987/88 to 2007/08, all hospitals, England

Data source: as for fig 1

Transfers from prison without restriction orders

4.30 The number of transfers shown at figure 70 above is not the total number of transfers in any year, as it excludes unrestricted patients. The Mental Health Unit claims to "authorise around 1,000 transfers under sections 47 and 48 per year"[369], implying perhaps one hundred unrestricted transfers in addition the transfers of restricted patients shown at figure 70. According to Information Centre data collections, there were 58 such transfers in 2007/08, but numbers of unrestricted transfers seem to fluctuate, as is shown at figure 72 below.

---

[369] Ministry of Justice Mental Health Unit Bulletin, March 2008, p. 4.

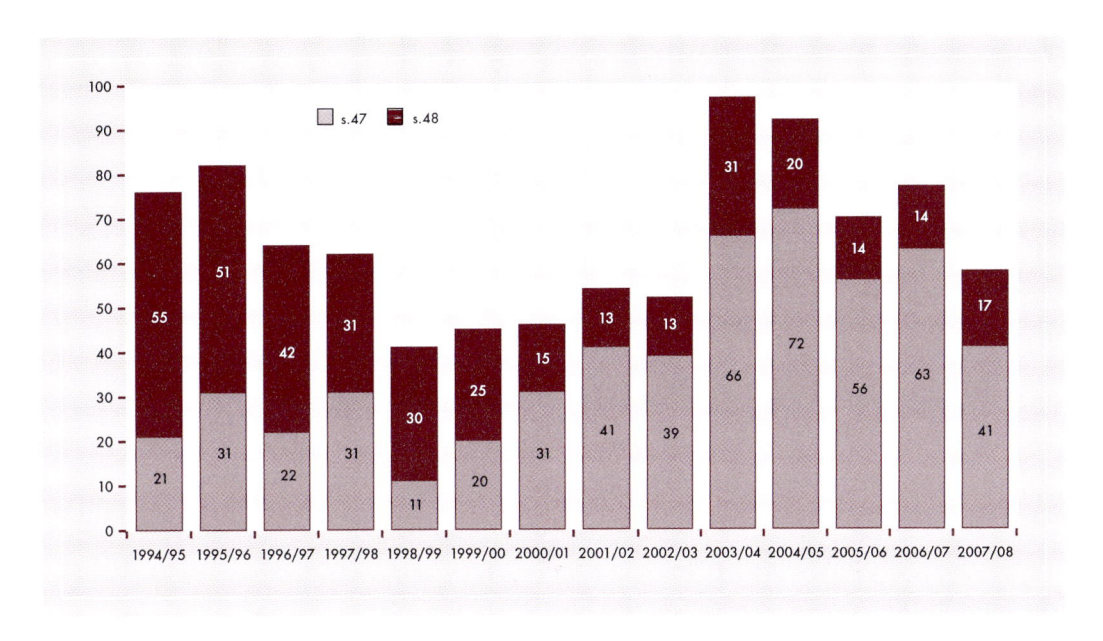

Fig 72: Prison transfers under ss.47 and 48 (without restrictions) 1994/05 to 2007/08

Source: as for fig 1

4.31 We know relatively little about these unrestricted transfers, and indeed the very existence of statistics showing unrestricted transfers under s.48 is something of a mystery, and the number of unrestricted transfers under s.47 a potential concern, given the stated policy of the Mental Health Unit that

> the Secretary of State will always apply restrictions (section 49) to a section 48 transfer and almost always to a section 47 transfer (the only exception being where the patient is very close to their earliest date of release from prison).[370]

4.32 Assuming that the statistics provided by detaining authorities to the Information Centre are correct, the small number of prisoners transferred under s.48 without restrictions (an annual average of 20 over the last decade) must either be either civil prisoners (i.e. those committed to prison for contempt of court or for non-payment of a fine) or detainees under immigration or asylum law[371]. In our last report we noted that in the twelve months to February 2007, eight immigration detainees had been transferred to hospital under s.48 (although not necessarily without restricted status), and discussed our concerns over the management of immigration detainees under the Mental Health Act[372]. This would be a very fruitful area for further monitoring or research.

4.33 There may also be a need to look more closely at unrestricted s.47 transfers. According to the Information Centre data, there have been 60 such transfers annually on average over the last five years (or an average of 44 per year over the last decade). We do not assume that the transfer of a patient 'very close to their earliest date of release from

---

[370] ibid.

[371] Only such classes of prisoner can be transferred under s.48 without restriction, should the Secretary of State authorise this. Remand prisoners, for example, can only be transferred as restricted patients: see MHA s.49(1).

[372] MHAC (2008) *Risk, Rights, Recovery; Twelfth Biennial Report 2005-2007*, para 7.23 *et seq*.

prison' is necessarily a bad thing, and indeed if patients do need to be transferred at such a stage of their imprisonment then it is surely right that they are not subject to restriction orders. Neither do we necessarily conflate transfers near to the earliest date of release with transfers at the end of a sentence: but we discuss our serious concerns over the latter below and would welcome further opportunities for monitoring or research into the nature and circumstances of the use of the Act represented by these statistics. We also hope that the Mental Health Unit will in future provide statistics on all of the transfers that it approves, and not just those to which it applies restricted status. Such data should also provide information on gender and ethnicity of transferees, for monitoring purposes and to ensure compliance with duties under anti-discrimination law.

Prison transfers in Wales

4.34 Figure 73 below shows the transfers of prisoners under restricted and unrestricted orders in Wales over the last 12 years. Figure 74 below shows the sector – independent or NHS – into which such prisoners were transferred.

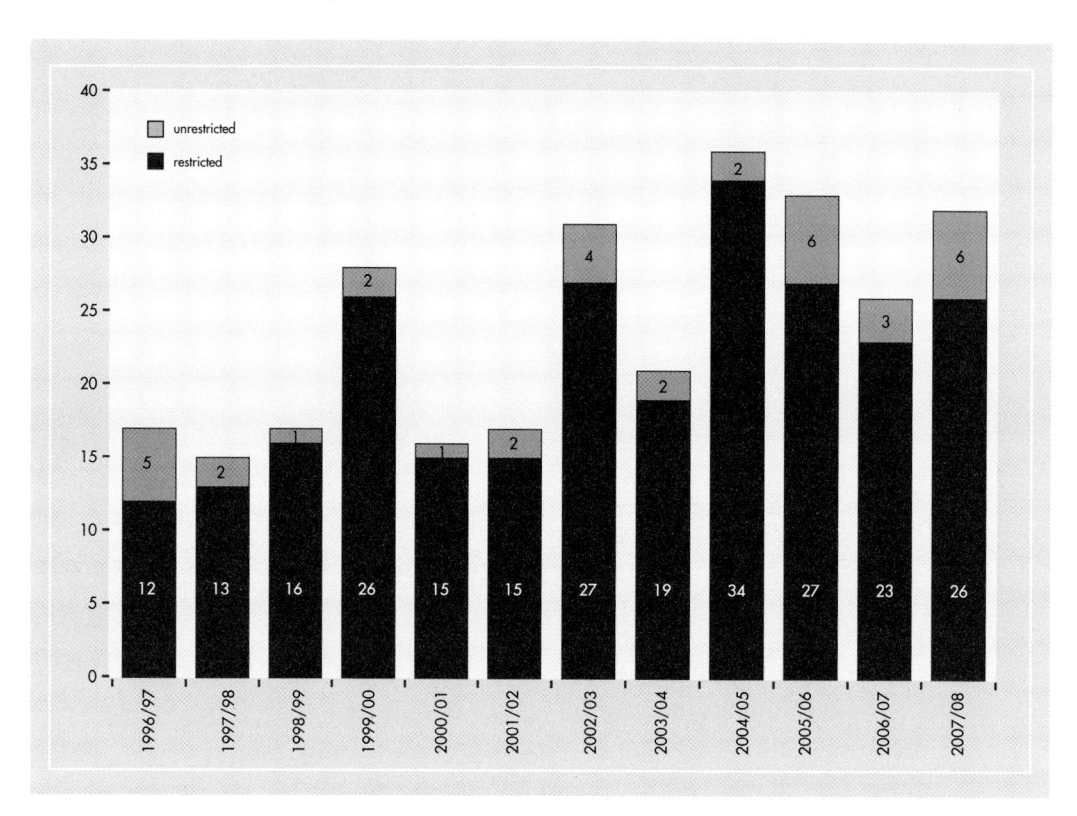

Fig 73: All prison transfers (s.47 and 48), restricted and unrestricted, Wales, 1996/97 to 2007/08

Data source: Welsh Assembly Government Statistics for Wales

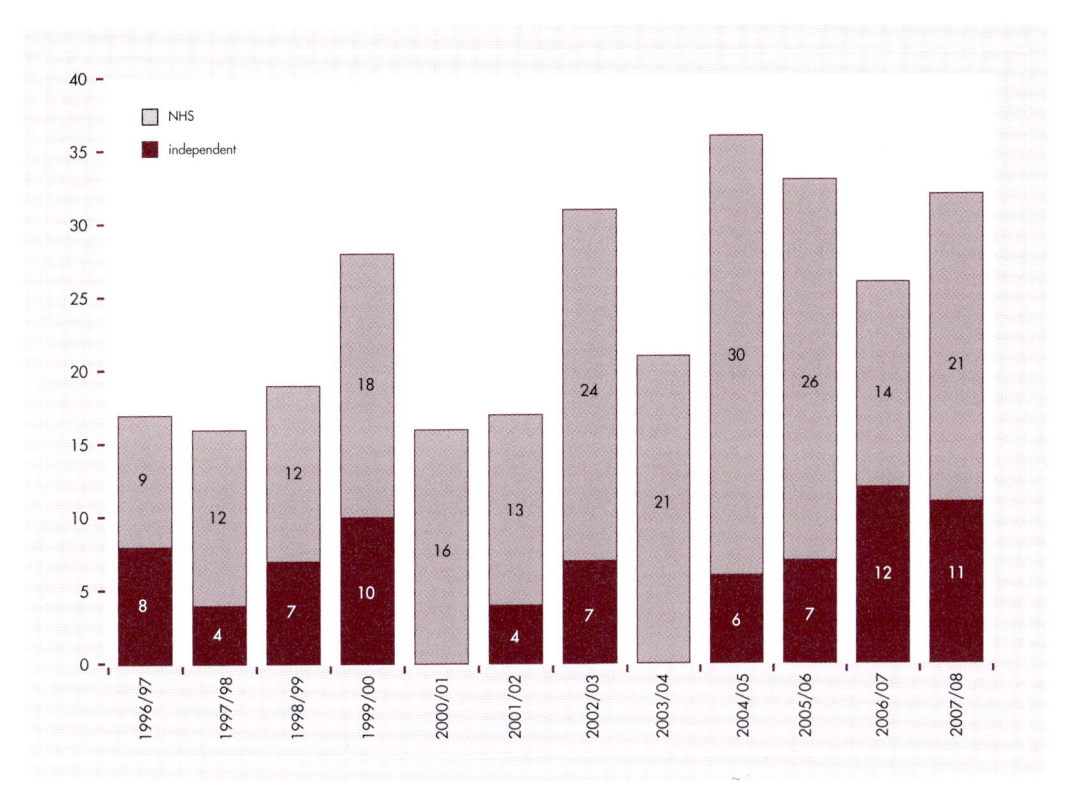

Fig 74: Prison transfers (s.47 and s.48, restricted and unrestricted), NHS and independent hospitals, Wales, 1996/97 to 2007/08

Data source: Welsh Assembly Government Statistics for Wales

Treatability

4.35　In our last report we highlighted the 2006 European Court of Human Rights' judgment *Jean-Luc Rivière v France*[373], which held that the detention of a seriously mentally ill and actively suicidal person in prison without proper facilities or treatment for his mental disorder could amount to inhuman and degrading treatment, and as such be in breach of Article 3 of the European Convention on Human Rights. We note with interest suggestions that the revisions to the Mental Health Act may strengthen potential claimants' cases in England and Wales. Rebecca Fitzpatrick has argued that the revised Mental Health Act's adoption of a single generic category of mental disorder, coupled with the replacement of a 'treatability test' by a test that 'appropriate medical treatment is available',

> makes it more likely that certain prisoners suffering from serious personality disorders (particularly those that are self-harming or putting others at risk) now meet the criteria for detention in hospital rather than in prison and so should be transferred. Successful judicial review, human rights and other legal challenges may follow, where prisoners do not receive appropriate treatment.[374]

---

[373] *Jean-Luc Rivière v France* (11 July 2006, app no 33834/03). See MHAC (2008) *Risk, Rights, Recovery: Twelfth Biennial Report 2005 – 2007*, para 7.9.

[374] Rebecca Fitzpatrick (2009) "'Mad', 'Bad', Dangerous'…? The impact of the Mental Health Act 2007 on our prison population." *Hill Dickinson Healthcare Focus*, January 2009. Reprinted in *Health Service Journal*, 7 January 2009, *The Mental Health Act and the prison population*, Becky Fitzpatrick.

4.36 However, we recognise the resource limitations that preclude the wholesale transfer of all seriously mentally disordered prisoners to psychiatric facilities outside of the prison estates: there are insufficient numbers of hospital beds to take them. It may be that this gap can be bridged in part by the provision of specialist in-reach psychiatric care for prisoners, although we are reluctant to concede that prison can ever be an appropriate environment for a seriously mentally disordered person. The Secretary of State for Justice remains under a duty expeditiously to take reasonable steps to obtain medical advice and transfer the prisoner to psychiatric hospital, if appropriate, where there are reasonable grounds that a prisoner requires treatment there[375].

4.37 There is, however, a potential hazard to some prisoners if it is true that the criteria for transfer to hospital have been widened by the revisions to the 1983 Act, which is explored in the next section.

Late transfers from prison and the fear of preventative detention

4.38 We accept that there are difficult decisions to be made, both by prison mental health workers and by the Ministry of Justice Mental Health Unit, in deciding which mentally disordered prisoners are most in need of transfer. It is clear that the demand must outstrip the supply of available hospital places. The Mental Health Unit has described its approach to prioritisation as follows:

> We give priority in issuing warrants to those cases where there is an inherent urgency (e.g. patient is refusing fluids or suicidal, close to their date of release and when the bed is available)[376].

4.39 It is, of course, inevitable that such cases should be brought to the front of the transfer queue, and the MHAC is not critical of taking such an approach. However, we remain concerned that the Mental Health Unit's prioritisation of prisoners who are near to their release date may sometimes have more to do with concerns for public safety than clinical need.

4.40 From its Third Biennial Report in 1989[377], the MHAC has expressed concerns about the transfer of prisoners to hospital under the Act shortly before the expiry of their sentences. We continue to meet with such patients, who express their shock and sense of injustice at their situation. These patients can often be a management problem in the hospitals to which they are taken, as they will be reluctant to engage with therapeutic aspects of hospital life[378].

4.41 In our Eleventh Biennial Report, we raised some concerns over the apparent levels of scrutiny applied over whether a patient transferred late in his sentence met the criteria for detention under the Act[379]. The medical recommendations for transfer did not, in

---

[375] *R (on the application of D) v Secretary of State for the Home Department and National Assembly for Wales* [2004] EWHC 2857 (Admin), para 33.

[376] Ministry of Justice Mental Health Unit Bulletin, March 2008, p. 4.

[377] MHAC (1989) *Third Biennial Report 1987-1989*, para 11.2.

[378] MHAC (2008) *Risk, Rights, Recovery; Twelfth Biennial Report 2005-2007*, para 7.19.

[379] MHAC (2006) *In Place of Fear? Eleventh Biennial Report 2003-2005*, para 5.74 *et seq*.

our view, make a clear case that the criteria were met. Correspondence from the Mental Health Unit to one of the medical referees had stated that "we are eager to get him transferred to a hospital under s.47/49 of the MHA before [his prison release] date", and we commented that

> it was clear that there were pressures on [Mental Health Unit] administrators (whose primary function was deemed to ensuring public protection) to provide a medical rationale for continued detention in this case, and that the rationale was read into the medical reports finally obtained[380].

4.42 In the above case, we wrote to the Mental Health Unit questioning its actions, copying the letter to the Mental Health Review Tribunal with a request that it be disclosed to all parties when the Tribunal considered any appeal. However, we did acknowledge that, in this case, a rationale for detention under the Act *might* have been made (as this was the Mental Health Act before the 2007 Amendment Act, in essence this meant addressing whether the patient's condition met the 'treatability' test[381]). Our point was that the rationale for detention had not been made at the time of transfer, and that this made the transfer questionably lawful.

4.43 This general point was addressed in the Court of Appeal in December 2008[382], albeit over a different case than that we highlighted in our report. In September 2008, a prisoner in a Young Offenders Institute had been transferred (in circumstances that we describe below) under s.47 of the Act to a medium secure unit. The medical opinions used to support the transfer were based on old assessments and only one considered whether the treatability test was met. The Court of Appeal (confirming the view at first hearing) found that it would have been very difficult for the decision maker at the Ministry of Justice to be satisfied that the two reporting doctors had applied their minds to treatability; that the decision maker herself had not applied her mind to that question; and the decision was therefore unlawful. Lord Justice Waller stated that

> The decision under section 47 was being taken right at the end of the appellant's sentence and it was thus a decision that involved depriving him of his liberty. That may often not be the position when section 47 is used because the transfer is in the course of a sentence of imprisonment and the patient's detention in hospital is in exchange for lawful detention in prison. That, as it seems to me, heightens the scrutiny which should be applied both by the Secretary of State as to the evidence on which that decision should be taken, and heightens the scrutiny which the court must apply to the decision of the Secretary of State.
>
> Where section 47 is proposed to be used at the very end of the sentence, and hopefully that will only be in very exceptional cases, the onus must be on the Secretary of State to show that the mind of the decision maker has focused on each of the criteria which it is necessary to satisfy if there is to be power to issue a warrant directing transfer to a hospital.
>
> *(para 31)*

---

[380] *ibid.*, para 5.75.

[381] i.e. that the nature and degree of a prisoner's mental disorder justifies treatment in hospital, and (as this was a case of psychopathic disorder), that such treatment is likely to alleviate or prevent a deterioration of the disorder. On the changes to this test, see para 4.35 above.

[382] *R (on the application of TF) v the Secretary of State for Justice* [2008] EWCA Civ 1457.

4.44 The first hearing judgment set out the failure to comply with the requirements of mental health and human rights law:

> ... at the time the decision was taken to issue the warrant the Secretary of State could not have been satisfied by reports from at least two registered medical practitioners that hospital treatment was likely to alleviate or prevent a deterioration of this claimant's condition. It was therefore unreasonable in the *Wednesbury* sense for him to decide to issue the warrant ... Further, the claimant's detention pursuant to that warrant seems to me to have been in violation of article 5(1) of the European Convention of Human Rights, that detention being neither in conformity with domestic law, nor ... pursuant to the lawful ordering of execution of measures involving the deprivation of liberty of a person of unsound mind -- see *Winterwerp v Netherlands* [1979] 2 EHRR 387[383].

4.45 Having found the warrant directing transfer and the subsequent detention to be unlawful, Mrs Justice Cox (presiding over the first hearing) exercised discretion not to grant relief on the grounds that, had the Secretary of State "carried out further enquiries and sought to clarify the [medical] opinions ... with particular regard to the statutory requirements of section 47, in advance of the decision [to allow the transfer], he would still have made the transfer direction and that direction would have been unimpeachable both in domestic law and under the Convention"[384]. The Court of Appeal overturned this, ruling that "the judge went wrong in seeking to keep an invalid order in place by the exercise of a discretion to refuse relief"[385] and "the court simply cannot render a detention lawful that which was unlawful simply by refusing to grant relief"[386].

4.46 Before leaving the particulars of this case to one side, we wish to flag the circumstances of the transfer of prisoner *F* as a particularly striking example of how the exercise of warrants for transfer to hospital at the end of prisoners' sentences can be disorientating, alarming and seemingly unjust to the prisoner: indeed, quite markedly *Kafkaesque*. The following is Mrs Justice Cox's summary of the exercise of the warrant, starting with its issue on the day before release from prison was due:

> On the same day that the warrant was issued by the [Secretary of State], a notice of supervision relating to [F]'s release plan whilst in the community was being prepared. This informed [F] that his sentence expired on 12th September 2008 and that on his release from custody he would be under the supervision of a probation officer or local authority social worker for three months until 11th December 2008. He was given details as to where and to whom he should report and the conditions of supervision with which he must comply.

> On the morning of 12th September this notice of supervision was handed to [F] by one of the prison officers who explained its terms and asked him to sign it, which he did. However, at the same time as [F] was preparing for and expecting to be released from custody, preparations were being made for the execution of the warrant and for service upon him of the transfer direction order. Staff from Kneesworth Hospital arrived at Stoke Heath and waited for [F] in the reception department which is located within the main perimeter fence and has no direct access to the main street outside, exit from the prison being achieved only through a series of corridors and locked gates.

---

[383] *R (on the application of F) v the Secretary of State for the Home Department* [2008] EWHC 2912 (Admin), para 36.

[384] ibid., para 39.

[385] *R (on the application of TF) v the Secretary of State for Justice* [2008] EWCA Civ 1457, para 8.

[386] ibid., para 11.

At about 9.30 am on 12th September in accordance with normal practice [F] was escorted from the wing to the reception department where he changed into civilian clothes and collected his property. There he was served with the order for transfer and then escorted from Stoke Heath to Kneesworth by the hospital staff. [F] knew nothing about his transfer to hospital until he arrived in reception and was served with the order.[387]

4.47 We should perhaps emphasise that we place no blame here on the staff from the medium secure unit, who played no part in what their eventual patient might view as the simulation of discharge proceedings. We are in fact sympathetic to those staff whose role it was to escort and/or subsequently care for a patient who had been distressed by this manner of hospitalisation.

4.48 In response to the judgment in this case, the Ministry of Justice has issued the following statement and instruction to clinicians, which we reproduce in full;

LAST-MINUTE TRANSFERS

Although section 47 allows the Secretary of State to transfer a sentenced prisoner to hospital at any time before his release date, transfers to prison should not be sought in order to prolong an individual's time in detention. A transfer to hospital late in sentence is likely to be counterproductive for public safety. A person who is transferred to hospital when they are expecting to be released is unlikely to cooperate with any treatment, and may well become more disaffected and dangerous. They are more likely in these circumstances to pose a risk of harm to other vulnerable patients. Adherence to MAPPA arrangements is more likely to promote their safe management.

In the recent case of *TF*, the High Court stated: "If the decision is being taken as in this case right at the end of the sentence what must also be in the Secretary of State's mind I suggest is that a decision to direct a transfer cannot simply be taken on the grounds that a convicted person will be a danger to the public if released (as understandable as that concern must be) but can only be taken on the grounds that his medical condition and its treatability (to use a shorthand) justify the decision."

For these reasons, the Mental Health Unit will turn down requests for transfers late in sentence unless there is some good evidence that hospital treatment will be of benefit to the prisoner and reasons why such a transfer could not have been achieved earlier in sentence (such as recent new evidence of a change to the person's mental state).[388]

4.49 We very much welcome this statement, and in particular the acknowledgement that late transfers are likely to be counter-productive, even if the only consideration were that of public safety. We hope that the statement will be translated into future practice to prevent situations such as that of *F* from happening again.

Rehabilitation and transferred prisoners

4.50 On occasion we have met with prison transferees who, although they have not been transferred at the end of their sentence, and indeed may be grateful to be in a place of treatment, complain of having lost freedoms or opportunities available to them in prison.

---

[387] *R (on the application of F) v the Secretary of State for the Home Department* [2008] EWHC 2912 (Admin), paras 18-20.

[388] Ministry of Justice *Mental Health Unit Bulletin*, February 2009, page 2.

4.51 A seemingly trivial example, but one of great importance to many patients, is the legal restriction on smoking now applicable to hospitals. Transferred prisoners, being likely to be subject to restriction orders, may have limited opportunities to leave the ward environment to smoke outdoors, and in some hospitals cannot even smoke there (see paragraph 1.95 above). In January 2008 we met with a patient who had very recently been transferred from prison to Rampton Hospital. The patient was very upset that in the preparation for transfer he had not been told that the hospital is a no-smoking site and that he would be unable to smoke. This had come as a shock to him and he stated that he felt mentally unprepared to deal with his withdrawal symptoms. We sought assurance that, in future, potential patients and those responsible for planning their care are fully informed of the Trust's smoking policy.

4.52 In spring 2008 the MHAC met with a patient detained under s.47/49 in an independent medium secure hospital. She had been transferred there from prison nine months earlier, for treatment of both mental illness and personality disorder. She told us that she thought the staff were nice, but complained of the 'childish' nature of ward-based activities and that she felt patients were left with insufficient intellectual stimulation. In prison she had been studying English and creative writing, but the funding for this had not followed her to hospital and she had at that time no access to equivalent education facilities. The failure to maintain continuity of education provision from prison to hospital was a setback to this patient, both in terms of her general morale and in her progress towards recovery and rehabilitation.

4.53 We have discussed in our last report[389] the very unfair decision in 2006 to remove transferred prisoners' eligibility for welfare benefits until the expiry date of their sentence, at the same time as other patients received substantial increases in their income[390]. This continues to cause difficulties in many forensic services, greatly disadvantaging such patients in the day-to-day life of the ward and in terms of opportunities for rehabilitation. It is not acceptable that patients should be held back from progressing towards discharge or transfer to lesser security by being unable to afford activities, such as shopping for themselves or taking escorted leave outside of the hospital grounds. We discuss wider concerns over costs associated with leave at paragraph 2.37 above.

4.54 As this report goes to press, the Ministry of Justice issued its second stage consultation on voting rights of convicted prisoners, and announced a separate consultation on the position of convicted persons detained under the Mental Health Act. Were the MHAC in existence for this consultation, we should have reiterated the points made in paragraph 7.65 *et seq* of our Twelfth Report. We therefore draw this to the attention of the Care Quality Commission as our successor body.

---

[389] MHAC (2008) *Risk, Rights, Recovery; Twelfth Biennial Report 2005-2007*, para 7.65 to 7.70.

[390] From April 10 2006, long-stay patients on incapacity benefit received an increase from £16.40 to £78.50 per week; patients on severe disability allowance received an increase from £16.40 to £47.45 per week; income support increased from £16.49 to a maximum of £57.45; retirement pension was increased from £16.40 to a maximum of £97 per week. By contrast, transferred prisoners lost their entitlement to the £16.40 per week; some, but not all hospitals replaced this with hospital pocket money (in Rampton Hospital's case, with an increase to £16.85 per week). See Harper S, Ferriter M, Cormac I (2008) 'Impact of the increase in state benefits on the pattern of expenditure by patients in a high security hospital' *Mental Health Review Journal*, vol 13 issue 3, p.4-7.

5

Deaths of Detained Patients

Deaths of Detained Patients

5.1 The Commission asks to be notified, by the detaining authority, of any death of a patient who is detained under the 1983 Act. The primary purpose of such notification is to ensure that we take appropriate monitoring action in response to individual cases: we will often attend inquests, for example, either to observe or as a 'properly interested person'. This chapter presents analysis of MHAC data collected through such notifications in the four calendar years 2005 to 2008. These findings are presented so as to be broadly comparable with our previous reports of earlier years' data[391].

Total deaths recorded 2005 – 2008

5.2 Over the four year period 2005 – 2008, we were notified of 1,392 deaths of detained patients. Over three-quarters of these (1,123) were ascribed to natural causes. Of the unnatural deaths, we have identified 205 as probable suicides, 30 as accidental deaths (some of which may in fact be suicide), two deaths due to patients being given incorrect medication and four possible other iatrogenic deaths. We have been unable to ascertain the cause of the remaining 28 deaths. We have largely relied on information from coroners for these classifications, although in a number of cases the coroners' inquest is still ongoing. It is also clear that there are no absolute lines of division between categories: classifying a number of cases is problematic, particularly in ascribing suicidal intent to actions resulting in death, but also in determining whether a death should be construed as natural causes or accident, etc.

Ethnicity and deaths of detained patients

5.3 Figure 75 below shows the ethnic origin of detained patients who died of natural and unnatural causes. The number of patients falling into categories other than 'White British' are too small to produce statistically significant differences, although it continues to be

---

[391] See Bannerjee S, Bingley W, Murphy E (1995) *Deaths of detained patients – a review of reports to the Mental Health Act Commission.* London, the Mental Health Foundation; MHAC (2001) *Deaths of Detained Patients in England and Wales. A report by the Mental Health Act Commission on information collected from 1 February 1997 to 31 January 2000.* Nottingham, MHAC, Feb 2001; and MHAC (2006) *Eleventh Biennial Report 2003-2005; In Place of Fear?,* chapter 4.279 – 4.312 for previous data.

notable that the proportion of patients from Black and Minority Ethnic categories overall (i.e. all those except the "British White" category) rises for unnatural deaths compared to natural deaths. As we observed in our Eleventh Biennial Report, it is possible that this is a reflection of the proportionately younger profile of most BME groups compared to the British White group.

Ethnic category	Ethnic category as % of natural deaths (n= 1,123)	Ethnic category as % of unnatural deaths (n= 241)
White British	82.7	73.5
White Irish	1.9	2.4
White Welsh	0.6	1.2
Any Other White Background	5.0	8.5
White & Black Caribbean	0.1	0.3
White & Black African	-	0.3
White & Asian	0.1	0.3
Any Other Mixed Background	0.3	0.6
Indian	-	1.5
Pakistani	0.5	0.6
Bangladeshi	0.1	0.9
Any Other Asian Background	0.4	0.6
Caribbean	3.8	3.4
African	1.1	2.3
Any other Black Background	0.2	0.9
Chinese	0.3	-
Any Other Ethnic Group	0.6	0.9
Not Stated	1.1	1.5
Total	**100**	**100**

Fig 75: Natural and unnatural deaths by ethnic category, 2005 – 2008

Source: MHAC data

Deaths by natural causes

Age at time of death

5.4   Not surprisingly, deaths of detained patients by natural causes predominantly involve elderly patients. The data for the four years 2005 to 2008 at figure 76 below echoes the findings of our previous reports in this respect.

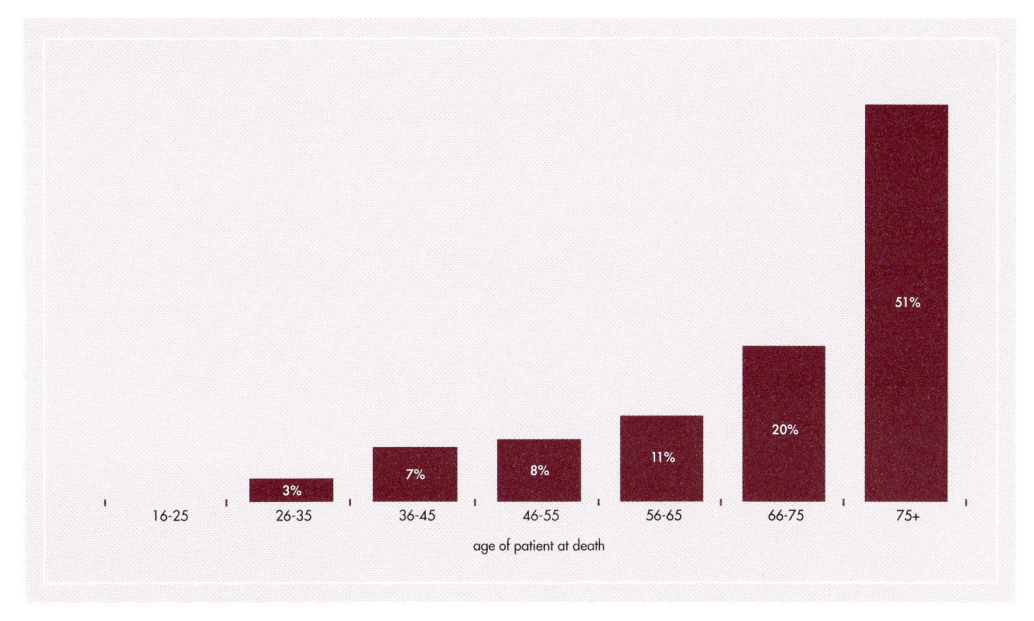

Fig 76: Percentage of all natural causes deaths by age-band, detained patients, England and Wales, 2005 – 2008

Source: MHAC data

Cardiac and respiratory arrest

5.5 Mental health and learning disability patients can be vulnerable to cardiac or respiratory arrest through coexisting physical illness, self-harm, and the effects of medication, including rapid tranquilisation[392]. Our data suggests that approximately one in five 'natural causes' deaths involving detained patients noted between 2005 and 2008 can be directly attributed to such causes. It is possible, of course, that some of these deaths have at least an iatrogenic element, in that medication or other treatment causes or exacerbates physical decline, and as such are questionably of 'natural causes' at all.

5.6 The National Patient Safety Agency (NPSA) has issued a requirement to all mental health and learning disability services to ensure that they have the equipment and staff training to react appropriately to such medical emergencies on psychiatric wards (see figure 81 below). Given the prevalence of incidents of cardio-respiratory arrest and associated crises in psychiatric units, and examples collected by the NPSA of poor handling of such situations[393], it is extremely important that this requirement is met.

Natural causes deaths following ECT treatment

5.7 Thirty-nine patients, all of whose deaths were ascribed to natural causes, had received ECT in the week prior to their death. Of these patients, all but three were aged over 60 years: two patients were in their late fifties, and one was 33 years old. Excepting these three patients, the average age of patients at death was 77 years. More than two-thirds

---

[392] NPSA (2008) *Rapid Response Report NPSA/2008/RRR010: Resuscitation in Mental Health and Learning Disability settings, Supporting Information.* November 2008.

[393] Between 1 January 2006 and 31 March 2008 the NPSA found 26 incidents where staff did not have the ability to manage the care of mental health or learning disability patients who experienced cardiac or respiratory arrests, or where equipment, including basic airways equipment and Automated External Defibrillators, was unavailable. NPSA (2008) *op cit.*

(26) were women. In all but one case, some kind of depressive illness or schizoaffective disorder was clearly indicated in the psychiatric diagnoses: the exception had a recorded diagnosis of 'unspecified organic personality and behavioural disorder'[394].

5.8 The causes of death for this group did not appear to show any different pattern from other deaths by natural causes, and many causes of death found at post-mortem seem to reflect the age of patients concerned. Many of these patients appear to have stopped taking food or fluid of their own volition, no doubt as a consequence of depressive stupor or other depressive state. In some of these cases, especially where ECT had been given within 24 hours of the death itself, the consequences of such food and fluid refusal appear to have been directly contributory to the cause of death. This was the case, for example, with the 33 year old woman whose last ECT treatment was administered only an hour before her death; and also with a 63 year old man who had four ECT treatments 'with minimal improvement', and had been transferred twice to general hospital for rehydration. It is clear from these cases that ECT was being attempted as a last resort to save a patient in a critical physical state.

5.9 In two cases, an event (aspiration[395]) that directly contributed towards the cause of death occurred during the ECT treatment itself. The patients were an 82 year old woman and an 85 year old man. The latter was transferred to a general hospital for intravenous antibiotics and, although discharged back to the mental health trust as medically fit, died shortly thereafter. The former died on a medical ward. The causes of death were recorded as "aspiration pneumonia (ECT)" and "bronchopneumonia" respectively.

Deaths by unnatural causes

5.10 This report is being prepared as the Coroners and Justice Bill is making its passage through Parliament. We hope that this Bill brings some clarity to proceedings following deaths of detained patients. The Bill proposes that a coroner will investigate the death of a detained patient whether or not the death is considered to be due to natural or unnatural causes[396]: at present only the latter are subject to an inquest. As some media reports have emphasised, this can cause distress to patients' families who believe that failures in care were a contributory factor to a death classified as due to natural causes[397]. However, a jury need only be called where the senior coroner has reason to suspect that the detained patient's death was a violent or unnatural one, or the cause of death is unknown. Thus, for example, where a post-mortem examination appears to reveal a natural cause of death, the inquest will be heard without a jury[398]. Prior to the introduction of the Bill, Government amended Rule 43 of the Coroners Rules 1984 to widen coroners' remit to make reports

---

[394] i.e. *International Classification of Diseases* (ICD-10) category F69 (World Health Organisation, 2007).

[395] i.e. – the entrance of foreign materials, usually oral or gastric contents such as food, saliva, or nasal secretions, into the bronchial tree, leading to pneumonia through either infection or a chemical inflammatory process. This is known as an iatrogenic risk in general anaesthesia, but may possibly have resulted from the ECT process (i.e. the fit) itself.

[396] See *Coroners and Justice Bill*, s.1.

[397] Nina Lakhani 'Families demand full inquests for deaths in secure hospitals' *Independent on Sunday*, 27 January 2008.

[398] See *Coroners and Justice Bill*, s.7.

to prevent future deaths, and to require that services who receive such reports respond in writing to them[399]. We welcome this change.

5.11 The Corporate Manslaughter and Corporate Homicide Act 2007 came into force in April 2008. Thus, NHS or independent bodies can be found guilty of an offence if the ways in which their activities are managed or organised by its senior management cause a patient's death or amounts to a gross breach of a relevant duty of care[400]. Section 2(1)(d) of the Corporate Manslaughter Act will extend its coverage to duties of care flowing from custody (including detention under the Mental Health Act), but its implementation has been delayed. Government has committed to implement this section in full within three to five years from April 2008, although in July 2008 the Department of Health was reported to have agreed to an early extension of the Act to fully cover detained patients before that time[401]. As of the end of March 2009, no announcement of a date of commencement had been made. We hope that, once implemented, case law over this Act will find that detaining authorities owe reciprocally heightened duties of care to those whom they make subject to Mental Health Act powers, although this will remain to be seen.

5.12 It may be that the thresholds for prosecution under the Corporate Manslaughter Act remain so high that patients' families seek other means of legal redress. The House of Lords opened up an alternative route in this reporting period[402]. In the case in question, a patient who had been detained for over three months under s.3 walked out of hospital and jumped in front of a train, and her family considered that the precautions taken to stop her absconding had been inadequate. After initially being refused permission to bring a claim of breach of the right to life under Article 2 of the European Convention on Human Rights, they were granted such permission by the Court of Appeal. The Trust, supported by the Secretary of State for Health, challenged this and sought to narrow the test for establishing breach of Article 2. The Trust argued that the test applicable in healthcare situations for such a breach should be restricted to a failure to have in place proper systems for protecting life, and that Article 2 should not be read to imply an operational duty to take measures to protect a particular life in healthcare settings. As such, the test for a breach of Article 2 argued for by the Trust and supported by government was "at the least gross negligence of the kind sufficient to sustain a charge of manslaughter"[403], a threshold that even 'ordinary' medical negligence would not meet[404]. Their Lordships rejected these arguments, finding that cases in the European Court itself supported a broader reading of the state's Article 2 duties towards those whom it deprives of liberty, which should be extended to detained patients. Thus the protective obligation upon detaining authorities might be read to require that they take such measures as are within the scope of their powers which, judged reasonably, might have been expected to avoid an identified risk of

---

[399] See www.justice.gov.uk/docs/coroners-reports-future-deaths.pdf for guidance on the new provision.

[400] *Corporate Manslaughter and Corporate Homicide Act 2007*, s.1.

[401] Ministry of Justice (2008) *Corporate Manslaughter and Corporate Homicide Act 2007 – Progress towards implementation of custody provisions.* July 2008.

[402] *Savage v South Essex Partnership NHS Foundation Trust* [2008] UKHL 74 .

[403] *ibid.*, para 88, quoting Mr Justice Swift from the first instance hearing.

[404] *ibid.*, para 91.

suicide[405]. This may open the way to legal redress for many more families than could ever be provided by the final implementation of the Corporate Manslaughter Act.

5.13 In the four years 2005 to 2008, the MHAC was notified of 241 unnatural deaths of detained patients. As stated at paragraph 5.2, the great majority were the result of self-harm or suicide: we have classified at least 85% (205) as probably suicide, and it is likely that the true figure is anything up to 98%, as a number of the 30 'accidental' deaths undoubtedly resulted from self-harming behaviour. The age range of these 241 patients is shown at figure 77 below.

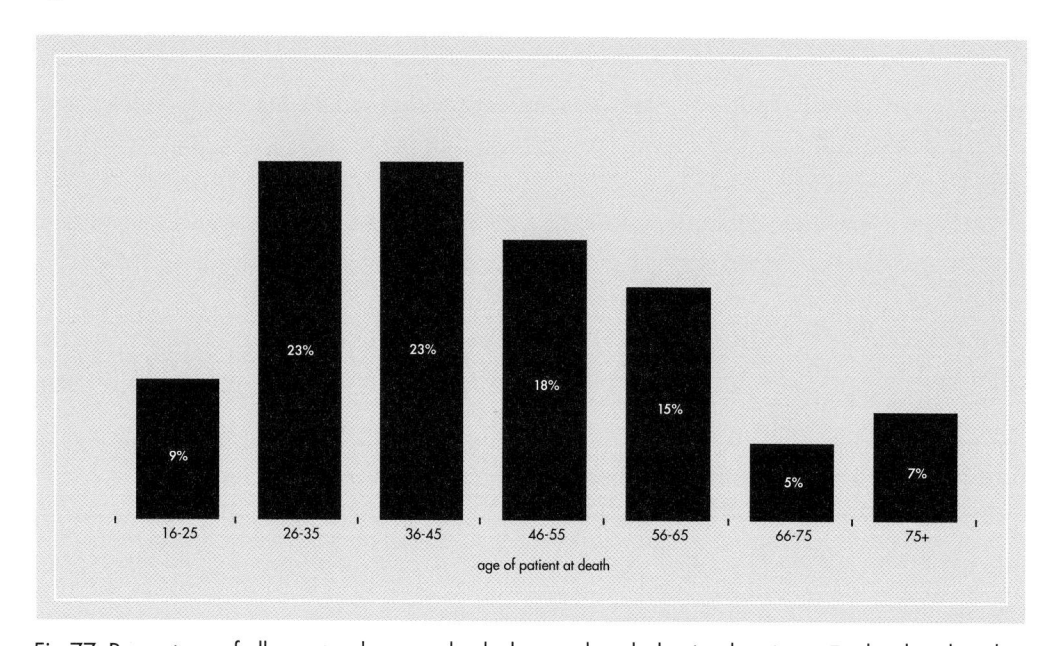

Fig 77: Percentage of all unnatural causes deaths by age-band, detained patients, England and Wales, 2005 – 2008

Source: MHAC data

5.14 The number of unnatural deaths amongst detained patients is too small to draw upon for meaningful statistical data. However, we set out at figure 78 below the causes of unnatural deaths of detained patients over the last nine years, and note the relatively constant proportions of each cause over time. Over half die of some form of hanging, self-strangulation or suffocation.

---

[405] *ibid.*, para 79, quoting *Van Colle v Chief Constable of the Hertfordshire Police* [2008] UKHL 50.

	2000	2001	2002	2003	2004[406]	2005	2006	2007	2008	Total	Total %
Hanging	22	25	17	24	26	27	18	20	15	204	41%
Self strangulation	1	2	1	1	1	2	1	4	4	18	4%
Self suffocation	7	3	3	-	2	3	-	5	3	26	5%
Jumped before train	9	8	5	9	1	2	14	6	9	63	13%
Jumped before road vehicle	1	3	2	1	1	2	14	6	7	37	7%
Jumped from height	7	9	4	4	6	8	6	7	4	48	10%
Self poisoning by drug / alcohol o.d.	6	4	6	3	1	1	7	11	8	47	10%
Drowning	2	6	2	1	1	9	2	1	-	26	5%
Fire	2	-	2	1	2	1	2	-	-	10	2%
Hosepipe to car exhaust	0	2	-	-	1	-	-	-	1	4	1%
Iatrogenic	1	-	-	2	1	2	-	1	-	7	1%
Death caused by another person	2	-	1	-	1	-	1	-	-	5	1%
Total	**60**	**62**	**43**	**46**	**45**	**57**	**65**	**61**	**51**	**496**	**100%**

Fig 78: Methods (where known) of unnatural deaths, detained patients, England and Wales, 2000 – 2008

Source: MHAC data

5.15 The proportion of patients dying by hanging or strangulation or suffocation is roughly similar to the proportion that die on hospital premises, as is shown at figure 79. This shows two categories of deaths in hospital premises – one for deaths actually taking place on psychiatric wards, and the other for deaths taking place on medical or surgical wards. In practice the difference between these two categories is largely consequential upon whether the patient is found dead (or cannot be resuscitated) on the psychiatric ward itself, or is found alive (or can be resuscitated) on the psychiatric ward and is subsequently taken to another hospital or hospital ward for further physical intervention. At least 40 of the 45 deaths that took place on medical or surgical wards were of patients who had been transferred there in such circumstances. As is discussed below at paragraph 5.57 *et seq*, the majority of incidents on psychiatric wards that lead to the death of a patient involve some form of suspension from a ligature or suffocation.

---

[406] Totals from 2004 revised from those published in MHAC (2006) as more data now available.

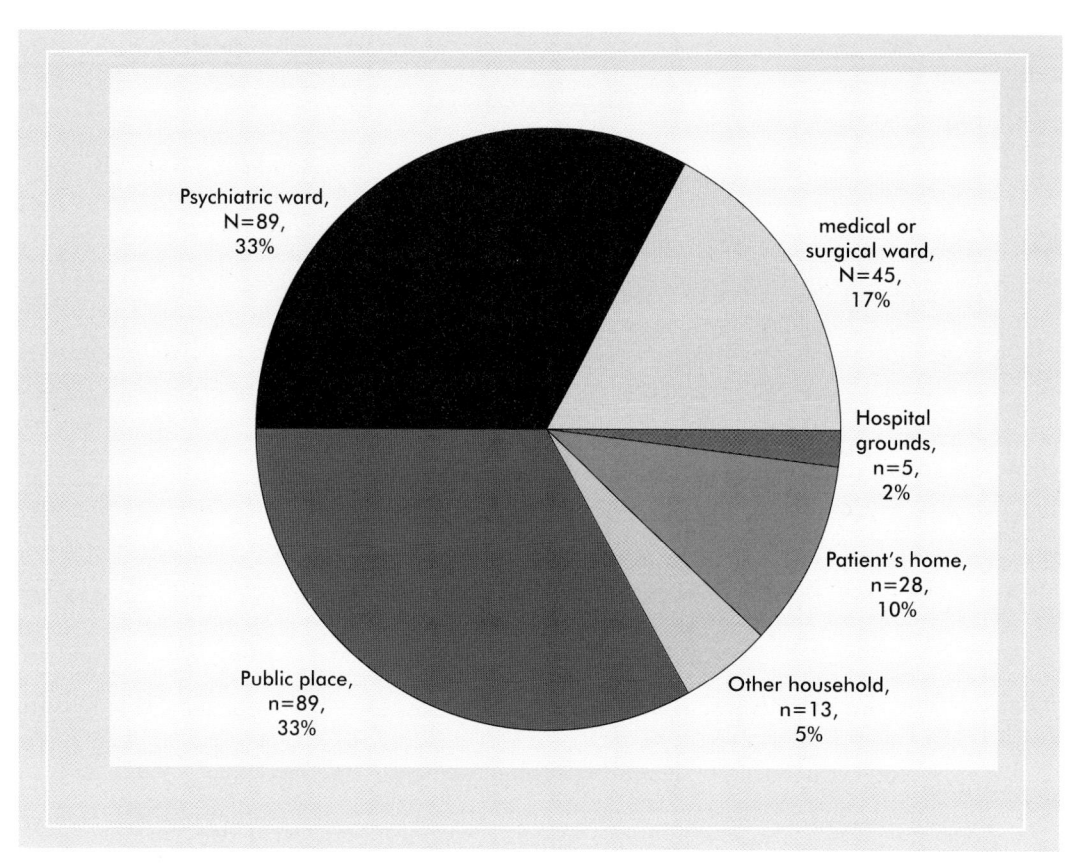

Fig 79: Deaths of detained patients by all unnatural causes, 2005 to 2008: location of death

Source: MHAC data

5.16 It is also notable that the proportion of patients who die in a public place is roughly equivalent to those who jump in front of vehicles (including trains) or jump from a height. As with the rough match between patients who die in hospital and means of death involving hanging or strangulation or suffocation, this may be a simple reflection that such means of death are the most accessible in the circumstances.

Accidental deaths

5.17 Only a small number of deaths of detained patients reported to the coroner are classified as being the direct result of an 'accident', although a number of deaths by 'natural causes' may have some accidental event – such as a fall in the case of elderly patients – as at least part of their causation.

5.18 One death as a result of complications following a fall was recorded in 2005 for a woman in her late forties. This patient had a history of anorexia and depression and was of extremely low weight, and consequently very frail. The fall fractured the patient's hip, exacerbating a previous fracture, and death resulted from septicaemia and bronchial pneumonia. This case highlighted problems with the interface between the acute medical and mental health sectors within the Trust concerned. The mental health team felt that they were being pressured to accept the patient back into their care before she was sufficiently physically stable (she was, for example, still receiving intravenous antibiotics); whilst the acute medical team felt that they had received no practical support provided for the mental health needs of the patient in the form of mental health nursing staff, etc.

Following a post-incident review, a protocol for the transfer of mental health patients to acute medical care was adopted by the Trust to address these problems.

5.19 We discuss wider concerns relating to the use of the Act in acute hospitals in chapter 2.121 above.

Fall prevention and mechanical restraint

5.20 In our Eleventh Biennial Report we suggested that a number of techniques used to reduce the incidence of falls in elderly patient services amount to mechanical restraint. This is often in apparent contradiction to the Code of Practice stipulation that "restraint which involves tying … to some part of a building or its fixtures should never be used"[407]; despite professional advisers to the Department of Health having questioned the efficacy of such methods; and despite reported deaths caused through entanglement in harnesses designed to keep patients in chairs or beds[408]. At the time of that report (2006), the Department of Health had discussed with the MHAC instigating notifications of the use of mechanical restraint to inform future Government actions[409]. Such discussions stalled at the point when we suggested that, to ensure the usefulness of data collected from such notifications, the Secretary of State should exercise her powers to extend the MHAC remit beyond detained patients for the purposes of the notification procedure, and fund the administration of the notification so that it was not at the expense of visiting detained patients in hospital. We therefore flag these concerns for both government and the Care Quality Commission's future consideration.

Control and restraint deaths

5.21 Three inquests held in 2008 concerned deaths of detained patients attributable to the the use of face-down restraint. Kurt Howard died aged 32 in Cefn Coed Hospital, Swansea, in June 2002. Azrar Ayub died aged 24 in Prestwich Hospital, Manchester, in May 2004. Geoffrey Hodgkin died aged 37 in St James Hospital, Portsmouth, in November 2004. We described the death of Mr Hodgkin in our last report, alongside a description of the death of Andrew Jordan, aged 28, as a consequence of face-down restraint during a Mental Health Act assessment in 2003[410].

5.22 Between 2005 and 2008 the MHAC was notified of only one death of a detained patient involving restraint as a possible cause, and this case has yet to go to inquest. The circumstances of the death, however, do not suggest that prolonged face-down restraint was used, and although the possibility of restraint asphyxia as a contributory factor cannot be excluded completely, it seems unlikely that this will be found to have been the primary cause of death.

---

[407] *Mental Health Act Code of Practice for England* (2008 revision), para 15.31. In the previous edition of the Code (1999) this statement can be found at para 19.10.

[408] MHAC (2006) *Eleventh Biennial Report 2003-2005; In Place of Fear?*, chapter 4.222.

[409] *ibid.*, chapter 4.220.

[410] MHAC (2008) *Risk, Rights, Recovery: Twelfth Biennial Report 2005-2007*, para 2.128.

5.23 It is, of course, impossible to talk of trends amongst the very few cases discussed here, and therefore we cannot tell whether the lack of cases of face-down restraint deaths between 2005 and 2008 is the result of safer practice or chance. We are not confident that staff operating in mental health services have sufficient training or support to rule out further tragedies.

5.24 The year 2008 was noted as the tenth anniversary of the death through face-down restraint of David "Rocky" Bennett[411]. The 2003 inquiry report into Mr Bennett's death recommended national guidance and training on restraint techniques, including a recommendation that no patient should be held in a prone position for more than three minutes[412]. We have discussed this in previous reports, noting that although Government did not accept the latter recommendation, a time-limit such as three minutes would in any case be little more than a guideline, but that mandatory training on physical restraint techniques, provided by regulated training bodies, is a clear need across mental health services that should be addressed[413]. We have also noted the publication of NICE guidelines into restraint practice[414], and although this does not specifically mention face-down restraint, it would clearly be a step forward were all staff aware of its recommendations[415]. Following the inquest into the death of Geoffrey Hodgkin, the coroner wrote to the Chief Medical Officer requesting that he issue clearer and more detailed guidance on restraint, and both the coroner for the inquest into Mr Bennett's death, and Sir John Blofeld, who chaired the independent inquiry into that death, have expressed frustration at the lack of progress[416].

5.25 The three inquest findings from 2008 underline that a lack of training and staff knowledge contributed to the deaths of these patients. We have outlined pertinent points raised at the inquests at figure 80 below. Common to all three incidents was inadequate staff awareness of risks and patient well-being, including awareness of the dangers of prone-position restraint. The policies and practice guidance available to staff were not followed. In the case of Kurt Howard, the lack of seclusion facilities denied staff an alternative option for the management of the disturbed behaviour: in the case of Azrar Ayub control of the restraint process was lost *en route* to the seclusion facility, which was placed on another ward. Service managers and commissioners should be aware that, whilst policies of not using seclusion or the absence of seclusion facilities may present an image of a less coercive hospital regime, in practical terms it may lead to extended physical restraint of patients whose behaviour would pose a threat to themselves or others if uncontained.

---

[411] See MHAC (2001) *Ninth Biennial Report 1999-2001*, chapter 6.26; MHAC (2003) *Placed Amongst Strangers, Tenth Biennial Report 2001-2003*, chapters 10.31, 11.29, 16.18. MHAC (2006) *In Place of Fear? Eleventh Biennial Report 2003-2005*, chapter 4.215 .

[412] Norfolk, Suffolk and Cambridgeshire Health Authority (2003) *Independent Inquiry into the Death of David Bennett,* December 2003, p. 52.

[413] See MHAC (2006) *In Place of Fear? Eleventh Biennial Report 2003-2005*, chapter 4.215; MHAC (2008) *Risk, Rights, Recovery. Twelfth Biennial Report,* chapter 2.129.

[414] National Institute of Clinical Excellence (2005) *Violence: the short-term management of disturbed / violent behaviour in inpatient psychiatric settings and emergency departments.* Feb 2005.

[415] See MHAC (2006) In Place of Fear? *Eleventh Biennial Report 2003-2005*, chapter 4.215- 4.217 & fig 85; MHAC (2008) *Risk, Rights, Recovery. Twelfth Biennial Report*, chapter 2.127.

[416] *Lack of staff training puts mentally ill at risk on wards'* Nina Lakhani, The Independent, 13 April 2008. Sir John Blofeld is quoted as follows: "we spent a lot of time making carefully considered recommendations and it is disappointing if no actions have been taken. If the police and prison services can issue control and restraint guidance, this ought to be possible for mental health staff. I wish to goodness they would get on with it".

Kurt Howard (2002)	Azrar Ayub (2004)	Geoffrey Hodgkins (2004)
Restraint not carried out in accordance with training. Adaptation was needed due to inadequate and unsuitable environment (i.e. there was no seclusion facility) and inadequate staff numbers.	Full control of the restraint was lost during the course of the movement to the seclusion room. Insufficient consideration was given to the patient's welfare during this process. The jury believed that a member of staff unintentionally may have knelt on Mr Ayub's back.	Prone restraint position was unsuitable and the duration was not in accordance with the restraint plan. Mr Hodgkin's head was not monitored at all times during restraint. Towels used during restraint and biting the towel may have reduced oxygen intake.
Staff not adequately trained in control and restraint techniques.	Not all staff adequately trained in control and restraint techniques.	Not all staff adequately trained in control and restraint techniques. Non-clinical staff involved in restraint.
The recognised training programme in place did not particularly emphasise the problems that could occur with the prone position. Risk assessments inadequate – neither up to date nor audited. Policies not followed.	Staff insufficiently aware of dangers of prone restraint. Policies not followed, including seclusion policy (in relation to observation, recording and request for doctor to attend). More checks should have been taken as to well-being when seclusion commenced. Observation poor and doctor not called to attend.	Inadequate risk assessment and care planning in relation to restraint. Staff insufficiently aware of dangers of prone restraint. Policies not followed. Not all staff adequately trained in basic life support. Delays in commencing resuscitation including lack of immediate availability and known location of crash trolley.

Fig 80: Summary of some findings at inquest in three cases of deaths during face-down restraint

Source: MHAC notes on inquest hearings and narrative verdicts

5.26 The independent inquiry into the death of David Bennett was published in December 2003. Two of these three deaths occurred in the months following that publication. Of the 22 main recommendations in the David Bennett Inquiry, the following may be directly relevant to one or more of these cases:

- All who work in mental health services should receive training in cultural awareness and sensitivity.

- All managers and clinical staff, however senior or junior, should receive mandatory training in all aspects of cultural competency, awareness and sensitivity. This should include training to tackle overt and covert racism and institutional racism.

- Under no circumstances should any patient be restrained in a prone position for a longer period than three minutes.

- A national system of training in restraint and control should be established as soon as possible and, at any rate, within twelve months of the publication of this report.

- All medical staff and registered nurses working in the mental health services should have mandatory first-aid training, including CPR training.

- Records should be kept of all psychiatric units' use of control and restraint on patients. The Department of Health should audit the use of control and restraint.

Choking

5.27 Mental health and learning disability patients can be particularly vulnerable to choking, through dysphagia associated with illnesses like dementia; food bolting; pica; or through intoxication, substance abuse or intentional self-harm.[417] And, of course, accidents do happen.

5.28 The National Patient Safety Agency (NPSA) recorded three choking-related deaths in mental health or learning disability units between January 2006 and March 2008, and 22 other choking incidents leading to at least moderate harm, thirteen of which required transfer to accident and emergency units[418]. Not all of these incidents will have involved patients detained under the Mental Health Act. The reports of these incidents suggested that, in some units, staff knowledge or skills were inadequate; resuscitation equipment was either unavailable or misused; and some transfers to A&E were unnecessary and delayed treatment. In November 2008 the NPSA issued the requirement on services outlined at figure 81 below.

5.29 We recorded choking as a cause of unnatural death in two cases during 2007, and four cases in 2008. One of the 2007 cases, in which a patient died as a result of swallowing paper tissues and water, is discussed at paragraph 5.49 below. The 2008 cases all occurred after March 2008 (one in April, two July, and one in October), and so will not appear in the NPSA's published data. In one case, the patient was in the presence of two nursing staff (charged with keeping him under 2:1 observation) when he choked on a piece of toast with fatal consequences. In at least two other incidents, the choking incident occurred at mealtime, when staff would have been immediately available.

5.30 In some of these choking incidents, staff had no access to appropriate instruments to extract foodstuffs lodged in the patient's throat. The inquest into a patient's death in Broadmoor Hospital in 2003 (where the nurse had inadvertently pushed a blockage further into the choking patient's throat whilst trying to remove it manually) had recommended that McGill forceps be available on every ward: these are cheap instruments that could save lives. The MHAC further recommends that compliance with the NPSA requirements below is closely monitored in 2009, and that patients and staff will be less likely to be involved in such distressing events as a result.

---

[417] NPSA (2008) *Rapid Response Report NPSA/2008/RRR010: Resuscitation in Mental Health and Learning Disability settings, Supporting Information.* November 2008.

[418] *ibid.,* table 2.

> **Medical & Nurse Directors providing MH or LD inpatient care (NHS & independent sector) should ensure by 20 MAY 2009 that:**
>
> 1. Their rolling programme of basic life support (BLS) training for all staff is based on Resuscitation Council (UK) standards that include the management of choking.
>
> 2. All patient areas have immediate access to appropriate BLS equipment (e.g. self-inflating bag-mask devices, or mouth-to-mask devices).
>
> 3. All patient areas where a cardiac arrest might be expected at least once every five years should have access to Automated External Defibrillators (AEDs) within three minutes.
>
> 4. All units where rapid tranquilisation, physical intervention, or seclusion may be used have access to staff trained in immediate life support (ILS) and to all equipment specified in NICE Guideline 25 (including AEDs).
>
> 5. Wherever feasible, their training includes regular practices or drills in addition to classroom teaching.
>
> 6. A leadership role for resuscitation issues is identified (including within organisations whose resuscitation training is contracted out) and levels of attendance at life support training are routinely audited, reported to a senior level of the organisation, and any lapses acted on.
>
> Source; NPSA Rapid Response Report 10/08: resuscitation in mental health and learning disability settings, 26 November 2008.

Fig 81: NPSA requirement on basic life support training in mental health and learning disability units

Drug and alcohol intoxication or overdose

5.31 A number of deaths (at least 18 between 2005 and 2008) occurred through the use of illicit drugs. In many of these it seems likely that the patient returned to opiate drug use upon leaving hospital but, after a period of enforced abstinence, the dosage or combination with other substances (including alcohol) proved fatal.

5.32 In one case of death from alcohol poisoning in 2008, a patient detained under s.3 was returned by the police from what should have been half an hour's leave. He had been out for approximately two hours and was so intoxicated that he could not walk or talk. He was placed in a wheelchair near the nursing station so that staff could keep an eye on him. He was observed to be intermittently conscious, and was snoring loudly when unconscious. Staff neither recognised the dangers of leaving the patient collapsed in a wheelchair with his head flopping forward, nor that snoring in a patient intoxicated by drink or drugs is a symptom of restricted respiration. The death may perhaps have been avoided had he been left on his side in the recovery position. Following this case, the coroner for Cheshire wrote to the Secretary of State suggesting a national policy for the management of the intoxicated patient, but was informed that "it is not the Department [of Health]'s role to determine...practice nationally". Whilst this may be the case, the MHAC urges that such mechanisms as are available to influence services should be used to prevent such avoidable tragedies, and we therefore have drawn this to the attention of the Care Quality Commission.

> **Recommendation:** The MHAC recommends that all mental health services should have a policy for the management of the intoxicated patient, and that the Care Quality Commission should, within its compliance criteria for hospitals' registration, ensure that hospitals have such a policy, backed up with suitable training, as a part of their organisational management of substance abuse.

Iatrogenic and related deaths

5.33 We have categorised three 'unnatural' deaths between 2005 and 2006 as 'iatrogenic'. Two of these, from 2005, concerned a 76 year-old male who died as a result of complications following surgery for a physical condition, and a 53 year old women for whom 'lithium toxicity' was cited as a contributory factor to her death from bronchopneumonia. It seems likely that there is some overlap between such cases and others recorded as natural deaths (such as the case involving aspiration during ECT mentioned at paragraph 5.9 above), and it may be that the MHAC data contains a number of similar deaths with an iatrogenic aspect that are not recognised as such.

5.34 In 2007, a 78 year old male died of an idiosyncratic reaction to antipsychotic drugs administered to him as a detained patient. We make no general observations on this case.

5.35 Two related deaths reported to the MHAC were the result of patients being given *incorrect* medication. In 2005, an 88 year old woman, described as suffering from paraphrenia and early-stage dementia, was mistakenly administered opioid analgesic drugs prescribed for another patient, with fatal respiratory effect. In 2007, a 34 year old male patient (diagnosed with schizophrenia and personality disorder) was given clozapine tablets by another patient, and died in his bedroom of cardio-respiratory failure and clozapine toxicity. His own prescription, to which he gave consent, contained the antidepressant sertraline and the antipsychotic olanzapine.

Community patients and medicines management

5.36 As patients subject to compulsion are increasingly cared for outside the hospital environment with the involvement of both primary care and secondary mental health services, and where the 'responsible clinician' may not be the prescriber of medication for mental disorder, co-ordination between potential prescribers is imperative not only for good legal practice, but also for patient safety.

5.37 In 2007, a detained patient died at home after taking overdoses of both the antidepressant sertaline and the analgesic dihydrocodeine. He had been granted s.17 leave with a view to discharge from detention onto aftercare under supervision. The drugs taken are known to react with each other (for example by increasing the plasma concentration of the antidepressant, thus lowering its overdose threshold), although as the toxicology report showed five times the maximum therapeutic dose of antidepressant and 20 times the maximum therapeutic dose of the analgesic, either of which could have been fatal independently. It was assumed that the patient had been secretly storing medication, as he had been discharged onto s.17 leave with only four days' medication supply. However, at inquest a general practitioner from primary care medical centre at which the patient was registered revealed that she had been unaware of hospital-based prescription of medication, and had also been prescribing supplies at monthly intervals, and had last done so on the day of his death.

5.38 There are a number of lessons from this death which are highly pertinent to the management of patients on long-term s.17 leave or Supervised Community Treatment. Clearly, it is vital that there is co-ordination between primary and secondary services over responsibilities for medication management, and in planning and monitoring the community placement of patients. This should include involvement with Care Programme Approach meetings, and sharing of any alerts and critical incidents. It should also be clear to all parties who is responsible for the legal and clinical co-ordination of the patient's treatment. In this case, such co-ordination was complicated by fact that patients were registered with the GP practice, rather than any individual GP. Such arrangements are increasingly common following the introduction of new GP contracts. Systems need to be in place to ensure that medical records are sufficiently flagged to alert any GP working in such practices (or any locum covering for the absence of another GP) of the legal status of the patient, not least to ensure appropriate and safe medication management.

Leave and absence without leave as a factor in unnatural patient deaths

5.39 Slightly more than half of all unnatural deaths of detained patients take place in hospitals, and so a significant minority involve patients who are granted leave of absence under s.17, or who are absent without leave (AWOL) from hospital. The 'AWOL' category includes both patients who fail to return from authorised leave on time, and patients who absent themselves directly from hospital. The numbers of all unnatural deaths between 2005 and 2008 showing the proportions on leave or AWOL is shown at figure 82 below.

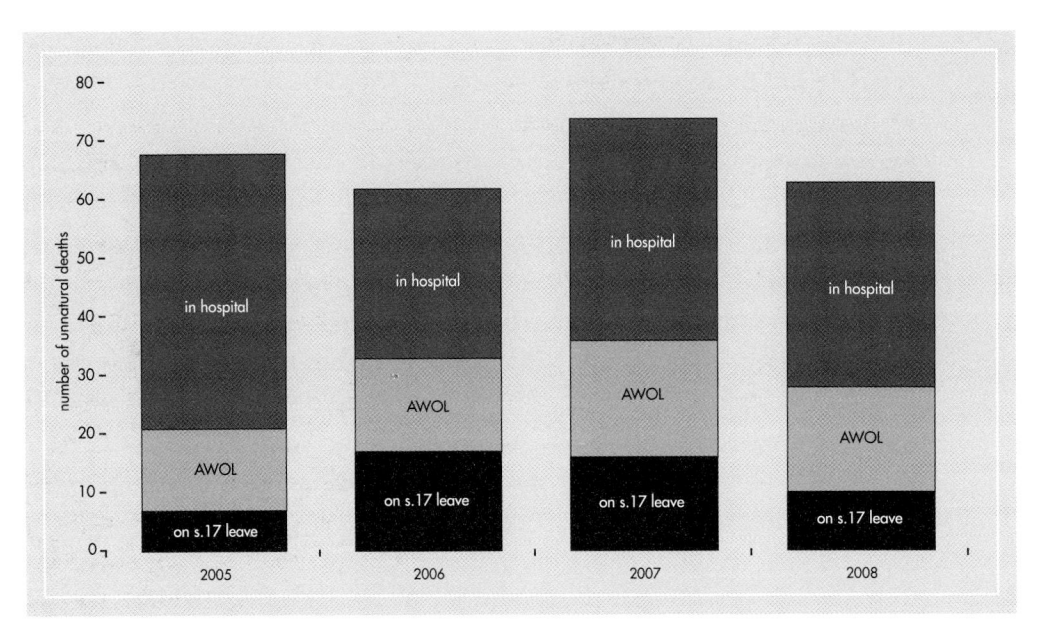

Fig 82: Deaths of detained patients by all unnatural causes, 2005 to 2008: leave status

Source: MHAC data

5.40 In one death from 2005, a patient suffering from psychotic depression who had been detained under s.3 for over ten weeks had spoken of intrusive thoughts regarding suicide using tablets, a plastic bag or a rope, although she denied having suicidal intent or having made any plans. She also had a recent history of non-adherence to the boundaries of leave granted under s.17. Documentation of risk assessment and care planning was inadequate, and so it is difficult to determine the basis upon which she was granted the overnight s.17 leave during which she hanged herself. It was clear, however, that the leave was granted without stipulating the time for return to hospital the next day, and the AWOL procedure was not implemented until after eight o'clock in the evening.

5.41 In another case from 2005, a patient who had been admitted under s.2 ten days earlier drowned herself in a reservoir, having put stones in her pockets. She had been granted overnight leave, also without a stated return time, and again the alarm was not raised until eight in the evening of the day she was due back. There appeared to have been no adequate risk assessment following her admission; the patient had not been given a care-plan or copy of her leave form; and leave had not been discussed within the multi-disciplinary team before being granted. Shortly before being granted leave the patient had been on 15 minute observations, and records did not show when this observation status had ended.

5.42 In 2006, a patient who had been in hospital for some months was granted leave from detention in hospital under s.3 to go to his 'new flat'. It appears that he had difficulty accessing the property, due to non-completion of housing benefit documentation, and indeed he remained on the ward for the first three days of his granted leave period. His Responsible Medical Officer at that time was not made aware of concerns about the patient until the second day after he had left the ward without care-plan, risk assessment or aftercare meeting to ensure his safety on leave. Two days later his body was found under a viaduct in a nature reserve, with injuries suggesting a fall from a height. Despite it being known that the patient had accommodation difficulties, it appears that there was neither a current risk assessment nor care plan. The administration of the leave was clearly poor, especially regarding communication between professionals, and signs that should have led to the authority for leave being reconsidered were missed. In this case, a clear failing was the lack of any s.117 aftercare meeting or discussion prior to the leave being agreed.

5.43 A patient detained under s.37 was allowed unescorted leave from an independent hospital on one morning in 2006, but telephoned the hospital during the morning and asked for leave to be extended until five in the afternoon. A search of the area around the hospital was undertaken, and the police were alerted at half past six in the afternoon. British Transport Police found her body on a railway line later the next day. The patient had a history of self-harm, including overdose and arson of her own flat. Despite some very good therapeutic work at the hospital, she had neither a current care plan nor risk assessment at the time of her death (each of these having been last completed eight months before), even though her mood had been noted as fluctuating in the week leading up to her death.

5.44 These cases demonstrate how risk-assessment, s.17 and AWOL procedures are central to patient safety. This is not a new finding, and indeed many investigations into the deaths of patients who were detained for their own safety have concluded that some failings in these aspects of their care were contributory to the patient's death. Services should therefore ensure that:

- Care plans should be complied regularly to be responsive to changing circumstances (i.e. at least monthly);
- Risk assessments should be completed before the granting of patient leave;
- Section 17 leave forms should state precise boundaries for the leave granted, and be copied to the patient and other relevant parties such as carers;
- Section 117 meetings must be held prior to any sustained period of leave being granted;
- the patient's belongings should be searched for any suicide note as a part of AWOL procedure.

5.45 We hope, however, that the need to take risk into account in granting leave will not lead to overly defensive practices that curtail patients' opportunities for rehabilitation and recreation, or further encourage the use of locked doors and other mechanistic approaches to patient security. Notwithstanding our past concerns over some of the language used in the *National Confidential Inquiry into Suicide and Homicide by People with Mental Illness* report *Avoidable Deaths*[419], we recognise and applaud its statement that there is a balance to be struck between patient autonomy and patient safety, and in terms of prevention of suicide 'the solution does not have to be coercive'.

---

[419] Appleby L, Shaw J, Kapur N N et al (2006) *Avoidable Deaths: five year report of the National Confidential Inquiry into Suicide and Homicide by People with Mental Illness.* University of Manchester. For the MHAC concerns over the use of terminology such as 'leaving a ward without permission' and 'absconsion' used in that report, see MHAC (2006) *In Place of Fear? Eleventh Biennial Report 2003-05*, para 2.104 et seq.

Suicides

5.46 The number of suicides in the general population appears to be falling. Between the first and second reports of the *National Confidential Inquiry into Suicide and Homicide by People with Mental Illness* (covering the years 1997-2000 and 2001-2004 respectively[420]), reported suicides in the general population fell by nine per cent. But this decrease is not reflected in the number of suicides where the person had been in contact with mental health services in the year prior to death: these have remained roughly consistent from the start of the Inquiry[421]. As the *Avoidable Deaths* inquiry report recognises, this does not necessarily indicate that mental health services are failing to make progress in suicide prevention: indeed the consistency of the number and rate of suicides of people in contact with mental health services at a time of falling national suicide rates could simply indicate that a larger proportion of those at risk of suicide are coming into contact with services than before[422].

5.47 The *Avoidable Deaths* inquiry report suggests that its findings, in particular relating to non-compliance with medication and suicide, "indicate the potential for prevention" through the use of Supervised Community Treatment[423]. Whilst it is true, as the report notes, that fourteen per cent of patient suicides (of all patients, whether subject to the powers of the Act or not) were preceded by non-compliance, we should be careful not to assume causality where none might exist. It is important that services do not interpret such findings simplistically and focus on the delivery of medication to the exclusion of more person-centred aspects of the care and treatment of those at risk.

Observation levels

5.48 We discuss observation at 1.136 *et seq* above. It appears to be the case that services are not always clear about the levels of observation appropriate to identified risks, or what such observation levels imply in terms of nursing practice. The following is from an MHAC visit to a London hospital in the winter of 2008:

> It appears that one patient has made two suicide attempts in the last two months. The nursing notes read 'X remains suicidal, continues to be nursed on 1:1 nursing obs.' It is recorded that at 14.30, X was found with her head down the toilet saying she wants to end it. A health care assistant raised the alarm and staff came to her rescue. This occurred while the patient was on 1:1 observation, but not by the healthcare assistant who raised the alarm. The observation record for the corresponding time does not mention the incident. It states "complaining of not wanting to be in the hospital". The MHAC would like to see the incident records for both suicide attempts.

---

[420] Appleby L, Shaw J, Sherratt J et al (2001) *Safety First: report of the National Confidential Inquiry into Suicide and Homicide by People with Mental Illness*. London: Stationery Office. Appleby *et al* (2006) *Avoidable Deaths, op cit*.

[421] In the first Inquiry report (*Safety First*), data for the years 1997 to 2000 showed an annual average of 5,355 suicides, 1,340 of whom were people in contact with mental health services. In the second report (*Avoidable Deaths*), data for the years 2001 to 2004 showed an annual average of 4,920 suicides, 1,360 of whom were people in contact with mental health services.

[422] *Avoidable Deaths*, p.32.

[423] *ibid.*, p.93.

5.49 In response to concerns expressed by a patient's family over risk assessment and observation levels, after that patient had hanged herself on the ward, one hospital reported that it was satisfied that the level of observation was changed appropriately in response to changes in the patient's condition: when "it was identified that she was a high risk of suicide… her level of observation was increased from 15 to five minutes". In fact, this patient killed herself at a time when she was not considered at "high risk of suicide", and was therefore on 15-minute observations: our point is, however, that observing someone every five minutes who is considered a "high risk of suicide" leaves ample time between observations for a lethal act, and falls short of the standards suggested by the NICE guidance, which are outlined in chapter one above at figure 28. In one unusual example from 2007, a patient subject to observation every ten minutes swallowed dry tissues and then drank water, leading to death by cardio-respiratory failure, asphyxiation and choking. Although the MHAC accepted that staffing levels and risk-assessments were appropriate following its enquiries subsequent to this death, it may be that, where assessments recognise a risk that warrants observation at a frequency greater than every fifteen minutes, or at least where a high risk of suicide is recognised, only continuous observation should be considered a safe approach. This is not to say that there is no place for less stringent observation techniques, as we discuss at paragraph 1.137.

5.50 At paragraph 5.54 below we discuss the cases from the 2005 to 2008 data of six patients who managed to hang or strangle themselves whilst purportedly under continuous observation. During this four-year period we were notified of two other unnatural deaths that can confidently be ascribed to deliberate acts by the patient, involving detained patients purportedly subject to continuous observation. In both cases the patient suffocated. In one of these cases, the patient tied a plastic bag over his head, indicating the absence of meaningful continuous observation. In the other case, the patient was in a secure room being observed through glass panel. He had a history of pretending that he had a problem so as to attack staff who came to his aid. He put a pillowcase over his head and after a short time lay face down on his bed. He ignored staff requests to stop this, and by the time extra staff had arrived to enable the room to be entered, he was dead. This case demonstrates an important lesson: staff who are undertaking continuous observation of a patient deemed to be at risk must be facilitated to take immediate action in response to observed risk, or else the observation serves little purpose.

Deaths – hanging

5.51 Figure 83 shows the location of hanging or self-strangulation incidents that led to deaths of detained patients between 2005 and 2008.

5.52　The pattern of locations for deaths by hanging or self strangulation has changed little from our first data collections. MHAC data from 1999 has indicated that approximately three-quarters of hangings of detained patients take place on the psychiatric ward[424]. Patients who hang themselves whilst on leave are likely to do so at their own homes; patients who do so whilst absent from hospital are probably more likely to use a public place.

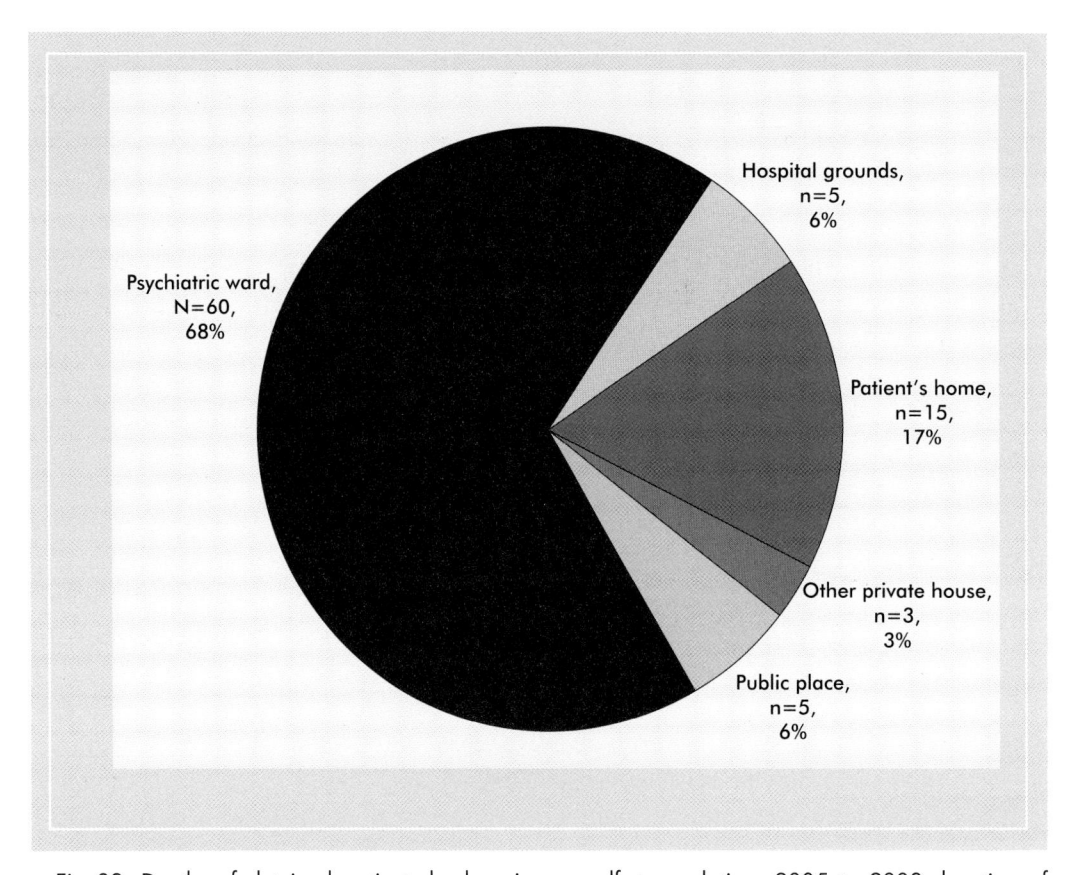

Fig 83: Deaths of detained patients by hanging or self-strangulation, 2005 to 2008: location of incident

Source: MHAC data

5.53　Thirty-nine per cent of all deaths on wards by hanging or self-strangulation between 2001 and 2008 took place when the patient concerned was formally subject to observation by staff at fifteen minute intervals or less (including some who were subject to continuous observation, discussed below), as shown at figure 84 below. Such circumstances applied in the deaths of 20 (37%) of the 54 patients who hanged or strangled themselves on hospital wards between 2005 and 2008.

---

[424] Between 1999 and 2000 the MHAC found that 78% of hangings took place on the psychiatric ward (MHAC (2001) *Deaths of Detained patients in England and Wales. A report by the Mental Health Act Commission on information collected from 1 February 1997 to 31 January 2000*. Nottingham, MHAC, Feb 2001, para 86). During 2000 to 2004, between 62% and 72% of hangings were ward-based. The 10% margin resulted from uncertainty where the hanging itself took place in cases where the 'place of death' was recorded as 'other medical or surgical units'. In the eight cases of such reported places of death between 2005 and 2008, it is clear in each case that the hanging took place on the ward, after which the patient was transferred to a medical ward for emergency medical attention (MHAC (2006) *Eleventh Biennial Report 2003-2005; In Place of Fear?* para 4.304).

	2000	2001	2002	2003	2004	2005	2006	2007	2008	total
continuous	4	1	2	0	0	2	1	1	2	13 (10%)
intermittent (up to 15 mins)	3	9	1	8	3	5	2	5	2	38 (29%)
general[425]	6	13	7	12	7	10	11	7	6	79 (61%)
total patients on ward at time of death	13	23	10	20	10	17	14	13	10	130 (100%)

Fig 84: Deaths of detained patients on psychiatric wards by hanging, 2000 – 2008: observation status of patients at time of death

Source: MHAC data

5.54 Six patients who died of hanging or self-strangulation since 2005 were purportedly under continuous observation (i.e. either level III or IV in the NMC guidelines, as shown at fig 28, chapter 1.136 above). In the five years prior to 2005, seven hangings or strangulations were reported of patients supposedly under such observation (figure 84). Overall, 10% these deaths of patients under 'continuous observation' account for 10% of all hangings or self strangulations taking place on psychiatric wards. It seems unlikely that a patient under continuous observation can have opportunity to hang or strangle him or herself. Indeed, the reporting to the MHAC of such deaths reveal that continuous observation cannot have been taking place in any meaningful sense: for example, such patients have been reported to have been "*found* hanging", or "*found* on ward with a ligature around her neck", etc.

5.55 An example of how observation levels can be poorly operated in practice was demonstrated to us by the case in 2008 of a young detained male patient who, whilst under five-minute observations, strangled himself with a sheet in the bathroom of a medium secure unit. At the time of his death there were 16 patients on his ward: ten of whom were on five-minute observations; five others on fifteen minute observations; and one on continuous observation. The staffing complement was two trained nurses and three agency health care assistants. It was clear that one health care assistant was responsible for all but the continuous observation, and that she had countersigned the continuous observations. To achieve such a workload, the health care assistant would be required to observe each patient in her care on a 25 second rotation throughout her shift: a physical impossibility, especially as patients moved around the unit. It was, perhaps, hardly surprising that there were suspicions of retrospective falsification of nursing records (indeed, one handover note seen by a Commissioner appeared to record the deceased patient as 'settled' on the night after he had died).

5.56 One patient found hanging in 2007 was reported to show signs of rigor mortis (not usually noticeable until around three hours after death) upon discovery, despite also being reported as being subject to 15-minute observations.

---

[425] In our *Eleventh Biennial Report 2003-2005; In Place of Fear* (fig 121), we counted all detained patients who died by hanging and who were not under at least 15-minute observation in this category. This will have included patients on leave, or AWOL, for whom observation at any level was a practical impossibility. In fig 84 above we have included only patients whose death appears to have taken place on the psychiatric ward (but see n.424 above) who were either subject to observation at a frequency of less than every 15 minutes. or not subject to any special observation levels at all.

Notable ligatures and load-bearing support

5.57 Throughout its existence, and with particular focus in its later years, the MHAC has pointed out ligature points on its visits and requested that they be removed or made safe. As the citation from the Lunacy Commission shows, this was also a feature of visits by our precedent bodies. On an MHAC visit to one north-east England hospital in September 2008 we wrote that:

> "In the dormitories occupied by the suicidals, blind cords might well be dispensed with, and in the single rooms where such cases sleep, the wire over the ventilating apertures are not perhaps free from objection"
>
> *Report of the Commissioners in Lunacy, visit to West Riding Asylum (later High Royds Hospital), May 10th 1889.*

a number of ligature points were observed in patient areas. These included the design of most bed frames, exposed pipe work on some washbasins, radiator controls, design of wash basin taps, shower fitments, wardrobe door hinges, door handles, window handles and suspended ceilings in some bedrooms. The part suspended ceilings in some bedrooms pose a security / ligature risk. Ceiling tiles are not secured therefore the space above can be used to secrete contraband or weapons or to access service pipes etc to use as a ligature point.

5.58 As we have written in past reports, a death reported to be the result of 'hanging' does not necessarily involve suspension by the neck from a height, with the subsequent 'hangman's fracture' (displacement of the epistropheus or second cervical vertebra)[426]. Patients also use various forms of ligature, sometimes attached to a load-bearing support that may even be at floor level, and in doing so die through strangulation, leading to asphyxisation, cardiac arrest or failure of blood supply to the brain. Such deaths are described in some of the following reports to the MHAC of 'hangings' since 2005:

> Patient found lying in bedroom, was on 30 min observations.
> Patient was allowed into the grounds and was left for 10 minutes and was then found to be kneeling down with a hose pipe around his neck. He died on the way to hospital
> Patient found on ward with a ligature (a pair of tights) around her neck
> Death by asphyxiation – patient found in room where he had hanged himself with his bed sheets attached to a window
> Patient found in his room by staff hanging from the toilet door with a dressing gown belt tied around his neck
> Patient hanging by his tie from the bathroom door
> Patient found hanging by a canvas belt attached to a screw on his bedroom wall
> Patient hanged himself from the bathroom door using a pair of jeans
> Patient hanging from conduit on ceiling with bed sheet
> Patient hanging from the shower room door – used plastic laundry bags to make a ligature
> Patient found hanging by his track suit bottoms from top of en-suite door
> Patient hanging by dressing gown cord
> Patient found hanging by shoe laces on wardrobe door
> Patient had upturned bed and used a belt

Fig 85: Methods of hanging detailed in reports to the MHAC, 2005 – 2009

---

[426] MHAC (2001) *Deaths of Detained patients in England and Wales*, paras 134 *et seq*; MHAC (2006) *Eleventh Biennial Report 2003-2005; In Place of Fear*, para 4.308.

5.59 Some of the ligatures used in the above list have not previously been reported to the MHAC. In particular, plastic laundry bags were an unrecognised hazard, and the hospital concerned now controls access to these. The use in hanging incidents of items of clothing such as jeans, track-suit bottoms and tights, or indeed domestic necessities such as bed-sheets, presents difficulties for risk-management, given that, in all but the most extreme circumstances, it would not be reasonable to deprive patients of such items and issue 'safety' replacements. This reinforces the importance of eliminating, as far as is possible, all load-bearing points that may be used to anchor such items, whether for the purposes of suspension from a height or for making a ligature. It is also vital that overrides for locks on bedroom or bathroom doors are readily at hand for nursing staff: in the case in a medium secure unit discussed above, the patient's self strangulation took place in a locked bathroom, and staff were initially unable to locate the device for opening the door from the outside.

Doors and door hinges

5.60 Following the death of the young man who hanged himself using his track-suit bottoms, the hospital concerned made alterations to door handles and hinges to present less opportunity as a ligature point. Some services have replaced bedroom and bathroom doors that open only in one direction with doors which, by opening both ways, remove the ligature point made by hinges and also ensure that staff can gain access. Doors in places that are difficult to observe – such as those to en-suite facilities – should be fitted with piano hinges or other safe alternatives. However, even doors that are made safer in this way can usually perform a load-bearing function. Although architectural design can help ensure a safe environment (and can certainly pose direct hazards to patient safety), the safety of patients can only be as good as the risk assessments and observation practices carried out by staff.

Self-Suffocation

5.61 As is shown at figure 78 above, between 2000 and 2008 some 5% of unnatural deaths of detained patients (26 deaths overall) were the result of self-suffocation. In one such case from 2007, a patient detained under s.3 suffocated herself with a plastic bag that had been used to line a waste-bin in a ward toilet. She was on five-minute observations. Both the availability of the bag and the level of observation were surprising, given that the patient had clearly expressed suicidal wishes, and a desire to suffocate herself, and had acted on this desire in the recent past. Two days before her death her nursing notes record her to have been at significant risk: "this week on two occasions she has put a plastic bag over her head in an attempt to suffocate herself".

5.62 Although it may be difficult to prevent access to plastic bags and similar hazards in wards with general security levels, particular care clearly should be taken where patients are assessed to be at risk of self-harm, and institutional use of plastic bags should be avoided wherever possible.

Breaking the news to relatives

5.63   It is vital that hospitals have in place policies and arrangements to ensure that patients' families are dealt with professionally and sensitively in the event of a serious incident or patient's death. Mental health services should be a source of help for families experiencing the shock, grief, anger and guilt arising from such incidents, and, although we recognise that families may project feelings of guilt or anger onto the detaining authority, such authorities must not exacerbate this through apparent indifference or unintentional cruelty. Hospital managers should also recognise that such events can be traumatising for staff who were involved in the incident, leading to inadvertent insensitivity or even irrational acts.

5.64   In the case of one death by self-strangulation in a medium secure unit during this reporting period, the police who were called to the scene wished to inform the patient's family through the appointed Family Liaison Officer, but a senior member of staff insisted on taking on this job himself. He telephoned the patient's family from the ward office, telling them that the patient had strangled himself but that they were working on him. Ten minutes later he called the family again to say that attempts to save the patient had failed. The family's distress was compounded by their discovery, upon receiving the coroner's report, that their family member had been dead for four hours at the time of the first telephone call to them.

5.65   Whilst hospitals must act within the limits of their duty to protect personal data, it is important that concern to ensure patient confidentiality does not create a bureaucratic culture that is inadvertently hostile to relatives of patients at times of great sensitivity. Following the death of one patient in 2007, the hospital had effectively prevented the deceased patient's family from access to records until the intervention of the MHAC at the point of the inquest hearing. The hospital administration had taken the view that the recipient of the papers should be the Nearest Relative: in this case the patient's centenarian father, who lived with another of his sons and was unable to provide requested proofs of identity (e.g. a utility bill, etc). The family were thus made distrustful of the hospital, suspecting it of attempting to hide things from them. In our view, the hospital administration was not deliberately obstructive, but its careful rectitude in the matter of proof of identity was disproportionately harmful to the family and its own discharge of a duty of care. Had the hospital had a means of reaching out to the family, this unnecessary antagonism might have been avoided.

5.66   More generally, the MHAC often encounters families of deceased patients who have received inadequate levels of communication and support from mental health services. In many cases, this is caused simply by slow responses to request for information, and by such responses being rather formal written documents in organisational language unsuited to its purpose.

5.67   In 2005, the Department of Health provided guidance on developing bereavement services in the NHS[427] which should already inform hospital policies and practice. In particular, policies and training over handling bereavement should be informed by the principles set out in this guidance, and should aim to ensure that the hospital response in the event of a patient death is a source of bereavement support and information. Hospitals may find the Royal College of Psychiatrists' *Bereavement Information Pack*[428] of use. We further recommend that all mental health services should have family liaison officers to provide a human face and point of contact for families of patients in the event of the unexpected death of a patient.

> **MHAC recommendation:** family liaison officers
>
> All mental health services caring for detained patients should have senior staff designated as family liaison officers in the event of deaths and serious untoward incidents.
>
> - The Trust should appoint a named case officer who identifies his/herself to the family as soon as possible after the death.
>
> - It should be the responsibility of the case officer to meet the family face to face as part of their job. The officer should visit the family, not summon them to meetings.
>
> - The case officer should be a relatively experienced and senior officer with a good understanding of grief and bereavement. He or she should, as far as is possible, not be liked to any part of the organisation which might be criticised in the enquiries.
>
> - The case officer should undertake to act as the conduit between the Trust and the family, solving practical problems and ensuring that questions are answered as fully as possible. All communication should be channelled through the officer where possible.

5.68   Hospital managers should also be alert to other ways in which they might provide inadequate support to or care for the needs of deceased patients' families. In one case, for example, although the patient's husband had been able to spend time with the body before it was taken to the mortuary, after delivery to the mortuary it became difficult for the family to see her again. The Trust recognised in its incident review that portering arrangements in such situations need to be directed the needs of the family, even if this might be inconvenient for staff. It is important that relatives and others are able to see and spend time with the body of the person who has died, at a convenient time and with as few restrictions as possible[429]. All hospital mortuary services should comply with the good

---

[427] Department of Health (2005) *When a Patient Dies – Advice on Developing Bereavement Services in the NHS*. Oct 2005.

[428] *Bereavement Information Pack: for those bereaved by suicide or other sudden death*. Kate Hill, Keith Hawton, Aslög Malmberg, Sue Simkin, RCPysch, 1997. Available to download from http://www.rcpsych.ac.uk/publications/books/rcpp/1901242080.aspx

[429] Department of Health (2005) *When a Patient Dies*, para 62.

practice guidance for mortuary staff published by the Department of Health in 2006[430]. We recognise, however, that in many cases following the sudden death of a detained patient, there will be some limitations on the extent to which relatives will be able to see and care for the body of the patient. Such limitations (for example, in terms of cleaning the body, brushing hair or changing clothes, or having medical devices such as drips or tubes removed) should be explained to relatives with consideration and sympathy.

Breaking the news to other patients

5.69   The death of any inpatient, or patient who has recently been on the ward, has a major impact on everyone, not least the other patients. How information is shared, therefore, and opportunities for expressing feelings about the event and the individual speak volumes to the patients about the way the hospital and its staff regard them and the value they place on them as individuals.

5.70   The following is a Commissioner's report from a visit to one unit where a death had recently occurred:

> It was very apparent that the recent death of a patient had had a considerable impact on the ward. The fact that this patient was well known to a number of the other patients over the years naturally meant that some were particularly affected. It appears, however, that patients were not called together at any time to inform them of the news, which instead was left to circulate by word of mouth and rumour following dramatic events durng the night the patient died. Neither was there therefore any public acknowledgement of this person's passing. One patient who spoke to the Commissioner about this had known the deceased over a number of years and was still visibly distressed but said nobody had spoken to him about it or offered him the opportunity to talk if he so wished. A patient who had been in the hospital a number of times when other deaths have occurred said he could only recall one occasion when patients were called together and the situation handled with some care and sensitivity. He indicated that he felt that the very act of some public affirmation of a patient's death was an indication of the hospital's care and respect for its patients. The possible, unintended, but very serious consequence of failing to deal properly with as significant an event as the death of a patient is that the rest of the patients can be left feeling that their lives are deemed insignificant to staff, the institution and even fellow patients. During her visit the Commissioner detected a sense of such a feeling existing among some of the patients on this ward.
>
> *West Midlands, November 2008*

Hospitals should provide guidance to staff, setting out a policy on dealing with these difficult situations on the ward and the needs of the patients.

---

[430] Department of Health (2006) *Care and respect in death: Good practice guidance for NHS mortuary staff.* August 2006.

Epilogue
The end of the Mental Health Act Commission?

The MHAC was founded to monitor the exercise of powers and duties of mental health law, after more than a two decade hiatus during which the inspectorate role itself had practically vanished. In the parliamentary debates leading up to that disappearance (formally enacted by the Mental Health Act 1959) the opposition sought to include a statutory duty upon the Minister to retain a visiting and reporting function:

> Dr. Edith Summerskill[431]: Under the Bill, the Board of Control [the successor to the Lunacy Commission] is to disappear, but the Minister will employ the officers. What we are asking is that those officers shall continue to carry out such duties, in respect of the regular visiting of hospitals and the issuing of reports of such visits, as the Minister may direct.[432]

Dr Summerskill did not then have her way. The monitoring of mental hospitals passed, without specific legal duties, to the Ministry of Health, as it was not for parliament to dictate what the Minister should instruct his officials. The Minister spoke at length on the reports that the remnants of the Board of Control, now rebadged as his own officials, might make. In the first place reports made by Ministry staff following their visits and inspections were to be "corn-piled" for the Minister himself to "discharge his duty of raising the standards of administration in the hospitals and acting as a clearing-house for all constructive ideas and improvements". Any further action would depend on the individual case, and although it was expected that in most cases the report would find its way to the hospital managers, it was assumed that publication would not be appropriate or helpful[433].

The ensuing two decades saw several hospital scandals relating to poor treatment of mental health and learning disabilities patients. In the run-up to the 1983 Act, independent visiting and monitoring of mental hospitals was reintroduced, albeit through an organisation with quango status[434], the MHAC.

What the Health and Social Care Act 2008 calls the abolition of the MHAC is not a re-run of 1959. Then, the Ministry of Health abolished and took over the human and material assets of the independent – or at least "arms' length" – monitoring body. Now, in England, the legal duties, and human and material assets or liabilities of one arm's length body are being transferred to another.

---

[431] Dr (later Baroness) Edith Summerskill, 1901 – 1980, was then MP for Warrington (Lab), and had been a Minister of National Insurance in the post-war Atlee Government, a member of the Labour Party National Executive Committee and Chair of the Labour Party.

[432] *Hansard*, HC Deb 05 May 1959 vol 605 column 235-6

[433] *Hansard*, HC Deb 05 May 1959 vol 605 cc238-9. This appears to reflect later practice of the Board of Control: see the introduction to this report.

[434] i.e. "quasi-autonomous non-governmental organisation". See Cavadino M (1995) 'Quasi-government: the case of the Mental Health Act Commission' *International Journal of Public Sector Management*, Vol 8 No 7, pp. 56-62.

Furthermore, what Dr Summerskill called for in the 1959 debates has, this time, come to pass: the core of the MHAC's work is preserved as a legal duty for the CQC. The title of 'Mental Health Act Commissioner' has been retained by the CQC for those who visit hospitals. Those of us that may be counted amongst the assets and liabilities of the MHAC may therefore look forward to a continuing role in monitoring the Act and visiting detained patients under the new body, and indeed might hope to shed some of the limitations, both legal and resource-based, on the scope of our work hitherto.

But being part of a big organisation has its own challenges, not least in getting into the public sphere the findings, observations and discussions included in Biennial Reports over the lifetime of the MHAC. We do not yet know what will be expected of the annual reporting duty placed upon the CQC in its dealings with the Mental Health Act, but we hope that we will continue to have some vehicle for public discourse over our findings, and that this will not be too squeezed into a mould dictated by more general monitoring methodologies. We hope that future parliamentary debates will not say of CQC what was said in 1959 about the Board of Control:

> Mr Charles Hale[435]: ... in a later stage of the Standing Committee debate I expressed the view that reports from the Board of Control to the House had never been very full or adequate. The reports which many of us read with pleasure from the Prison Commissioners are, in many ways, models of their kind. They are one of the few documents in which the appendices are often more interesting than the report, because they give individual and humane examples of cases. The reports from the Board of Control are examples of what is usually said to be the supreme quality of wit – they concentrate on brevity.[436]

In the end, however, the abolition of the MHAC is, in common with the abolition of its legal predecessors, rather more metamorphoses than annihilation. From our perspective, some of these past metamorphoses failed to produce butterflies – in particular, perhaps, the transformation of the officials of the Board of Control into officers of the Ministry of Health after the Second World War – but we have their lessons to build upon.

The Mental Health Act Commission is dead. Long live Mental Health Act Commissioners!

Mat Kinton
March 2009

---

[435] Charles Leslie Hale (later Baron Hale), 1902-1985, was then MP for Oldham (Lab).

[436] *Hansard* HC Deb 05 May 1959 vol 605 cc235.

Appendix A

Brian D M Smith
1925 – 2008

A founder member of the Mental Health Act Commission, Brian Smith died in the year that the NHS celebrated its 60th birthday. It is appropriate, in this the last of the Commission's biennial reports, not only to celebrate Brian's career and contribution to the Commission (he was a Commissioner from 1983 to 1993) but also to use those memories as a vehicle for looking back on the Commission's first decade.

Rejected on medical grounds for service in the RAF (much to his chagrin but also possibly his good fortune – he was one of two in his class at school who survived the war) he became in 1944 the Assistant Master of St Michaels Workhouse in Enfield. Thus began a career in public service and, beginning 4 years later, in particular the NHS that lasted 40 years. He was what was then called a "hospital administrator" – a band of mostly men who, in effect, for not much money (certainly as compared with NHS Executive Directors of today) devoted their lives to managing the NHS through frequent crisis, restructurings, inadequate resources, periodic less than subtle undermining from clinical colleagues and a high political profile that has never diminished in the service's 60 years.

Studying part time at the LSE he obtained his Diploma in Public Administration and Membership of the Association of Hospital Administrators and so armed, he followed a career in the health service that took him from London through Preston, Luton, Stevenage, back to London and then onto Lincolnshire where his career culminated as Area Health Administrator for Lincolnshire; from which he retired in 1982. Highlights along the way included planning the new Lister Hospital in Stevenage and planning and delivering the new 580 bed Pilgrim Hospital in Boston as well as, in his role as a Fellow of the Kings Fund, devising some of their first courses for senior public sector managers.

His retirement coincided with the establishment of the Mental Health Act Commission. There are many ways of assessing the objectives that lay behind the initial membership of the Commission. What is not in doubt is that leaders or potential leaders of the various professional groups who made up its membership were sought. Whilst it is invidious to mention names it is illustrative to pick a few: the redoubtable Kathleen Jones (Professor of Social Policy at York University); Bob Bluglass (the first Professor of Forensic Psychiatry ever appointed in the UK); Gillian Shepherd (who went onto be Secretary of State for Education and now graces the House of Lords); Tessa Jowell (now Paymaster General and Minister for the Olympics); Molly Meacher (now in the House of Lords); Tim Kirkhope MEP; and, a later member, Genevra Richardson (who chaired the Government's review of the Act in 1998 and is now Professor of Law at Kings College London).

In 1983 the inspectorate landscape was lightly populated: essentially the Hospital Advisory Service and the National Development Team. The Commission was not an inspectorate although many (both within and more often without the Commission) wanted it to be and debating, defining and redefining its role has been a feature of its existence. What is clear is that at its outset its founders wanted it to comprise what David Halberstam called the "best and the brightest" and that their multi-disciplinary wisdom would influence those services that were the subject of the Commission's jurisdiction. Brian Smith was a natural choice to join this galaxy. A man of the utmost integrity with a remarkable commitment to individual (and in particular patient) rights, he bought to the organisation wisdom; shrewdness; political skills (with a small "p" borne of having operated in one of the most complex working environments in the world; the NHS); an ability to work creatively with clinical colleagues and a constructively critical, but never wavering, loyalty to the organisation. Always collegiate and pragmatic, his particular focus on how the Commission should handle complaints and operate effectively in the High Security Hospitals (especially Rampton which he visited) was very influential. He was a mentor and advisor to all four of us during our time at the Commission. Above all, he was a thoroughly nice man of great human warmth.

The Commission's performance as a watchdog institution will always be debated and in its first 10 years it spent a lot of its energy (which unsurprisingly was considerable having regard to the pedigree of its 90 members) not only undertaking its remit but also debating what compulsory mental health care should look like, as well as its own structure and ways of working. What is probably true to say is that it enjoyed a high credibility. Visits from the Commission were remarkably important for the services visited; end-of-visit feedbacks were attended always by the Chief Executive and other senior officers. At their best (and they were not always thus) visit reports were masterpieces of observation and recommendation, especially when they successfully communicated a justified concern for which there was limited evidence. There was a downside of course: some Commissioners overemphasised on occasion their own preoccupations; the voice of the patient (as opposed to concern about, which was always central) was not strong, although many Commissioners had personal experience of mental ill health; and there were frequent misunderstandings about the Commission's remit. Having said that, the Commission throughout its life has represented the very best of what might be termed enlightened concern about and recognition of one of the most serious acts that the state can ever undertake: the deprivation of an individuals liberty on account of their mental disorder.

In acknowledging and celebrating the life of and contribution to the Commission of Brian Smith all those who were Commissioners in the organisation's 26 years of work are also acknowledged and celebrated.

Sir Louis Blom-Cooper QC, Chairman 1987 to 1994

Elaine, Baroness Murphy of Aldgate, Vice Chairman 1988 to 1994

Mike Napier CBE, QC, Chairman North East Region 1983 to 1993

William Bingley, Chief Executive 1990 to 2000.

Appendix B

Mental Health Act Commissioners, 1983-2009

Mr	I	Adam	Mr	A	Barstead	Mr	Martin	Brown
Mrs	E	Abrahams	Mr	Andrew	Beaumont	Mr	Robert	Brown
Mr	David	Abrahart	Mr	Michael	Beebe	Mr	T	Brownie
Ms	Melissa	Agart	Mrs	Glora	Beeching	Mr	Michael	Bryant
Mr	Christopher	Aggett	Mrs	Vivien	Bellau	Mrs	Janet	Buckley
Mr	Nisar	Ahmed	Mr	P	Bennet	Ms	H	Burke
Ms	Anne	Aiyegbusi	Mrs	Caroline	Bennett	Mr	Brian	Burke
Mr	Vincent	Alexander	Mrs	O	Benyon	Ms	Julie	Burton
Mrs	Shahida	Ali	Miss	I	Bernstein	Mr	J	Bury
Mr	John	Allam	Dr	Colin	Berry	Mrs	B	Butler
Dr	A	Allen	Mrs	Kathy	Berry	Mr	Gary	Bye
Dr	Hilary	Allen	Ms	Linda	Berry	Prof	Patrick	Callaghan
Miss	C	Allison	Mr	Alfred	Best	Mr	J	Camp
Mr	P	Allot	Mr	Reginald	Bevan	Mrs	Susan	Campbell
Ms	B	Allwood	Mr	Allan	Bevan	Ms	Georgina	Campbell
Dr	A	Ananthakopan	Dr	Dawn	Black	Mr	Michael	Cann
Dr	T	Ananthanarayanan	Mr	J	Black	Dr	E	Carr
Mrs	Annie	Anderson	Dr	Dorothy	Black	Ms	F	Cassells
Mr	Simon	Armson	Dr	J	Blackburn	Mr	D	Castell
Dr	J	Ashcroft	Mr	John	Blavo	Ms	Maxine	Caswell
Dr	Barry	Ashcroft	Sir	Louis	Blom-Cooper	Mrs	S H	Cawthra
Mr	Salim	Atchia	Dr	Tony	Blowers	Ms	Patricia	Chadderton
Mr	Ajibola	Awogboro	Prof	Robert	Bluglass	Mrs	Barbara	Chaffy
Mrs	Inge	Axt-Simmonds	Ms	C	Bollinger	Mr	Christopher	Chambers
Ms	Genevieve	Bediako-Bonsu	Ms	Linda	Bolter	Ms	Pamela	Chan
Mr	Anthony	Backer-Holst	Mrs	Chistina	Bond	Mr	R	Chapman
Mr	Richard	Backhouse	Miss	Anita	Bowden	Mr	Hugh	Chapman
Mr	S	Badland	Mr	John	Bowyer	Ms	Noelle	Chesworth
Mr	G	Badland	Ms	Helen	Bramley	Mr	Eric	Chitty
Ms	Sheridan	Bailey	Ms	Valerie	Bramley	Ms	Elisa	Cioffi
Ms	Hilary	Bainbridge	Dr	David	Brandford	Mr	Felix	Cofie
Ms	Deborah	Baldwin	Mr	B	Branett	Mr	Jeff	Cohen
Mr	Allen	Ball	Mrs	Katherine	Brass	Mrs	E	Coleman
Ms	Carey	Bamber	Mrs	L	Breach	Mrs	M	Coleman
Mr	Robert	Bamlett	Mrs	Sarah	Breach	Ms	Louize	Collins
Dr	Sube	Bannerjee	Ms	Susan	Brindle	Lord		Colville
Mrs	C	Baptiste-Cyrus	Dr	Oliver	Briscoe	Mr	Brendan	Commons
Dr	Marian	Barnes	Dr	Anne	Broadhurst	Ms	Sarah	Cooke
Ms	Jane	Barnes	Mr	E	Bromley	Ms	Sharon	Cookson
Mr	B	Barnett	Ms	Melanie	Brooks	Mr	J	Cooley
Dr	Alan	Barrett	Mr	Peter	Brotherhood	Ms	Margaret	Coombs
Mr	Kevin	Barrett	Dr	Maria	Broughton	Mrs	Alison	Cooney

Mr	A	Cooper	Ms	Pat	Edwards	Ms	Gillian	Gower
Dr	R	Cope	Dr	Anwar	El Khomy	Mr	Monty	Graham
Ms	Jill	Cox	Mr	Anselm	Eldergill	Mr	J	Graham-White
Ms	Susan	Cragg	Ms	F	Eliot	Mrs	J M	Grant
Mr	M	Crane	Mrs	J	Endean	Mr	Michael	Green
Mrs	Valarie	Cranwell	Mrs	Phillipa	Entwistle	Ms	Patricia	Gregory
Lady		Crawshay	Mr	Nihat	Erol	Mr	Huw	Griffiths
Ms	Jennifer	Creek	Dr	M	Evans	Dr	John	Grimshaw
Ms	Lyn	Critchley	Mr	M	Evans	Ms	Catherine	Grimshaw
Miss	Judith	Croton	Mr	T	Evans	Mrs	P	Guinan
Mr	P	Croughton	Mr	William	Evans	Prof	Michael	Gunn
Mr	Christopher	Curran	Prof	Phil	Fennell	Prof	H	Gwynne-Jones
Ms	Penny	Cushing	Dr	Suman	Fernando	Ms	Anne	Hall
Mr	Alan	Dabbs	Mr	Harry	Field	Ms	Sandra	Hallam
Dr	Omar	Daniels	Mr	John	Finch	Miss	Margaret	Halliday
Ms	Salle	Dare	Dr	H	Firth	Mr	Gordon	Halliday
Dr	Cyril	Davies	Mr	T	Fisher	Mr	J	Halliwell
Mr	Howard	Davis	Dr	N	Fisher	Ms	M	Halstead
Ms	Ann	Davison	Mr	Paul	Fisher	Dr	K	Hamadah
Dr	Ken	Day	Mr	R	Fletcher	Mr	Norman	Hamilton
Ms	Annette	De La Cour	Ms	Angela	Flower	Mr	Tomasz	Hanchen
Mr	Paul	De Ponte	Mr	Michael	Follows	Mrs	J B	Hanham
Mrs	Joan	Deeley	Mr	Madhun	Foolchand	Mr	R	Hargreaves
Mr	Anthony	Deery	Mrs	Jane	Forman-Hardy	Dr	R	Harper
Mr	Barry	Delaney	Dr	M	Forth	Dr	P	Harper
Ms	Suki	Desai	Dr	C	Foster	Dr	Max	Harper
Mr	Sunil	Dharmabanahu	Mrs	Judith	Foster	Dr	J	Harrington
Dr	Donald	Dick	Dr	Sadie	Francis	Miss	Catherine	Harris
Prof	Bridget	Dimond	Mrs	Ros	Fraser	Dr	R	Hartley
Mr	L	Dodds	Mrs	J	Freeman	Miss	Caroline	Harvey
Mr	Malcolm	Dodds	Miss	Diana	Frempong	Mrs	Sanota	Harvey
Ms	Kathyrn	Doeser	Mr	M	Frost	Mrs	Jospehine	Hassell
Dr	Robert	Dolan	Ms	Elizabeth	Frost	Dr	Agnes	Hauck
Mrs	Margot	DosAnjos	Ms	Carolyn	Fyall	Canon	Arthur	Hawes
Mr	Richard	Dosoo	Ms	Steve	Gannon	Miss	Sharon	Hayles
Mrs	Petrina	Douglas-Hall	Mrs	Ann	Gallagher	Mrs	J	Healey
Mr	D	Downham	Mr	R	Gardner	Ms	G	Heath
Mrs	Gillian	Downham	Ms	Michelle	Garner	Mr	Stephen	Hedges
Miss	C	Drew	Dr	Sammy	Gaspar	Mr	M	Hefferman
Mr	Anthony	Drew	Dr	Hema	Ghadiali	Ms	Annette	Henry
Dr	Keith	Dudleston	Ms	E	Gilham	Prof	M	Herbert
Dr	Desmond	Dunleavy	Ms	Claire	Gilham	Ms	Katherine	Herzberg
Mr	L	Dunn	Dr	Neville	Gittleson	Ms	Pauline	Heslop
Mr	T	Eager	Mr	M	Godridge	Ms	J	Hesmondhalgh
Mr	Ray	Earle	Mr	Malcolm	Golightley	Dr	Pearl	Hettiaratchy
Mr	Anthony	Eaton	Mrs	C	Goonatillake	Mr	John	Hewett
Mr	M	Edwardes-Evans	Dr	B	Gordon	Mr	David	Hewitt
Mr	P	Edwards	Dr	Edward	Gordon	Mrs	Christine	Hewitt
Dr	H	Edwards	Mrs	Julie	Gossage	Dr	David	Hide

Mr	Peter	Higson		Dr	R	Kennon		Mr	Leslie	Marshall
Mr	Michael	Hill		Mr	G	Kerr		Mrs	Lotte	Mason
Mr	David	Hill		Mr	Nairon	Khan		Mr	Richard	Mason
Mr	A	Hillier		Cllr	T	Kirkhope		Dr	Robert	Mather
Mr	Philip	Hindson		Mr	Stephen	Klein		Dr	G	Mathur
Mr	Ben	Hoare		Ms	Silba	Knight		Ms	Sarah	Matthews
Mr	Robert	Holdsworth		Dr	Stephen	Knights		Ms	Julie	McAllister
Dr	John	Holliday		Ms	Gillian	Koraonkar		Mrs	P	McCaig
Mr	Derek	Holmes		Mr	Gordon	Lakes		Miss	Mary	McCann
Mr	William	Horder		Mrs	E	Land		Mr	Colin	McCarthy
Mr	Bakhtiar	Hormoz		Ms	Joan	Langan		Mr	Derek	McCarthy
Mr	John	Horne		Dr	Gordon	Langley		Mr	Howard	McClarron
Ms	Barbara	Howard		Ms	Althia	Lawrence		Mr	Peter	McCormick
Dr	E	Howarth		Mrs	Sue	Ledwith		Dr	M	McCoubrie
Mrs	I	Howd		Mr	A	Lee		Mr	Brian	McGinnes
Mr	Philip	Howes		Mrs	Soo	Lee		Mr	E	McGuinness
Mr	P	Hughes		Mr	David	Lee		Ms	Suzanne	McKeever
Dr	H	Hughes-Roberts		Mr	Philip	Lee		Ms	Alison	McKenna
Mrs	Heather	Hurford		Mr	M	Lee-Evans		Dr	John	McKenna
Dr	J	Hurst		Mr	G	Lees		Ms	Patricia	McKenzie
Mr	P	Hutchinson		Mrs	S	Lees		Ms	J	McKenzie
Ms	Lacey	Ingham		Mr	Neville	Lees		Mr	John	Mclean
Dr	R	Ingrey-Senn		Dr	I	Lennox		Mrs	Sue	McMillan
Mr	Chinyere	Inyama		Mr	H	Leopoldt		Ms	G	McMorrow
Mr	J	Jackson		Ms	Penny	Letts		Mrs	Molly	Meacher
Dr	V	Jain		Mrs	A R M	Lewis		Mrs	L	Meade
Mr	Mohammed	Jamil		Ms	Hazelanne	Lewis		Mrs	E	Meade
Dr	J	Jancar		Mrs	Jillian	Lewis		Miss	Naomi	Mehta
Ms	Sue	Jarvis		Rev	Brian	Lillington		Mr	T	Meirion Wynne
Dr	Peter	Jefferys		Mr	Richard	Lingham		Dr	Eric	Mendelson
Dr	Tim	Jerram		Miss	Georgina	Linton		Mrs	Jean	Meredith
Miss	C	John		Mrs	Vicki	Lipscomb		Ms	Lindsey	Messenger
Ms	D	Johnson		Dr	S	Llewellyn		Ms	Linda	Metcalfe
Ms	Kathryn	Johnson		Mrs	Carys	Llewelyn-Jones		Dr	Ihsan	Mian
Mrs	C	Jones		Mrs	Margaret	Lloyd		Mrs	Inge	Midforth
Prof	Katherine	Jones		Miss	D	Lockie		Mr	Garry	Millard
Mr	Richard	Jones		Canon	Frank	Longbottom		Dr	E	Miller
Prof	M	Jones		Dr	Judith	MacKenzie		Mr	Alan	Milligan
Mr	G	Jones		Ms	Jane	MacKenzie		Dr	Alfred	Minto
Mr	Robert	Jones		Ms	Elizabeth	MacMin		Dr	Nathaniel	Minton
Ms	Linda	Jones		Mrs	Mita	Madden		Mr	R	Moody
Ms	Esther	Jones		Dr	M	Malcolm		Dr	S	Moore
Rt Hon	Tessa	Jowell MP		Dr	Tim	Malcolm		Mr	Paul	Moore
Mr	Lionel	Joyce		Mr	Steve	Manikon		Mr	John	Moran
Dr	Ola	Junaid		Dr	Sivanathan	Manjubhashini		Mrs	Edith	Morgan
Mr	L	Kaye		Mrs	Hilary	Markson		Mr	Bill	Morgan
Mrs	A	Kelbrick		Mr	James	Marlow		Mr	Alban	Morley
Dr	Alison	Kelly		Miss	Laraine	Marriott		Mrs	M	Morris
Mrs	M	Kendrick		Mr	Yens	Marsen-Luther		Mrs	Glynis	Morton

Mr	Peter	Moxley		Mrs	Parminder	Parmar		Ms	Evangeline	Rogers
Mr	Simon	Mumford		Mrs	Jill	Patel		Dr	A	Rolfe
Mr	Michael	Murkin		Lord	Kamlesh	Patel		Ms	Helen	Ross
Prof	Elaine	Murphy		Mrs	Jane	Patterson		Dr	Martyn	Rowton-Lee
Mr	Robert	Murphy		Ms	Lesley	Pavincich		Mr	G	Royle
Dr	S	Nagraj		Ms	Sarah	Paxton		Dr	Ron	Ryall
Mr	B	Napier		Mr	Trevor	Peel		Ms	Nigar	Sadique
Ms	Maureen	Napier		Mr	Albert	Persaud		Ms	Y	Saloojee
Mr	Mike	Napier		Mr	Randolph	Peters		Mrs	Anita	Samuels
Mrs	Anna	Navarro		Mrs	Marisa	Phillips		Ms	Lyne	Saunders
Mr	Mark	Naylor		Dr	Robin	Phillpott		Dr	Anu	Sayal-Bennett
Mr	George	Nazer		Mr	Samuel	Pierre		Prof	J	Scott
Ms	Lucia	Ndoro		Mr	J	Pinschof		Mrs	A	Scott Fordham
Dr	C	Neal		Dr	J	Pippard		Ms	Lucy	Scott-Moncrieff
Dr	David	Neal		Mr	Robert	Plumb		Ms	Jennifer	Scudamore
Dr	T	Nelson		Mrs	Sally	Plumb		Mr	Kevin	Seacy
Ms	Mary	Nettle		Mr	John	Price		Dr	Poppy	Seberatnam
Mr	Ian	Newton		Mr	J	Prins		Mr	John	Sedgeman
Mr	R	Nichol		Prof	Herschel	Prins		Dr	B	Sekhawat
Mr	Leroy	Nicholas		Ms	Julia	Prior		Mrs	Christine	Selim
Mr	R	Nichols		Mr	Egon	Prtak		Mrs	Bridget	Sensky
Mr	Joe	Nichols		Dr	I	Pryce		Ms	Jennye	Seres
Mrs	Rosemary	Nicholson		Dr	Gwyn	Pryce		Mr	John	Sharich
Ms	Jayne	Norgate		Mr	Kuruvilla	Punnamkuzhy		Mrs	D	Shaw
Mr	R	North		Ms	Mary	Purcell		Mrs	C	Sheehy
Insp.	Nicholas	North		Mr	David	Ramage		Mrs	Kay	Sheldon
Miss	Iris	Nutting		Mrs	Sue	Ramprogus		Lady	Gillian	Shephard
Mr	A	Oakley		Mr	Sunil	Ramrecha		Miss	D	Shepherd
Ms	E	O'Farrell		Dr	Y	Rao		Ms	A	Shields
Mr	Michael	Ogley		Dr	John	Rao		Ms	Linda	Sinclair
Ms	Pamela	Oglivie		Ms	V	Rao		Mr	John	Sinclair
Mr	J	Ogunremi		Mrs	Elaine	Rassaby		Mr	G	Smith
Dr	T	O'Hare		Mrs	Carole	Rees-Williams		Mr	Brian	Smith
Mr	Bernard	O'Hare		Mr	Edmundson	Reid		Dr	Marilyn	Smith
Prof	M R	Olsen		Miss	I	Reinbach		Mrs	Christine	Smithson
Mrs	Jeraine	Olsen		Mrs	Louise	Relton		Dr	S	Soni
Mrs	Justina	Oraka		Mr	Steven	Richards		Mr	Robert	Southern
Ms	Kate	O'Regan		Prof	Genevre	Richardson		Ms	M	Southwell
Prof	M	Osen		Ms	N	Rickman		Mrs	Reshma	Spafford
Mrs	D	Ottley		Ms	Marion	Rickman		Mrs	S	Spence
Mrs	Elizabeth	Owen		Mrs	Rachel	Riddle		Mrs	Jacqueline	Spencer
Prof	Femi	Oyebode		Mrs	Mair	Roberts		Dr	Ian	Spencer
Mr	J	Palacios		Ms	Helen	Roberts		Ms	J	Spenser
Dr	Elizabeth	Parker		Dr	Geoff	Roberts		Ms	Penny	Spinks
Ms	Camilla	Parker		Mr	A	Robinson		Ms	Sandra	Squires
Mr	John	Parker		Mrs	Josephine	Robinson		Mr	Ray	Stables
Dr	Robert	Parker		Mr	Neil	Robinson		Ms	Penny	Stafford
Mr	D	Parkin		Mr	Robert	Robinson		Ms	D	Steele
Mr	Alan	Parkin		Ms	Jenny	Rogers		Mr	Gregory	Steele

Ms	Pashe	Stott	Mrs	Mashid	Turner	Mrs	Nonn	Williams
Mr	S	Stratton	Ms	June	Tweedie	Prof	Richard	Williams
Mrs	Beryl	Stroll	Ms	Vimala	Uttarkar	Mr	Barry	Williams
Mrs	Helen	Swaffield	Mr	Paul	Veitch	Mr	J	Williams
Dr	Marion	Swan	Mr	H	Vickers	Mr	Trevor	Williams
Dr	P	Sykes	Mr	Philp	Wales	Mrs	Rhian	Williams-Flew
Dr	L	Tarlo	Mr	Jeremy	Walker	Mr	Alastair	Williamson
Mr	Mark	Taylor	Lady	Margaret	Wall	Mr	Len	Wilson
Mr	Michael	Taylor	Dr	Gerald	Wallen	Mr	Thomas	Wilson
Mr	P	Taylor	Mr	Ivor	Ward	Mr	Barry	Windle
Mr	Harry	Teaney	Mr	Alan	Watson	Mr	M	Wiseman
Dr	G	Tennant	Ms	V	Watson	Mr	Tony	Wishart
Dr	T	Tennent	Mr	C	Watts	Mr	Jeff	Withington
Mrs	Helena	Thomas	Dr	M	Way	Mr	Ron	Wix
Ms	Catherine	Thompson	Mr	N	Weaver	Mr	E	Wong
Mr	Paul	Thompson	Mr	Roderick	Webster	Mr	David	Woodcock
Mr	Ashley	Thompson	Mr	S	Weldon	Mr	Charles	Woods
Mr	Brian	Thorne	Prof	Malcolm	Weller	Mr	Jon	Woolmore
Mr	T	Ticknell	Ms	Mavis	Wenham	Mr	Tony	Wrigglesworth
Mr	R	Timson	Prof	Donald	West	Mr	Alan	Wright
Ms	Glenys	Tipton	Mr	Phillip	Westcott	Mr	T	Wright
Mr	David	Torpy	Ms	Kate	Whalley	Mrs	Momena	Wright
Mr	Glenn	Townsend	Mr	J	White	Mr	Benjamin	Wyke
Mrs	Christa	Trollope	Ms	C	Whitting	Prof	Aubrey	Yates
Mr	Robert	Tunmore	Mr	Merlin	Wilce	Mrs	Lorraine	Yearsley
Ms	Jacqueline	Turnball	Dr	C	Williams	Mr	Paul	Yeomans
Mrs	S	Turner	Dr	Anthony	Williams	Dr	Tony	Zigmond

Index

The locators in the index refer to paragraph numbers. Figures are indicated by the paragraph number immediately preceding the figure, and are italicised with the letter 'f'; notes by the italicised number and 'n'; and recommendations by the italicised number and 'r'.

absconding, 2.58 *see also* absence without leave
absence without leave, 2.56–2.57
    deaths, 5.39–5.45, *5.39f*
    return to hospital, 2.60–2.61
    statistics on, 2.58–2.59
Academy of Medical Royal Colleges, 2.122
accidental death, 5.2, 5.17–5.19
    self-harming behaviour, 5.13
ACPO (Association of Chief Police Officers)
    data collection on police powers, *2.140r*
Acting Together project, 1.15
activities, access to, 1.86–1.90, *1.88f*, 1.144
Acute Trusts, *2.128r*
    KP90 statistics, 2.121
    liaison psychiatry teams, 2.122–2.123
    medicine management, 3.24
    Mental Health Act powers, 2.121, 2.124
        obligations, 2.125–2.126
    Mental Health Trusts, 2.126
acute wards, 1.7–1.8, 1.61–1.63
    activities, 1.86–1.90, *1.88f*
    acuity of patients, 2.116–2.117
    comfort provisions, 1.75–1.76
    environments, 1.71–1.77
    locked doors, 1.64–1.67, *1.64f*
    medical, 5.18–5.19
    nursing staff, 1.9–1.11, 1.84
    over-occupancy, 1.68–1.70, *1.69f*
    repairs, 1.74
    self-harm, *1.65f*
    staffing levels, 1.78–1.85, *1.79f, 1.82f, 1.83f*
Administrative Justice and Tribunals Council Stakeholder Advisory Group, 2.110
admissions
    delays in, 2.29
    independent sector, 1.25, *1.25f*, 1.27
    informal patients, 1.27
    threshold for, 1.20–1.22
    ward environments, 1.7–1.12
adolescents
    on adult wards, 1.6, 1.49–1.58, *1.51f, 1.53f, 1.54f, 1.55f, 1.58f*

    care standards, 1.48–1.49
    consent to treatment, 3.88–3.89, *3.88f, 3.89f*
    ECT treatment, 3.88, 3.90–3.92
    ethnicity, 1.58, *1.58f*
    secure services, 1.59–1.60
advance decisions, 3.18–3.22, 3.80
advocacy services, 3.22
    for adolescents, 1.56, 1.59
    IMHAs, 1.111–1.113
    seclusion, 1.156
aftercare provision, 2.141
    discharge from, 2.145–2.147
    funding of, 2.142
age, of patients
    children and adolescents, adult wards, 1.51–1.52, *1.51f*
    death, natural causes, 5.4, *5.4f*
    death, unnatural causes, 5.13, *5.13f*
    detained, 1.30–1.31, *1.30f*
    electro-convulsive therapy (ECT), 3.48, *3.48f*
    Supervised Community Treatment, 2.79, *2.79f*
agency staff, 1.83, *1.83f*
AJTC (Administrative Justice and Tribunals Council), 2.110
alcohol related deaths, 5.31–5.32, *5.32r*
AMHPs *see* Approved Mental Health Professionals
anger management, 1.158
antipsychotic medication
    administration of, 3.10
    combination prescribing, 3.15
    high dosage, 3.12, 3.14, 3.37
    side effects, 3.13
    weight gain, 3.16
appeals, points of law, 2.96
appeals against detention *see* managers' hearings; Tribunal, the appraisals, psychiatrists, 2.20, *2.20r*
Approved Clinicians, 2.9, 2.15
    patient capacity and consent, 3.39
    s.12 approval, 2.18
    training, 2.127, *2.128r*
Approved Doctors, 2.17–2.20, *2.20r*
    change of address, 2.19

Approved Mental Health Professionals, 1.112, 2.21–2.23
    assessment of detainees, 2.137
    conveyance for patients, 2.28–2.29
    interviews with patients, 2.24, 2.25–2.26
    Supervised Community Treatment, 2.67, 2.70–2.72
Article 5 ECHR, 2.11
aspiration, 5.9, *5.9n*
assessment
    Approved Mental Health Professionals, 2.22–2.23
    s. 136 detainees, 2.136–2.137
    uncooperative patients, 2.24–2.27
Association of Chief Police Officers, 1.5
autistic spectrum disorder, 2.56
autonomy, of patients, 1.98, 5.45
Avoidable Deaths report, 5.45, 5.46
AWOL *see* absence without leave

bed management, 1.21
benefits, state
    staff meals, 2.37
    transferred prisoners, 4.53, *4.53n*
    withdrawal of, 2.45
bereavement services, 5.66–5.68, *5.67r*
Black and Minority Ethnic groups, 1.37 *see also* ethnic minorities
    deaths, while detained, 5.3, *5.3f*
    s. 136 detention, 2.140
    second opinions, 3.32–3.34, *3.32f*, 3.33, *3.33f*
    Supervised Community Treatment, 2.80–2.81, *2.80f*
BME *see* Black and Minority Ethnic groups
boredom, 1.144, 4.52
Broadmoor High Security Hospital, 1.27

camera phones, 1.115, 1.117
CAMHS *see* Child and Adolescent Mental Health Services
capacity, of patient
    advance decisions, 3.21
    assessment, 3.9
    deep-brain stimulation, 3.63
    ECT treatment, 3.49–3.51
    recognition of, 3.4
    refusal, consent to treatment, 2.76, 3.4
        Supervised Community Treatment, 3.70–3.72
    thresholds for, 3.54–3.55
cardiac arrest, 5.5–5.6

care, 1.8 *see also* community care services
    homes, 2.84, 2.145–2.147
care plans, *see also* Care Programme Approach
    consent to treatment, 3.15
    leave, 2.33
    lower security sectors, 1.104
    necessity for, 5.40–5.44
    seclusion, 1.157
Care Programme Approach, 1.99–1.100, 1.102, 5.38
    medicine management, 3.24
Care Quality Commission, 1.6 *see also* Epilogue
    community care services, 1.23
    consent to treatment, 3.6
    de facto detention, 2.66
    establishment of, 1.1
    functions, 1.2–1.3
    human rights, 1.32
    IMHA services, 1.113
    intoxicated patients, 5.32, *5.32r*
    long-term leave, 2.62–2.64
    mail for patients, 1.125
    mechanical restraint, 5.20
    second opinion service, 3.36
    statutory duties, 1.24
    Supervised Community Treatment, 2.75
    transport for patients, 2.29
    Tribunal secretariat data, 2.120, *2.120r*
    voting rights, detained prisoners, 4.54
Care Services Improvement Partnership
    medication management, 3.24
carers, 2.32
case management, 2.98
certification, 2.75
certification of consent, 3.7
Child and Adolescent Mental Health Services, 1.56
children
    on adult wards, 1.6, 1.49–1.58, *1.51f, 1.53f, 1.54f, 1.55f, 1.58f*
    care standards, 1.48–1.49
    consent to treatment, 3.88–3.89, *3.88f, 3.89f*
    ECT treatment, 3.88, 3.90–3.92
    ethnicity, 1.58, *1.58f*
    learning difficulties, 1.44
Chinese patients, 1.37
choking, 5.27–5.30, *5.30f*, 5.49
City 128 Study of Acute Psychiatric Wards, *1.77f*, 1.82, *1.82f, 1.88f*, 1.105
    observation, 1.137

Codes of Practice *see* Mental Health Act Codes of Practice
coercive measures, 1.93–1.94, 1.101, 1.143
    Black patients, 2.81
    Supervised Community Treatment, 2.76, 2.115
Commission for Racial Equality, *1.39n*
commissioning bodies, independent sector, 1.26
common law
    children, 3.91
    Supervised Community Treatment, 3.64
communications
    mail, 1.123–1.124
        High Security Hospitals, 1.125–1.127, *1.126f*
        Medium Security Hospitals, 1.133–1.135
    telephones
        mobile, 1.114–1.117
        monitoring of, 1.131–1.132
        ward-based, 1.118–119
community care services, 1.23–1.24
    learning disability patients, 1.47
    long-term leave patients, 2.62–2.64
    Supervised Community Treatment, 2.72
community orders, 2.4–2.8, 4.15–4.19, *4.15f, 4.16f*
community treatment orders (CTOs), 2.82
compassion and care, 1.8
compliance notices, 1.3
conditional discharges, 2.69, 2.87, 2.88
    second opinions, *3.17n*
confidentiality, 5.65
Consensus statement on high-dosage antipsychotic medication and polypharmacy, 3.37
consent to treatment, 3.39–3.40 *see also* second opinion appointed doctor system
    Acute Trusts, 2.125
    compliance, 3.15
    concurrent refusal, 3.38, 3.40–3.42
    guidance on, 3.5
    record keeping, 3.7–3.9
    status, detained patients, *3.15f*
coroners, 5.10
Coroners and Justice Bill 2009, 5.10
Corporate Manslaughter and Corporate Homicide Act 2007, 5.11
costs, mental health services, 1.22
Count Me In census, 1.4, 1.30, *2.74n*
Court of Protection, 2.66
court proceedings, security, 4.22–4.23, *4.23r*
CPA *see* Care Programme Approach
CPN (Community Practice Nurse), 2.78

CQC *see* Care Quality Commission
CRHTs *see* Crisis Resolution and Home Treatment teams
criminal justice system detentions *see also* prison population
    consent status, 3.15
    hospital orders, 4.5, 4.8–4.14, *4.12f, 4.14f*
    probation, 4.15–4.19, *4.15f, 4.16f*
    women, 4.20–4.21, *4.20f*
crisis plans, 3.22
Crisis Resolution and Home Treatment teams (CRHTs), 1.22–1.23
cultural awareness, 5.26
culture, on wards, 1.93–1.94, 1.98

data collection
    s. 136 police powers, 2.140, *2.140r*
    Supervised Community Treatment, 2.75–2.76
    Tribunal, the, 2.120, *2.120r*
DBS *see* deep-brain stimulation
de facto detention, 2.65–2.66
deaths, detained patients *see also* suicide
    accidental, 5.17–5.19
    choking, 5.27–5.30, *5.30f*, 5.49
    community patients, 5.36–5.38
    drugs or alcohol, 5.31–5.32, *5.32r*
    ethnicity, 5.3, *5.3f*
    iatrogenic, 5.2, 5.5, *5.9n, 5.14f*, 5.33–5.35
    inquests, 5.10
    during leave or absence, 5.39–5.45
    location, 5.15–5.16, *5.15f*, 5.51–5.52, *5.52f*
    manslaughter, 5.11–5.12
    natural causes, 5.4–5.9, *5.4f*
    notification of, 1.6, 5.1–5.2
    other patients, 5.69–5.70
    relatives, 5.63–5.68, *5.67r*
    under restraint, 1.145, 5.21–5.26, *5.25f*
    unnatural causes, 5.13–5.14, *5.14f*
deep-brain stimulation, 3.63
defensive measures, 1.93
    locked wards, 1.65, *1.65f*
dehydration, 5.8
Department of Health, 1.38–1.39, *1.39n*
    Community Treatment orders, 2.82
    guidance
        mobile phones, 1.114–1.115
        psychological therapies, 3.23
        victim information, 2.48
    Supervised Community Treatment, 3.72–3.73

depression
    transcranial magnetic stimulation, 3.59–3.60
deprivation of liberty, 2.66, 4.43
    care homes, 2.84
    right to life, 5.12
    Supervised Community Treatment, 2.82–2.85
detention
    access to IMHAs, 1.111
    Acute Trusts, 2.125
    aftercare funding, 2.142–2.144
        s. 3 patients, 2.145–2.147
    age profile, 1.30–1.31, *1.30f*
    children, 3.88
    community orders, 4.18
    concurrent consent and refusal, 3.38
    consent to treatment, 3.2
    criteria for prisoners, 4.41–4.42, 4.43
    ethnicity, 1.36–1.37, *1.36f*
    gender ratios, 1.28–1.29, *1.28f, 1.29f*
    illegal, 2.19–2.20
    learning disability, 1.42–1.47
    leave histories, 2.46
    Mental Health Act 1983 powers, 2.3, *2.3f*
        England, 1.17, *1.17f*, 1.18, *1.18f*
        Wales, *1.18f*, 1.19
    by police, 2.129–2.130
    reasons for, 2.114–2.117
    retained mail, 1.123–1.124
    s.12 approved doctor, 2.17–2.20, *2.20r*
    second opinions, 3.2, 3.4
    smoking, 1.95
    statistics, *2.74n*
    Supervised Community Treatment, 2.77–2.78
    uncooperative patients, 2.24–2.27
    women, 1.32–1.36
diet, in hospital, 1.89–1.90
doctors
    holding powers, 2.1, 2.128
    on-call cover, 1.150
DOL *see* deprivation of liberty
drug or alcohol related deaths, 5.31–5.32, *5.32r*

eating disorders, 3.88
ECHR *see* European Convention on Human Rights
ECT treatment *see* electro-convulsive therapy (ECT)
educational facilities, 4.52
elderly people *see* older people
electro-convulsive therapy (ECT), 3.44, *3.44f*, 3.45–3.46, *3.46f*
    advance decisions, 3.18
    age range, 3.48, *3.48f*
    capacity status, *3.46f*, 3.47, *3.47f, 3.52f*, 3.53–3.55
    children and adolescents, 3.88, 3.90–3.92
    deaths, 5.7–5.9
    in emergency, 3.50, 3.56–3.58, *3.57f, 3.58f*
    gender profile, *3.44f, 3.46f*, 3.47–3.48, *3.47f, 3.48f*
    Mental Health Act 2007, 3.45, 3.49, 3.50–3.51, 3.55
    refusal of consent, 3.51, 3.52, *3.52f*, 3.53
    Second Opinions, *3.1f, 3.44f*, 3.45, *3.48f*, 3.51, *3.52f*
emergency treatment, *3.1n*, 3.4, 3.43, *3.43f*
    ECT treatment, 3.50, 3.56–3.58, *3.57f, 3.58f*
England
    detentions, 1–17–1.18, *1.17f, 1.18f*, 2.3, *2.3f*
        independent sector, 1.25, *1.25f*
Enhancing the Healing Environment programme, 1.72
escaping, 2.58 *see also* absence without leave
escort, for leave, 2.54
ethnic minorities, *1.36f*, 1.37
    children and adolescents, 1.58, *1.58f*
    data collection, 2.140
    deaths, detained patients, 5.3, *5.3f*
    language difficulties, 1.38–1.40
    racism, institutional, 1.38–1.39, *1.39n*
    racist abuse, 1.41
    s. 136 detention, 2.140
    Supervised Community Treatment, 2.80–2.81, *2.80f*
Europe, 1.21, *1.21n*
European Convention on Human Rights
    compulsory treatment, 3.5, 3.17
    detention, 2.11
    mentally ill prisoners, 4.35
    rehabilitation, 2.46
European Working Time Directive, 1.150
    telephone contact, 2.14
exercise opportunities, 1.89–1.90, 2.55

Fair Deal campaign, 1.61, 1.92
falls, detained patients, 5.18, 5.20
family liaison officers, 5.64, *5.67r*
fire risk, of smoking, 1.95–1.96
First-tier Tribunal (Health, Education and Social Care Chamber), 2.96
First-tier Tribunal (Mental Health) *see* Tribunal, the
FLORID, 1.110
forensic services *see* prison population

fresh air, 1.90
From Strength to Strength, 1.16

gender
    children and adolescents
        adult wards, 1.53–1.55, *1.53f, 1.54f, 1.55f*
        ECT treatment, 3.88
    detained patients, 1.28–1.29, *1.28f, 1.29f*
    electro-convulsive therapy (ECT), *3.44f, 3.46f,* 3.47–3.48, *3.47f, 3.48f*
    Supervised Community Treatment, 2.79, *2.79f, 2.80f,* 2.81
General Medical Council (GMC), 3.5, 3.16
general practitioners (GPs), 2.90, 3.85, 5.37–5.38
goodwill, of staff, 2.40
ground leave, 2.52–2.55

Health and Social Care Act 2007, *2.75n*
health checks, high dosage medication, 3.37
Healthcare Commission, 1.23, 1.37
    review of acute services, 1.102
Healthcare Inspectorate Wales, 1.1, *1.3n*
    consent to treatment, 3.6
    functions, 1.2
    human rights, 1.32
    seclusion practices, 1.160
    second opinion service, 3.36
    Tribunal secretariat data, 2.120, *2.120r*
High Security Hospitals
    absconding, data collection, 2.58
    mail, 1.123–1.124
        appeals against withholding, 1.125–1.127, *1.126f*
    pornography, 1.128–1.130
    telephone monitoring, 1.131–1.132
holding powers, 2.1–2.3, *2.1f, 2.2f, 2.3f*
    delays in assessment, 2.22–2.23
    doctors, 2.128
hospital managers
    and relatives, 5.63–5.68, *5.67r*
    and victims, 2.48–2.51
hospital orders, 4.5, 4.8–4.14, *4.12f, 4.14f*
    with restrictions, 4.13
hospitals
    Supervised Community Treatment, 2.86–2.88
HSHs *see* High Security Hospitals

iatrogenic deaths, 5.2, 5.5, *5.14f,* 5.33–5.35
    aspiration, *5.9n*

IMHAs *see* Independent Mental Health Advocates (IMHAs)
immigration detainees, 4.32
incapacity, detained patients, 3.31
    ECT treatment, 3.49
independent hospitals, 1.25–1.26, *1.25f*
    hospital order patients, 4.14, *4.14f*
    informal patients, 1.27
Independent Mental Health Advocates (IMHAs), 1.111–1.113
Independent Police Complaints Commission, *2.56n,* 2.130
    s. 136 police powers, 2.140, *2.140r*
Indian patients, 1.37
informal patients
    aftercare funding, 2.142
    assessments, 2.137
    children and adolescents, 3.90–3.91
    detention, 1.18, *1.18f,* 1.19, 2.65–2.66
    ECT treatment, 3.49, 3.90–3.91
    holding powers, 2.1–2.3, *2.1f, 2.2f*
    independent sector, 1.27
    reduction in, 2.116
    Supervised Community Treatment, 2.85
information, for patients
    care and treatment, 1.106–1.110
    Supervised Community Treatment, 2.77–2.78
    on Tribunals, 1.109
injections, 3.10
inquests, 5.10
insanity, as defence, 4.3–4.7
internet access, 1.110, 1.120–1.121
    restrictions on content, 1.122

King's Fund, 1.72

language barriers, 1.38–1.40, 2.106
learning disability patients
    cardiac arrest, 5.5–5.6
    choking, 5.27–5.28, *5.30f*
    data collection, 1.45, *1.45n*
    detention of, 1.42–1.47, *1.47f*
        independent sector, 1.44, 1.46, *1.46f*
        NHS facilities, 1.45, *1.45f*
        under Part 3 of the Act, 1.47
    leave, 2.37, 2.44
least restriction principle, 1.66
leave, for patients
    audits of, 2.39

241

authorisation of, 2.31
carers, 2.32
costs of, 2.37, 4.53
deaths on leave, 5.39–5.45, *5.39f*
delays in, 3.26
detention, 2.4–2.8
escorts for, 2.37, 2.39
ground leave, 2.52–2.55
importance of, 2.46
informal patients, 2.65
long-term, 2.62–2.64, 2.76
meals for staff, 2.37
medication management, 3.85–3.87, 5.37–5.38
or Supervised Community Treatment, 3.69, 3.83
rationed, 2.38
resource limitations, 2.37–2.40
restricted patients, 2.41–2.46
victim consultation, 2.47–2.51
leave beds, 2.37
legal aid
　eligibility for, *2.95n*
　managers' hearings, 2.95
　solicitors' remuneration, 2.108–2.110
legal rights, 1.106–1.109, 2.77
　IMHAs, 1.112
Legal Services Commission
　guidance to solicitors, *2.95n*
　solicitors' availability, 2.109
　Tribunal adjournments, *2.99n*, 2.101
legal status, patients, 2.77
life support training, *5.30f*
ligature points, 5.57–5.60
Local Health Boards, Wales, 1.111
locked wards, 1.64–1.67, *1.64f*

magnetic stimulation, 3.59–3.60
mail, 1.123–1.124
　High Security Hospitals, 1.125–1.127, *1.126f*
　Medium Security Hospitals, 1.133–1.135
　pornography, 1.128–1.130
managers' hearings
　delays in, 2.91
　information for patients, 2.92–2.94
　legal representation, 2.95
Managing Urgent Mental Health Needs in the Acute Trust, 2.122, *2.128r*
manslaughter, 5.11–5.12
MAPPA arrangements, 4.48
MCA *see Mental Capacity Act 2005*

medical assessment, *2.71n*
medication
　cardiac arrest, 5.5
　deaths from, 5.2, 5.33–5.35, 5.36–5.38
　high-dose, 3.37
　long-term leave patients, 2.63
　Second Opinions, *3.1f*
　self-administration, 3.24
medicine management, 3.24–3.26
　electronic, 3.27
medium secure units
　ground leave, 2.55
　leave, limitations on, 2.37
Medium Security Hospitals
　mail, 1.133–1.135
Mental Capacity Act 2005, 2.85, 3.9, 3.31
　adolescents, 3.91
　deep-brain stimulation, 3.63
　Supervised Community Treatment, 3.64
Mental Health Act 1959, 1.123–1.124
Mental Health Act 1983, 1.2, 2.21
　Part 2, 1.18, *1.18f*
　Part 3, *1.18f*, 1.19, 2.67, 2.69
　Part 4, 2.22, 3.60
　s. 2, 1.53, 2.2–2.3, *2.2f, 2.3f*
　　community orders, 2.4–2.8
　s. 3, 2.2–2.3, *2.2f, 2.3f*
　s. 5, 2.1, *2.1f, 2.2f*
　s.12, 2.17–2.20, *2.20r*, 2.24
　s.13(2), 2.24
　s.17 leave, 2.34
　　long-term, 2.62–2.64
　　or Supervised Community Treatment, 3.69, 3.83
　　resource limitations, 2.37–2.40
　s. 32, 1.38, 1.106–1.109
　s. 37/41, 4.5, 4.8–4.14, *4.12f, 4.14f*
　　leave, 2.41–2.51
　s. 47, 4.43, 4.45, 4.48
　s. 47/49, 4.5, 4.31, 4.41
　s. 57, 3.61, 3.63
　s. 62, 3.56, *3.57f,* 3.58, *3.58f*
　s. 117 aftercare, 2.141–2.147
　s. 130A, 1.111
　s. 131A, 1.48–1.49
　s.134, 1.134
　s.134(2), 1.127
　s. 136, 1.5
　　data collection, 2.140

242

places of safety, 2.129
public places, 2.138–2.139
seclusion, 1.156
statistics, 1.4–1.5
treatment, regulation of, 3.1
withholding of mail, 1.123
Mental Health Act 2007
detention, 2.115
Part 4A, 3.64, 3.70, 3.73–3.74
Second Opinions, *3.1n*
Supervised Community Treatment, 2.77, 2.96
victim information, 2.48–2.51
Mental Health Act Administrator, 2.123
responsibility of professionals, 2.90
Mental Health Act Codes of Practice (general)
advance decisions, 3.19
consent to treatment, 3.5
patients in court, 4.22
restraint, 5.20
Mental Health Act Code of Practice for England
absences without leave, 2.57
AWOL patients, 2.61
deprivation of liberty, 2.83, 2.85
ECT and children, 3.92
information for patients, 1.106
leave, 2.34
leave form, 2.32
locked doors, 1.66, 1.67
managers' hearings, 2.91–2.92
mobile telephones, 1.114–1.115
places of safety, 2.130, 2.136
responsible clinician, 2.13
seclusion, 1.157, 1.160–1.163
security at court, 4.22–4.23
statutory consultees, 3.84
Supervised Community Treatment, 2.67–2.68, 2.83
appropriateness of treatment, 3.76–3.79
consent to treatment, 3.68–3.69
user involvement, 1.91–1.92
ward-based telephones, 1.118
Mental Health Act Code of Practice for Wales, 1.66, 2.34
absences without leave, *2.57n*
AWOL patients, 2.61
information for patients, 1.106
places of safety, 2.130, 2.136
responsible clinician, 2.13
seclusion, 1.160–1.163

security at court, 4.22–4.23
statutory consultees, 3.84
Supervised Community Treatment, 2.67–2.68
Mental Health Act Commission (MHAC) *see also* Appendix A, Epilogue
dissolution, 1.1
focus, 2.121
guidance, 2.33–2.34, *2.34f*
remit, 1.2–1.3, 3.1
Mental Health Act Commissioners, 1.3, 2.62
Mental Health Act Reviewers, *1.3n*
Mental Health (Amendment) Act 1982, 3.17
Mental Health Lawyers Association, 2.109
Mental Health Minimum Data Set, 2.59
Mental Health Review Tribunal (MHRT) *see* Tribunal, the Mental Health Trusts, Acute Trusts, 2.126, *2.128r*
Mental Health Unit *see* Ministry of Justice Mental Health Unit
MHAC *see* Mental Health Act Commission
MHLA *see* Mental Health Lawyers Association
MHMDS *see* Mental Health Minimum Data Set
MHRT *see* Tribunal, the
MHU *see* Ministry of Justice Mental Health Unit
MIND, second opinions, *3.17n*
Ministry of Justice Mental Health Unit, 2.41, 2.43–2.44
guidance, victim information, 2.48
transfers from prison, 4.38–4.39, 4.41–4.42, 4.48
victim consultation, 2.47
mixed-sex wards, 1.33
children and adolescents, 1.54–1.55, *1.54f, 1.55f*
M'Naghten rules, 4.3
money, for patients, 2.37, 2.42, 2.45
mortality, of patients, 1.82, *1.82f*
mortuary services, 5.68
mother and baby units, 1.34

National Audit Office, 1.23, 4.19
National Autistic Society, 2.56
National Confidential Inquiry into Suicide and Homicide by People with Mental Illness, 5.45, 5.46, 5.47
National Institute for Clinical Excellence (NICE)
observation, 1.136, *1.136f,* 5.49
psychological treatment, 3.23
restraint practice, 5.24
National Mental Health Minimum Dataset, 1.4
National Patient Safety Agency (NPSA), 5.6, *5.30f*
guidelines on choking, 5.28–5.30, *5.30f*

National Service Framework, 2.72
nearest relatives, 1.112, 5.65
    legal rights, 2.22
neurosurgery, 3.61–3.62
New Ways of Working workbook, 1.80–1.81
NICE *see* National Institute for Clinical Excellence
NMD *see* neurosurgery
non-psychiatric sector *see also* Acute Trusts
    use of Mental Health Act powers, 2.121–2.124
Not just visiting DVD, 1.14
NPSA *see* National Patient Safety Agency
nursing homes, 2.145–2.147
nursing staff
    dangers of jewellery, 1.146–1.147
    holding powers, 2.1
    skills of, 1.9–1.11
    as statutory consultees, 3.84
nursing standards
    acute wards, 1.9–1.11

observation, by nursing staff, 1.136–1.144
    effect on other patients, 1.141–1.143
    secluded patients, 1.159
    suicide risk, 5.48–5.50
    terminology for, *1.136f*
occupational therapy, 1.86–1.87
older people
    care standards, 1.76
    risk of falls, 5.20
    social services assessments, 2.22
out of area placements, 1.60
over-occupancy, 1.68–1.70, *1.69f*

PACE (*Police and Criminal Evidence Act*), 2.136
partnerships, in treatment, 1.13, 3.16
personality disorder, 4.35
pharmacy services, 3.16, 3.24–3.26
photographs, of patients, 1.115
physical environment, acute wards, 1.71–1.77
PICU *see* Psychiatric Intensive Care Units
places of safety, 2.129–2.130
    hospital based, 2.135
    police cells, 2.132–2.134, 2.136
    transfer between, 2.132
    Wales, 2.130
police
    AWOL patients, 2.60–2.61
    places of safety, 2.129–2.130, 2.132–2.134, 2.136

powers to detain, 1.5, 2.136, 2.140, *2.140r*
powers to search, 2.136
Supervised Community Treatment patients, 2.89
on wards, 1.149, 1.151–1.153
Police and Criminal Evidence Act, 2.136
polypharmacy, 3.37
pornography, access to, 1.128–1.130
possessions, security of, 1.77, *1.77f*
powers of attorney, 3.22
Practice Directions, Tribunal, 2.97, 2.103–2.104
prison population, 4.1–4.2
    adolescents, 1.60
    learning difficulties, 2.44
    mental health services, 2.41–2.46
    personality disorders, 2.44
    transfer to hospital, 4.8–4.14, *4.12f, 4.14f, 4.27f*
        criteria for, 4.41–4.42, 4.43
        delays in, 4.24, 4.26
        equivalent treatment, 4.24–4.27
        last minute, 4.40–4.42, 4.43–4.49
        loss of freedoms, 4.50–4.52
        not allowed, 4.6–4.7
        prioritisation, 4.38–4.39
        rehabilitation, 4.50–4.54
        treatability test, 4.35–4.37
        voting rights, 4.54
        Wales, 4.34, *4.34f*
        welfare benefits, 4.53
        without restriction orders, 4.30–4.33, *4.30f*
        women, 4.28–4.29, *4.29f*
Prison Reform Trust, 4.24–4.25
Pritchard test, 4.3, 4.5
privacy and dignity
    under observation, *1.136f*, 1.139–1.140, 1.142–1.143
    rights to, 1.115, 1.118–1.119
probation, 4.15–4.19, *4.15f, 4.16f*
professional attitudes, 1.7–1.8
Psychiatric Intensive Care Units (PICU), 1.54
    adolescents, 1.59
psychological treatments, 3.23
psychotic illness, 1.35
public, rights to refuse mail, 1.133
public places, 2.138–2.139
public safety, 4.39, 4.48–4.49

quality assurance framework, 1.26

race equality, 2.81
Race Relations (Amendment) Act 2000, 1.39, *1.39n*, 2.140
racism, institutional, 5.26
record keeping, 2.30–2.34
    consent and capacity, 3.7–3.9
    electronic, 3.27
    high-dosage medication, 3.37
    information to patients, 1.108–1.109, 2.78
    long-term leave patients, 2.64
    managers' hearings, 2.93
    non-psychiatric sector, 2.123–2.124, 2.125
    nursing reports, 2.105
    restraint, 1.148
    suicides, 5.48, 5.55
recovery models, 1.91–1.92
recruitment, nursing staff, 1.85
refusal of treatment, 2.76
    concurrent consent, 3.38
Regional Tribunal Judges, 2.98
rehabilitation
    funding for leave, 2.46
    transferred prisoners, 4.50–4.54
reinstitutionalisation, 4.13
relatives, 1.112
    death of patient, 5.63–5.68, *5.67r*
residential homes, 2.145–2.147
resource limitations, 2.32, 2.37–2.40
respiratory arrest, 5.5–5.6
responsible clinician, 1.112, 2.9–2.11
    co-ordination with others, 5.36–5.38
    consent and capacity, 3.7
    identification of, 2.12–2.16
    leave for patients, 2.43–2.44
    liaison with victims, 2.48–2.51
    off-duty, 2.13–2.14
    powers and duties, 2.12
    standing-in, 2.14–2.16
    Supervised Community Treatment, 2.67, 2.71–2.72, 2.83
        medication, 2.89
    training requirement, 2.127, *2.128r*
responsible medical officer, 2.127 *see also* responsible clinician
    withholding of mail, 1.123–1.124
restraint, 1.141–1.143
    dangers of jewellery, 1.146–1.147
    deaths under, 1.145, 5.21–5.26, *5.25f*
    doctor attendance, 1.150
    fall prevention, 5.20

    guidance for, 5.24–5.26
    record keeping, 1.148, 5.26
    seclusion, 1.154, 5.25
    staff responsibilities, 1.149
    training needs, 1.145–1.146, 5.23–5.26, *5.24n*
restricted liberty
    Supervised Community Treatment, 2.87
restricted status
    conditional discharge, 3.66
    consent to treatment, 3.15, *3.15f*
    former prisoners, 4.26–4.27, *4.27f*
    leave, 2.41
        resource limitations, 2.44
        suspension of, 2.42–2.43
resuscitation training, *5.30f*
rights, of patients
    Acute Trusts, 2.125
    awareness of, 2.113
    deprivation of liberty, 4.44
    to information, 1.106–1.110, 2.77, 2.106
    mentally ill prisoners, 4.35–4.37
    mobile phones, 1.115
    to privacy and dignity, 1.115, 1.118–1.119
    right to life, 5.12
    to Tribunal, 2.106–2.107
RiO electronic record system, 3.27
risk assessment, 1.94, 2.35–2.36
    absconding, 2.56–2.57, 2.59
    consent to treatment, 3.8, 3.15
    leave, 5.40–5.45
    ligature points, 5.57–5.60
    observation levels, 5.48–5.50
    prisoners, 4.8–4.11
Royal College of Psychiatrists, 1.61
    bereavement guidelines, 5.67
    high-dose medication, 3.37
    places of safety, 2.131
    s. 136 police powers, 2.140, *2.140r*
    second opinions, *3.17n*
    young people, 1.48

Safety and Security Directions, 1.131
safety measures
    doors, 5.60
    ligature points, 5.57–5.59
    plastic bags, 5.61–5.62
Scotland
    deep-brain stimulation, 3.63
    neurosurgery, *3.62n*

SCT *see* Supervised Community Treatment
seclusion practices, 1.154–1.155
    inadequate, 5.25
    long-term, 1.161–1.163
    night-time review, 1.160
    patient involvement, 1.157–1.158
    statutory provision, 1.56
    unsafe, 1.158–1.159
second opinion appointed doctor system (SOAD), 1.2
    changes to treatment, 3.35–3.36, *3.35f*
    children, 3.88–3.89, *3.88f, 3.89f*
        ECT treatment, 3.90–3.92
    detained patients
        age range, 3.32, *3.32f*
        Black and Minority Ethnic groups, 3.32–3.34, *3.32f, 3.33f*
        capacity status, 3.31, *3.31f*
        gender, 3.30, *3.30f*
        limits of treatment, 3.42
        refusal of consent to treatments, 3.38, 3.41
    growth of service, 3.1, *3.1f,* 3.28, *3.28f*
    recruitment needs, 3.29
    safeguards for patients, 3.4–3.6
    Supervised Community Treatment, 2.75–2.76, *2.75f,* 3.17, 3.68
        appropriateness of treatment, 3.73, 3.75–3.83
        delays in, 3.29
        refusal of treatment, 3.71–3.75
    training, 1.14
Secretary of State powers, 2.107
security, of possessions, 1.77, *1.77f*
segregation, 1.163
self-administration, medication, 3.24
self-harming behaviour, *1.65f, 1.82f*
    deaths, 5.13
    observation, *1.136f,* 1.137
    seclusion, 1.158, 1.160
serious untoward incident, 2.59
service level agreements, 2.126–2.127, *2.128r*
Service User Reference Panel, 1.3, 1.14
    newsletter, 1.16
service users
    involvement in decisions, 1.13–1.16, 1.91–1.93, 1.99–1.104
    Mental Health Act powers, 1.3
    support for each other, 1.105
sexual dysfunction, 3.16
side effects, treatment, 3.16
smoking
    ban, 1.71, 1.95

    restrictions, 1.95–1.98
    transferred prisoners, 4.51
SOAD *see* second opinion appointed doctor system
social circumstances reports, 2.102–2.103
social workers
    Approved Mental Health Professionals, 2.21
    assessment, 2.23, 2.137
    older people, 2.22
solicitors
    need for, 2.118
    remuneration, 2.109, 2.110
    Tribunal work, *2.95n*
        withdrawal from, 2.109–2.110
specialist services, 1.26, 1.27
    mother and baby units, 1.34
    for women, 1.35
St Lucia, 4.3
staff
    acute wards, 1.62
    deaths, effects of, 5.63, 5.70
    goodwill, 2.40
    mandatory ratios, 1.80
    shortages of, 1.66, 1.78–1.85, *1.79f,* 5.55
    training, 1.81
Star Wards scheme, 1.73
state benefits *see* benefits, state
SUI (serious untoward incident), 2.59
suicide, 5.2, 5.13–5.15, *5.14f*
    drop in, 5.46
    by hanging, 5.49, 5.51–5.56, *5.52f, 5.53f,* 5.58–5.60
    on leave, 2.36
    ligature points, 5.57–5.59
    medication
        hoarding, 5.37
        non-compliance, 5.47
    observation levels, 1.137, 5.48–5.50, 5.53–5.56, *5.53f*
    other patients, 5.69–5.70
    relatives, 5.63–5.68, *5.67r*
    risk of, 1.105, 5.12, 5.40–5.45
    self-strangulation, 5.51–5.54
    self-suffocation, 5.61–5.62
Supervised Community Treatment, 2.67–2.68, 2.73
    access to IMHAs, 1.111
    advance decisions, 3.18
age and gender, 2.79, *2.79f*
    appropriateness, 2.69–2.71
        of treatment, 3.73, 3.76–3.83
    community services, 2.72

consent status, 3.66–3.67, *3.67f*
consent to treatment, 3.64–3.65
deaths, 5.36–5.38
delays in implementing, 2.71
deprivation of liberty, 2.82–2.85
discharge practices, 2.86–2.88
ethnicity, 2.80–2.81, *2.80f*
hospital residence, 2.86–2.88
isolation, 2.78
long-term leave, 2.64
medication management, 3.85, 3–87
Mental Health Act Commission, 1.2, 1.14
non-compliance with medication, 5.47
recall to hospital, 3.83
refusal of treatment, 3.68–3.72, 3.76–3.83
responsibilities of professionals, 2.89–2.90
revocation, 2.76
rights to information, *1.106n*, 2.78
second opinions, 3.3
    effective use of, 3.17
        refusal of treatment, 3.71–3.72
        statutory consultees, 3.84
use of provision, 2.74–2.76
victim information, 2.48
supervised discharge provisions, 2.84, 2.87, *2.87n*
supported housing, long-term leave, 2.63
SURP see Service User Reference Panel

telephones
    mobile phones, 1.114–1.117
    monitoring of, 1.131–1.132
    ward-based, 1.118–119
theft, *1.77f*
thresholds, of capacity, 3.54–3.56
TMS *see* transcranial magnetic stimulation
toilet facilities, seclusion, 1.159
training needs
    bereavement, 5.67
    of Commissioners, 1.14
    incapacity of patients, 3.31
    life support, *5.30f*
    medical emergencies, 5.6, *5.6n*
    restraint practice, 1.145–1.146, 5.23–5.26, *5.24n*
    staff proportions, *1.79f*
transcranial magnetic stimulation, 3.59–3.60
transport, for patients
    on detention, 2.28–2.29
    leave, 2.37
    return when AWOL, 2.60
treatability test, 4.35, 4.42, 4.43, *4.43n*
treatment
    delays in, 2.22
    human rights, 3.5
    second opinion safeguards, 3.1
    understanding of, 3.16
Tribunal, the, 2.96
    adjournments, 2.101, *2.101f*, 2111
    administration, 2.99
    cooperation of parties, 2.98
    delays, 2.99–2.100
    discharge before hearing date, 2.119
    functions, 1.3
    legal aid, 2.95, *2.95n*, 2.108
    legal representation, access to, 2.109–2.110
    nursing reports, 2.104–2.105
    outcomes, 2.111–2.113, *2.111f*
        success rates, 2.113–2.114, 2.117–2.118
    rights to, 2.106–2.107
    Rules and Practice Directions, 2.97, *2.98n*, 2.103–2.104
    social circumstances reports, 2.102–2.103
    staff training, 2.99
    Supervised Community Treatment, 2.68
    transfer of prisoners, 4.42
    withdrawn applications, *2.111f*, 2.112, 2.119
Tribunals, Courts and Enforcement Act 2007, 2.96

unfitness to plead, 4.3–4.7
unsound mind, 4.1–4.2
Upper Tribunal, 2.98

value, of individuals, 5.69–5.70
victim liaison officers, 2.47
victims, liaison with
    leave, restricted patients, 2.47–2.51
    unrestricted patients, 2.48–2.51
visiting
    of Commissioners, 1.14, 1.15
    in private, 1.3
voluntary patients *see* informal patients
voting rights, prisoners, 4.54

Wales *see also* Mental Health Act Code of Practice for Wales
    detentions, *1.18f*, 1.19, 2.3, *2.3f*
        independent sector, 1.25, *1.25f*
    forms for treatment, *3.39n*

    holding powers, 2.1–2.2, *2.1f, 2.2f*
    hospital orders, 4.14, *4.14f*
    IMHAs, 1.111
    prisoners, transfer to hospital, 4.34, *4.34f*
ward environments
    acute wards, 1.71–1.77
    boredom, 1.144
    police presence, 1.149, 1.151–1.153
warrants, transfer from hospital, 4.44–4.46
weight gain, drug-induced, 1.89–1.90, 3.16
welfare benefits *see* benefits, state
Women detained in hospital, 1.32
women patients
    court disposals, 4.20–4.21, *4.20f*
    detention, 1.14, 1.32–1.33
    safety of, 1.33
    specialist services, 1.34–1.35
    transfer from prison, 4.28–4.29, *4.29f*
World Health Organization, 1.21

young people, transfer from prison, 4.43–4.49